Welcome to the Spring 2015 issue of *Acoustic & Digital Piano Buyer*, a semiannual publication devoted to the purchase of new, used, and restored acoustic pianos and digital pianos. *Piano Buyer* is the supplement and successor to the well-known reference *The Piano Book*, which, since 1987, has been the principal consumer guide to buying a piano in the U.S. and Canada. Partially supported by advertising, *Piano Buyer* is available free online at www.pianobuyer.com. It can also be purchased in print from the website and in bookstores.

Piano Buyer is a hybrid book/magazine. The "book" part consists of a collection of how-to articles on the many aspects of buying a piano. These basic articles are repeated in every issue to serve the many new buyers continually entering the piano market. The "magazine" part consists of features that change with each issue to cover topics of more temporary or niche interest, and to provide variety. Each issue contains several of these excellent features, many of which remain relevant for years. If you missed any of them, you'll find them under the website's Archive tab. The brand, model, and price reference material in the second half of the publication is updated, as needed, with each issue.

In this issue we offer several new articles for your reading pleasure. The 1911 publication *Pianos and Their Makers*, by Alfred Dolge, lists 124 piano-manufacturing firms in the New York City area; of them, only Steinway & Sons remains today. But of the hundreds of thousands of instruments these companies produced, many are still in existence and in need of restoration, and to serve that need, the piano-building tradition of a century ago is carried

on by the many fine rebuilding shops of present-day New York. In "Rebuilding the New York Way," author Sally Phillips takes a look at several of these shops, and relates some of their owners' more interesting stories and challenging rebuilding projects (p.68).

Also in this issue we offer reviews of two piano lines: one acoustic, one digital. Through the late 1990s and early 2000s, Petrof pianos, from the Czech Republic, were positioned in the North American marketplace as low-cost European alternatives to other well-known, established brands. In 2009, Petrof's line of grand pianos was revised, with new designs, materials, and a higher level of build quality, all intended to compete with the great pianos of Europe and America. Here, Dr. Benjamin Boren reviews the three smallest models of this six-model line (p.49).

The Yamaha Clavinova, one of the industry's longest-running and most popular lines of digital piano, turns 30 this year. Jim Aikin, himself a 30-year veteran of reporting on electronic keyboards for industry publications, reviews for us a couple of models from the new Clavinova CLP-500 line. These models feature

sounds sampled from not only a Yamaha CFX concert grand, but a Bösendorfer Imperial as well. Aikin isn't yet ready to give up his Yamaha acoustic grand, but it's a close call (p.117).

Piano Buyer's ratings of new pianos are probably the publication's most read, most misunderstood, and most controversial feature. As the quality of low-end pianos rises, and the differences between brands become increasingly subtle and subjective, our ratings have come to represent less our judgments of the instruments, and more our sense of how manufacturers and dealers position them in the marketplace—partly by price, but also by reputation and country of origin. But we've never been completely satisfied with this, in part because readers who lack time, interest, and/or ability to make their own judgments frequently ask that we help them by recommending specific models. We've risen to the challenge with "Staff Picks," our unapologetically subjective assessments of the best in today's acoustic, digital, and hybrid pianos (p.43).

Don't forget to explore the rest of our website. If you're shopping for a new piano, our two searchable online databases of 3,000 acoustic and more than 200 digital models will help you quickly home in on the instruments that match your requirements for size, furniture style, budget, and features. If you're shopping for a used instrument, try our Piano Buyer Classifieds; using its powerful search engine, browse among thousands of used pianos for sale. If you're in need of

(continued on page 2)

Acoustic & Digital PIANO BUYER

PIANOBUYER.COM

®

The Definitive Guide to Buying New, Used, and Restored Pianos

THE PIANO BOOK

SPRING 2015 Supplement to THE PIANO BOOK

Acoustic & Digital Piano Buyer is published semiannually, in March and September, by:

Brookside Press LLC
P.O. Box 601041
San Diego, CA 92160 USA
info@pianobuyer.com

800.545.2022
617.522.7182
617.390.7764 (fax)
www.pianobuyer.com

Acoustic & Digital Piano Buyer copyright © 2015 by Brookside Press LLC
All rights reserved

"The Piano Book" is a Registered Trademark of Lawrence Fine
"Piano Buyer" is a Registered Trademark of Brookside Press LLC

ISBN 978-192914540-9

Distributed to the book trade by Independent Publishers Group,
814 North Franklin St., Chicago, IL 60610
(800) 888-4741 or (312) 337-0747

Publisher and Editor
Advertising Director
Larry Fine
larry@pianobuyer.com

Piano Review Editor
Dr. Owen Lovell
owen@pianobuyer.com

Contributing Editor and
Piano Industry Consultant
Steve Cohen
steve@pianobuyer.com

Design and Production
Julie Gallagher, Harry St. Ours

Acoustic Piano
Technical Consultants
Sally Phillips
Del Fandrich

Digital Piano
Technical Consultant
Alden Skinner

Copyeditor
Richard Lehnert

Contributors to this issue:
Jim Aikin, Benjamin Boren, Ori Bukai, Brian Chung, George Litterst, Sally Phillips, Alden Skinner, Chris Solliday, Christopher Storch

See www.PianoBuyer.com for more information.

(continued from page 1)

piano-related services—tuning, rebuilding, sales, teaching, or moving—use our Local Services Directory. And when you're ready to take a break, treat yourself to some comic relief with our latest blog, *Piano-Buying Stories*.

Finally, if you're reading this online, consider buying a print copy of *Piano Buyer*. It's a handsome volume, printed in color on glossy paper, and will make a great reference, coffee-table book, or gift. You can purchase it through the website or in bookstores.

Piano Buyer exists to make shopping for a piano easier and more enjoyable. If you have a suggestion for how we can do that better, please e-mail me at *larry@pianobuyer.com*.

—Larry Fine, *Publisher*

AUTHENTIC SAUTER TIMELESS
—Pianofortemanufaktur—

*"Your piano is
too good for me."*
-Ludwig Van Beethoven*

*"Playing a Sauter feels like
touching a piece of heaven.
I just love them."*
-Manuel Valera**

Photo credit: Jimmy Ryan

*Letter to the owner of the piano workshop where the future founder of Sauter
worked on Mr. Beethoven's pianos

www.SauterPiano.com

**2013 Grammy Nominated Cuban composer and jazz pianist. Recipient of Chamber
Music America's New Jazz Works and the ASCAP Young Jazz Composer Award

100% Made in Germany • Family Owned for Seven Generations • Manufactured in the Black Forest since 1819

WWW.SAUTERPIANO.COM ◆ 509-946-8078

Inside This Issue

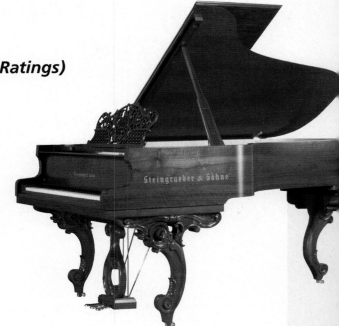

DIGITAL PIANOS

HYBRID & PLAYER PIANOS

NEW-PIANO BUYERS' REFERENCE

ACOUSTIC PIANOS

DIGITAL PIANOS

THE PRODIGIOUS POWER OF PIANO PLAYING

BRIAN CHUNG

PRACTICE MAKES PERFECT. You've probably heard that saying a hundred times, especially if you've ever studied the piano. Mom said it, so it must be true, right?

Well, hold on a minute—nothing against Mom, but let's get real: "Practice makes perfect" is a terrible motto for piano players. First of all, it's incorrect—how can anything become "perfect" if, every time, you practice it *wrong*? And second, it can't even come close to capturing the prodigious power of playing the piano. So, with all due respect to that venerable axiom, trash it—and make way for a motto that proclaims the *real* benefits of piano playing: *Practice makes prosperous.*

People usually associate the word *prosperous* with wealth. While that's certainly part of its meaning, many dictionaries suggest a broader definition: to be *prosperous* is to *flourish*, to *thrive . . .* to *be successful.* Therefore, the phrase *practice makes prosperous* declares boldly that *those who play the piano are far more likely to flourish, thrive, and experience success in life than those who do not.* Quite a stretch, you say? Read on.

Thriving Children

Consider what happens when eight-year-old Bobby decides to embrace serious piano practice. Not only does he embark upon a wondrous musical adventure (possibly the greatest benefit of all) but, perhaps unconsciously, he acquires a diversity of skills far beyond the musical notes:

- **He learns to *work hard.*** Anyone who excels at the piano has made a commitment to practice with vigor and determination.

- **He learns to *focus.*** In a world where iPods, MySpace, Facebook, Twitter and mobile texting have made multi-tasking the de facto way of life, young people are at risk of losing the art of concentration. Piano practice reminds Bobby how to focus on *one thing*—and do it well.

- **He learns to be *responsible.*** Serious pianists learn that faithful, consistent practice—even when they don't *feel* like doing it—will bring great satisfaction over time.

- **He learns to *pay attention to details*.** As his skills mature, Bobby learns to observe the fine points and use the most subtle nuances to create art.

- **He learns to be *self-reliant.*** While practicing, Bobby can't always rely on Mom and Dad for help. To succeed, he must learn to work well on his own.

- **He learns to be *creative.*** Creativity is a musician's lifeblood. Pianists use it not only to express musical ideas, but also to conquer the physical and mental obstacles that arise when learning new music.

- **He learns to *persevere.*** There is little satisfaction in learning only *half* of a piece of music. The determined pianist finds joy in following through to the very end.

> Those who play the piano are far more likely to flourish, thrive, and experience success in life than those who do not.

These are only some of the skills Bobby will acquire as he devotes himself to diligent piano practice. So, how will such practice make him prosperous?

Ask employers what they look for when interviewing young job candidates for their top positions. Most are looking for a well-defined set of character traits. Specifically, they want people who know how to work hard, can focus well and avoid distractions, are responsible, will pay attention to details, are self-reliant and creative, and will persevere on a project from start to finish. Sound familiar?

You see my point. The skills Bobby learns by practicing the piano will be of immeasurable value to him not only in job interviews, but in every area of his life. People who have these skills are more likely to flourish in college, thrive in the work world, advance in their careers—and generally enjoy success in any field of endeavor.

Test scores support this contention. Studies show that students of music typically score higher on SATs than do non-music students—on average, 57 points higher on the verbal section and 41 points higher in math.[1] Further, a 1994 study showed that college undergraduate students who majored in music had the highest rate

---

[1] *Profile of SAT and Achievement Test Takers.* The College Board, compiled by Music Educators National Conference, 2001.

OUTSTANDING OVATION

2014 Supplier
Excellence Award
Music Inc. Magazine

2014 Digital Home
Keyboard of the Year
MMR Dealers' Choice

2014 Product
Excellence Award
Music Inc. Magazine

2014 Digital Pro Digital
Piano Line of the Year
MMR Dealers' Choice

2014 Best Home Digital
Under 1500 Euros
Tastenwelt Magazine

2014 Editor's Choice
NAMM: Best in Show
Music Inc. Magazine

2014 "Rock On"
Company (Japan)
Silver Prize

2013 Supplier
Excellence Award
Music Inc. Magazine

2013 Editor's Pick
Best of the Best
Worship Leader Magazine

2012 Digital Home
Keyboard of the Year
MMR Dealers' Choice

2012 Product
Excellence Award
Music Inc. Magazine

2012 Good Design Award
Japan Institute
of Design Promotion

2011 Acoustic Piano
of the Year
MMR Dealers' Choice

2010 Product
Excellence Award
Music Inc. Magazine

2010 Good Design Award
Japan Institute
of Design Promotion

2010 Acoustic Piano
of the Year
MMR Dealers' Choice

2009 Supplier
Excellence Award
Music Inc. Magazine

2009 Acoustic Piano
of the Year
MMR Dealers' Choice

2008 Good Design Award
Japan Institute
of Design Promotion

2008 Editor's Pick
Best of the Best
Worship Leader Magazine

2008 Acoustic Piano
of the Year
MMR Dealers' Choice

2007 Digital Home
Keyboard of the Year
MMR Dealers' Choice

2005 Acoustic Piano
Line of the Year
MMR Dealers' Choice

2004 Acoustic Piano
Line of the Year
MMR Dealers' Choice

2003 Acoustic Piano
Line of the Year
MMR Dealers' Choice

2003 Supplier
Excellence Award
Music Inc. Magazine

2003 Readers' Choice Award
Tastenwelt Magazine
(Europe)

2002 Digital Home
Keyboard of the Year
MMR Dealers' Choice

THANKS TO ALL WHO HAVE MADE OUR SUCCESS POSSIBLE.

KAWAI
The Future of the Piano

KAWAIUS.COM

of acceptance to medical school (66%).[2] *Practice makes prosperous.* Prepare your children for success in life: Introduce them to the piano.

Thriving Adults

But how about *you*? Are you among the 82% of adults who have always wanted to learn how to play an instrument?[3] Did you know that adults can gain as much as younger people from playing the piano?

Even if you've already achieved career success and significant wealth, there can be *so* much more to a prosperous life. Consider what happens when Nancy, a baby boomer and successful business owner, decides to join a recreational group piano class for adults:

- **She immediately feels *relief from stress*.** After hours of intense daily pressure at work, Nancy finds it easy to unwind at the piano. The class moves at a comfortable pace and no one is ever required to play solo—which means zero stress. In her personal practice and in class, Nancy can just relax and have fun.

- **She's *making new friends*.** Because recreational piano classes are taught in groups, Nancy enjoys getting to know others who share a common interest. Many of her classmates are professional people like her who, after raising a family, are finally getting to try the things they've always wanted to do. The warm camaraderie among class members is a wonderful surprise.

- **She enjoys *playing her favorite songs*.** Nancy always dreamed of learning her two favorite Beatles tunes. Now, she's thrilled to play these and many other classic hits for friends and family.

- **Her *mind and spirit are enlivened*.** The process of learning something completely new has been intellectually and emotionally stimulating for Nancy. She enjoys a sense of adventure when exploring new musical concepts and genres with her classmates. Playing the piano has made her feel more fully alive.

Studies have shown that recreational group music-making can significantly improve the quality of life and personal well-being among those who embrace it. So even when you're playing the piano just for fun, *practice makes prosperous* in meaningful ways that far exceed the balance in your 401(k).

To give the piano a whirl, contact a local music store or independent piano teacher to find out about recreational piano classes in your area. Whether you're young or old, striving for success or just playing for fun, the prodigious power of playing the piano can change your life. 🎹

How about you?
Are you among the 82% of adults who have always wanted to learn how to play an instrument?

Brian Chung is Senior Vice President of Kawai America Corporation and a leading proponent of the benefits of making music. He is also a pianist, and co-author (with Dennis Thurmond) of *Improvisation at the Piano: A Systematic Approach for the Classically Trained Pianist* (Alfred Publishing, 2007). Visit his website at www.brianchung.net.

[2] Peter H. Wood, "The Comparative Academic Abilities of Students in Education and in Other Areas of a Multi-focus University," ERIC Document ED327480 (1990).
[3] *U.S. Gallup Poll.* 2008 Music USA NAMM Global Report (August, 2008): 139.

ACOUSTIC OR DIGITAL:
What's Best for Me?

ALDEN SKINNER AND LARRY FINE

FOR MANY, there will be no easy answer to this question. Many factors play into this seemingly simple decision, some practical, some not. Ideally, perhaps, the answer should be "Both"—take advantage of the "organic" qualities and connection with tradition of the acoustic piano, as well as the extreme flexibility of the digital. But assuming that, for a variety of reasons, "Both" isn't an option, careful consideration of the advantages and disadvantages of each will probably quickly reveal which will be best for you.

The advantages of the acoustic piano start with the fact that it's the "real thing," inherently capable of nuances that are difficult for the digital piano to emulate. The experience of playing an acoustic piano—the harmonics, the vibrations, the touch, the visual appeal, the interaction with the room, the connection with tradition—is so complex that digitals cannot reproduce it all. And, provided that it's a decent instrument and properly maintained, the acoustic will continue to serve you or a subsequent owner for several generations, after which it might be rebuilt and continue to make music.

If you're a beginner, the tone and touch of a good-quality digital piano should not interfere with the elementary learning process for a while, but is likely to become less satisfactory as you advance. If your aspiration is to play classical piano literature, the choice is clear: A digital may serve as a temporary or quiet-time practice instrument (some well-known classical pianists request that a digital piano be placed in their hotel rooms for practice and warmup), but the first time you play an acoustic piano that stirs your soul, there will be no turning back. Although digitals continue to draw closer to the ideal, there is, as yet, nothing like the total experience of playing a fine acoustic instrument.

The downside of an acoustic piano? Initial cost is generally higher, they're harder to move, the best ones take up a lot of space, and tuning and maintaining them adds several hundred dollars a year to their cost. And—most important—*all they will ever be or sound like is a piano.*

So why do sales of digital pianos outnumber sales of acoustics by more than two to one? Because, in addition to making a piano sound, digitals can also sound like any other instrument imaginable. State-of-the-art digital pianos can allow a player with even the most basic keyboard skills to sound like an entire orchestra. Many models have features that will produce an entire band or orchestra accompanying you as the soloist. Digital pianos can also be used as player pianos. They can enhance learning with educational software. They can be attached to a computer, and you can have an entire recording studio at your fingertips, with the computer printing the sheet music for anything you play. Many fine players whose main piano is a quality acoustic also have a digital, providing the technology for band and/or orchestral compositions, transcriptions, and fun!

Add to all that the advantages of lower cost, convenience, lack of maintenance expense, the ability to play silently with headphones, meeting the needs of multiple family members, the obvious advantages for piano classes, and computer connectivity, and you have a powerful argument for the digital.

While digital pianos have a lot of advantages, it's important to also consider the disadvantages. In addition to those related to learning and playing classical music, mentioned above, the life expectancy of a good digital piano is limited, primarily by obsolescence (digitals haven't been around long enough to know how long they will physically last), while the life expectancy of a good acoustic piano is upward of 50 years. Acoustic pianos hold their value rather well, while digitals, like other electronics, quickly drop in value. Obviously, then, if you're buying a starter instrument and plan to upgrade later, from a financial perspective you would do better to start with an acoustic piano.

Both variations have places in our musical lives. Now, which is right for you?

(If you're still unsure, you might want to consider a hybrid piano—see our story on the subject in this issue.)

> **Both variations have places in our musical lives. Now, which is right for you?**

~Celebrating~

30 YEARS
in North America

Kayserburg
Pianos for Artists

PEARL RIVER
The World's Best Selling Piano

Ritmüller
Since - 1795

It's been a great 30 years, but we've only just begun!

The Pearl River Piano Group is celebrating a momentous anniversary in North America. Since we began distribution in the US and Canada, our company has added two remarkable lines, Ritmüller and Kayserburg, and year by year earned outstanding reviews for our achievements in the piano industry. Under the stewardship of Master Designer, Lothar Thomma and Master Technician, Stephan Mohler, Pearl River has led the industry in combining 21st Century technology with old world craftsmanship. Even though we're already the world's largest piano manufacturer, we're continually perfecting the pianos we build. To learn more, visit **PearlRiverUSA.com**.

PEARL RIVER
The World's Best Selling Piano

Guangzhou Pearl River Piano Group Co., Ltd.
Distributor in North America:
GW Distribution, LLC. (845) 429.3712

Introduction

An acoustic piano can be one of the most expensive—and difficult—purchases most households will ever make. The "difficult" aspect arises from several factors that are peculiar to pianos and the piano business. First, a "modern" piano is essentially a 19th-century creation about which few people—even those who have played piano all their lives—know very much, and about which much of what they *think* they know may not be accurate or current. Thus, a person who sets out to buy a piano is unlikely to have a social support network of family and friends to serve as advisors, as they might if buying a car, house, or kitchen appliance. Even music teachers and experienced players often know little about piano construction or the rapidly changing state of piano manufacturing. They often rely on their past experience with certain brands, most of which have changed significantly.

Second, acoustic pianos are marketed nationally in the United States under some 70 different brand names (plus dozens of additional names marketed locally) from a dozen countries, in thousands of furniture styles and finishes—and that's just new pianos! Many once-popular brands have long gone out of business, yet pianos still bearing their name are made overseas, often to much lower standards, and marketed here. Add in more than a century's worth of used pianos under thousands of brand names in an almost infinite variety of conditions of disrepair and restoration. Just thinking about it makes me dizzy.

Third, new pianos can vary in price from $2,000 to $200,000. But unlike most consumer items, whose differences can be measured by the number of functions performed, or buttons, bells, whistles, and conveniences contained, most pianos, regardless of price, look very similar and do pretty much the same thing: they're shiny and black (or a wood color), play 88 notes, and have three pedals. The features advertised are often abstract, misleading, or difficult to see or understand. For this reason, it's often not clear just what you're getting for your money. This can lead to decision-making paralysis.

Last, while many piano salespeople do an honest and admirable job of guiding their customers through this maze, a significant minority—using lies, tricky pricing games, and false accusations against competing dealers and brands—make the proverbial used-car salesman look like a saint. And once you get through haggling over price—the norm in the piano business—you may be ready for a trip to a Middle East bazaar.

As you shop for a piano, you'll likely be bombarded with a great deal of technical jargon—after all, the piano is a complicated instrument. But don't allow yourself to be confused or intimidated. Although some technical information can be useful and interesting, extensive familiarity with technical issues usually isn't essential to a successful piano-shopping experience, especially when buying a new piano. (A little greater familiarity may be advisable when buying a used or restored instrument.) Most technical information you'll come across relates to how the manufacturer designed the instrument. You should focus on how the instrument sounds, feels, and looks, not how it got that way. In addition, technical features are often taken out of context and manipulated by advertising and salespeople—the real differences in quality are often in subtleties of design and construction that don't make good ad copy.

For 20 years, *The Piano Book* has acted as a textbook on how to buy a piano, but over the years many people have asked for something a little simpler. *Acoustic & Digital Piano Buyer* is the answer, and this article is the beginning. For those readers who love reading about the finer technical details, *The Piano Book* is a must read. But in the interests of brevity and simplicity, we decided in this publication to keep technical details to a minimum.

The purpose of this article is modest: to provide an overview of the piano-buying process, with an emphasis on the decisions you'll have to make along the way, and on the factors that will affect any acoustic piano purchase. To do this succinctly, it will be necessary to make a number of generalizations, which you can discard in favor of more complete or nuanced explanations

as you advance toward your goal. References are given to other articles in this publication, or to *The Piano Book*, for further information on selected topics. In addition, for answers to specific questions that arise while you shop, I recommend visiting the Piano Forum at Piano World (**www.pianoworld.com**), the premiere website for everything related to pianos and pianists.

Vertical or Grand?

Probably the most basic decision to make when buying a piano—and one you may have made already—is whether to buy a vertical or a grand. The following describes some of the advantages and disadvantages of each.

Vertical Advantages

- Takes up less space, can fit into corners
- Lower cost
- Easier to move

Vertical Disadvantages

- Sound tends to bounce back into player's face, making subtle control of musical expression more difficult.
- Action is not as advanced as grand; repetition of notes is slower and less reliable in most cases, and damping is sometimes less efficient.
- Keys are shorter than on grands, making subtle control of musical expression more difficult.
- Cabinetwork is usually less elegant and less impressive.

Vertical pianos are suitable for those with simpler musical needs, or where budget and space constraints preclude buying a grand. Despite the disadvantages noted above, some of the larger, more expensive verticals do musically rival smaller, less expensive grands. They may be a good choice where space is at a premium

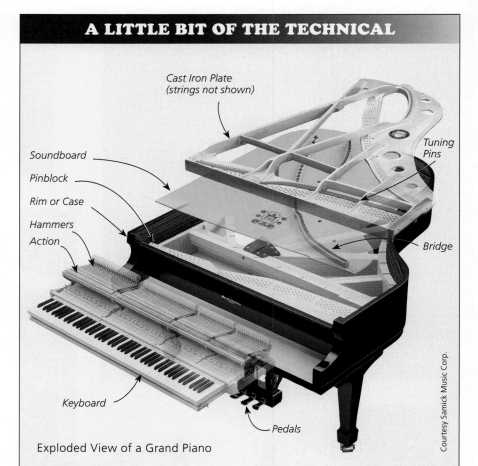

A LITTLE BIT OF THE TECHNICAL

Exploded View of a Grand Piano

Courtesy Samick Music Corp.

A little bit (but not too much) of technical information about the piano is useful to have while shopping for one. Important words are in **boldface**.

A piano can be thought of as comprising four elements: mechanical, acoustical, structural, and cabinetry.

Mechanical: When you press a piano **key** (usually 88 in number), the motion of your finger is transmitted through a series of levers and springs to a felt-covered wooden **hammer** that strikes the strings to set them vibrating. This complex system of keys, hammers, levers, and springs is known as the **action**. Also, when you press a key, a felt **damper** resting against each string lifts off, allowing the string to vibrate. When you let the key up, the damper returns to its resting place, stopping the string's vibration. **Pedals**, usually three in number, are connected to the action and dampers via **trapwork**

levers, and serve specialized functions such as sustaining and softening the sound. The right-foot pedal is called the **damper** or **sustain pedal**; it lifts all the dampers off all the strings, allowing the strings to ring sympathetically. The left-foot, **soft pedal** (on a grand piano, the **una corda pedal**) softens the sound. The function of the middle pedal varies depending on the type and price level of the piano (more on that later). As a **sostenuto pedal**, it selectively sustains notes or groups of notes, a function required only rarely in a small percentage of classical compositions. Other possible functions for the middle pedal include a damper pedal for the bass notes only, and a mute pedal that reduces the sound volume by about half.

Acoustical: Piano **strings** are made of steel wire for the higher-sounding notes (**treble**), and steel wire wrapped with copper for the lower-sounding

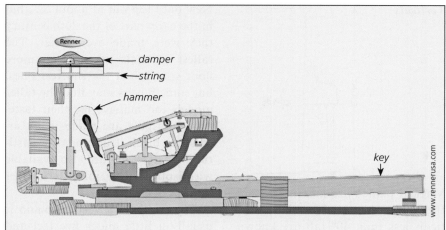

The key and action parts of a single note from a grand piano

[For online animation, click here.]

notes (**bass**). They are graduated in thickness, length, and tension, and strung tightly across the structural framework of the piano. Each note has one, two, or three strings associated with it. Each such set of strings is known as a **unison** because all the strings in a set vibrate at the same pitch. The strings lie across narrow hardwood **bridges** that transmit their vibrations to a wooden **soundboard**, usually made of spruce. The relatively large area of the soundboard amplifies what would otherwise be a rather weak sound and broadcasts the sound to the ears. The dimensions, arrangement, and positioning of all the acoustical elements in a piano is known as the piano's **scale design**. The scale design varies with the model and is a major determinant of the piano's tone.

Structural: The strings are strung across a gold- or bronze-colored **plate** (sometimes called a **frame** or **harp**) of cast iron, which is bolted to a substantial wooden framework. This heavy-duty structure is necessary to support the many tons of tension exerted by all the taut strings. A **vertical**, or upright, piano is one in which the structural element stands vertically, and is most commonly placed against a wall. A **grand** piano is one in which the structural

element lies horizontally. In a vertical piano, the wooden framework consists of vertical **back posts** and connecting cross beams. In a grand, wooden **beams** and the familiar curved **rim** comprise the framework. One end of each string is anchored to the plate toward the rear of a grand or the bottom of a vertical piano. The other end is coiled around a **tuning pin** embedded in a laminated hardwood **pinblock** hidden under the plate at the front (grand) or top (vertical). A piano is **tuned** by turning each tuning pin with a special tool to make very slight adjustments in the tension of its string, and thus to the string's frequency of vibration, or **pitch**.

Cabinetry: The piano's **cabinet** (vertical) or **case** (grand) provides aesthetic beauty and some additional structural support. A grand piano's rim is part of both the wooden structural framework and the case. Accessory parts, such as the music desk and lid, are both functional and aesthetic in purpose.

Although the acoustical and structural elements have been described separately, in fact the plate, wooden framework, soundboard, bridges, and strings form a single integrated unit called the **strung back**. A piano, then, consists of a strung back, an action, and a cabinet or case.

but a more subtle control of musical expression is desired.

Grand Advantages

- Sound develops in a more aesthetically pleasing manner by bouncing off nearby surfaces and blending before reaching player's ears, making it easier to control musical expression.
- More sophisticated action than in a vertical. Grand action has a repetition lever to aid in the speed and reliability of repetition of notes, and is gravity-assisted, rather than dependent on artificial contrivances (springs, straps) to return hammers to rest.
- Longer keys provide better leverage, allowing for significantly greater control of musical expression.
- Casework is usually more elegant and aesthetically pleasing.

Grand Disadvantages

- Takes up more space
- Higher cost
- Harder to move

What Size?

Both verticals and grands come in a wide variety of sizes. The important thing to know here is that size is directly related to musical quality. Although many other factors also contribute to tonal quality, all else being equal, the longer strings of larger pianos, especially in the bass and mid-range sections, give off a deeper, truer, more consonant tonal quality than the strings of smaller pianos. The treble and bass blend better and the result is more pleasing to the ear. Also, longer grands usually have longer keys that generally allow superior control of musical expression than shorter grands. Therefore, it's best to buy the largest piano you can afford and have

space for. Small differences in size between models are more significant in smaller pianos than in larger ones. However, a difference in size of only an inch or two is generally irrelevant, as it could be merely due to a larger cabinet or case.

Verticals

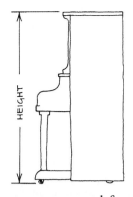

Vertical pianos are measured from the floor to the top of the piano. Verticals less than 40" tall are known as spinets. They were very popular in the post–World War II period, but in recent years have nearly died out. Verticals from 40" to about 43" or 44" are called consoles. Spinet and console actions must be compromised somewhat in size or placement within the piano to fit them into pianos of this size. The tone is also compromised by the shorter strings and smaller sound-board. For this reason, manufacturers concentrate on the furniture component of spinets and consoles and make them in a variety of decorator styles. They are suitable for buyers whose piano needs are casual, or for beginning students, and for those who simply want a nice-looking piece of furniture in the home. Once students progress to an intermediate or advanced stage, they are likely to need a larger instrument.

Studio pianos, from about 44" to 47", are more serious instruments. They are called studios because they are commonly found in the practice rooms of music schools. Manufacturers make them in both attractive furniture styles for the home and in functional, durable, but aesthetically bland styles for school and other institutional use. If you don't require attractive furniture, you may save money by buying the school style. In fact, many buyers prefer the simple lines of the institutional models.

Verticals about 48" and taller, called uprights, are the best musically.

New ones top out at about 52", but in the early part of the 20th century they were made even taller. The tallest verticals take up no more floor space than the shortest ones, but some buyers may find the taller models too massive for their taste. Most uprights are made in an attractive, black, traditional or institutional style, but are also available with exotic veneers, inlays, and other touches of elegance.

The width of a vertical piano is usually a little under five feet and the depth around two feet; however, these dimensions are not significantly related to musical quality.

Grands

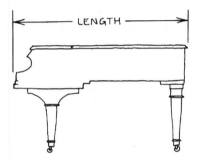

Grand pianos are measured with the lid closed from the very front of the piano (keyboard end) to the very back (the tail). Lengths start at 4' 6" and go to over 10' (even longer in some experimental models). Widths are usually around 5' and heights around 3', but only the length has a bearing on musical quality.

Grands less than 5' long are the musical equivalent of spinets and consoles; that is, they are musically compromised and are mainly sold as pieces of furniture. Grands between about 5' and 5½' are very popular. Although slightly compromised, they can reasonably serve both musical and furniture functions and are available in many furniture styles. (By the way, piano professionals prefer the term *small grand* to *baby grand*. Although there is no exact definition, a small grand

Baldwin

PROFESSIONAL SERIES GRANDS

Quality Features That Made Baldwin America's Favorite Piano

- All Maple inner and outer rim
- Wet sand cast plate
- Solid Sitka Spruce Soundboard
- Abel Hammers
- Real Ebony sharp keys

Available in 5 sizes –
BP148 (4'10")
BP152 (5')
BP165 (5'5")
BP178 (5'10") *
BP190 (6'3") *

*Now available with Magic-Lid!

Baldwin

is generally one less than about 5½' long.) Above 5½', pianos rapidly improve, becoming professional quality at about 6'. Pianos intended for the home or serious professional top out at about 7' or 7½'. These sizes may also satisfy the needs of smaller concert venues. Larger venues require concert grands, usually about 9' long.

When considering what size of piano is right for your home, don't forget to add two to three feet to the length of a grand or the depth of a vertical for the piano bench and pianist. Shoppers tend to underestimate what will fit and buy smaller pianos than necessary. Sometimes, the next-size-larger instrument can give you a great deal of tonal improvement at little additional cost. Dealers can usually lend you templates corresponding to different piano sizes to lay down on your floor so you can measure what will fit.

Budget

Your budget is probably the most important factor in your choice of piano, but it's hard to make a budget when you don't know how much pianos cost. Here is some rule-of-thumb information to get you started:

Most new vertical pianos sell in the range of $3,000 to $10,000, though some higher-end ones cost two or three times that, and a few cost less. Entry-level grand pianos generally go for $5,000 to $10,000, mid-range grands from $10,000 to $30,000, and high-end grands for $30,000 to $100,000 or more. Unrestored but playable used pianos cost from perhaps 20 to 80 percent of the cost of a comparable new instrument, depending on age and condition, with 15-year-old used pianos coming in at about 50 percent. The cost of restored instruments will be discussed later. More complete and accurate information can be found in the articles on **new** and **used** pianos, and in the "**Model & Pricing Guide**" reference section, elsewhere in this issue.

Rent or Buy?

If the piano is being purchased for a beginner, there is a significant possibility that he or she will not stick with playing the piano. To handle this and other "high-risk" situations, most dealers offer a rental/purchase program. In the typical program, the dealer would rent you the piano you are considering purchasing for up to six months. You would pay round-trip moving expenses upfront, usually $300 to $400, plus a monthly rental fee, typically $50 to $100 for a vertical piano. (Rental/purchase programs do not usually apply to grand pianos.) Should you decide to buy the piano at any time before the end of the six-month term, all money paid up to that point would be applied to the purchase. Otherwise, you would return the piano and be under no further obligation.

Two pieces of advice here: First, make sure you rent the piano you ultimately wish to buy, or at least rent from the dealer who has that piano, and not simply the piano or dealer with the lowest rental rate—if you eventually decide to buy from a different dealer, you'll forfeit the rental payments already made to the first dealer. However, if you decide to buy a different piano from the same dealer from whom you rented, it's possible that dealer would agree to apply some or all of the rental payments to the new piano—but check on this in advance. Second, clarify issues of price before you decide whether to rent or buy. Specifically, find out whether you'll be allowed to apply the rental payments toward, for example, today's sale price, rather than toward the regular price six months from now—or conversely, if you'll be held to today's price should there be a sale six months from now. Keep in mind, however, that a "sale" is generally a reduction in price designed to entice you to buy now.

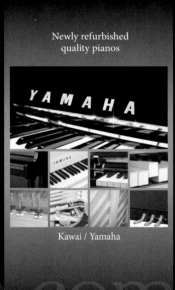

Quality

Like just about everything else you can buy, pianos come in a range of quality levels. When we speak of *quality* in a piano, we are referring to how it sounds, plays, and looks, and how well it will hold up with time and use. These are functions of the care taken in the design of the instrument; the quality of the materials used and how they are assembled; and the amount of handwork put into the final musical and aesthetic finishing of the instrument. With a new piano, we are also concerned, to a lesser extent, with how much pre-sale service is required by the dealer to make the instrument ready—a dealer is less likely to perform a lot of "make-ready" on an inexpensive piano. Also important are the terms of the warranty and the manufacturer's (or other warrantor's) reputation for honoring warranties. The prestige value of the name and the history of the brand may also be perceived as a form of quality by some buyers. *The Piano Book* goes into great detail about what creates quality in a piano.

As you can imagine, any discussion of quality in pianos is likely to involve a lot of subjectivity and be somewhat controversial. However, a useful generalization for the purpose of discussing quality can be had by dividing pianos into two types: performance-grade and consumer-grade. Performance-grade pianos are made to a single, high quality standard, usually in relatively small quantities, by companies that strongly favor quality considerations over cost. Consumer-grade pianos, on the other hand, are built to be sold at a particular price, and the design, materials, and level of workmanship are chosen to fit that price. Most consumer-grade pianos are mass-produced at a variety of price levels, with materials and designs chosen accordingly. Throughout much of the 20th century, the United States produced both types of piano in abundance. At the present time, however, most performance-grade pianos are made in Europe and the United States, while virtually all consumer-grade pianos are made in Asia. Due to globalization and other factors, the distinction between the two types of piano is beginning to blur. This is discussed at greater length in the article "The New-Piano Market Today," elsewhere in this issue.

The above explanation of quality in pianos is very general, and some aspects of quality may be more applicable to your situation than others. Therefore, it pays to take some time to consider exactly what you expect from your piano, both practically and in terms of lifestyle. Practical needs include, among others, the level of expressiveness you require in the piano's tone and touch, how long you want the instrument to last or intend to keep it, and what furniture it must match—as well as certain functional considerations, such as whether you use the middle pedal, desire a fallboard (key cover)

that closes slowly, or need to be able to lock the piano. Lifestyle needs are those that involve the prestige or artistic value of the instrument, and how ownership of it makes you feel or makes you appear to others. Just as a casual driver may own a Mercedes, or one devoid of artistic abilities may own great works of art, many who don't play a note purchase expensive pianos for their artistic and prestige value.

A couple of the practical considerations require further discussion. Concerning expressiveness: What kind of music do you play or aspire to play? One can play any kind of music on any piano. However, some pianos seem better suited in tone and touch than other kinds to some kinds of music. Quality in piano tone is often defined in terms of the instrument's ability to excel at pleasing players of so-called "classical" music because this kind of music tends to make the greatest expressive demands on an instrument. So if you aspire to play classical music seriously, you may wish to one day own a fine instrument capable of the nuanced tone and touch the music demands. On the other hand, if classical music isn't your thing, you

can probably get away with a much less expensive instrument.

A key factor concerns how long you want to keep the instrument: Is it for a beginner, especially a youngster, and you're not sure piano lessons will "stick"? Is it a stepping stone to a better piano later on? Then an inexpensive piano may do. Do you want this to be the last piano you'll ever buy? Then, even if your playing doesn't yet justify it, buy a piano you can grow into but never grow out of.

A note about how long a piano will last—a question I hear every day. The answer varies for pianos almost as much as it does for people. A piano played 16 hours a day in a school practice room might be "dead" in ten years or less, whereas one pampered in a living room in a mild climate might last nearly a century before requiring complete restoration to function again. A rule-of-thumb answer typically given is that an average piano under average conditions will last 40 to 50 years. If past experience is any guide, it would not be unreasonable to predict that the best-made pianos will last about twice as long as entry-level ones, given similar conditions of use and climate. However—and this is the important point—most pianos are discarded not because they no longer function—in fact, they may go on to long lives as used pianos for other people—but because they no longer meet the needs or expectations of their owners or players. A player may have musically advanced beyond what the instrument will deliver, or the owner may now be wealthier and have higher expectations for everything he or she buys—or perhaps no one in the house is playing anymore and the piano is just taking up space. Thus, the important consideration for most buyers, especially buyers of new or relatively young pianos, is how long the piano in question will

meet their needs and expectations, rather than how long that piano will last.

You'll get a better sense of what quality means in a piano if you play a wide variety of them, including ones that cost less than what you plan to spend, as well as ones you can't afford. Warning: The latter can prove dangerous to your bank account. It's not unusual for a buyer to begin shopping with the intention of buying a $3,000 vertical, only to emerge some time later with a $30,000 grand!

New or Used?

The next choice you'll have to make is whether to buy new or used. The market for used pianos is several times the size of the market for new ones. Let's look at the merits of each choice:

New Piano Advantages

- Manufacturer's warranty
- Little chance of hidden defects
- Lower maintenance costs
- Easier to shop for
- Usually more local choices
- Longer piano life expectancy
- Greater peace of mind after purchasing

New Piano Disadvantages

- Higher upfront cost
- Significant depreciation loss if resold within first few years
- Limited choice of attractive old styles and finishes

Used Piano Advantages

- Lower upfront cost
- Greater choice of attractive old styles and finishes
- Can be more fun and interesting to shop for (if you like shopping for old things)
- Restorer may detail instrument to an extent that rivals new piano
- Piano likely to be already significantly depreciated, resulting in little or no loss if resold

Used Piano Disadvantages

- No manufacturer's warranty (though there may be a dealer's or restorer's warranty)
- Greater chance of hidden defects (unless completely restored)
- Higher maintenance costs (unless completely restored)
- Shorter piano life expectancy (unless completely restored)
- Can be maddeningly difficult and confusing to shop for
- Need to pay technician to examine and appraise it
- Usually fewer local choices
- Possible need to size up restorer's ability to do a good job

Despite the longer list of disadvantages, most people buy used because of the lower upfront cost and because they feel they can manage the risks involved. The most important rule by far in managing risk is to have the piano professionally examined and appraised by a piano technician prior to purchase. This is especially important when buying from a private-party seller because there is no warranty, but it should also be done for peace of mind when buying from a professional seller, particularly if the piano is over ten years old. This will cost between $100 and $200 and is well worth the money. If you don't already have a piano technician you trust, hire a Registered Piano Technician (RPT) member of the Piano Technicians Guild (PTG). You can locate one near you on the PTG website, www.ptg.org. (To be designated an RPT, one must pass a series of tests. This provides the customer with some assurance of competence.)

A subset of used pianos consists of instruments that have been professionally restored. The complete restoration of a piano is known as *rebuilding*. There is no universally agreed-on definition of what is

Reinstalling the cast-iron plate during the rebuilding of a grand piano

www.spaldingpiano.com

included in a rebuilding job, so you have to ask specifically what has been done. A minimal partial restoration is called *reconditioning*—often just cleaning up the piano, replacing a few parts, and adjusting it. Vertical pianos are almost never completely rebuilt because the cost cannot be recouped in the sale price. However, verticals are frequently reconditioned. A complete rebuilding of a top-quality grand piano by a top-notch rebuilder generally costs from $20,000 to $40,000—and that's if you own the piano. If you're buying the piano too, figure a total cost of from 75 to more than 100 percent of the cost of a new piano of similar quality. A partial rebuilding of a lower-quality brand might cost half that, or even less.

Buying a used or restored piano is generally more difficult than buying a new one because, in addition to making judgments about the underlying quality of the instrument, you also must make judgments about its condition or about the skill and trustworthiness of the restorer—there's a greater concern about being burned if you make a mistake. Some find this too stressful or time-consuming. Others find the hunt fascinating, and end up discovering an

entire world of piano buffs, and piano technical and historical trivia, in their community or online. It helps to remember that a new piano becomes "used" the moment it is first sold. Although junk certainly exists, used pianos actually come in a bewildering variety of conditions and situations, many of which can be quite attractive, musically and financially. The subject is vast. *The Piano Book* has a chapter devoted to it, including how to do your own preliminary technical examination of a piano. A summary of the most important information, including a description of the most common types of used pianos, where to find them, and how much to pay, can be found in the article "Buying a Used or Restored Piano" elsewhere in this issue.

The Piano Dealer

The piano dealer is a very important part of the piano-buying experience, for several reasons. First, a knowledgeable and helpful salesperson can help you sort through the myriad possibilities and quickly home in on the piano that's right for you. Second, a dealership with a good selection of instruments can provide you with enough options to choose from that you don't end up settling for less than what you really want (although you can make up for this to some extent by shopping among a number of dealers). Third, all pianos arrive from the factory needing some kind of pre-sale adjustment to compensate for changes that occur during shipment, or for musical finishing work left uncompleted at the factory. Dealers vary a great deal in their willingness to perform this work. There's nothing worse than trying to shop for a piano, and finding them out of tune or with obvious defects. It's understandable that the dealer will put the most work into the more expensive pianos, but

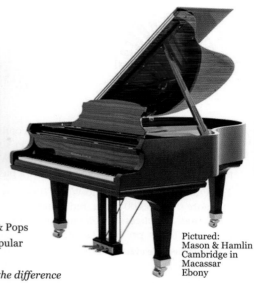
a good dealer will make sure that even the lower-cost instruments are reasonably playable. Last, a good dealer will provide prompt, courteous, skilled service to correct any small problems that occur after the sale, and act as your intermediary with the factory in the rare event that warranty service is needed. Knowledge, experience, helpfulness, selection, and service—that's what you're looking for in a dealer.

Shopping Long-Distance via the Internet

The question often arises as to whether one should shop for a piano long-distance via the Internet. It turns out that this is really two different questions. The first is whether one should locate a dealer via the Internet, possibly far away, then visit that dealer to buy a piano. The second is whether one should buy a piano sight unseen over the Internet.

If you're shopping for a new piano, you'll probably have to visit a dealer. This is because dealers are generally prohibited by their agreements with manufacturers from quoting prices over the phone or via the Internet to customers outside their "market territory," the definition of which differs from brand to brand. But once you set foot in the dealer's place of business, regardless of where you came from, you're considered a legitimate customer and all restrictions are off, even after you return home. There are no such restrictions for advertising or selling used pianos.

Customers, of course, don't care about "market territories." They just want to get the best deal. Given the ease of comparison shopping via the Internet, and the frequency with which people travel for business or pleasure, dealers are increasingly testing the limits of their territorial

restrictions, and more and more sales are taking place at dealerships outside the customer's area. This is a delicate subject in the industry, and the practice is officially discouraged by dealers and manufacturers alike. In private, however, dealers are often happy when the extra business walks in the door (though they hate like heck to lose a sale to a dealer outside their area), and some manufacturers are choosing to look the other way.

There are obvious advantages to shopping locally, and it would be foolish not to at least begin there. Shopping, delivery, and after-sale service are all much easier, and there can be pleasure in forging a relationship with a local merchant. That said, every person's lifestyle and priorities are different. A New Yorker who frequently does business in San Francisco may find it more "local" to visit a piano dealer

in downtown San Francisco, near his or her business meeting, than to drive all over the New York metropolitan area with spouse and children on a Saturday morning. In the marketplace, the customer is king. As people become more and more at ease with doing business of all kinds long-distance with the aid of the Internet, it's inevitable that piano shopping will migrate in that direction as well. In recognition of this trend, several manufacturers now mandate that when a customer buys a piano from a dealer outside the customer's local area, the local authorized dealer of that brand will actually deliver the piano, and will receive a small percentage of the sale from the selling dealer in return for handling any warranty issues that may arise.

Buying a piano sight unseen (which, in view of the above discussion, must involve used pianos, not new) is something entirely different. Obviously, if you're at all musically sensitive, buying a piano without trying it out first is just plain nuts. But, as much as I hate to admit it, it may make sense for some people. In the piano business, we like to say (and I say it a lot) that a piano is not a commodity; that is, a product of which one example is more or less interchangeable with another. Each piano is unique, etc., etc., and must be individually chosen. But for someone who is buying a piano for a beginner, who has no preference in touch and tone, and just wants a piano that's reasonably priced, reliable, and looks nice, a piano may, in fact, actually be a "commodity." I might wish it were otherwise, just as an audiophile might wish that I wouldn't buy a stereo system off the shelf of a discount department store, but we're all aficionados of some things and indifferent about others, and that's our choice. Furthermore, just as people who buy electronic keyboards frequently graduate to acoustic pianos, the person who today buys a piano over the Internet may tomorrow be shopping at a local dealer for a better piano with a particular touch and tone. Although it isn't something I'd advise as a general rule, the fact is that many people have bought pianos over the Internet without first trying them out and are pleased with their purchase (and some people, probably, are not so pleased).

If you're thinking of making a long-distance purchase, however, please take some precautions (not all of these precautions will be applicable to every purchase). First, consider whether it's really worth it once you've taken into account the cost of long-distance shipping. Find out as much as you can about the dealer. Get references. Get pictures of the piano. Hire a piano technician in the dealer's area to inspect the piano (use the Piano Technicians Guild website, www .ptg.org, to find a technician) and ask the technician about the dealer's reputation. Make sure the dealer is experienced with arranging long-distance piano moves, and uses a mover that specializes in pianos. Find out who is responsible for tuning and adjusting the piano in your home, and for repairing any defects or dings in the finish. Get the details of the warranty, especially who is responsible for paying the return freight if the piano is defective. Find out how payment is to be made in a way that protects both parties. And if, after all this, you still want to buy long-distance, my best wishes for a successful purchase.

Negotiating Price and Trade-Ins

The prices of new pianos are nearly always negotiable. Only a handful of dealers have non-negotiable prices. If in doubt, just ask—you'll be able to tell. Some dealers carry this bargaining to extremes, whereas others start pretty close to the final price.

Many dealers don't like to display a piano's price because not doing so gives them more latitude in deciding on a starting price for negotiation, depending on how they size up the customer. This makes shopping more difficult. Use the price information in the "Model & Pricing Guide" of the current issue of *Acoustic & Digital Piano Buyer* to determine the likely range within which a given model will sell. Don't give in too quickly. It's quite common for the salesperson to call a day or two later and offer a lower price. If there's an alternative piano at another dealership that will suit your needs just as well, it will help your negotiating position to let the salesperson know that.

Due to the high cost of advertising and conducting piano megasales (such as college sales, truckload sales, etc.), prices at these events are often actually *higher* than the price you could negotiate any day of the week, and the pressure to buy can be enormous. Shop at these sales only after you've shopped elsewhere, and look for the real bargains that occasionally exist.

If you're buying a new piano to replace one that's no longer satisfactory, you'll probably want to trade in the old one. Dealers will usually take a trade-in, no matter how bad it is, just to be able to facilitate the sale. In fact, in many cases the dealer will offer you what seems like a king's ransom for the old one. The downside is that when a generous trade-in allowance is given on the old piano, the dealer is then likely to offer you a less-generous price on the new one. To see if you're being offered a good deal, you'll have to carefully analyze the fair-market value of the old piano and what would be a likely price for the new one without a trade-in. Sometimes it will be to your advantage to sell the old piano privately, though in that case you'll need to take into account the hassle factor as well.

For more information about new-piano prices and negotiating, see the introduction to the "Model & Pricing Guide," elsewhere in this issue, as well as in *The Piano Book*.

Used-piano prices may or may not be negotiable. If the used piano is being sold by a dealer who primarily sells new pianos at negotiable prices, then the used-piano prices are probably also negotiable. Prices of restored pianos sold by the restorer are less likely to be negotiable, as technical people are usually less comfortable with bargaining. Prices of pianos for sale by private-party sellers are usually negotiable, in part because the seller often has little idea of what the piano should sell for and has just made up a price on the basis of wishful thinking. But even knowledgeable sellers will usually leave a little wiggle room in their price.

Electronic Player-Piano Systems

Prior to the Great Depression, most pianos were outfitted with player-piano mechanisms—the kind that ran on pneumatic pressure and paper rolls. Today's player pianos are all electronic; they run on CDs, iPods, floppy diskettes, or electronic downloads from the Internet, and are far more versatile and sophisticated than their pneumatic ancestors. Now you don't have to wait until Junior grows up to hear something interesting from the piano! A substantial percentage of new pianos, especially grands, are being outfitted with these systems. In fact, many pianos are being purchased as home-entertainment centers by buyers who have no intention of ever playing the piano themselves.

Several companies make these systems. Yamaha's Disklavier system is built into select Yamaha models at the Yamaha factory. PianoDisc and QRS Pianomation, the two major after-market systems, can be installed in any piano, new or used, typically by the dealer or at an intermediate distribution point. If installed properly by a trained and authorized installer, none of these systems will harm the piano or void its warranty. However, such installations are complicated and messy and must be done in a shop, not in your home.

The most basic system will play your piano and accompany it with synthesized orchestration or actual recorded accompaniment over speakers attached to the piano. These systems generally add about $4,000 to $7,000 to the price of the piano. Add another $1,500 to $2,000 to enable the piano to record your own playing for future

PianoDisc

Typically, the control box for an electronic player-piano system is attached to the underside of the keybed.

playback. For a little bit more, you can mute the piano (stop the hammers from hitting the strings), turn on a digital piano sound, and listen through headphones. The range of prices reflects the variety of configurations and options available, including what music source you use (CD, iPod, MP3 player, etc.) and how much memory storage you purchase, among others. There are also higher-level systems at twice the price that provide touch screens with wireless connection for instant downloading of songs from the Internet. See the article "Buying an Electronic Player-Piano System" elsewhere in this issue for more information.

Furniture Style and Finish

Although for most buyers the qualities of performance and construction are of greatest importance in selecting a piano, a piano is also a large piece of furniture that tends to become the focal point of whatever room it is placed in. This is especially true of grands. Add to that the fact that you'll be looking at it for many years to come, and it becomes obvious that appearance can be an important consideration. For some buyers, it may be the most important consideration.

Vertical pianos without front legs are known as *Continental* style (also called *Contemporary, European*

Contemporary, or *Eurostyle*). They are usually the smallest (42 to 43 inches high) and least expensive pianos in a manufacturer's product line.

Pianos with legs supported by *toe blocks* are sometimes known as *Institutional* or *Professional* style, particularly when the cabinet also has little in the way of decoration or embellishment.

School pianos are a subset of the institutional-style category. Generally 45 to 47 inches in height, these are institutional-style pianos made specifically for use in school practice rooms and classrooms. They usually come equipped with long music racks for holding multiple sheets of music, locks for both the lid and the fallboard, and heavy-duty casters for easier moving. They are generally available in ebony or satin wood finishes. Sturdy and sometimes plain-looking, they are also often purchased by non-institutional customers for less furniture-conscious locations. (If you're buying a piano for an institution, please read "Buying Pianos for an Institution," elsewhere in this issue.)

Institutional or Professional Style

Samick Music Corp.

School Style

Pramberger Piano Co.

Decorator Style: French Provincial Cherry

Pramberger Piano Co.

Decorator Style: Traditional Mahogany

Pramberger Piano Co.

Continental Style

Wyman/Orla

Decorator Style: Mediterranean Oak

Samick Music Corp.

Hybrid Style

Wyman/Orla

Straight Leg

Spade Leg

Victorian Style
with Ice-Cream Cone legs

Petrof

Queen Anne Style

Samick Music Corp.

Yamaha Corp.

Vertical pianos with free-standing legs not reinforced by toe blocks are generally known as *Decorator* style. Common decorator styles are Queen Anne and French Provincial, generally in cherry (or Country French in oak), all with curved legs; Italian Provincial, typically in walnut with square legs; Mediterranean, usually in oak with hexagonal legs; and Traditional, most often in mahogany or walnut, with round or hexagonal legs. Matching music racks and cabinet decoration are common furniture embellishments. Furniture-style preference is an entirely personal matter. A practical consideration, however, is that front legs not supported by toe blocks have a tendency to break if the piano is moved frequently.

Hybrids styles, containing features of both institutional and decorator styles, are common, especially in Asian pianos.

Grand pianos come in far fewer styles than verticals. As you shop, it is likely you will see only a few different styles, in a number of woods and finishes.

The traditional grand piano case is likely familiar to everyone. It has

rather straight or slightly tapered legs, often flaring slightly just above the floor (called a *spade* leg), and usually a rather plain, solid music rack.

Victorian style (sometimes called *Classic* style) is an imitation of a style in fashion in the late 1800s, with large, round, fluted legs and a fancy, carved music desk. Variations of the Victorian style have "ice-cream cone" or other types of round-ish legs.

As with verticals, grands also come in Queen Anne and French Provincial styles, with curved legs, and in other period styles. In addition to the leg style, these usually differ in the treatment of the music rack and cabinet embellishment as well.

Pianos come in a variety of woods, most commonly ebony (sometimes called ebonized), which is not actual ebony wood, but an inexpensive, sturdy veneer that has been painted black; as well as mahogany, cherry, walnut, and oak. Exotic woods include bubinga, rosewood, and many others, available on higher-priced uprights and grands. In pianos of lesser quality, sometimes a less expensive wood will be stained to look like a more expensive one. Pianos are

also available in ivory or white, and it's often possible to special-order a piano in red, blue, or other colors.

In addition to the wood itself, the way the wood is finished also varies. Piano finishes come in either high polish (high gloss) or satin finishes. Satin reflects light but not images, whereas high polish is nearly mirror-like. Variations on satin include matte, which is completely flat (i.e., reflects no light), and open-pore finishes, common on European pianos, in which the grain is not filled in before finishing, leaving a slightly grainier texture. A few finishes are semigloss, which is partway between satin and high polish. As with furniture style, the finish is an entirely personal matter, though it should be noted that satin finishes tend to show fingerprints more than do high-polish finishes.

Most piano finishes are either lacquer or polyester. Lacquer was the finish on most pianos made in the first three-quarters of the 20th century, but it is gradually being supplanted by polyester. In my opinion, lacquer finishes—especially high-gloss lacquer—are more beautiful

than polyester, but they scratch quite easily, whereas polyester is very durable. (Lacquer finishes can be repaired more easily.) Hand-rubbed satin lacquer is particularly elegant. Sometimes, when a customer desires a piano in a satin finish but the dealer has in stock only the high-polish polyester model, the dealer will offer to buff it down to a satin finish at a cost of $500 to $1,000. This is commonly done, and it works, but usually doesn't look as nice as the factory-made satin finish.

Touch and Tone

Touch, in its simplest form, refers to the effort required to press the piano keys. Unfortunately, the specifications provided by the manufacturers, expressed in grams, don't do justice to this complicated subject. The apparent touch can be very different when the piano is played fast and loud than when it is played soft and slow, and this difference is not captured in the numbers. If you are other than a beginner, be sure to try it out both ways.

Advanced pianists tend to prefer a touch that is moderately firm because it provides better control than a very light touch and strengthens the muscles. Too light a touch, even for a beginner, can cause laziness, but too firm a touch can be physically harmful over time. The touch of most new pianos today is within a reasonable range for their intended audience, but the touch of older pianos can vary a lot depending on condition. A piano teacher may be able to assist in evaluating the touch of a piano for a beginner, particularly if considering an entry-level or used piano.

Piano *tone* is also very complex. The most basic aspect of tone, and the one most easily changed, is its brightness or mellowness. A *bright* tone, sometimes described by purchasers as *sharp* or *loud*, is one in which higher-pitched overtones predominate. A *mellow* tone, sometimes described as *warm*, *dull*, or *soft*, is one in which lower-pitched overtones are dominant. Most pianos are somewhere in between, and vary from one part of the keyboard to another, or depending on how hard one plays. The key to satisfaction is to make sure that the tone is right for the music you most often play or listen to. For example, jazz pianists will often prefer a brighter tone, whereas classical pianists will often prefer one that is mellower, or that can be varied easily from soft to loud; i.e., that has a broad dynamic range. However, there is no accounting for taste, and there are as many exceptions to these generalizations as there are followers. A piano technician can make adjustments to the brightness or mellowness of the tone through a process known as *voicing*.

Another aspect of tone to pay attention to is *sustain*, which is how long the sound of a note continues at an audible level, while its key is depressed, before disappearing. Practically speaking, this determines the ability of

a melodic line to "sing" above an accompaniment, especially when played in the critical mid-treble section.

Most pianos will play loudly quite reliably, but providing good expression when played softly is considerably more challenging. When trying out a piano, be sure to play at a variety of dynamic levels. Test the action with your most technically demanding passages. Don't forget to test the pedals for sensitivity commensurate with your musical needs.

Room acoustics have a tremendous effect on piano tone, so you'll want to note the extent to which the

THE PIANO AS SCULPTURE

Both grands and verticals are available in *Designer* versions, with such decorative features as inlays and marquetry, carving, wood veneer or chrome accents, burl woods, two-tone effects, decorative moldings, painting, and more. Some designer pianos are outrageous or defy categorization, while others attempt to be very "modern," or combine both the modern and the traditional.

The highest form of piano art is embodied in *Art-Case* pianos. These are usually highly decorated instruments, their embellishments organized around a theme and designed by a famous furniture designer, who in his work may make use of inlays, paintings, gem stones, or just about any other medium one can think of. These pianos are very expensive and considered works of art as well as musical instruments.

Under the heading "Piano Art," examples of designer and art-case pianos are scattered throughout this publication for your appreciation and amusement.

PianoMart.com

Buy or Sell A Piano

acoustics of the dealer's showroom differ from those of your home, and make allowance for it. Hard surfaces, such as bare walls, tile, and glass will make the tone brighter. Absorbent surfaces—upholstered furniture, heavy drapes, plush carpeting—will make it mellower. Once the piano is in the home, a technician may be able to make adjustments to the tone, but to avoid unpleasant surprises, it's best to buy a piano whose tone is already close to what you want. Adjusting the room acoustics through the strategic use of wall hangings, scatter rugs, and furniture can also help. See the article "Ten Ways to Voice a Room," elsewhere in this issue.

The Piano Warranty

The majority of pianos never generate a warranty claim. That said, few people would sleep well worrying about potential problems arising in such a major purchase. Key

warranty issues are: what is covered, for how long, and who stands behind the warranty. The overwhelming majority of new-piano warranties cover the cost of parts and labor necessary to correct any defect in materials or workmanship. The warrantor (usually the manufacturer or distributor) also generally reserves the right to replace the piano should it choose to in lieu of repair. The warrantee (the customer) generally makes warranty claims to the dealer who, upon approval of the warrantor, makes the necessary repairs or replaces the instrument, as applicable. If the dealer is out of business, or if the customer has moved, warranty claims are made to the new local dealer of that brand, if any, or directly to the warrantor.

Warranties are in effect from the date of purchase and generally run between five and fifteen years, depending on the manufacturer. Note that there is little correlation between the length of warranty and

the quality of the piano, as decisions on warranty terms are often made based on marketing factors. For example, a new manufacturer might well offer a longer warranty to help bolster sales.

The Magnuson-Moss Warranty Act mandates that warranties be either *full* or *limited*. In the piano industry, the only significant difference is that full warranties remain in effect for the entire stated term, regardless of piano ownership, whereas limited warranties cover only the original purchaser. If you plan on possibly selling or trading up within a few years, a full warranty offers protection to the new owner, increasing the piano's value to them, and may justify a little higher selling price or trade-in value.

The final key issue about piano warranties concerns who stands behind the warranty. In most cases the warranty is backed by the actual manufacturer. This is advantageous, as the manufacturer has a major capital investment in its factory and has probably been in business for many years. The likelihood is that it will be around for the entire five- to fifteen-year period of your warranty. In today's piano market, however, many brands are manufactured under contract for a distributor, and the warranty is backed only by that distributor. Often, the distributor's only investment is a small rented office/warehouse and a few dozen pianos. Pianos are also often made to order for a particular dealership under a private brand name and are sold—and warranted—only by that dealership and/or its affiliates. In those cases, the warranty is further limited by the financial strength of the distributor or dealership, which can be difficult for the shopper to evaluate. In these situations, caution is called for.

When purchasing a used or restored piano, there is no warranty from a private, non-commercial seller, but a commercial seller will usually provide some kind of warranty, even if for only a few months. Pianos that have been completely restored typically come with a warranty with terms similar to that of a new piano, though of course it is backed by only the restorer.

Miscellaneous Practical Considerations

Bench

In all likelihood, your purchase of a new piano will include a matching bench. Benches for consumer-grade pianos are usually made by the piano manufacturer and come with the piano. Benches for performance-grade pianos are more often provided separately by the dealer.

Benches come in two basic types: fixed-height and adjustable. Consumer-grade pianos usually come with fixed-height benches that have either a solid top that matches the piano's finish, or a padded top with sides and legs finished to match the piano. The legs of most benches will be miniatures of the piano's legs, particularly for decorative models. Most piano benches have music storage compartments. School and institutional-type vertical pianos often come with so-called "stretcher" benches—the legs are connected with wooden reinforcing struts to better endure heavy use.

Adjustable benches are preferred by serious players, and by children and adults who are shorter or taller than average. The deeply-tufted tops come in a heavy-duty vinyl and look like leather; tops of actual leather are available at additional cost. Adjustable benches vary considerably in quality. The best ones are expensive ($500 to $750) but are built to last a lifetime.

Finally, if the piano you want doesn't come with the bench you desire, talk to your dealer. It's common for dealers to swap benches or bench tops to accommodate your preference, or to offer an upgrade to a better bench in lieu of a discount on the piano.

For more information, see "Benches, Lamps, Accessories, and Problem Solvers," elsewhere in this issue.

Middle Pedal

As I mentioned near the beginning of this article, the function of the middle pedal varies. In some circumstances, you may need to consider whether the function of the middle pedal on a particular instrument will meet your musical needs.

On most new vertical pianos, the middle pedal operates a mute that reduces the sound volume by about 50 percent, a feature often appreciated by family members of beginning students. If your piano lacks this

feature, after-market mute mechanisms are available for grands and verticals through piano technicians or dealers. On older verticals and a few new ones, the middle pedal, if not a mute, usually operates a bass sustain, although occasionally it's a "dummy" pedal that does nothing at all. I've never known anyone to actually use a bass-sustain pedal, so it might as well be a dummy.

On most grands and a few expensive uprights, the middle pedal operates a sostenuto mechanism that selectively sustains only those notes whose keys are down at the moment the pedal is pressed. This mechanism is called into action for only a relatively few pieces of classical music, yet it is generally considered obligatory for any "serious" instrument. Only inexpensive new and used grands omit the sostenuto, usually in favor of a bass sustain. (The obligatory nature of the sostenuto pedal—or any middle pedal—on a grand piano is a largely American phenomenon. Until fairly recently, many "serious" European pianos made for the European market had only two pedals.)

Fallboard *(Keyboard Cover)*

Vertical pianos use one of three basic fallboard designs: the Boston fallboard, a sliding fallboard (both of which disappear when open), or a one-piece "drop" fallboard with integrated music shelf.

The Boston fallboard is found on most furniture-style pianos and characteristically is a two-piece, double-hinged assembly. It is easily removed for service, and the rigidity provided by the hinges keeps the fallboard and the piano's side arms from being scratched when the fallboard is opened or closed.

The sliding fallboard, a one-piece cover that slides out from under the music desk to cover the keys, is considerably less expensive. However, if it is pulled unevenly and/or upwardly, it can scratch the fallboard or the inside of the piano's side arms.

The one-piece "drop" fallboard is commonly found on larger uprights. It is simply hinged at the back and lifts up to just past vertical, where it lies against the upper front panel of the piano. Attached to its underside is a small music shelf that is exposed when the fallboard is opened, then manually unfolded.

Grand pianos use a smaller one-piece "drop" fallboard that opens under the music desk. Fallboards on many newer grands are hydraulically damped so as to close slowly over the keys, eliminating the possibility of harming the player's or a young child's fingers. Aftermarket kits are available for pianos that lack this feature.

WHEN I BEGAN servicing pianos during the 1970s, most pianos sold in the U.S. (with the important exception of the growing number of pianos from Japan) were made in the U.S. by about a dozen different makers, which together turned out hundreds of thousands of pianos annually. By current standards, many were not particularly well made. Today, only three companies make pianos in the U.S. in any real quantities, which combined amount to no more than a few thousand instruments per year. However, over 30,000 new acoustic pianos are sold here annually under some 70 different brand names, made by more than 30 companies in a dozen countries. The quality is the best it's ever been. Here are the highlights of what's happened:

- The Japanese "invasion" of the 1960s onward was followed by a wave of pianos from Korea in the 1980s and '90s. Together, these imports put most low- and mid-priced American makers out of business.
- Rising wages in Korea in the 1990s caused much of that country's piano production to move to Indonesia and China.
- The economic emergence of China during the 2000s resulted in a new wave of low-priced, low-quality pianos appearing in the U.S. and globally.
- Foreign firms and investors have combined low-cost Chinese and Indonesian labor with high-quality design and manufacturing expertise, parts, and materials from Western countries to greatly increase the quality of low-priced Chinese and Indonesian pianos.
- Cheaper equipment for computer-aided design and manufacturing has allowed for their more widespread use by small and large firms alike, with a consequent increase in precision of manufacturing at all price levels.
- Since the 1990s, a dozen or more European makers of high-quality pianos have been aggressively marketing their pianos in the U.S., challenging entrenched interests and creating more choice and higher quality in the high end of the piano market. They are currently hampered, however, by a disadvantageous exchange rate.
- To better survive in a global economy, high-end companies have diversified their product lines to include low- and mid-priced pianos, setting up factories or forming alliances with companies in parts of the world where labor is cheaper. At the same time, makers of low- and mid-priced pianos are creating higher-priced models using parts and expertise usually associated with the high-end companies, thus blurring the line between the high and low ends of the piano market.

> Over 30,000 new acoustic pianos are sold here annually under some 70 different brand names, made by more than 30 companies in a dozen countries.

China

The first piano factory in China is said to have been established in 1895, in Shanghai (perhaps by the British?). During the 1950s, the Communists consolidated the country's piano manufacturing into four government-owned factories: Shanghai, Beijing, and Dongbei (means "northeast") in the northern part of the country, and Guangzhou Pearl River in the south. Piano making, though industrial, remained primitive well into the 1990s. In that decade, the government of China began to open the country's economy to foreign investment, first only to partnerships with the government, and later to completely private concerns.

As China's economy has opened up, the nation's rising middle and upper classes have created a sharp increase in demand for pianos. Tempted by the enormous potential of the Chinese domestic market, as well as by the lure of cheap goods manufactured for the West, foreign interests have built new piano factories in China, bought existing factories, or contracted with existing factories for the manufacture of pianos. The government has also poured money into its own factories to make them more competitive and to accommodate the growing demand.

Except for the government involvement, the piano-making scene in China today is reminiscent of that in the U.S. a century ago: Hundreds of small firms assemble pianos from parts or subassemblies obtained from dozens of suppliers and sell them on a mostly regional basis. The government factories and a few large foreign ones sell nationally. Most of the pianos sold in the Chinese domestic market are still primitive by Western standards. Primarily, the quality has markedly improved where foreign technical assistance or investment has been involved; only those pianos are good enough to be sold in the West.

Although in China the government factories have long had a monopoly on sales through piano dealers, that hold is gradually being eroded, and the government entities are experiencing great competitive pressure from all the smaller players. Combined with the inefficiencies and debt inherent in government operations, the current competitive situation is probably making the government think twice about continuing to subsidize the piano industry. Already, one of its factories, Dongbei, has been privatized through its sale to Gibson Guitar Corporation, parent of Baldwin Piano Company; and another, Guangzhou Pearl River, has successfully completed an initial public offering to become a public company.

Besides Baldwin, Pearl River, and the government-owned factories, other large makers in China for the North American market are Parsons Music (Hong Kong), Yamaha (Japan), Young Chang (Korea), and, for the Canadian market, Kawai (Japan)—all of whom own factories in China. Other foreign-owned companies that own factories in China or contract with Chinese manufacturers to make pianos for the U.S. market include AXL (Palatino brand), Bechstein (W. Hoffmann Vision brand), Blüthner (Irmler Studio brand), Brodmann, Cunningham, Heintzman, Perzina, Schulze Pollmann, and Wilh. Steinberg. Many American distributors and dealers contract with Beijing, Pearl River, and other makers, selling pianos in the U.S. under a multitude of names. Steinway & Sons markets the Essex brand, designed by Steinway and manufactured by Pearl River.

And one company, Hailun, is owned and operated by a Chinese entrepreneur, Chen Hailun.

From about 2000 to 2005, most sales of Chinese pianos in the U.S. were based on the idea of luring customers into the store to buy the least expensive piano possible. Dealers that staked their business on this approach often lost it. A growing trend now is to manufacture and sell somewhat higher-priced pianos that have added value in the form of better components, often imported to China from Europe and the U.S., but still taking advantage of the low cost of Chinese labor. The best ones are not just a collection of parts, however, but also have improved designs developed with foreign technical assistance, and sufficient oversight to make sure the designs are properly executed.

The oversight is especially important. Chinese piano manufacturers have been quite aggressive in acquiring piano-making knowledge, and are happy to use their alliances with Western distributors in furthering that end. There has been a tendency, however, for Chinese factory managers to ignore the advice and requests of Western distributors once their inspectors leave the factory, resulting in product that does not meet the standards or specifications contracted for. The distributors have gradually discovered that the only way to overcome this problem is to own the factory themselves, to maintain a constant presence at the factory, or to constitute such a large percentage of the Chinese company's business that they, the Westerners, can control production. Alternatively, a Western company can examine all the pianos in its home country before sending them on to dealers, but this is less satisfactory than stopping problems at the source. Western distributors of Korean pianos used to complain of a similar problem with Korean factory managers during the height of that country's piano industry in the 1980s and '90s. As in Korea, the situation in China is rapidly improving as the Chinese become accustomed to Western ways of doing business and more focused on quality control.

Pianos made in China now dominate the North American market, constituting more than a third of all new pianos sold in the U.S. A decade ago, most were just barely acceptable technically, and musically undesirable. Over the years, however, both the technical and musical qualities have taken big leaps forward. While some remain at the entry level, others rival the performance of more expensive pianos from other parts of the world. Reports sometimes suggest less consistency than with pianos from other countries, and a continuing need for thorough pre-sale preparation by the dealer (who sometimes must weed out the bad ones and return them to the factory), but otherwise few major problems. The prices of the better models are rising, but for entry- and mid-level buyers, many Chinese brands are still good value.

Indonesia

Indonesia is China's closest competitor in terms of price and quality. But unlike China, in which many small and large companies, domestic and foreign, are involved

Portland's Own *Piano Shop on the Left Bank:*
www.classicportland.com

Visitors to *Classic Pianos* of Portland, Oregon are surprised to discover the ambiance of an old-world *Restoration Shop* and three distinctive *Piano Salons* within a museum-like atmosphere of used brick walls, waxed concrete and rough plank floors, original wall art created from antique piano parts, and hanging re-bronzed piano harps.

Adjacent to the piano shop is a circa 1912 craftsman mission chapel that once served as offices for the Episcopal Diocese of Oregon. Now restored and enlarged to include a condominium for out of town guests, this quaint structure for auditioning pianos has been renamed *The Schimmel House (Das Schimmel Haus).*

Classic Pianos, located at the East End of the Ross Island Bridge, crossing over the Willamette River into Portland's historic southeast "*Brooklyn Neighborhood*," has reached national and international recognition. Guests often comment that it's a chapter right out of Thad Carhart's national bestseller, *THE PIANO SHOP ON THE LEFT BANK:* "Discovering a Forgotten Passion in a Paris Atelier."

CLASSIC COLLECTION — Fully restored 1928 *Steinway & Sons* Model B Louis XV. Sold and shipped to Dr. and Mrs. J. Berg of San Luis Obispo, California.

Classic Pianos is owned by Maurice Unis and his three sons, Brian, Aaron, and Taylor. Winner of every *Top Dealer Award* from European, Asian, and American, piano manufacturers, *Classic Pianos* represents *Bösendorfer, Schimmel, Yamaha, Mason & Hamlin, and* also showcases a *CLASSIC COLLECTION* of vintage-restored *Steinway & Sons* and *Mason & Hamlin* grands.

Classic Collection sales and shipments coast-to-coast in U.S. and Canada

CUSTOMER COMMENTS: "In the course of a nation-wide search, we finally discovered Classic Pianos.... We could not have made a better choice. Classic Pianos is home to an amazing group of professionals. "
— Julie Berg, San Luis Obispo, California
Pianist, Teacher, and College Educator

VISITOR COMMENTS: "I was overwhelmed: I had never, previously, encountered such a galaxy of new pianos… among the finest obtainable in the United States, in Europe, and in the Orient."
— Lucien Needham , Alberta, Canada
Associate, Graduate, and Fellow, *Guildhall School of Music*

COMMENTS BY CONCERT PIANISTS: "I have known Maurice Unis, and some of his associates, for over 25 years. His understanding of technical rebuilding and piano restoration is, in a word, 'unparalleled.' "
— Mark Westcott, Portland, Oregon
Master of Music, Eastman School of Music
Winner of Five International Competitions, including Third Prize
Van Cliburn International Piano Competition, 1969.

"Your masterful approach to tuning, voicing, regulating, and restoring heirloom Mason & Hamlin and Steinway grands recalls another bygone era of the Golden Age of Pianos. Bravo!"
— Eric Himy, Washington, DC
Master of Music, *The Juilliard School*, New York.
Winner of numerous piano competitions, including the
Gold Medal at the 1988 *World Piano Competition*

CLASSIC 🎵 PIANOS

A PASSION FOR PIANOS
3003 SE Milwaukie Avenue   Portland, Oregon 97202   Telephone: (503) 239-9969
www.classicportland.com

in piano manufacturing, virtually all pianos made in Indonesia are the products of three large, foreign players: Yamaha, Kawai, and Samick. For the U.S. market, Yamaha makes an entry-level grand and most of their smaller verticals in Indonesia; Kawai makes all its small and medium-sized verticals there, and one entry-level grand; and Samick makes all its pianos for sale in North America there, both grand and vertical.

Overall, the manufacturing quality is similar to China's, but Indonesia got to this level of quality more rapidly and is perhaps more consistent. This may have been due to the smaller number and, on average, larger size of Indonesia's piano manufacturers, as well as to cultural and political differences between the countries. Development of manufacturing in Indonesia was aided by the fact that the country was already a democratic (more or less), capitalist nation with strong ties to the West, and accustomed to Western ways of working and doing business, with English widely spoken. The government does not own or manage the factories.

One of the big challenges in Indonesia, as in the rest of tropical Asia (which includes southern China), is climate control inside the factories, and the proper handling of wood to avoid problems later on when the instruments are shipped to drier countries and the wood dries out. All three companies, as well as Pearl River in southern China, have done a good job of meeting this challenge, but caution and proper climate control by the consumer are especially advised when these pianos are to be used in very difficult, dry indoor climates.

Korea

The Korean piano industry has had a tumultuous history, from its beginnings in the war-torn 1950s through its meteoric global rise in the 1980s; through labor unrest, the Asian economic crisis, and the abrupt collapse of the country's piano industry in the 1990s; and most recently through bankruptcies, reorganizations, aborted takeovers, and more bankruptcies. Today, both Samick and Young Chang seem to be on relatively stable financial footing, the latter having just emerged from bankruptcy after being purchased by Hyundai Development Company. As mentioned earlier, due to high labor costs in Korea, both companies have moved most of their manufacturing elsewhere, limiting production at home to the more expensive models.

Quality control in the Korean models is now nearly as good as in pianos from Japan, but getting there has taken 30 years of two steps forward, one step back. The reasons for the slow development are probably numerous, but undoubtedly some are cultural in nature: Western piano-company personnel have often reported that their Korean counterparts can be proud people, reluctant to take advice from Americans (not that they necessarily should—unless they're trying to sell products to Americans).

Musically, the two companies' pianos have never really gained clear, aesthetic identities of their own, other than as very acceptable musical products. Periodic redesigns by German engineers, or American engineers with Germanic names (always sought by piano makers), have brought some progress, but never as much as was hoped for. Part of the reason for the lack of identity may be that there have been such a multitude of product lines made in different factories to constantly changing specifications that nothing has settled down long enough to stick. Internal politics and dealing with quality-control problems have also taken up much energy over the years.

Things are settling down now for both companies. Samick, in its upper- and mid-level lines, is producing some of its nicest pianos ever. Young Chang is playing catch-up, but also has some good designs, with new ones in the pipeline. Both companies' top-level products have much to offer at good prices.

Japan

Japan's two major piano manufacturers, Yamaha and Kawai, began making pianos around 1900 and 1927, respectively, with export to the United States beginning in earnest in the early 1960s. The first few years of export were spent learning to season the wood to the demands of the North American climate, but since then the quality control has been impressive, to say the least, and the standard to which other piano manufacturers aspire. Both companies also have outstanding warranty service, so customers are never left hanging with unsatisfactory instruments. As in Korea, labor costs in Japan have risen to the point where both companies have been forced to move much of their manufacturing elsewhere, making only their more expensive models in Japan. With some exceptions, their grands and tallest uprights are made in Japan, small and mid-sized verticals in other Asian countries.

> **Quality control in the Korean models is now nearly as good as in pianos from Japan, but getting there has taken 30 years of two steps forward, one step back.**

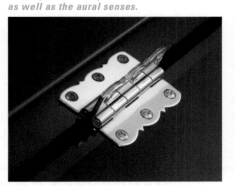

The tone of Japanese pianos tends to be a little on the bright and percussive side (Yamaha more than Kawai), though less so than in previous years, and pleasing in their own way. In addition to their regular lines, both companies make high-end lines with more "classical" qualities, as well as entry-level lines that reflect a compromise between price and quality. The pianos are very popular with institutions and are real workhorses. Although more expensive than most other Asian pianos, a Japanese-made Yamaha or Kawai piano is hard to beat for reliability. Kawai also manufactures the Boston brand, designed by Steinway and sold through Steinway dealers.

United States

Only three companies manufacture pianos here in any numbers: Steinway & Sons, Mason & Hamlin, and Charles R. Walter. A couple of other makers are in very limited production: Astin-Weight in Salt Lake City, whose factory was shut down several years ago by storm damage, says it still makes a few pianos; and pianos are once again being assembled in Chicago under the Kimball name using parts sourced from around the world. A few boutique makers, such as Ravenscroft, build high-end pianos to order. Baldwin, for a century one of the largest American producers, finally ceased most production at its American factory in 2009, having moved nearly all piano production to its two plants in China.

Steinway & Sons has been making high-quality pianos in New York City since its founding in 1853 by German immigrants. For most of the past century, the company has had little competition in the U.S.: when one desired to buy a piano of the highest quality, it was simply understood that one meant a

Steinway. The last decade or two has seen a gradual erosion of that status by more than a dozen European firms and our own Mason & Hamlin. Although each by itself is too small to make a dent in Steinway's business, their combined effect has been to claim a substantial share of the market for high-end pianos in the home. (Steinway still dominates the concert-grand market and, to some extent, the institutional market.) This has been made easier by the fact that in certain respects these European-made pianos are visibly and audibly of higher quality than American-made Steinways (to be distinguished from Steinways made at the company's branch factory in Hamburg, Germany, which are of the highest quaity).

Steinways have classic designs and use proven materials and methods of construction, but the musical and aesthetic finishing of the American-made pianos has too often been left uncompleted at the factory in the expectation, frequently unmet, that the dealers would finish it off. Fortunately, the past few years have seen a reversal of this trend in the form of many small improvements at the factory, as well as perhaps better performance by dealers. Though there is room for further improvement, the ratio of compliments to complaints, in my experience, has become more favorable. The recent replacement of American Steinway management by personnel from Steinway's European branches may also be having a salutary effect.

Mason & Hamlin, Steinway's principal competitor in the early part of the 20th century, went into a long period of decline after the Great Depression. After a series of

The rush to sell to Americans has caused some European companies to reconsider the tonal designs of their instruments.

bankruptcies and reorganizations in the 1980s and '90s, Mason & Hamlin was purchased in 1996 by the Burgett brothers, owners of PianoDisc, a leading manufacturer of player-piano systems. Since then, from an old brick factory building in Haverhill, Massachusetts, the Burgetts have completely restored the company to its former excellence, and then some. They and their staff have designed or redesigned a complete line of grand pianos and modernized century-old equipment. Rather than compete with Steinway on Steinway's terms, Mason & Hamlin has repositioned itself as an innovator, seeking out or developing high-quality but lower-cost parts and materials from around the world, and combining them with traditional craftsmanship to produce a great piano at a somewhat lower price.

Charles R. Walter, a piano design engineer by profession, has been making high-quality vertical pianos in Elkhart, Indiana, since the 1970s, and grands for over ten years. The factory is staffed in large part by members of his extended family. The instruments are built using the best traditional materials and construction practices. Right now, times are tough for small companies such as this, which produce an excellent product but are neither the high-priced celebrated names nor the low-cost mass producers. If you're looking to "buy American," you can't get any more American than Charles R. Walter.

Europe

European makers that regularly sell in the U.S. include: Bechstein,

Blüthner, August Förster, Grotrian, Sauter, Schimmel, Seiler, Steingraeber, and Wilh. Steinberg (Germany); Bösendorfer (Austria); Fazioli and Schulze Pollmann (Italy); Estonia (Estonia); and Petrof (Czech Republic). Most are of extremely high quality; even the least of them is very good. Until two decades ago, most of these brands were virtually unknown or unavailable in the U.S., but as the European demand for pianos contracted, many of the companies found that Americans, with their large homes and incomes, would buy all the grand pianos they could produce. The liberation of Eastern Europe resulted in an increase in the quality of such venerable brands as Estonia and Petrof, which had suffered under Communist rule, and these brands, too, became available and accepted here.

The rush to sell to Americans has caused some European companies to reconsider the tonal designs of their instruments and to redesign them for better sound projection, tonal color, and sustain—that is, to sound more like American Steinways. Considering that some of these companies are five or six generations old and have redesigned their pianos about that many times in 150 years, this degree of activity is unusual. Some of the redesigns have been great musical successes; nevertheless, the loss of diversity in piano sound is to be mourned.

Several German companies have started or acquired second-tier lines to diversify their product lines, and have gradually shifted much of their production to former Soviet-bloc countries with lower labor costs, producing brands such as W. Hoffmann (by Bechstein) in the Czech Republic, and Wilhelm Schimmel, formerly Vogel (by Schimmel), in Poland. Today, there is enough commonality in business practices, laws, and attitudes toward quality among the countries of Europe that the distinction between Eastern and Western Europe carries little meaning—except for labor costs, where the savings can be great.

Globalization, Quality, and Value

The worldwide changes in the piano industry are making it more difficult to advise piano shoppers. For many years, the paradigm for piano quality has been an international pecking order: pianos from Russia, China, and Indonesia at the bottom; followed by Korea, Japan, and Eastern Europe; and, finally, Western Europe at the top, with pianos from the U.S. scattered here and there, depending on the brand. This pecking order has never been foolproof, but it has served a generation of piano buyers well enough as a rule of thumb.

Now this order is being disturbed by globalization. High-end and low-end makers are, to some extent, adopting each other's methods and narrowing the differences between them. On the one hand, some Western European and American makers of high-end pianos are partially computerizing the manufacture of their "hand-built" pianos, quietly sourcing parts and subassemblies from China, and developing less expensive product lines in Eastern Europe and Asia. On the other hand, some Korean and Chinese makers are importing parts and technology from Germany, Japan, and the U.S., producing pianos that sometimes rival the performance of more expensive pianos from the West. Global alliances are bringing new products to market that are more hybridized than anything we've seen before. Although the old pecking order still has

The worldwide changes in the piano industry are making it more difficult to advise piano shoppers.

some validity, the number of exceptions is increasing, causing temporary confusion in the marketplace until a new order emerges.

At the same time that the range of quality differences is narrowing, the range of prices is widening, bringing into greater prominence issues of "value." Eastern European brands have emerged as "value" alternatives to Western European brands, the latter becoming frightfully expensive due to high labor costs and the rapid appreciation of the euro against the dollar. Some of the better pianos from China, Korea, and Indonesia have become value alternatives to Japanese pianos. Brands that don't scream "value" are being squeezed out of the market.

As mentioned above, one of the consequences of globalization is that parts and materials formerly available only to high-end makers are now for sale to any company, anywhere, that's willing to pay for them. Thus, you'll see a number of Asian firms marketing their pianos with a list of well-regarded brand-name components from Germany and North America, such as Renner, Röslau, Mapes, and Bolduc. The question then naturally arises: Given that high-end pianos are so expensive, and that today one can buy for so little a Chinese-made piano with German design, German parts, and perhaps even a German name, is it still worth buying a performance-grade piano made in the West? Are there any differences worth paying for?

There's no question that high-end components, such as Renner hammers and Bolduc soundboards, add to the quality and value of consumer-grade pianos in which they're used. But in terms of quality, components such as these are only the tip of the iceberg. Although the difference between performance- and consumer-grade pianos has narrowed, in many ways the two types of manufacturers still live in different worlds. Differences are manifested in such things as the selection, drying, and use of wood; final regulation and voicing; and attention to technical and cosmetic details.

Makers of performance-grade pianos use higher grades of wood, selected for finer grain, more even color, or greater hardness, strength, and/or acoustical properties, as the use requires. Wood is seasoned more carefully and for longer periods of time, resulting in greater dimensional stability and a longer-lasting product. Veneers are more carefully matched, and finishes polished to a greater smoothness. Action assemblies purchased from suppliers may be taken apart and put back together to more exacting tolerances than originally supplied. The workspace is set up to allow workers more time to complete their tasks and a greater opportunity to catch and correct errors. Much more time is spent on final regulation and voicing, with an instrument not leaving the factory, in some cases, until a musician has had an opportunity to play it and be satisfied. Of course, the degree to which these manifestations of quality, and many others not mentioned, are present will vary by brand and circumstance, but underlying them all is this philosophical difference: with performance-grade pianos, the driving force behind decision-making tends to be the quality of the product; with consumer-grade pianos, cost is a greater factor.

A MAP OF THE MARKET FOR NEW PIANOS

The chart and commentary that follow are intended to provide the newcomer to the piano market with a simple summary of how this market is organized. Although summarizing the market requires making a certain number of subjective judgments, this summary is intended less as a ranking of quality than as a description of how manufacturers and dealers position their products in the marketplace. That is, if a dealer carried every brand, how would he or she position those brands, in terms of relative quality, when presenting them to prospective purchasers? This positioning is usually done along lines of price, country of origin, and reputation; however, while these factors are often associated with quality, that association is far from perfectly consistent.

PERFORMANCE-GRADE PIANOS			
Highest Quality/Prestige *Verticals:* $30,000–$60,000 *Grands 5' to 7':* $75,000–$140,000	*Very High Quality/Prestige* *Verticals:* $32,000–$36,000 *Grands 5' to 7':* $61,000–$97,000	*Very High Quality* *Verticals:* $20,000–$40,000 *Grands 5' to 7':* $50,000–$90,000	*High Quality* *Verticals:* $15,000–$25,000 *Grands 5' to 7':* $45,000–$75,000
C. Bechstein Blüthner Bösendorfer Fazioli Grotrian Sauter Steingraeber & Söhne Steinway & Sons (Hamburg)	Steinway & Sons (New York)	Bechstein (B) Estonia August Förster Haessler Shigeru Kawai Mason & Hamlin Petrof Schimmel (Konzert/Classic) Seiler (Germany) Yamaha (CF)	Rönisch Schimmel (International) Schulze Pollmann (Masterpiece) Wilh. Steinberg (Signature) Charles R. Walter

INTERMEDIATE-GRADE PIANOS		
European Affiliated *Verticals:* $8,000–$17,000 *Grands 5' to 7':* $25,000–$50,000	*Deluxe Consumer (Japanese)* *Verticals:* $9,000–$18,000 *Grands 5' to 7':* $21,000–$55,000	*Deluxe Consumer (Other Asian)* *Verticals:* $7,500–$15,000 *Grands 5' to 7':* $22,000–$40,000
Brodmann (AS) W. Hoffmann Irmler (Professional) Schulze Pollmann (Studio) Seiler (ED) Wilh. Steinberg (Nomos) Wilhelm Schimmel/Vogel	Boston (Japan) Kawai (RX/GX) grands Kawai verticals (Japan) Yamaha (C/CX) grands Yamaha verticals (Japan)	Kayserburg (Artist) Wm. Knabe (Concert Artist) Perzina verticals J.P. Pramberger (Platinum) Albert Weber

Note: Unless otherwise stated, brand names refer to both grand and vertical models.

CONSUMER-GRADE PIANOS			
	Samick/ Young Chang	**Yamaha/Kawai**	**Other Companies**
Upper Level Verticals: $4,500–$10,000 Grands 5' to 7': $15,000–$35,000		Boston verticals (Indonesia) Kawai (GE) grands Kawai verticals (Indonesia) Yamaha (GC) grands Yamaha verticals (Indonesia)	Baldwin Brodmann (PE) Cunningham Hailun Irmler (Studio) Perzina grands Ritmüller (Premium)
Mid-Range Verticals: $5,500–$8,000 Grands 5' to 7': $12,000–$21,000	Wm. Knabe (Academy) Pramberger (Signature) Johannes Seiler Weber Young Chang	Kawai (GM) grands Yamaha (GB) grands	Essex Heintzman Kingsburg verticals Palatino Ritmüller (Performance) G. Steinberg Story & Clark (Signature)
Economy Verticals: $4,000–$6,500 Grands 5' to 7': $9,500–$16,000	Wm. Knabe (Baltimore) Pramberger (Legacy) Samick	Cable-Nelson (Yamaha)	Altenburg Brodmann (CE) Cline Cristofori/Lyrica Everett Falcone A. Geyer Hallet, Davis & Co. Hobart M. Cable Kingsburg grands Hardman, Peck Pearl River Ritmüller (Classic) Schumann Story & Clark (Heritage) Wyman

To better understand this chart, please read the accompanying commentary.

Note: Unless otherwise stated, brand names refer to both grand and vertical models.

Why don't we strictly judge piano quality in *Piano Buyer*? During the last half of the 20th century, a great many pianos, especially low-end instruments manufactured in the U.S. and in developing countries, had significant defects that made separating good instruments from bad relatively easy. That is no longer the case. Due to globalization and the computerization of manufacturing, virtually all pianos now sold in the West are competently made and without major defects, and the differences between them are increasingly subtle and subjective. In addition, price is sometimes more a reflection of labor costs in the country of origin than of quality. While it's still clear that high-end pianos are better than entry-level ones, comparisons of instruments that are closer in price are less conclusive, and much more subject to the whims of personal preference, how well the pianos have been prepared for sale, room acoustics, and so forth. Furthermore, even those responsible for the technical design of pianos often can't agree on which features and specifications produce the best instruments! In such a context of extreme subjectivity, contradictory expert opinion, and a changing market, making too many judgments about piano quality tends to give a false impression of scientific objectivity, and inhibits shoppers from making their own judgments and possibly discovering something wonderful for themselves.

For these reasons, we have chosen to take a less active but, we think, more honest approach to giving piano-buying advice, by providing newcomers to the market with a simple frame of reference and a few personal recommendations (see our new "Staff Picks" section beginning on page 43), and otherwise letting them explore and discover for themselves what appeals to them.

The key to proper use of this chart, then, is not to follow it religiously, but to understand that, given its nature, it should be used only as a learning tool. In addition, use common sense when comparing one brand with another. Compare verticals with other verticals of similar size, and grands with similarly sized grands, or models whose selling prices fall within the same range. Don't get hung up on small differences between one subgroup and the next—the distinctions can be quite subtle. Furthermore, the preparation of the piano by the dealer can be at least as important to the quality of the product you receive as some of the distinctions listed in the chart. Note that, for the sake of simplicity, there may be quality differences within a single product line that are not indicated here; and a few brands have been omitted due solely to lack of sufficient information about them. **Within each group or subgroup, the brands are listed in alphabetical order. No judgment of these brands' relative quality should be inferred from this order.**

Prices shown for each group represent, in round numbers, a typical range of Suggested Maximum Prices (SMP) of new pianos in the least expensive styles and finishes (significant discounts from these prices are likely—see page 201 for explanation).

A generalization useful to understanding the piano market is that pianos can be divided into two types, Performance Grade and Consumer Grade, both of which are necessary to meet the needs of the wide variety of piano buyers.

Performance-Grade Pianos

Performance-grade pianos generally have several of the following attributes:

- They are built to a single high standard, almost without regard to cost, and the price charged reflects whatever it takes to build such a piano and bring it to market.
- A greater proportion of the labor required to build them is in the handwork involved in making custom refinements to individual instruments, often with fanatical attention to detail.
- Most are made in relatively small quantities by firms that have been in business for generations, often under the ownership of the same family. As a result, many have achieved almost legendary status, and are often purchased as much for their prestige value as for their performance.
- These are the instruments most likely to be called into service when the highest performance level is required, particularly for classical music.
- Most performance-grade pianos are made in Europe or the United States.

Performance-grade pianos are divided here into four subcategories, based on our perception of their reputation in both the musical and technical spheres of the piano business. The first two subcategories are reserved for those brands whose prestige figures prominently in their value. Of course, this prestige is based in large part on their extremely high quality, but marketing success and historical accident also play important roles in the reputations of these and other high-end brands. Also, preferences among performance-grade pianos in general are greatly dependent on musical taste in tone and touch. For these reasons, a number of brands in the third subcategory have devoted followings and, practically speaking, may be just as good despite not having as much prestige associated with their names. The brands in the fourth subcategory are considered runners-up; however, most of these are also considerably less expensive, and may be a better value when the highest levels of quality or prestige are not needed.

Consumer-Grade Pianos

Consumer-grade pianos are built to be sold at a particular price, and adjustments to (i.e., compromises in) materials, workmanship, and method and location of manufacture are made to meet that price. Most are mass-produced in Asia, with less in the way of custom refinement of individual instruments.

Consumer-grade pianos are subcategorized here mostly, but not entirely, by price. As mentioned earlier, in the current piano market, price is not a perfect indicator of technical or musical quality. However, price becomes a better indicator of quality when *quality* is understood to include all factors that consumers value—not only an instrument's performance, but also the brand's reputation and its track record for durability, reliability, warranty service, and resale value.

This is especially relevant for consumer-grade pianos, where purchasers often are more interested in these other factors than in the instrument's performance. It also means, however, that some brands may be rated a little higher or lower than they would be if rated on musical performance alone. In a few cases we've made small adjustments when we felt that considerations of price alone seriously under- or overvalued a brand.

As can be expected, upper-level consumer-grade pianos generally have premium components and better performance than lower-level instruments. The economy models are basic, no-frills pianos suitable for beginners and casual users, but which a conscientious student may outgrow in a few years. As piano quality in general improves, the distinctions between levels become more subtle and difficult to discern.

Intermediate-Grade Pianos

As discussed earlier, globalization and the computerization of manufacturing have, to some extent, blurred the distinctions between performance- and consumer-grade pianos. Increasingly, makers of performance-grade instruments have been creating lower-cost brands by manufacturing instruments and components in countries with cheaper labor, while makers of consumer-grade pianos have been bringing to market higher-quality models by perfecting automation and sourcing parts worldwide. This has created difficulties in classifying brands by means of a two-grade system, both because some brands defy such classification, and because of the bottleneck that results from the attempt to rate too many brands relative to one another in a restricted space. To alleviate this problem, we've spun off a third type of piano, called Intermediate Grade.

Intermediate-grade pianos are of two types. One, here called Deluxe Consumer, consists of former consumer-grade brands that in recent years have become so advanced in their designs, materials, and manufacturing technologies that they now rival some performance-grade pianos in musicality, and are sometimes recommended as substitutes for them, often at considerably lower prices. The second type, here called European Affiliated, consists of lesser product lines of companies, mostly European, that are principally known for their performance-grade models. Increasingly, instruments from this latter group are being partly made in China or Indonesia, then shipped to Europe for completion. Exactly how much of their manufacture is actually done in Europe—which, after all, is offered as a justification for their higher price—is sometimes

a well-kept secret and the subject of much speculation. As the quality of pianos throughout the market rises and becomes more homogeneous, debate about these dual-origin models tends to seesaw between "What a rip-off for what's basically a Chinese (or Indonesian) piano" and "What a great deal for an instrument that's virtually the same as a high-end European one." We'll let you be the judge of which of these extremes is closer to the truth.

STAFF PICKS

*by **Piano Buyer** staff*

Due to the highly subjective nature of piano ratings, in "A Map of the Market for New Pianos" (page 40), we purposely avoided making too many judgments about the quality of the various brands. Instead, we provided, as a frame of reference, a

Brand/Model	Classics/ Perennial Favorites	Musical Standouts	Good Values	Price ($)	Comments
ACOUSTIC PIANOS					
Baldwin BP178 (5' 10")			✔	21,990	
Baldwin BP190 (6' 3")			✔	26,190	
Bechstein, C. Concert 8 (51.5")	✔	✔		70,600	One of the all-time great upright pianos.
Blüthner 2 (7' 8")	✔	✔		121,932	
Bösendorfer 200 (6' 7")	✔			125,798	A lovely and distinct chamber instrument.
Boston GP215PE (7' 1")		✔		51,400	
Brodmann PE187 (6' 2")		✔	✔	18,580	Design said to be based on that of a Steinway model A.
Cunningham Studio Grand (5' 4")		✔	✔	16,890	
Estonia L168 (5' 6")		✔	✔	39,608	Estonia grands are an excellent value among high-end pianos. The tone of the L190 has lyrical beauty and is without harshness.
Estonia L190 (6' 3")		✔	✔	48,139	
Förster, August, 190 (6' 4")		✔		67,718	
Grotrian Cabinet (6' 3")		✔		80,040	Uniquely diverse timbre. Subject of book *Grand Obsession*, by Perry Knize.
Haessler 186 (6' 1")		✔		72,797	
Hailun HU5-P (50")		✔	✔	9,316	A "total package"—balanced tone, responsive action.
Hailun HG178 (5' 10")		✔	✔	22,312	
Hardman, Peck & Co. R45F (45")			✔	4,790	Beautiful cabinet, well constructed.
Kawai K300 (48")	✔		✔	9,390	
Kawai GX-2BLK (5' 11")	✔			33,190	A must-try for those shopping for a grand under 6' long.
Kawai, Shigeru, SK-6L (7')		✔		73,400	
Kayserburg KA-132 (52")		✔		16,190	Lovely, singing tone.
Knabe, Wm., WKV131 (52")		✔	✔	10,700	
Mason & Hamlin A (5' 8")	✔			56,360	
Mason & Hamlin AA (6' 4")		✔		64,191	
Mason & Hamlin BB (7')	✔	✔		72,707	Prodigious bass register sounds like that of a concert grand.
Pearl River EU122 (48")			✔	5,590	
Perzina UP-112 Kompact (45")			✔	7,260	Impressive low-bass performance from a small, inexpensive vertical.
Perzina UP-122 (48")		✔	✔	8,300	
Perzina UP-130 (51")		✔		10,580	A vertical piano that can hold its own against some far more expensive peers.

(continued)

ACOUSTIC PIANOS (continued)

Brand/Model	Classics/Perennial Favorites	Musical Standouts	Good Values	Price ($)	Comments
Petrof P125 (49.25")		✔		26,990	
Pramberger PS-175 (5' 9")			✔	15,112	
Ritmüller UH-121R (48")		✔	✔	7,790	One of our favorite vertical pianos at this price.
Ritmüller GH-148R (4' 10")		✔	✔	11,590	Amazingly good performance for such a small piano.
Sauter 220 "Omega" (7' 3")		✔		128,100	An incredibly capable tool for any serious pianist—and for fun, take a look under the lid.
Schimmel K132 (52")		✔		34,780	
Schimmel C213 (7')		✔		60,480	
Schimmel K219 (7' 2")		✔		80,800	A fantastic instrument from Schimmel's new Konzert series.
Schumann U22TD (48")			✔	5,030	
Seiler ED-186 (6' 2")		✔	✔	29,590	Clear treble tone and good sustain.
Seiler, Johannes, GS-160 (5' 3")		✔	✔	16,180	Pleasantly mellow with an elegant look.
Steingraeber & Söhne C212 (7')		✔		135,414	Remarkable tonal subtlety.
Steinway & Sons M (5' 7")	✔			66,300	
Steinway & Sons O (5' 10.5")	✔			74,800	
Steinway & Sons A (6' 2")	✔			85,300	
Steinway & Sons B (6' 10.5")	✔	✔		96,900	Very popular model in college and conservatory teaching studios, and the standard against which other high-end grands are measured.
Story & Clark H60 (5' 3")			✔	17,495	When you take into account all the technology it comes with (player piano and MIDI record), this piano is a great value.
Walter, Charles R. 1520/1500 (43"/45")	✔	✔		14,338	Proof that a 43" piano can be musical, and it's made in the U.S.A.
Weber W150 (4' 11")		✔	✔	11,580	Surprisingly musical and satisfying tone for such a short grand.
Weber W185 (6' 1")		✔	✔	16,980	Satisfyingly beautiful tone at a good price.
Yamaha U1 (48")	✔	✔		10,699	The standard against which every 48" vertical is inevitably compared.
Yamaha C3X (6' 1")	✔			48,998	A workhorse in countless teaching studios and institutional practice rooms.
Yamaha C5X (6' 7")		✔		54,398	
Yamaha C7X (7' 6")	✔			69,898	Very popular in recording studios; musically versatile in the hands of the right technician.
Yamaha Silent Piano b2SG2 (45")			✔	9,358	An affordable acoustic with the flexibility of a digital.

(continued)

Brand/Model	Classics/ Perennial Favorites	Musical Standouts	Good Values	Price ($)	Comments
DIGITALS & HYBRIDS					
Blüthner e-Klavier PRO-88		✔		3,164	An elegantly-styled slab with a unique piano sample.
Casio Privia PX-5S			✔	999	A professional instrument at a consumer price.
Casio Privia PX-860			✔	1,099	Impressive sound from a shallow cabinet.
Kawai CN35			✔	2,599	A great feature package for the price.
Kawai CA97		✔		4,627	Solid action performance, Soundboard Speaker System, and nice variety of piano samples.
Kawai VPC1		✔		1,849	Not a digital per se, but rather a dedicated controller keyboard for software (virtual) pianos, with Kawai's great RM3II action.
Kurzweil CUP-2		✔		4,299	An extremely compact contemporary design conceals a wealth of voices and features.
Roland HP504			✔	2,599	A way-above-average starter instrument with Ivory Feel keyboard.
Roland V-Piano Grand		✔		19,950	Enclosed in an elegant grand-piano cabinet, the V-Piano gives you the technology to design your own piano.
Yamaha Clavinova CVP-605		✔	✔	6,236	A price/performance sweet spot in ensemble digital pianos.
Yamaha Arius YDP-181	✔		✔	1,700	A direct descendant of the venerable YDP-223 from 2002. A perennial best-seller.
Yamaha AvantGrand N2/N3		✔		12,362/ 18,698	A game changer that redefined our expectations for the sound and feel of a non-acoustic piano.

summary of the way pianos are presented in the marketplace by manufacturers and dealers. However, we feel we owe some *specific* recommendations to the many readers who have requested them, in part to simplify the buying process for shoppers who lack the time, ability, or interest to make their own discoveries. To emphasize the subjective nature of these recommendations, we provide them in this list rather than through the Map. This way, too, we don't have to pass judgment on each and every brand and model.

It's important to understand that in any artistic field, "expert" recommendations are only partially recognitions of inherent quality; in other ways, they are simply personal preferences. Thus, while you can probably count on pianos recommended by us to be "good" instruments, it

doesn't follow from that that you will necessarily like them as much as we do. Our recommendations also say virtually nothing about brands and models that are *not* on the list. Either we haven't had the opportunity to try them out (or, at least, not under favorable conditions), or they just didn't stand out to us as being really special—but that doesn't mean there's anything wrong with them, or that you wouldn't want to take one home with you.

This list focuses on home- and studio-size instruments and does not include concert grands. A work in progress, it is by no means comprehensive, and will likely grow and evolve with future issues of *Piano Buyer*.

Classics/Perennial Favorites are models with a long-standing reputation for performance and durability. They are generally top sellers from well-known manufacturers.

Musical Standouts represent pianos that play and sound great to us. Although the list understandably tends to favor larger instruments, we've also included several smaller models that are noteworthy for having great sound for their size.

Good Values are pianos whose performance per dollar, in our opinion, is particularly attractive.

Vertical piano sizes are shown in inches, grand piano sizes in feet and inches. Prices shown for acoustic pianos are the Suggested Maximum Prices (SMP) of the least expensive style and finish (significant discounts from these prices are likely—see page 201 for explanation). Prices shown for digitals and hybrids are the Estimated Prices of the least expensive finish (see page 263 for explanation). ▭

THE BOSTON PERFORMANCE EDITION
DESIGNED BY STEINWAY & SONS

Designed by Steinway & Sons, the Boston piano is unrivaled in its class and unmatched in value. Because the design and materials are specified by Steinway & Sons, you can be confident that you are purchasing a truly great piano that is widely used at music schools and festivals around the world. Enhancements in recent years to the current "Performance Edition" introduced a maple inner rim, the patented Octagrip™ Pinblock, and other improvements that truly elevate the Boston piano into a class by itself in the mid-price range. Every new Boston grand or upright piano comes with *The Steinway Promise* – which means that at any time within ten years of the date of purchase, you can trade in your Boston piano and receive 100% of the original purchase price in trade toward a new Steinway & Sons grand piano.

**TO LEARN MORE ABOUT THE BOSTON PERFORMANCE EDITION,
CALL 1-800-STEINWAY (1-800-783-4692)
OR VISIT WWW.STEINWAY.COM/BOSTON**

Introducing the *CX* SERIES

2010 – The CFX revolutionized the Beauty and Power of the concert grand piano…

2012 – The CX is introduced…

2014 – The legacy continues…

The New Soundboard resonates with the emotions of the performer.

New contoured Bridges and Ribs dramatically improve projection.

New Hammers based on those of the CFX Piano.

Advanced design. Expert engineering. Over twenty years of research. This is the birth of a new series of pianos that builds on the legacy of Yamaha's CFX concert grand piano.

⦿ YAMAHA

Based in the Czech Republic, piano builder Petrof celebrated its 150th anniversary in 2014. Through the late 1990s and early 2000s, Petrof pianos were positioned in the North American marketplace as a low-cost European alternative to other well-known, established brands. Their grand-piano models, reviewed in the Spring 2010 issue of **Piano Buyer**, were named, from smallest to largest, with Roman numerals: V, IV, III, II, I. In 2009, Petrof's grand-piano lineup was revised, with new designs, materials, and a higher level of build quality. The new models—from smallest to largest: Bora, Breeze, Storm, Pasat, Monsoon, and Mistral—were designed to compete with the great pianos of Europe and America. Features include custom-tapered soundboards, genuine ebony bridge caps in the high treble, laser-placed front and rear duplexes, single stringing (as in some of the most expensive European pianos), and a choice of two action suppliers. We asked guest reviewer Dr. Benjamin Boren to take a look at the three smaller Petrof models: Bora, Breeze, and Storm.—*Editor*

As a pianist who has played mostly pianos owned by the universities I've attended and at which I've taught and performed, I've rarely had the opportunity to try out instruments by makers other than Baldwin, Bösendorfer, Mason & Hamlin, Steinway, and Yamaha. I had heard of the Petrof brand, but had neither seen nor played one before. With the help of Joe Brattesani of World Class Pianos, in the San Francisco peninsula city of Burlingame, California, I was able, for this review, to sample three recently upgraded models: the Bora (5' 2"), the Breeze (5' 6"), and the Storm (6' 2").

Even before playing, I noticed the pianos' aesthetic appeal; they are beautifully constructed, and feature eye-catching wood veneer around the inner rim. This particular Breeze had the "Klasik" (Classic) upgrade, which includes a filigree music desk and tapered, "ice-cream cone" legs, both tastefully elegant without being too ornate. These pianos also display, on the right keyblock, the European Excellence crest, an attractive feature that declares the instruments' solely European construction and use of at least 61% European-made parts and materials.

To test the pianos, I played repertoire from a recent recital: Mozart's Adagio in B Minor; Beethoven's Variations

Petrof P173 Breeze Klasik

in C-Minor, WoO 80; the complete Chopin Préludes; and Carl Vine's Sonata No. 1. To test how the pianos reacted to specific situations and textures, I also played excerpts from Debussy's *Clair de Lune*, Liszt's Sonata in B-Minor, Prokofiev's Piano Concerto No. 3, and various preludes and fugues by J.S. Bach, among other pieces. Certain capabilities, such as repeated notes, were tested separately from pieces. Generally, the instruments behaved similarly in almost every aspect, with the characteristics, as expected, becoming more pronounced and enhanced with each increase in size.

All three instruments produced a distinct, remarkably warm, rich sound, with considerable sustain in every register. The round tone rang with a bell-like quality, rendering percussive sounds difficult to create. They also possessed tremendous dynamic breadth for their size, easily generating the entire range between *pianissimo* and *fortissimo*. Each piano had lively middle and upper registers, and a lower register that was less immediately present. While this did not create any balance problems, pianists will need to use greater articulation to match the lower register with the others.

Using the damper pedal created tremendous resonance; additionally, the sound did not project as much as with larger, concert, grands, but rather stayed closer to the piano. Because of this, pianists will likely find themselves using the pedal sparingly; it also makes these pianos more suitable for rooms with dry acoustics. The *una corda* pedals all had the similar effect of shortening the sustain and dulling the resonance, but without creating a muffled or muted sound. While on brighter pianos I often like to experiment with this pedal for different colors, here I found it unnecessary, much preferring the natural sound.

Petrof's grand pianos are available with either the Petrof Original Action or a Renner action. The Breeze and Storm that I played featured the Petrof Original Action, the Bora a Renner action. I was told that, except for tuning, the pianos had not been prepped prior to my arrival; my remarks here are based on their condition directly from the factory. I found both actions delightfully sensitive, of medium weight, and remarkably well regulated. They allowed for excellent control in the quietest playing, yet responded with surprising sprightliness in fast passages and repeated notes, handling both with ease without overtiring me. I found that the Petrof Original Actions handled repeated notes slightly better than the Renner, and offered a modicum more control; however, pianists playing the most demanding repertoire will be happy with either.

Given these findings, I believe that these pianos are well suited to a wide variety of repertoire. Their lengthy sustain and round tone allowed Classical melodies to sing without needing pedaling to combat dryness, while their resonance, and wide ranges of dynamics and color, created lush, full sonorities for Romantic and French Impressionist repertoire. I was particularly impressed with the Bora, which, despite being only 5' 2", had excellent dynamic range and was capable of great nuance; it would be an ideal practice piano even for pianists of the highest level. The two smaller instruments are probably best used in a home setting; either would be an excellent practice and teaching piano. The largest model, the Storm, with its bigger sound, could be used in large classrooms or small performance halls. ▥

Benjamin Boren is an American pianist and pedagogue currently living in Burlingame, California. For more information and to contact him, please visit his website at www.benjaminboren.net.

PETROF GRANDS
Prices shown are for models finished in polished ebony.

Model	Size	Price
P 159 Bora	5' 2"	75,910
P 173 Breeze	5' 6"	79,990
P 194 Storm	6' 3"	83,964
P 210 Pasat	6' 10"	119,990
P 237 Monsoon	7' 9"	157,390
P 284 Mistral	9' 2"	217,084

*See page 201 for pricing information.

(This article is adapted from Chapter 5, "Buying a Used Piano," of The Piano Book, Fourth Edition, *by Larry Fine. Steve Brady updated the depreciation schedule and used-piano pricing information. Before reading this article, be sure to read "Piano Buying Basics"—especially the section "New or Used?"—elsewhere in this publication.)*

WHAT TO BUY:
A Historical Overview

1700–1880

The piano was invented about 1700 by Bartolomeo Cristofori, a harpsichord maker in Padua, Italy. Cristofori replaced the plucking-quill action of the harpsichord, which can pluck only with unvarying force and hence unvarying volume of sound, with a newly designed striking-hammer action, whose force could be precisely controlled by the player. Thus was born the *gravicembalo col piano e forte* (keyboard instrument with soft and loud). This name was later shortened to *pianoforte*, then *fortepiano*, and finally just *piano*. In the 1700s the new instrument, made mostly by craftsmen in their shops, spread quietly through upper-class Europe. A number of different forms of piano action and structure were invented, such as the Viennese action, the English action, the square piano, and so on. Replicas of early

Cristofori Piano, circa 1720

fortepianos are popular among certain musicians who prefer to play the music of that period on the original instruments for which that music was written.

In the 1800s the piano spread more quickly through the middle classes, and across the ocean to North America. Riding along with the Industrial Revolution, piano-making evolved from a craft into an industry. Many important changes took place during the 19th century: The upright piano was invented; the modern grand piano action was invented, incorporating the best aspects of the previous rival actions; the cast-iron plate was invented, vastly strengthening the structure and allowing the strings to be stretched at a higher tension, thus increasing the power and volume of sound; the range of the instrument was extended from about five octaves to the present seven-plus octaves; and, toward the end of the century, the square piano died out, leaving just grands of various sizes and the full-size upright. By 1880, most of these changes were in place; the pianos made today are not very different from those of a hundred or more years ago.

In your search for a piano, you're unlikely to run across instruments made before 1880, with two exceptions. The square piano, or square grand, as it is sometimes called, looks like a rectangular box on legs (see illustration), and was very

popular as a home piano during the 19th century. Its ornate Victorian case makes very pretty furniture—but it also makes a terrible musical instrument for 21st-century playing and practicing. Tuning, servicing, and repair are difficult and expensive, very few piano technicians know how to do it, and parts are hard to come by. Even at their best, these instruments are unsuitable to practice on, even for beginners.

Another piano to avoid is a type of upright made primarily in Europe from the middle to the end of the 19th century. The dampers on these piano are positioned *above* the hammers and actuated by wires in *front* of the action—the reverse of a modern-day upright. This over-damper system has been nicknamed the "birdcage action" because the damper wires form an enclosure that resembles a bird cage. Besides being very difficult to tune and service through the "bird cage," these pianos are usually so worn out that they won't hold a tuning longer than about ten seconds, and their actions work erratically at best. Many of these pianos were cheaply made to begin with, but they often have ornate cabinets and fancy features,

Square Grand, 19th Century

such as candlestick holders, that make them attractive to antique collectors.

Although most pianos you'll come across made prior to 1880 will have little practical or financial value, the few that have historical value are best left to specialists and collectors who can properly conserve them.

1880–1900

The years from 1880 to about 1900 were a transition period, as some old styles were slow to fade. But some pianos from this period may be suitable for you. A piano with only 85 instead of 88 notes may be perfectly satisfactory if you don't anticipate ever needing the highest three notes. The resale value of such a piano may be slightly lower than its modern equivalent, but so should be the price you pay for it. A piano with an old-style cast-iron plate that, while extending the full length of the piano, leaves the pinblock exposed to view is, for all practical purposes, just as structurally sound as one in which the plate covers the pinblock.

Avoid, however, the so-called "three-quarter-plate" piano, in which the plate ends just short of the pinblock. These pianos have a high rate of structural failure. Pianos with actions that are only very slight variations on modern actions are fine as long as the parts are not obsolete and absolutely unobtainable.

Most pianos this old will need a considerable amount of repair and restoration to be fully usable, so the best candidates from this period will be those instruments that justify the expense involved, such as Steinway, Mason & Hamlin, Bechstein, and Blüthner grands, or, in rare instances, a more ordinary brand that has been exceptionally well preserved. With occasional exceptions, the vast majority of uprights and cheaper grands that survive from this period are not worth repairing, unless for historical or sentimental reasons.

1900–1930

The period from about 1900 to 1930 was the heyday of piano manufacturing in America. The piano held an important place in the national economy and as a symbol of culture and social status. Hundreds

An old-fashioned, pneumaticallydriven player piano with punched-paper music roll and pumping pedals

of small firms turned out millions of pianos during this time; in fact, far more pianos were made annually then than are made today. If you're shopping for a used full-size upright or a grand, some of the pianos you'll see will probably be from this period. Smaller pianos weren't introduced until later. Although some well-preserved instruments from this period may be usable as is, most will need rebuilding, or at least reconditioning.

Those in the market for a used piano often ask for recommendations of specific brands from this period. This is a problem, because the present condition of the piano, the kind of use you'll be giving it, and the cost of the piano and repairs are far more important factors than the brand when considering the purchase of an old piano. Even a piano of the best brand, if poorly maintained or badly repaired, can be an unwise purchase. Time and wear are great levelers, and a piano of only average quality that has not been used much may be a much better buy. Nevertheless, since that answer never satisfies anyone, I offer a list (see box) of some of the brand names of the period that were most highly regarded. Please note that this list, which is by no means complete—or universally agreed on—applies only to pianos made before about 1930, since in many cases the same names were later applied to entirely different, usually lower, quality standards.

During this period, a large percentage of the pianos made were outfitted with pneumatically driven player-piano systems. When these mechanisms eventually fell into disrepair, they were often removed. Although there is still a small group of technicians and hobbyists dedicated to restoring these fascinating relics of the past, in most cases it is not economically practical to do so except for historical or sentimental reasons.

GRAY-MARKET PIANOS

If you're looking for a piano made within the last few decades, there is usually a plentiful supply of used Yamaha and Kawai pianos originally made for the Japanese market. However, there has been some controversy about them. Sometimes called "gray-market" pianos, these instruments were originally sold to families and schools in Japan, and some years later were discarded in favor of new pianos. There being little market for these used pianos in Japan—the Japanese are said to have a cultural bias against buying any used goods—enterprising businesspeople buy them up, restore them to varying degrees, and export them to the U.S. and other countries, where they are sold by dealers of used pianos at a fraction of the price of a new Yamaha or Kawai. Used Korean pianos are available under similar circumstances. (Note: The term "gray market" is used somewhat erroneously to describe these pianos. They are used instruments, not new, and there is nothing illegal about buying and selling them.)

Yamaha has taken a public stand warning against the purchase of a used Yamaha piano made for the Japanese market. When Yamaha first began exporting pianos to the United States, the company found that some pianos sent to areas of the U.S. with very dry indoor climates, such as parts of the desert Southwest and places that were bitterly cold in the winter, would develop problems in a short period of time: tuning pins would become loose, soundboards and bridges would crack, and glue joints would come apart. To protect against this happening, Yamaha began to season the wood for destination: a low moisture content for pianos bound for the U.S., which has the greatest extremes of dryness; a higher moisture content for Europe; and the highest moisture content for Japan, which is relatively humid. The gray-market pianos, Yamaha says, having been seasoned for the relatively humid Japanese climate, will not stand up to our dryness. The company claims to have received many calls from dissatisfied owners of these pianos, but cannot help them because the warranty, in addition to having expired, is effective only in the country in which the piano was originally sold when new.

My own research has led me to believe that while there is some basis for Yamaha's concerns, their warnings are exaggerated. There probably is a little greater chance, statistically, that these pianos will develop problems in conditions of extreme dryness than will Yamahas seasoned for and sold in the U.S. However, thousands of gray-market pianos have been sold by hundreds of dealers throughout the country, in all types of climates, for many years, and I haven't found evidence of anything close to an epidemic of problems with them. In mild and moderate climates, reported problems are rare. There are, however, some precautions that should be taken.

These pianos are available to dealers in a wide variety of ages and conditions. The better dealers will sell only those in good condition made since about the mid-1980s. In some cases, the dealers or their suppliers will recondition or partially rebuild the pianos before offering them for sale. Make sure to get a warranty that runs for at least five years, as any problems will usually show up within that period if they are going to show up at all. Finally, be sure to use some kind of humidity-control system in situations of unusual dryness. Remember that air-conditioning, as well as heating, can cause indoor dryness.

It's not always possible to determine visually whether a particular instrument was made for the U.S. or the Japanese market, as some original differences may have been altered by the supplier. The dealer may know, and Yamaha has a utility on its website (**www.yamaha.com/pianoserials/index.asp**) that will look up the origin of a particular Yamaha piano by serial number.

1930–1960

The rise of radio and talking pictures in the 1920s competed with pianos for the public's attention and weakened the piano industry, and the Great Depression decimated it. During the Depression, many piano makers, both good and bad, went bankrupt, and their names were bought up by the surviving companies. Sometimes the defunct company's designs continued to be used, but often only the name lived on. Still, piano making in the 1930s, though reduced in quantity from earlier years, was in most cases of a similar quality.

To revive the depressed piano market in the mid-1930s, piano makers came up with a new idea: the small piano. Despite the fact that small pianos, both vertical and grand, are musically inferior to larger ones, the public decided that spinets, consoles, and small grands were preferable because they looked better in the smaller homes and apartments of the day. There has always been a furniture aspect to the piano, but the degree to which piano makers catered to that aspect from the mid-'30s onward marked a revolution in piano marketing.

During World War II, many piano factories were commandeered to make airplane wings and other wartime products, and what piano making there was fell somewhat in quality because of a lack of good raw materials and skilled labor. Things changed for the better in the postwar period, and you'll sometimes find used pianos from this period, still in reasonably good condition or needing some reconditioning, from such brands as Steinway, Baldwin, Mason & Hamlin, Sohmer, Everett, Knabe, and Wurlitzer.

1960–Present

In the 1960s, the Japanese began exporting pianos to the U.S. in large numbers. Although at first they had some difficulty building pianos to

the demands of our climate, by the mid- to late-'60s their quality was so high and their prices so low that they threatened to put all U.S. makers out of business. In response, most of the mid-priced American makers cheapened their product to compete. As a result, the 20 years from about 1965 to 1985 are considered, from a quality standpoint, to be a low point in U.S. piano manufacturing. In any case, the Americans were unable to compete. The international takeover of the U.S. piano market accelerated in the 1980s as the Koreans began to export here, and by 1985 all but a few U.S. piano makers had gone out of business. As in an earlier period, some of their brand names were purchased and later used by others.

Please see the article "The New-Piano Market Today" for more information on the post-1960 period.

A used piano made within the past few decades can often be a very good deal, as these instruments may still show very few signs of age and wear, but with a price far below that of a new piano. The most recently made used pianos may even come with a warranty that is still in effect. Also, the influx of new, low-priced, Chinese- and Indonesian-made pianos has driven down the price of used pianos, in some cases rather substantially, as the imports offer the opportunity to buy a new piano for a price only a little higher than a decent used one previously commanded. If you're considering a piano from this period, you may wish to read applicable articles in this publication about new pianos, as well as current and past editions of *The Piano Book*. See also the accompanying article about so-called gray-market pianos.

Though in each decade both good and bad pianos have been produced, and each piano must be judged on its own merits, this brief historical overview may give you some idea of what to expect to see as you shop for a used piano. You can determine the age of a piano by finding its serial number (*The Piano Book* tells how) and looking it up in the *Pierce Piano Atlas* (www.piercepianoatlas.com), or perhaps by asking a piano dealer or technician to look it up for you.

How to Find a Used Piano

Finding a used piano essentially involves networking, a concept very much in vogue these days. Some networking can be done by computer, and some with old-fashioned phone calls and shoe leather. Here are some of your options—you may be able to think of others.

■ *Contact piano technicians, rebuilders, and used-piano dealers*

People who service pianos often have customers who want to sell their instruments. Some technicians also restore pianos for sale in their shops. Contacting these technicians or visiting their shops is a good way to acquaint yourself with local market conditions, to better understand what's involved in piano restoration, and to see an interesting slice of life in your community you might not otherwise encounter. If you decide to buy from a technician, you may pay more than you would a private party, but you'll have the peace of mind of knowing that the piano has been checked over, repaired, and comes with a warranty. Even though you trust the seller, it's a good idea to hire an independent technician to inspect the piano before purchase, just as you would if the piano were being sold by a private party, because even the best technicians can differ in their professional abilities and opinions.

■ *Visit dealers of new pianos*

New-piano dealers take used pianos in trade for new ones all the time, and need to dispose of them to recoup the trade-in allowance they gave on the new piano. Although many of the trade-ins will be older pianos, it's quite common for a customer to trade in a piano purchased only a few years earlier for a bigger or better model, leaving a nearly new piano for you to buy at a substantial discount on its price when new. Again, you may pay more than you would from a private party—usually 20 to 30 percent more—but it may be difficult to find something like this from a private party, and the dealer will likely also give some sort of warranty. Some of the best deals I've seen have been acquired this way. If you're also considering the option of buying a new piano, then you'll be able to explore both options with a single visit. On the other hand, sometimes dealers advertise used pianos just to get customers into the store, where they can be sold on a new piano. The used piano advertised may be overpriced, or may no longer be available. When you have a used piano inspected, make sure the technician you hire owes no favors to the dealer who's selling it.

■ *Shopping via the Internet*

The best way to use the Internet to shop for a used piano is to look for sellers, both commercial and non-commercial, within driving distance of your home. That way, you can more easily try out the piano, develop a face-to-face relationship with the seller, and get a better sense of whether or not you want to do business with them. Craigslist (www.craigslist.org), though not a piano-specific site, seems to have become the preferred classified-ad site for this purpose, as it's both free and is organized by city. If you travel frequently, you should check out sellers in other cities, too—easy to do on Craigslist. Other popular piano classified-ad sites include www.pianoworld.com (which also has extensive forums for exchanging information and getting answers to your questions), www.pianomart.com (smartly organized for easy searching), www.pianobroker.com, and our own Piano Buyer Classifieds (www.pianobuyer.com), which uses the Pianomart database and search engine. These sites either charge a monthly fee to list or a small commission upon sale, but are free to buyers.

You'll also find pianos for sale on the Internet auction site eBay. Search on a variety of keywords, as each keyword will bring up a different group of pianos for sale. This can be frustrating, as either too broad or too specific a search term may yield unsatisfactory results. The bidding process generally provides a window of time during which you can contact the seller for more information, see the piano, and have it inspected before placing a bid. This is definitely not a good way to buy a piano unless you have the opportunity to first try out the piano and have it inspected. On both eBay and the classified-ad sites mentioned above, many listings that appear to be non-commercial will actually turn out to have been placed by commercial sellers, who may have many more pianos for sale than the one in the ad you answered.

The website of the Piano Technicians Guild (www.ptg.org) has a listing of dealer websites and other resources that may be useful in locating used or restored pianos. If your situation is such that finding a local source of used pianos is unlikely, one reliable source that ships nationwide is Rick Jones Pianos in Beltsville, Maryland (www.rickjonespianos.com).

If you're thinking of making a long-distance purchase, the precautions mentioned in the section "Shopping Long-Distance via the Internet," in the article "Piano Buying Basics," bear repeating: First, take into account the cost of long-distance shipping and consider whether it's really worth it. If buying from a commercial source, find out as much as you can about the dealer. Get references. If you haven't actually seen the piano, get pictures of it. Hire a technician in the seller's area to inspect the piano and ask the technician about a commercial seller's reputation. Make sure the dealer has experience in arranging long-distance moves, and uses a mover that specializes in pianos. Find out who will be responsible for tuning and adjusting the piano in your home, and for repairing any defects or dings in the finish. Get the details of any warranty, especially who is responsible for paying the return freight if the piano is defective. Find out how payment is to be made in a way that protects both parties.

■ *Non-Internet Techniques*

In this age of the Internet, it's important not to forget older, more

conventional methods of networking that still work, such as placing and answering classified print ads in local newspapers and want-ad booklets; and posting and answering notices on bulletin boards anywhere people congregate, such as houses of worship, community centers, laundromats, etc. Other, more aggressive, techniques include contacting movers and storage warehouses to see if they have any pianos abandoned by their owners; attending auctions; contacting attorneys and others who handle the disposition of estates; and just plain old asking around among coworkers, friends, and acquaintances.

■ *Obtaining a Piano from a Friend or Relative*

It's nice when pianos remain in the family. I got my piano that way. But pianos purchased from friends and relatives or received as gifts are as

likely as any others to have expensive problems you should know about. It's very hard to refuse a gift, and perhaps embarrassing to hire a piano technician to inspect it before you accept it, but for your own protection you should insist on doing so. Otherwise you may spend a lot of money to move a "gift" you could have done without.

Which of these routes to finding a used piano you end up following will depend on your situation and what you're looking for. If you have a lot of time and transportation is no problem, you may get the best deal by shopping around among private owners or in out-of-the-way places. If you're busy or without a car but have money to spend, it may be more convenient to shop among piano technicians, rebuilders, or dealers, who may be able to show you several

pianos at the same time and spare you from worrying about future repair costs and problems. If you travel a lot to other cities or have few piano resources in your local area, the Internet can be a big help in locating an appropriate commercial or non-commercial source far away. (See the ads in this publication for movers that specialize in long-distance piano moving.) The best route also depends on where you live, as some communities may have a brisk trade in used pianos among private owners but few rebuilding shops, or vice versa, or have an abundance of old uprights but few grands.

Buying a Restored Piano

Three terms are often used in discussions of piano restoration work: *repair*, *reconditioning*, and *rebuilding*. There are no precise definitions of these terms, and any particular job may contain elements of more than one of them. It's therefore very important, when having restoration work done on your piano or when buying a piano on which such work has been done, to find out exactly what jobs have been, or will be, carried out. "This piano has been reconditioned" or "I'll rebuild this piano" are not sufficient answers. One technician's rebuilding may be another's reconditioning.

Repair jobs generally involve fixing isolated broken parts, such as a broken hammer, a missing string, or an improperly working pedal. That is, a repair does not necessarily involve upgrading the condition of the instrument as a whole, but addresses only specific broken or improperly adjusted parts.

Reconditioning always involves a general upgrading of the entire piano, but with as little actual replacement of parts as possible. For instance, reconditioning an old upright might include resurfacing

THE LARGEST SELECTION.

THE FINEST RESTORATION.

EASY SHIPPING
International delivery

30 DAY RETURNS
Guarantee you love it

WARRANTIES
5, 10, 15 & Lifetime options

NATIONAL NETWORK
of piano technicians

LindebladPiano.com   888.587.4266

Gluing a new soundboard into the rim of a grand piano

A rebuilt grand piano action with new hammers is ready for regulating and voicing.

the hammer felt (instead of replacing the hammers) and twisting (instead of replacing) the bass strings to improve their tone. However, definitions of *reconditioning* can vary widely: Many technicians would consider the replacement of hammers, tuning pins, and strings to be part of a reconditioning job in which more extensive work is either not needed or not cost-effective; others would call such work a partial rebuild.

Rebuilding is the most complete of the three levels of restoration. Ideally, *rebuilding* means putting

the piano into "like new" condition. In practice, however, it may involve much less, depending on the needs and value of the particular instrument, the amount of money available, and the scrupulousness of the rebuilder. Restringing the piano and replacing the pinblock in a grand, as well as repairing or replacing the soundboard, would typically be parts of a rebuilding job. In the action, rebuilding would include replacing the hammer heads, damper felts, and key bushings, and replacing or completely overhauling other sets of parts as well. Refinishing the piano case is also generally part of the rebuilding process. Because of the confusion over the definitions of these terms, sometimes the term *remanufacturing* is used to distinguish the most complete rebuilding job possible—including replacement of the soundboard—from a lesser "rebuilding." However, there is no substitute for requesting from the technician an itemization of the work performed.

When considering buying a rebuilt piano, or having a piano rebuilt, particularly an expensive one, the rebuilder's experience level should count heavily in your decision. The complete rebuilding of a piano requires many dissimilar skills. The skills required for installing a soundboard, for example, are very different from those required for installing a new set of hammers or for regulating the action. Mastering all of these skills can take a very long time. In a sense, you should be

Restoring the piano case to like-new condition

GRAND PIANO REBUILDING CHECKLIST

The following is a list of the tasks that might comprise a fairly complete rebuilding of a grand piano. Any particular job may be either more or less extensive than shown here, depending on the needs and value of the instrument and other factors, but this list can serve as a guide. See also *The Piano Book* for information about specific rebuilding issues pertaining to Steinway and Mason & Hamlin pianos.

Notice that the restoration can be divided into three main parts: the soundbox or resonating unit, the action, and the cabinet. The *soundbox* (also known as the *strung back* or *belly*) includes the soundboard, ribs, bridges, strings, pinblock, tuning pins, plate, and the structural parts of the case; the *action* includes the keyframe and action frame, keys and keytops, hammers, dampers, trapwork, and all other moving action parts; the *cabinet* includes cosmetic repair and refinishing of the case and of the nonstructural cabinet parts and hardware. Note that the damper parts that contact the strings are restored with the soundbox, whereas the damper underlever action is treated with the rest of the action.

There is very little overlap among the three types of work; each of the three parts could be performed alone or at different times, as technical conditions permit and/or financial considerations require. In a typical complete rebuilding job, restoration of the soundbox might comprise 45 percent of the cost, the action 30 percent, and the cabinet 25 percent, though these percentages will vary according to the particulars of the job.

Soundbox or resonating unit

- Replace or repair soundboard, refinish, install new soundboard decal (if not replacing soundboard: shim soundboard cracks, reglue ribs as necessary, refinish, install new soundboard decal)
- Replace pinblock
- Replace bridges or bridge caps
- Replace or ream agraffes, restore capo-bar bearing surface
- Refinish plate, paint lettering, replace understring felts
- Replace strings and tuning pins, tune to pitch
- Replace damper felts, refinish damper heads, regulate dampers

Action

- Replace hammers, shanks, and flanges
- Replace or overhaul wippen/repetition assemblies
- Replace backchecks
- Replace front-rail key bushings
- Replace balance-rail key bushings or key buttons
- Replace or clean keytops
- Replace key-end felts
- Clean keys
- Clean and refelt keyframe
- Replace let-off felts or buttons
- Clean and, if necessary, repair action frame
- Regulate action, voice
- Overhaul or replace damper underlever action and damper guide rail
- Overhaul pedal lyre and trapwork, regulate

Cabinet

- Repair music desk, legs, other cabinet parts, as needed
- Repair loose or missing veneer
- Strip and refinish exterior; refinish bench to match piano
- Buff and lacquer solid-brass hardware, replate plated hardware

shopping for the rebuilder as much as for the piano.

Many rebuilders contract out portions of the job, particularly the refinishing of the piano's case, to others who have special expertise. Although this has always been so, more recently groups of technicians, each with his or her own business and shop, have been openly advertising their close, long-term collaboration with one another on rebuilding jobs. In a typical collaboration of this type, one person might rebuild the strung back or soundbox (soundboard, bridges, pinblock, strings, tuning pins, cast-iron plate); another would rebuild the action and do the final musical finishing, such as regulating and voicing; and the third would refinish the case. Collaboration of this kind is a positive development, as it means that each technician does only what he or she does best, resulting in a better job for the customer. But make sure you know with whom you are contracting or from whom you are buying, and which technician is responsible for making things right if problems arise.

It may occur to you that you could save a lot of money by buying an unrestored piano and having a technician completely restore it, rather than buying the completely restored piano from the technician. This is often true. But the results of a rebuilding job tend to be musically uncertain. That is, if you are particular in your taste for tone and touch, you may or may not care for how the instrument ultimately turns out. For that reason, especially if a lot of money is involved, you might be better off letting the technician make the extra profit in return for taking the risk.

"Vintage" . . . or New?

"Vintage" pianos are those made during the golden years of piano-making in the United States—roughly, from 1880 to World War II. More specifically, the term usually refers to the Steinway and Mason & Hamlin pianos made during that period, though it's occasionally applied to other great American makes as well. In the last few decades the demand for these pianos, and consequently their prices, has mushroomed due to a (until recently) strong economy, increased entrepreneurial activity on the part

APPRECIATE OR DEPRECIATE?

Some piano manufacturers market their instruments as "investments" and tout their potential for appreciation in value. If that's the case, then why a *depreciation* schedule? Do pianos appreciate or depreciate?

It depends on how you look at it. Imagine parking a sum of money in a savings account earning 2 percent interest at a time when inflation is at 3 percent. Each year, the balance in the account grows . . . and *loses* purchasing power. This is something like the situation with pianos. After a large initial drop in value during the first five to ten years (because, unless given an incentive to buy used, most people would prefer a new piano), used pianos lose value in comparison with similar new ones at about 1.5 to 2 percent per year. However, because the price of *everything* (including pianos) is rising in price at 3 or 3.5 percent per year (the rate of inflation), the value of your used piano will appear to *rise* by 1 to 2 percent per year (the difference between the depreciation and the inflation).

Why do we figure depreciation from a comparable new piano instead of figuring appreciation from the original price of the used one? Theoretically, it could be done either way. But the price of a comparable new piano is easier to look up—one might have to do a lot of research to find out what grandma paid for her piano. And the price of the new piano embodies all the inflation that has occurred between the original purchase of the used piano and the present, avoiding the trouble of having to look up the change in the cost of living during that time. The case is even stronger for using this method with foreign-made pianos: Tying the value of a used piano to the cost of a comparable new one makes it unnecessary to calculate the changes in the currency exchange rate—and sometimes changes in the currency itself!—that have occurred since the used piano was new.

Figuring depreciation from a comparable new piano is not without its own problems, however. With so many piano brands of the past now defunct or made to entirely different standards (usually in China), the task of figuring out what constitutes a "comparable" new piano can sometimes be formidable, if not impossible.

---

of rebuilders and piano brokers, allegations by rebuilders and others that today's new pianos are not as well made as the older ones were, and the purchase of many older Steinways by Steinway & Sons itself for rebuilding in its factory.

What makes these vintage pianos so alluring? Many musicians and technicians believe that these instruments, when rebuilt, sound and play better than new pianos. However, no one knows for sure why this should be so, since most of the components in the piano are replaced during rebuilding. Some point to the fact that Steinway operated its own plate foundry until about World War II, afterward using a commercial plate foundry (which it now owns). Because this radical change in the manufacture of such an important component roughly corresponds with the end of the vintage era, and because the plate is one of the few original parts to survive the rebuilding process, some speculate that it holds the key to the difference. Others say it has to do with changes in the quality of the wood available to Steinway and other companies. Still others say it wasn't any single thing, but rather a combination of many fortuitous factors, including extremely skilled and talented craftsmen, that enabled these companies to make such special pianos during that period, but allegedly not afterward (though that doesn't explain why the rebuilt ones from that period should be better).

Steinway & Sons, for its part, disputes the entire idea that older Steinways are better, dismissing it as a romantic notion spread by purveyors of those pianos in their own financial interest. The company says it has done extensive testing of both plates and woods, and the idea that the older plates and woods were better has no scientific basis. It says it has also carefully inspected hundreds of older Steinways at its factory rebuilding facility, which is the largest Steinway rebuilding facility in the world, and finds no evidence that the older pianos were built better than today's—in fact, it believes that just the opposite is true. Steinway acknowledges that some pianists may prefer the sound of specific older pianos for subjective artistic reasons, but says that those considering the purchase of a restored, older instrument should do so to save money, not to seek better quality.

For more discussion of this topic, and of specific technical issues applicable to the rebuilding of a Steinway or Mason & Hamlin, please see *The Piano Book*.

How Much Is It Worth?

The valuation of used pianos is difficult. Prices of used pianos vary wildly, depending on local economies, supply and demand, and the cosmetics and playing condition of the instrument at hand, including the amount and quality of any restoration work done. As if this weren't enough, it's almost a certainty that no two piano technicians or piano salespeople would return exactly the same verdict on any given piano's value. Art being what it is, beauty is in the eye and ear of the potential purchaser, and values are very much subjective.

In addition, when considering a used piano being sold by a private, non-commercial seller, keep in mind that many such sellers really have no firm idea of how much their piano is worth, and have made up something based on little more than a wish. Therefore, don't let a high asking price keep you from making a more reasonable offer. Ask the seller how they arrived at their asking price. If you can back up your offer with your own technician's appraisal (including a list of the things that need to be fixed), credible listings of similar pianos, or other evidence of the piano's true value, you stand a good chance of getting the piano at or close to your price.

In this article, I've tried to assemble some information and tools to help buyers and sellers understand the appraisal process and determine the value of a piano within a reasonable range.

Fair market value is the price at which an item would change hands between a willing buyer and a willing seller, neither of whom is compelled to buy or sell, and each of whom has reasonable knowledge of the relevant facts.

Appraisers of used pianos and other consumer goods typically use three different methods to determine fair market value: *comparable sales*, *depreciation*, and *idealized value minus the cost of restoration.*

Comparable Sales

The *comparable sales* method compares the piano being appraised with recent actual selling prices of other pianos of like brand, model, age, condition, and location. Generally speaking, this is the most accurate method of determining value when one has access to a body of information on recent sale prices of comparable items. The problem here is that, with few exceptions, it's rare to

find several recently sold pianos that are perfect matches for all these criteria. There is no central repository for sales information on used pianos, and each appraiser or technician, over a lifetime, sees pianos that are so diverse and scattered as to these criteria that they are likely to be of only limited value as appraisal guides. (Exceptions might be technicians or dealers who specialize in used Yamaha, Kawai, or Steinway pianos, brands that have attained near-commodity status in the piano business.)

To handle this problem, I and my staff have attempted to approximate the fair market value of pianos of various types, ages, and conditions by querying a number of piano technicians about their memories of comparable sales. The result is the accompanying chart, "Prices of Used Pianos," though I stress that

PRICES OF USED PIANOS (US$)				
	Private Seller			Dealer	
	Worse	Average	Better	Reconditioned	Rebuilt
Vertical, pre-1950, average brand	0–300	300–750	600–1,000	1,000–1,500	N/A
Vertical, pre-1950, better brand	150–500	400–1,000	700–1,500	1,200–2,000	N/A
Vertical, pre-1950, best brand	500–1,000	1,000–3,000	2,000–5,000	3,000–6,000	10,000–16,000
Vertical, 1950–1980, average brand	200–600	400–1,000	1,000–1,500	1,200–2,500	N/A
Vertical, 1950–1980, better brand	400–800	700–1,500	1,000–2,500	2,000–4,500	N/A
Vertical, 1950–1980, best brand	700–2,000	1,500–2,500	3,000–5,000	4,000–7,000	7,000–10,000
Vertical, 1980–	Use Depreciation Schedule				
Grand, pre-1950, average brand, 5'	0–500	700–1,500	1,000–2,500	1,500–3,500	N/A
Grand, pre-1950, average brand, 6'	500–1,200	1,500–2,000	2,000–3,000	3,500–4,500	N/A
Grand, pre-1950, average brand, 7'	800–1,500	1,500–3,500	3,000–5,000	4,000–7,000	8,000–10,000
Grand, pre-1950, better brand, 5'	500–1,000	2,000–3,000	2,500–4,000	5,000–8,000	N/A
Grand, pre-1950, better brand, 6'	1,000–2,500	2,500–4,000	4,000–7,000	7,000–10,000	12,000–18,000
Grand, pre-1950, better brand, 7'	1,800–3,500	3,500–7,000	6,000–10,000	8,000–15,000	18,000–30,000
Grand, pre-1950, best brand, 5'	3,000–6,000	6,000–9,000	8,000–15,000	15,000–20,000	15,000–25,000
Grand, pre-1950, best brand, 6'	5,000–8,000	7,000–15,000	12,000–20,000	15,000–28,000	28,000–50,000
Grand, pre-1950, best brand, 7'	7,000–10,000	12,000–18,000	20,000–35,000	20,000–40,000	35,000–65,000
Grand, 1950–1980, average brand, 5'	500–1,200	1,500–2,500	2,000–4,000	3,000–5,000	N/A
Grand, 1950–1980, average brand, 6'	800–2,000	2,000–3,000	3,000–5,000	3,500–7,000	N/A
Grand, 1950–1980, average brand, 7'	1,500–2,500	2,500–4,000	4,000–7,000	4,000–8,000	8,000–12,000
Grand, 1950–1980, better brand, 5'	800–2,000	2,000–4,000	2,500–5,000	5,000–9,000	N/A
Grand, 1950–1980, better brand, 6'	1,500–3,000	2,500–5,000	4,000–9,000	8,000–12,000	12,000–22,000
Grand, 1950–1980, better brand, 7'	3,000–6,000	5,000–10,000	8,000–15,000	10,000–20,000	15,000–30,000
Grand, 1950–1980, best brand, 5'	4,000–7,000	7,000–10,000	9,000–18,000	16,000–21,000	17,000–25,000
Grand, 1950–1980, best brand, 6'	6,000–10,000	8,000–15,000	12,000–20,000	20,000–28,000	28,000–50,000
Grand, 1950–1980, best brand, 7'	8,000–12,000	14,000–20,000	18,000–30,000	20,000–40,000	35,000–65,000
Grand, 1980–	Use Depreciation Schedule				

we do not have enough data to do more than make rough estimates. This chart is most useful for determining the approximate value of many brands of older piano for which it would otherwise be difficult to find enough comparable sales to determine a value. Understandably, however, the price ranges shown in the chart are quite broad. The chart is organized by categories of vertical and grand piano broken down by age (pre-1950 and 1950–1980), quality (Average, Better, Best), and condition (Worse, Average, Better, Reconditioned, and Rebuilt). For prices of pianos made since 1980, I suggest using the depreciation method, described later in this article.

The price ranges given reflect the wide possibilities a buyer faces in the used-piano market. At the low end of each range is a price one might find in a poor economy or a "buyer's market," where supply exceeds demand. At the high end, the prices are consistent with both a better economy and a higher demand for the type of instrument indicated. In some categories, the prices we received from our sources varied all over the map, and we had to use a considerable amount of editorial discretion to produce price ranges that were not so broad as to be useless as guidelines, and to retain at least a modicum of internal consistency in the chart. For that reason, you should expect to find some markets or situations in which prices higher or lower than those given here are normal or appropriate.

The prices given here for pianos that are not reconditioned or rebuilt (those labeled Worse, Average, Better) are the price ranges you might expect to find when buying pianos *from private owners*. The Reconditioned and Rebuilt categories represent prices you might encounter when shopping for such pianos *at piano stores or from piano technicians*, with a warranty given. In some cases we have omitted the Rebuilt price because we would not expect rebuilding to be cost-effective for pianos of that general age and type. In every case, prices assume the least expensive style and finish; prices for pianos with fancier cabinets, exotic veneers, inlays, and so forth, could be much higher.

Quality

"Best brands" include Steinway, Mason & Hamlin, and the very best European makes, such as Bechstein, Blüthner, and Bösendorfer. "Better brands" include the well-regarded older names mentioned in the accompanying article for the pre-1930 period, such as Knabe and Chickering; and names such as Baldwin, Everett, Kawai, Sohmer, Yamaha, and others of similar quality for the 1950–1980 period. "Average brands" are pretty much everything else.

Condition

Worse, Average, and Better refer to the condition of the piano in comparison to the amount of wear and tear one would expect from the piano's age. However, even Worse pianos should be playable and serviceable. Note that because many buyers are quite conscious of a piano's appearance, pianos that are in good shape musically but in poor shape cosmetically will often sell at a price more consistent with the Worse range than with a higher one. This offers an opportunity for the less furniture-conscious buyer to obtain a bargain.

For a discussion of the definitions of *reconditioned* and *rebuilt*, please see the section "Buying a Restored

Piano" in this article. **For the purposes of this chart, however, we have adopted the requirement that a piano has not been** *rebuilt* **unless its pinblock has been replaced, and that a piano that has been restrung, but without a new pinblock, is considered to have been** *reconditioned.* Note that these definitions are not precise, and that both the quality and the quantity of the work can vary greatly, depending on the needs of the instrument and the capabilities of the restorer. These variations should be taken into account when determining the piano's value.

Depreciation

The *depreciation* method of determining fair market value is based on the fact that many types of consumer goods lose value over time at a more or less predictable rate. A *depreciation schedule,* such as the one here, shows how much an unrestored used piano is worth as a percentage of the actual selling price of a new piano of comparable quality. The problem here is that so many older brands are now made by companies different from the original, in different factories and parts of the world, and to different standards, that it can be difficult or impossible to determine what constitutes a "comparable" new piano. Thus, this method of figuring value is best used for pianos of relatively recent make when the model is still in production, or for older pianos whose makers have remained under relatively constant ownership, location, and standards, and for which, therefore, a comparable model can reasonably be determined.

Note that depreciation is from the *current* price of the model, not the original price, because the current price takes into account inflation and, if applicable, changes in the value of foreign currencies. The values are meant to reflect what the piano would sell for between *private,*

DEPRECIATION SCHEDULE			
Age in Years	Percent of New Value		
	Worse	*Average*	*Better*
1	75	80	83
2	72	77	80
3	69	74	77
5	63	68	71
10	52	57	60
15	43	48	51
20	36	41	44
25	29	34	37
Verticals only			
30	22	27	30
35–70	15	20	23
Grands only			
30–70	25	30	33
Steinways			
1	75	80	83
2	72	77	80
3	70	75	78
5	66	71	74
10	58	63	66
15	50	55	58
20	42	47	50
25	34	39	42
Verticals only			
30	28	33	36
35–70	25	30	33
Grands only			
30	31	36	39
50	30	35	38
70	28	33	36

non-commercial parties. I suggest adding 20 to 30 percent to the computed value when the piano is being sold *by a dealer,* unrestored, but with a warranty. These figures are intended only as guidelines, reflecting our general observation of the market. "Worse," "Average," and "Better" refer to the condition of the used piano for its age. A separate chart is given for Steinway pianos. Other fine pianos, such as Mason & Hamlin, or some of the best European brands, may command prices between the regular and Steinway figures.

Idealized Value Minus the Cost of Restoration

This is the difference between the cost of a rebuilt piano and the cost to restore the unrebuilt one to like-new condition. For example, if a piano, rebuilt, would be worth $50,000, and it would cost $30,000 to restore the unrebuilt one to like-new condition, then according to this method the unrebuilt piano would be worth $20,000. This method can be used when a piano needs extensive, quantifiable repair work. It's not appropriate to use this method for an instrument that is relatively new or in good condition.

Other Types of Valuation

Several other types of valuation are sometimes called for:

Replacement value is what it would cost to replace the used piano with a brand-new one. This value is often sought when someone has purchased an insurance policy with a rider that guarantees replacement of a lost or damaged piano with a new one instead of paying the fair market value of the used one. The problem here, again, is what brand and model of new piano to consider "comparable" if the original brand and model are no longer being made, or are not being made to the same standards.

Here it may be helpful to consult the **rating chart** in the ***Piano Buyer*** article "The New-Piano Market Today." Choose a brand whose relationship to today's piano market is similar to that the original brand bore to the piano market of its day. Whatever brand and model you choose, depending on how high a replacement value you seek, you can use either the manufacturer's suggested retail price (highest), the approximate street price (lowest), or something in between. These prices,

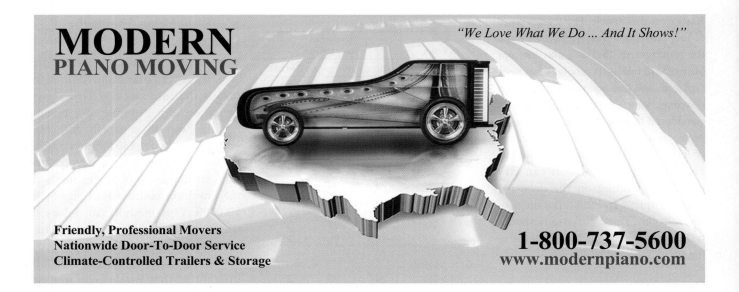
or information on how to estimate them, can be found in the "Model & Pricing Guide."

Trade-in value is what a commercial seller would pay for the used piano, usually in trade (or partial trade) for a new one. This is discounted from the fair market value, typically by at least 20 to 30 percent, to allow the commercial seller to make a profit when reselling the instrument. (In practice, the commercial seller will often pay the fair market value for the used piano, but to compensate, will increase the price of the new piano to the consumer.)

Salvage value is what a dealer, technician, or rebuilder would pay for a piano that is essentially unplayable or unserviceable and in need of restoration. It can be determined using the idealized-value-minus-cost-of-restoration method, but discounted, like trade-in value, to allow the commercial seller to make a profit.

Inspect, Inspect, Inspect

In closing, I'd like to remind you that your best protection against buyer's remorse is having the piano inspected by a piano technician prior to purchasing it, particularly if the piano is more than ten years old. Sometimes it will be sufficient to speak to the seller's technician about the piano, if he or she has serviced it regularly and has reason to believe that he or she will continue servicing it under your ownership. However, in most situations, you'll be better off hiring your own technician. You can find a list of Registered Piano Technicians in your area on the website of the Piano Technicians Guild, www.ptg.org.

More Information

If you're serious about buying a used piano, additional information in *The Piano Book* may be useful to you, including:

- How to remove the outer cabinet parts to look inside the piano

- How to do a preliminary inspection of a piano to rule out those that are not worth hiring a technician to inspect, including an extensive checklist of potential problem areas

- A discussion of issues that frequently come up in regard to the rebuilding of Steinway pianos

- A complete list of older Steinway models, from 1853 to the present

- How to locate the serial number of a piano

- A list of manufacturing dates and serial numbers for Steinway pianos.

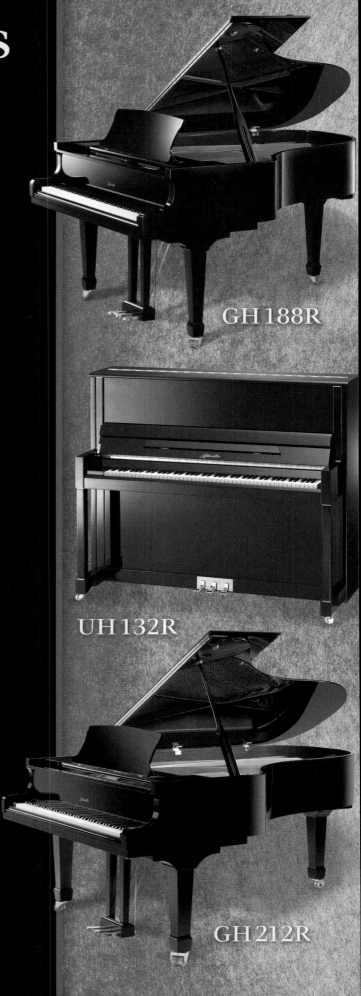

From 1789 to the present, over 100 different companies, most of them now long gone, have manufactured pianos in New York City. They have included Decker & Sons, Mathushek, Mehlin & Sons, Steinway & Sons, and Weber, to name a few of the better known. This extensive piano-manufacturing presence made New York the ultimate piano town, where craftsmen from Great Britain and continental Europe migrated and stayed, working in an industry that supplied the 19th and early 20th centuries' burgeoning world of pianists with nearly endless choice in price and quality.

While many of those older pianos are still in use, many others have or soon will have reached the end of their useful life, and will need rebuilding if their owners—families, churches, schools, museums, and universities—want to continue to use them as musical instruments. To serve that need, the piano-building tradition of a century ago lingers on in the many fine rebuilding shops of present-day New York.

Rebuilding a piano—restoring it to like-new condition by replacing its strings, pinblock, action, keys, soundboard, and bridges, and refinishing its case—is a long and complicated process. Further complicating this process is the possibility that the original manufacturer may no longer be in business and therefore is unable to supply parts or materials. If you can, envision craftspeople at work, puzzling over missing parts, re-creating mechanisms of bygone eras, and tirelessly researching and reproducing some of the 19th and early 20th centuries' most complicated musical cabinetry.

I contacted a number of New York–area rebuilders and asked them questions about their history, their operations, and the sources of some of their parts and materials. I also requested that they send me stories and photographs of interesting rebuilding projects they've undertaken, and to display the variety of work being done in their shops.

Here, in alphabetical order, are responses from some of the best-known New York rebuilders:

AC Pianocraft

42-24 Orchard Street, 4th Floor
Long Island City, New York 11101
718-361-9112
www.acpianocraft.com

AC Pianocraft has been rebuilding pianos since 1966, using methods learned by founder Ted Kostakis and his associates while working for many years at the Steinway & Sons factory, also located in Long Island City. Current owner Alex Kostakis, Ted's son, has continued rebuilding fine pianos for institutions and private clients using traditional materials and methods.

His years of being in the trade have given Alex many colorful stories of clients and pianos. While AC Pianocraft's specialties are pianos from Steinway, Mason & Hamlin, and other fine brands, they don't shy away from tackling the more interesting and challenging rebuilds of lesser makes.

The company recently took in for rebuilding a piano by Kranich & Bach, an old New York company that made pianos with lovely art cases, but had actions that were notorious for never working well even when new. Alex said that he at first tried to discourage the owner from having the work done because of the potential for an unsatisfying outcome. But when the customer decided to proceed, Alex ordered sample parts from many manufacturers, trying and modifying them until he came up with a solution. Ultimately, he completely redesigned and installed a new performance-quality action in the spectacular case for a very happy customer.

Beethoven Pianos

211 West 58th Street
New York, New York 10019
212-765-7300
800-241-0001
www.beethovenpianos.com

Offering a wide range of prices and brands, and with a rebuilding facility in the Bronx, Beethoven Pianos has been a fixture in the New York piano market for over 40 years. Owner Carl Demler says that although he does many rebuilding jobs for clients, most of his rebuilds of Steinway, Mason & Hamlin, and European pianos are for resale. In addition, he sells new pianos by Grotrian, Hailun, Ritmüller, and Sauter, among other brands. Demler says he uses only German-made Renner action parts in his rebuilds, but with New York Steinway hammers in the Steinways. Soundboard wood is sourced from a number of countries, depending on which will work best in a particular instrument. In addition to standard case styles, Beethoven specializes in rebuilding art-case pianos. With 10 employees, Beethoven rebuilds about 75 pianos a year. Demler emphasized his attention to detail and reliance on traditional techniques for Beethoven's continued success over four decades.

This interesting art case, created on a Steinway model B, shows AC Pianocraft's versatility and creativity in woodworking and case decoration.

Faust Harrison Pianos

Manhattan Location
207 West 58th Street
New York, New York 10019
212-489-3600
www.faustharrisonpianos.com

Faust Harrison has been rebuilding pianos since 1983, when founder Sara Faust, a concert pianist, began rebuilding to satisfy her own need for high-quality performance instruments. What began as a hobby became a small side business, then quickly grew into a large enterprise as word spread of the availability of quality rebuilt Steinways. The business is now run by Sara, her husband, Irving, and their adult children, Joshua and Jessica, and has 32 full-time employees at its four locations in Manhattan, White Plains, and Huntington (Long Island), New York, and in Fairfield, Connecticut.

Their new, 25,000-square-foot facility in White Plains is designed especially for rebuilding, with careful consideration of humidity control and lighting, separation of woodworking from other departments, and a state-of-the-art dust-collection system to facilitate the high-quality refinishing for which they are especially known. Joshua Faust highlights their unusually extensive inventory, which includes used and rebuilt vintage-era Steinways and other fine makes. He says they source all their soundboard material from André Bolduc, the Canadian soundboard supplier, in the form of soundboard blanks, and craft every aspect of the soundboard themselves in their White Plains facility. The company rebuilds some 100 pianos per year, and maintains a few dozen completed rebuilt pianos in their four locations for customers to try. Faust Harrison also sells new C. Bechstein, Brodmann, W. Hoffman, Mason & Hamlin, Schimmel, and Yamaha pianos.

The special furniture page of their web site (www.faustharrisonpianos.com/brands/steinway-special-furniture-pianos.shtml) shows and describes two interesting

Soundboard construction

Hand-rubbed lacquer mahogany finish

Case finish department at Faust Harrison

Steinway Art Deco pianos restored by Faust Harrison. The first piano, built by Steinway in 1940 from a commissioned design by renowned designer Arthur Dorwin Teague, spent years on a cruise ship that sailed between New Orleans and Rio de Janeiro, where it suffered the effects of high humidity. It was fully rebuilt and refinished for a client by Faust Harrison in 2004, and has since been chosen to eventually join the keyboard collection of the Metropolitan Museum of Art. Irving Faust says he has seen several Teague-designed Steinways over the past 35 years, but has never seen another to match this piano's intriguing style.

In 2005, Faust Harrison acquired a 1938 Steinway Arts & Crafts model S piano that they were reluctant to rebuild because its case was rather ugly. However, they saw that, with a bit of ingenuity and some master carpentry, including the fabrication of an entire new leg-and-lyre assembly, they could transform the case to match that of Teague's Steinway Art Deco design.

In 2006, Hugh Grant, Drew Barrymore, and hordes of production crew descended on the Faust Harrison showroom on 58th Street to shoot a scene for the film *Music and Lyrics*. In 2007, Faust Harrison received a call from a woman in Ohio who was looking to buy a special-style Steinway S. Irving described the 1938 Arts & Crafts piano to her, as well as their vision of transforming it to look like the Teague Art Deco. The cost was more than she was looking to spend, but she was intrigued and said that she'd think about it. That evening, by coincidence, she took her niece to see *Music and Lyrics*—and there on the big screen was a shot of the Faust Harrison showroom. The next morning, she called to order the piano.

Klavierhaus

119 West 56th Street
New York, New York 10019
212-245-4535
www.klavierhaus.com

The background of Klavierhaus's Hungarian-born owner, Sujatri Reisinger, includes restoration work not only on modern pianos, but on antique European instruments as well. Although Klavierhaus focuses its rebuilding primarily on the larger Steinway models B, C, and D because of their extensive use as performance pianos, the company also rebuilds C. Bechstein, Blüthner, Bösendorfer, Broadwood, Érard, Pleyel, and other fine European makes. Reisinger feels that his company's strength lies in its ability to customize an action or sound to conform to the customer's preferences in touch and tone.

Klavierhaus has recently moved to a new location at Le Parker Meridien Hotel, where it hosts concerts to showcase its pianos. Klavierhaus is also the New York and New England retail outlet for Fazioli Pianoforti, the Italian maker of fine pianos. The Klavierhaus rebuilding workshop is in Yonkers, New York.

Klavierhaus associate Nicholas Russotto was generous with his enthusiasm and stories about famous pianists and their visits:

Last year, Klavierhaus performed some work on Emanuel Ax's Hamburg Steinway C, which, after decades of hard use, had begun to show the wear typical of a concert pianist's main practice instrument. Klavierhaus took in the piano and, after performing the requested maintenance, awaited Ax's arrival to try the repaired instrument. When he called to make an appointment to come into the shop, it turned out that another Klavierhaus client, concert pianist Richard Goode, had booked the recital hall at the same time to hear one of his students play. To accommodate Goode, Klavierhaus staff moved Ax's piano into the showroom, just outside the recital hall.

While trying out his piano, Ax played the first several measures of Beethoven's Sonata Op.81a, "Les Adieux," a beautiful piece with a somewhat wistful "horn call" in its first measures. The proper articulation of this passage requires a tremendously fine touch; the voicing of the horn call can be accomplished in multiple ways, and each pianist has his or her own way of doing so. During the course of the conversation with Klavierhaus staff, Ax asked who was in the recital hall, and was delighted to hear that it was his friend Goode. After toying a bit with the first moments of "Les Adieux," Ax jumped up from the bench and exclaimed, "Well, I'll just go ask the master!" He entered the recital hall, and from outside, the Klavierhaus staff heard each of them trying different voicings and articulations of the horn-call passage. They were thrilled to witness this interaction between two great figures of the piano world.

Klavierhaus has undertaken many difficult and unusual rebuilding projects, two of which are described below:

- The House of Pleyel was a powerhouse of harpsichord and piano building for much of the 19th and early 20th centuries. This Pleyel piano, dating from 1874, was installed in an ornate harpsichord case very much in the Louis XV "Chinoiserie" style: flowers, birds, and butterflies are depicted in 14-karat gold on a red background, and the case is supported by six legs that terminate in hoof sabots. The decorative restoration work was done by Nam Thai. The instrument has a lovely, exceedingly polite sound suitable for smaller spaces or salons. It has a completely new action, made to duplicate the touch of the original.

- This Steinway & Sons model B, from 1907, was purchased by William Guggenheim as a Valentine's Day gift for his wife. Custom-painted by Robert Benvenuti for Lucien Alavoine and Company (one of the firms contracted to refresh the Waldorf-Astoria hotel in the 1920s), it is a stunning, one-of-a-kind example of Louis XVI décor.

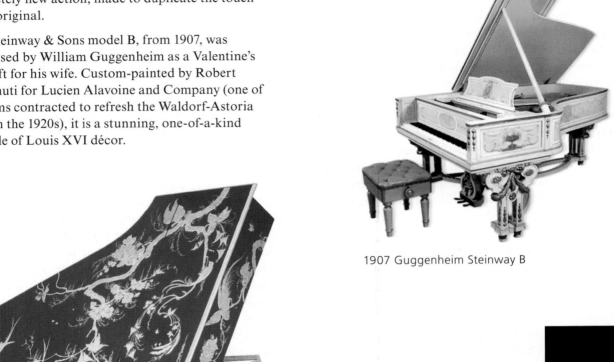

1907 Guggenheim Steinway B

Pleyel "Chinoiserie"

Lindeblad Piano Restoration

101 U.S. 46
Pine Brook, New Jersey 07058
888-587-4266
www.lindebladpiano.com

Lindeblad Piano Restoration is a family-owned business with six family members actively involved, in addition to other staff. It has been in business for more than 100 years, and rebuilds over 200 pianos a year. Lindeblad rebuilds all brands of upright and grand, both for sale and for private clients. At any time, more than 30 completed rebuilds are available to play at their shop. They offer a variety of warranty options on their sales of rebuilt pianos, including a 30-day guaranteed return policy.

Lindeblad maintains a strong online presence, including an inventory that can be browsed before visiting their showroom. The informative videos on their website thoroughly explain the quality of the work and their approach to issues that can come up in the rebuilding process, giving the consumer confidence in the quality of the finished product.

Below is a photo of a rare painted-case Steinway A recently restored by Lindeblad. The company worked with Fine Wood Conservation Ltd., an art-restoration facility in Brooklyn, New York, to restore the paintings on the case.

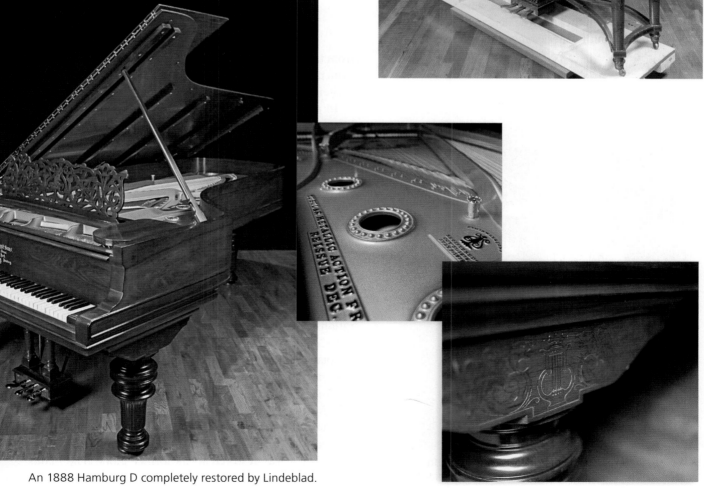

An 1888 Hamburg D completely restored by Lindeblad.

Steinway Restoration Center

Steinway & Sons
Steinway Place
Long Island City, New York 11105
718-204-3175
restoration.steinway.com

The Steinway Restoration Center, located at the Steinway & Sons factory in the Astoria section of Queens, New York, is engaged in three different areas of rebuilding. First, Steinway dealers contract with local clients to rebuild the clients' Steinway pianos, then send the pianos to the Restoration Center to have all or part of the work performed. Second, the Restoration Center rebuilds vintage-era Steinways and makes them available to Steinway dealers for resale. These pianos, known as the Steinway Heirloom Collection, are the only rebuilt Steinways for sale that are certified by Steinway & Sons as "100% genuine." Last, the Restoration Center contracts directly with private clients and institutions to rebuild their Steinway pianos. Steinway restores pianos for museums, concert halls, universities, and conservatories, including the Juilliard School and the Curtis Institute of Music. A Steinway piano rebuilt by the Restoration Center carries the same manufacturer warranty as a new Steinway. The company works with Steinway dealers and technicians all over North and South America to arrange shipment to and

From the Steinway Heirloom Collection

Bill Youse (top row, left) and the Steinway Restoration Center team gather around the completed Motown Steinway.

from the factory for these services. The pianos are insured from pick up to return, and include the resources available to Steinway dealers for follow-up tuning and maintenance.

In addition to rebuilding a piano's innards, Steinway has extensive resources for refinishing exterior cases, and, upon request, can work in traditional finishes such as hand-rubbed lacquer, varnish, or French polish, as well as the current standard high-polish polyester finish. The Restoration Center also employs the services of several specialty woodcarvers who can reproduce damaged or missing carvings or art work, as well as moldings, legs, music desks, or other case parts.

Bill Youse, a 40-year, third-generation Steinway employee, supervises the Restoration Center's 25 dedicated specialists. Many of these senior craftsmen have 30 to 40 years' experience at Steinway. They do well over 100 restorations a year, all Steinways. As the head of the Restoration Center, Youse is not only an expert in the mechanics of the piano, but has a wealth of knowledge about the historic case styling and rare woods used, now and in the past.

Youse recalls the opportunity in 2012 to restore the 1877 Motown Museum Steinway. Sir Paul McCartney had contacted Steinway to ask if they would work with him to see that the famous Steinway used in so many recordings at Motown was restored to its former glory. The piano had been in constant use for decades, and the repairs it

Valentine Toussaint works on the soundboard.

Luis Foreiro finishes an ornate leg.

Photos courtesy of Steinway & Sons
Photographer: Chris Payne

received during that time had been a creative combination of conservation and keeping the piano functioning. Several attempts at partial rebuilding had been made to this early Steinway, and the resulting functionality would not have been optimal for any piano, much less for a Steinway. The Motown Museum wanted the instrument brought back to its original working order, but also wanted to keep the worn and battered case. After several meetings of Museum conservators with the Steinway Restoration Center, a plan was completed and agreed on, and the rebuilt piano was returned to Detroit in late 2012. 🎹

Over the past 35 years, piano technician **Sally Phillips** has worked in virtually every aspect of the piano industry: service, retail, wholesale, and manufacturing. In her role as a concert-piano technician, she has tuned and prepared pianos for concert and recording work in such venues as Town Hall, Alice Tully Hall, and the Kennedy Center, and for such orchestras as the Cincinnati Symphony, the BBC Concert Orchestra, and the Vienna Philharmonic. At present, Phillips lives in Kentucky and works throughout the southeastern U.S. She can be contacted at sphillipspiano@hotmail.com.

SINCE THE PIANO'S INVENTION by Bartolomeo Cristofori in 1700, its evolution has been driven by the desire to meet the changing musical needs of the times, by advances in technology, and by the business and marketing requirements of the piano manufacturers. High-end pianos exemplify this evolutionary process.

Early pianos were limited by the technology of the day to a lightweight structure, and a design that produced a tone—bright and intimate, but with short sustain and low volume—that evolved from the sound of the harpsichord. This complemented both the musical styles favored by the Classical period, especially chamber music, and the smaller, more intimate venues in which music was then customarily performed. As technology advanced, it became possible—using cast-iron plates, stronger strings, and higher-tension scale designs—to produce more robust instruments capable of filling a large hall with sound. This suited the composer-virtuosos of the Romantic period, such as Liszt and Brahms, whose works for the piano demanded from the instrument greater power, and the ability to be heard above the larger orchestras of the day. However, this louder, more overtone-filled sound could also conflict with and overpower other chamber instruments and their performance settings.

The great American pianos, having come of age during the Romantic era, tend toward the Romantic tonal tradition. The great European piano makers, however, embedded in a culture steeped in centuries of musical tradition, have long had to satisfy the conflicting tonal styles of different ages, and this has resulted in a wide variety of instruments with different musical qualities. As the American market for European pianos grows, the European companies are further having to reconcile remaining true to their own traditions with evolving to please the American ear. While all brands make full use of technological advances and are capable of satisfying diverse musical needs, some tend toward a more pristine tone, with plush but low-volume harmonics, perfect for chamber music or solo performances in small rooms; others are bright and powerful enough to hold their own above the largest symphony orchestras; and many are in between.

The good news is that the best way to find the right piano for you is to play as many as you can—a simply wonderful experience!

What follows is a story with a valuable perspective from a well-respected dealer of performance-quality instruments.

—Editor

THE BEST PIANO: A STORY
by ORI BUKAI

"I'm tone deaf," declared the husband. "I can't tell the difference between one piano and another."

His wife nodded in agreement. "He *is* tone deaf. And while I can hear some differences, it's all so confusing. All we want is a piano that our kids can learn to play on. We don't need a *great* piano."

A short conversation ensued in which I learned, among other things, that this couple had three children, ranging in age from seven years to six months.

"Our daughter just turned seven," the wife said. "She's interested in piano lessons, but we're not sure how committed she'll be."

"You know kids," the husband shrugged. "She may want piano lessons now, but in a few months' time . . . ?"

"You're right," I said. "Kids change their minds all the time. I started piano lessons at the age of six, and stopped only a few months later. But the piano stayed in our home, and at the age of 12 I was drawn back to it. I played a few tunes by ear, and after a while I started lessons again. But . . . would you like your youngest child to play the piano as well?"

They looked at each other. It seemed that the possibility of their six-month-old baby taking lessons sometime in the future was something they hadn't considered.

"This means that whatever instrument we choose, it will probably stay in our home for a very long time," the woman said to her husband. "Perhaps we should look at a greater range of instruments than just the few we had in mind . . . ?"

"But still," he said, turning to me, "is there enough difference in the tone of the pianos to justify a greater investment, and a possible increase in our budget?"

Such conversations are not rare. Some people feel they won't be able to hear the differences between pianos, or that a high-end piano will be wasted on them. Others try to accommodate

The tone of a Blüthner piano combines effortless power with the smoothest pianissimo. Perfection of design created by piano masters. Hand crafted in Germany since 1853.

only what they perceive their needs to be at the time of purchase, rather than over the many years they may end up owning a piano.

Often, piano buyers form an idea of what they want and how much to spend, and consider only a few brands, without ever sufficiently researching the differences in manufacturers' philosophies and how these might affect the tone, touch, musicality, and price of the instrument. However, such information can help the consumer clarify his or her true needs and preferences. Many shopping for a piano all but ignore higher-end models, considering them beyond their needs or means. But for more than a few of these buyers, a better-quality piano may prove the better fit and value.

There are significant differences in manufacturing methods between performance-oriented instruments, which are often referred to as "handmade," and mass-produced instruments, in which some musical qualities are sacrificed to meet a lower retail price.

Performance-oriented manufacturers, especially at the highest level, are looking to capture a wide range of tonal characteristics. Some of these qualities, such as sustain, tonal variation, and dynamic range, are universally accepted as helping the playing of pianists of all levels sound more musical. All makers of high-end pianos strive to make pianos that excel in these areas. Other tonal characteristics, however, such as tonal color—the specific harmonic structure of the tone—can reflect a particular manufacturer's philosophy of what the best piano should sound like, and are the elements that separate one high-end make from another. A piano maker's decision to emphasize certain musical qualities over others is manifested through differences in the instrument's design, in the instrument's resulting tone and touch,

and in its appeal to a particular player or listener.

"Would you like to hear some higher-end instruments as well, just to compare?" I asked the couple.

"Yes, please," replied the woman.

And so we went on a tour of Piano Land, playing, listening to, and assessing the tone of a variety of instruments. "Ooohhh," said the wife in response to one particular make. "Aaahhh," sighed her husband, as the realization struck him: He actually *could* hear the differences between these pianos; not only that, he had some rather clear preferences.

"But which is the *best* piano?" he asked. There are quite a few instruments here, all so beautiful, but so different from each other. Which *is* the best?

This is a question customers ask me again and again when visiting our showroom—we represent most of the high-end makers, and side-by-

THE VIENNESE SOUND

WWW.BOESENDORFER.COM

side comparisons are always possible. And while, time after time, our customers do find the absolute "best," for each of those customers the "best" is represented by a different make, according to his or her preferences. The combination of musical qualities emphasized by one piano maker may speak to one customer while leaving another indifferent—who, in turn responds enthusiastically to an instrument made by another manufacturer that has left the first customer cold. Some people prefer a bold, outgoing, and powerful sound; others want a more delicate, clear, and melodic tone. Some like focused, defined, and pure tonal characteristics, while others look for instruments whose sound is more robust, deep, and dark.

At the top end of piano manufacturing, each instrument should have a high level of design, parts, materials, execution, workmanship, and attention to detail. However, it is personal preference—the buyer's response to the various manufacturers' interpretations of the "perfect sound"—that determines the answer to the question of "But which is the *best* piano?" The answer is different for every customer.

But which piano is the "best" is also a matter of other factors. Some high-end instruments might be considered the "best" in one setting, but not quite the best in another. A piano that sounds its best in a large concert hall with hundreds of people may not necessarily be the right fit for the typical living room.

"The best instrument," I replied to the couple, "is the one that you'll most enjoy listening to as your children—and perhaps, before you know it, your grandchildren—play and develop their musical skills. The 'best' piano is the one you'll be happy with over the many years it will live in your home, and that one day, when you have the time, perhaps may tempt you to take lessons yourself. The best piano is the one that will deliver to you and your family the joy of music, now and over the long run."

Ori Bukai owns and operates Allegro Pianos in Stamford, Connecticut, which specializes in the sale of new and restored high-end pianos. Visit his website at www.allegropianos.com.

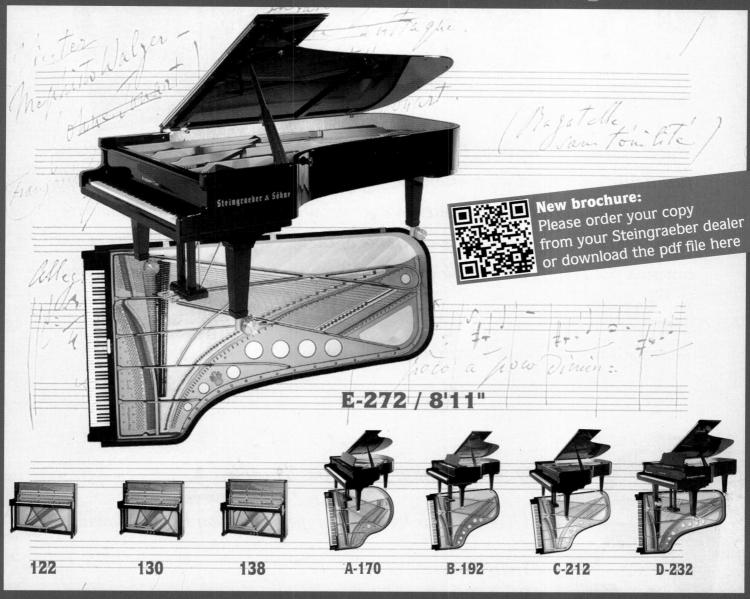

PETROF

PIANOS SINCE 1864

Dear Mrs. Petrof,

The concert in Bradenton, Florida on February 8th, 2015 was a total success, full house and standing ovation. We enjoyed so much playing on the Petrofs! They are truly great instruments. We must say that after playing a few previous concerts on different pianos (some of them very good!), the minute we touched the Petrofs we finally felt like we wanted to, comfortable and to our full capacity.

Anatoly Zatin & Vlada Vassilieva

Dear Mr. Zatin, Dear Mrs. Vassilieva

Thank you for the honor of performing on Petrof pianos.

Yours Sincerely,
Susan Petrof

Family Owned Since 1864
Made in the heart of Europe at our factory in
Hradec Kralove, Czech Republic

P.O. Box 1130 • Richland, WA 99352 • Office 509.946.8078 •Fax 815.550.1840

BUYING PIANOS FOR AN INSTITUTION

GEORGE F. LITTERST

[This article assumes you are already familiar with the basics of piano-shopping (see "Piano Buying Basics" and other appropriate articles in this publication), and treats only those aspects of the subject that are specific to the institutional setting.—Ed.]

Institutional Basics

Institutions vary so widely in size, makeup, and needs that it is impossible to cover in a single article all the variables that might apply. For example, the studio of a graduate-school piano professor might be 12 feet square, carpeted, and cluttered with bookshelves, desk, and chairs, but still needs a performance-grade instrument. A church sanctuary—often a carpeted, irregularly shaped room with a raised dais and filled with pews, glass windows, and lots of sound-absorbing people—needs a piano that can accompany the choir, be heard throughout a huge room, and also be used as a solo instrument for visiting artists. A school may need dozens of pianos for everything from tiny practice cubicles to a concert hall.

However, regardless of whether you're purchasing a piano for a church, school, performance space, or another institutional location, you need to start with some basic questions that will help identify the piano (or pianos) that are appropriate for your situation.

For example:

- Who will use the piano—beginners, advanced players, or concert artists?
- How often will the piano be played—in the occasional concert, or for 18 hours per day of intense student practice?

- How will the piano be used—lessons for graduate students? church services? recordings?
- Will the piano's location be fixed, or will it be moved often?
- In what size room will it primarily be used?

After answering these questions, this article will help you establish some basic parameters, including:

- Grand vs. Vertical
- Size
- New vs. Used
- Digital vs. Acoustic
- Traditional Acoustic vs. Acoustic with Record/Playback/Computer Features

Budget

Once you've narrowed down the parameters of your ideal instrument or group of instruments, you need to consider your budget. In doing so, it's best to remember that quality instruments properly maintained will last a long time. Accordingly, it's best to view the cost of each instrument not as a one-time expense, but as a total expense amortized over the life of the instrument.

When figuring out the true annual cost of an instrument:

- Spread out the instrument's purchase price over the span of its working life
- Factor in the cost of money, that is, the interest you would pay if you were to finance the purchase

(even if you don't actually plan to finance it)

- Include costs of tuning (typically three to four times a year, but far more often for performance instruments), regulation, and repairs

When you figure the cost of an instrument this way, you may even discover that certain more expensive instruments are more affordable than you thought.

Once you've determined your budget, and the size and other features of the instruments you desire, you can use the online searchable database accessible through the electronic version of this publication to assist you in finding the specific brands and models that will fulfill your needs.

Grand vs. Vertical

Many situations are adequately served by vertical pianos, including:

- Practice rooms where the piano is used primarily by, or to accompany, non-pianist musicians
- Places where there is no room for a grand
- Instruments that are not used for intense playing or difficult literature

A number of features of vertical pianos are commonly sought by institutional buyers:

- Locks on fallboard and tops
- A music desk long enough to hold multiple sheets of music or a score
- Toe-block leg construction with double-wheel casters—particularly important if the piano will be moved often

- Heavy-duty back-post and plate assembly for better tuning stability
- Climate-control systems
- Protective covers

Grand pianos, however, have keys, actions, and tonal qualities that are more appropriate for practicing and performing advanced literature, and are therefore preferred in situations where they are largely used by piano majors or performing pianists. Grands are preferred by piano majors even for small practice rooms, because the students use these instruments primarily to develop advanced technical facility, something that's almost impossible to do on vertical pianos. Commonly sought features of grands are:

- Mounting on a piano *truck* (a specialized platform on wheels) for moving the piano easily and safely
- Protective covers to avoid damage to the finish
- Climate-control systems
- Lid and fallboard locks

Size

Carefully consider the size of your space. You can easily spend too much on a piano if it's larger than the space requires, and you can easily waste your money if you purchase an undersized instrument. For more information about how room acoustics might affect the size of instrument you should purchase, see "Ten Ways to Voice a Room," elsewhere in this issue.

Of course, the tonal quality and touch of the instrument are related, in large part, to its size. If you're purchasing pianos for teaching studios in which artist faculty are instructing graduate piano majors, or for practice rooms used primarily by piano majors, there may be musical reasons for choosing larger grands despite the fact that the spaces are small. You'll be able to capture most of the advantages of a larger grand's longer keys with an instrument six to six-and-a-half feet long. Any longer will be overkill for a small teaching studio or practice room. A larger teaching studio may be able to accommodate and make good use of a seven-foot grand. The size of the piano is much less important in the training of beginning pianists or non-pianist musicians. There, other factors, such as the size of the room, will be the dominant considerations.

Vertical pianos made for institutions are almost always at least 45 inches tall. Smaller verticals may have inferior actions and tone, and cabinetry that is more prone to breakage. Verticals taller than about 48 inches are probably unnecessary for most small studio and practice rooms, but may be appropriate in larger spaces where a larger sound is needed but a grand is out of the question.

A special problem often occurs when a house of worship or small recital venue with limited funds tries to make do with a grand piano that's too small for the space. The pianist will tend to play much harder than normal, and overuse the sustain pedal, in an effort to make the piano heard at the back of the sanctuary or hall, causing strings and hammers to break and pedal systems to wear out prematurely. Generally, a small- to medium-size sanctuary will require a grand six to seven feet long to adequately fill the hall with sound, but this can vary greatly depending on the size of the hall, its acoustics, how large an audience is typically present, whether the piano is being used as a solo instrument or to accompany others, and whether the sound

The Yamaha model P22 has typical school-piano features, such as locks, a long music desk, toe-block leg construction, and double-wheel casters.

THE DEFINITIVE LIST

Only the following brands are certified by
The Association of German Piano Makers to be

100% MADE IN GERMANY.

Certified Brand	Piano Manufacturer
Blüthner THE GOLDEN TONE	Julius Blüthner Pianofortefabrik GmbH
AUGUST FÖRSTER	August Förster GmbH
GROTRIAN Because we love music	Grotrian Piano Company GmbH
Haessler	Julius Blüthner Pianofortefabrik GmbH
RÖNISCH	Carl Rönisch Pianofortemanufaktur GmbH
SAUTER Pianofortemanufaktur	Carl Sauter Pianofortemanufaktur GmbH & Co. KG
SCHIMMEL PIANOS	Wilhelm Schimmel Pianofortefabrik GmbH
Steingraeber & Söhne Perfektion seit 1852	Steingraeber & Söhne KG

Find out more at **www.pianos.de**

Bundesverband Klavier e.V.

is amplified. A piano dealer can help sort out these issues and recommend an appropriate instrument.

New vs. Used

Excellent acoustic pianos that are well maintained should last for decades. Given this fact, should your institution consider purchasing used instruments and thus save some money? If this is something you're considering, read "Buying a Used or Restored Piano" in this issue before continuing. When comparing a used piano to a new one, consult a trusted piano technician to get a sense of the used instrument's condition and remaining useful life. Then amortize the cost of the pianos, including expected repair costs, over their expected lifetimes to determine which is the better value.

If considering a used acoustic piano with embedded electronics, such as an electronic player piano, be careful to avoid purchasing an instrument whose technology is so obsolete that you can't use it productively. On the other hand, if your intention is to use a player piano's MIDI features mostly in conjunction with a computer, you do have one protection against obsolescence on your side: Although MIDI has been around since 1982, it's still an industry standard that works well and shows no sign of disappearing in the near future. Accordingly, you can continue to upgrade the features of an older MIDI piano merely by upgrading the software you use on your computer.

Acoustic vs. Digital

Digital pianos continue to improve every year, and the benefits realized for every dollar spent on a digital piano continue to grow with advances in technology.

Here are some examples of institutional situations in which a digital piano is generally the preferred instrument:

- Class piano, where students and teachers wear headsets and the teacher controls the flow of sound in the room with a lab controller
- Multipurpose computer/ keyboard labs where students need to work independently on theory, composition, and performance projects without disturbing others in the room
- A church that features a so-called "contemporary service" in which the keyboard player needs an instrument with lots of on-board sounds, registrations, and automatic accompaniments

In other situations, the preferred choice may not be so obvious. For example, if a school has a practice room

largely used by singers and instrumentalists (not pianists), should you supply a digital piano or a vertical?

When weighing these and similar questions, keep in mind:

- In an institutional setting, a typical, well-maintained acoustic piano has a life expectancy of 20 to 40 years; a higher-quality instrument might last 30 to 50 years. Because the digital piano is a relatively recent invention, we can't be as certain how long they will last in an institutional setting. A reasonable estimate for a good-quality digital instrument might be 10 to 20 years. However, digital instruments are subject to a rapid rate of technological advance that may eventually limit the instrument's usefulness, even though it still functions. On the other hand, the digital piano won't need tuning, and may go for years before it needs any other maintenance.
- Some digital pianos are simply a substitute for the acoustic equivalent. Others have additional features that may be highly desirable, such as connectivity to a computer, orchestral voices, and record and playback features.
- Some acoustic pianos are also available with digital-piano–like features, such as record and playback, and Internet and computer connectivity. If your choice comes down to an acoustic piano (for its traditional piano features of touch and tone) and a digital

SEILER

— Flügel und Pianos —

1849

The Art of European Piano Building.

FOLLOW US:

www.seilerpianousa.com

Seiler Pianos | 1329 Gateway Drive   Gallatin, TN 37066 | Tel: 615-206-0077

piano (for its embedded technologies), you may need to consider a hybrid digital/acoustic instrument. (See the article on hybrid pianos in this issue of *Piano Buyer*.)

Assessing Pianos Before Purchase

Assessing digital pianos is a relatively straightforward matter. You simply play and compare the features of various makes and models and make your selection. If you choose Model X, it doesn't matter if you take possession of the actual floor model that you tried: All Model X digital pianos will be the same.

Acoustic pianos are a different animal. There is more variation among pianos of the same model from a given manufacturer. However, it is important to note that some manufacturers have

a reputation for producing uniformly similar instruments, while others have a reputation for producing more individually distinctive instruments.

If you're purchasing a single acoustic piano or a small number of acoustic pianos, you can and should take the opportunity to audition each one of them and make your selection carefully. If you're purchasing a concert or other very large grand, you may need to travel to the manufacturer's national showroom in order to make your selection. If so, factor the cost of the trip into your budget. In some situations it may be possible to audition a large grand in the space in which you intend to use it. This will give you an opportunity to know for sure that you're making the right decision. On the other hand, if you're purchasing a dozen practice room

upright pianos, or are completely replacing your inventory of instruments, it's more practical to audition just a sample of each model and make your purchase decision on that basis.

Keep in mind that any fine acoustic piano can be adjusted within certain parameters by a concert-quality technician. If a piano sounds too bright when it is uncrated, skilled needling of the hammers can result in a noticeable mellowing of the sound. Similarly, a new action may require some additional adjustment (called *regulation*) to provide you with a keyboard that is optimally responsive.

Preparation, Tuning, and Maintenance

All pianos require maintenance, and acoustic pianos more than digitals. New acoustic pianos need to be

---

LOAN PROGRAMS:
AN ALTERNATIVE TO PURCHASING

Often, institutions find themselves needing to acquire a number of pianos at one time. Perhaps the institution needs to replace a large number of aging instruments or to furnish a newly expanded facility or program—or a school may want to acquire a number of new instruments each year to demonstrate to prospective students that it has a music program of high quality. Such situations can pose a budgetary dilemma—the simultaneous purchase of even a few pianos can cause fiscal stress. Fortunately, relief is sometimes available in the form of a school loan program.

On the surface, a school loan program may seem too good to be true: free pianos, loaned for an academic year. At the end of the year, the pianos are sold. More free pianos the next year.

In truth, a school loan program can work only when it makes sense for both the school and the local dealer. (Although the manufacturer may be a

participant in the program, the contract is normally with the local dealer.) Both sides of the agreement have obligations to the other.

For example, a school *may* receive any of the following, depending on the structure of the program:

- Free or very-low-cost use of a significant number of pianos
- Free delivery
- Free tuning and maintenance
- Name association with a prestigious manufacturer

A school may also have any of these obligations:

- Liability for damage
- Delivery charges
- Tuning and maintenance costs
- Requirement to purchase a certain percentage of the instruments
- Requirement to supply an alumni mailing list to the dealer for advertising purposes

- Requirement to provide space for an end-of-year piano sale

When evaluating a loan program, it's generally a good idea to consider:

- The quality of the dealership that stands behind the program
- The appropriateness of the mix of pianos offered
- The school's vulnerability if the program were to be discontinued by the dealership after the current year

That last point is a key issue. What happens if you replace your inventory of old pianos with loaned instruments and the loan program becomes unavailable the next year? Suddenly and unexpectedly, you are faced with having to buy replacement instruments.

Generally speaking, it is a good idea to include with your loan program a purchase component so that you are building your inventory of quality instruments over the course of the loan.

---

properly prepared before they're deployed. All acoustic pianos should be tuned regularly, and regulated as needed. Acoustic pianos with record and play-back systems also may need periodic calibration of their embedded systems. See the accompanying article for more information on the maintenance of acoustic pianos in institutions.

Who Should Make the Purchase Decision?

As the foregoing discussion suggests, there are many intersecting practical, artistic, and financial factors to be considered when making an institutional purchase of a piano or group of pianos. This raises the question: Who should make the purchase decision?

No single answer fits all situations. By tradition, a church's decision-making process may be handled by the music director, the pastor or priest, or perhaps by a lay committee. In a school of music, decisions may be delegated to the chair of the piano department, the chair of the music department, the dean of fine arts, or some other individual or faculty committee.

In many instances, well-intentioned individuals with no knowledge of pianos find themselves having to make a final decision. It is important that those involved in the process commit themselves to understanding the intersecting issues, and bring into the decision-making process appropriate people from the artistic, technical, and/or financial sides. At a minimum, that means the piano technician, and the most advanced, or most frequent, professional users. If a digital-technology–based instrument is being considered, someone should be involved who can speak to those technical issues as well. A department chair who has not actually used the technology in question may or may not be in a position to evaluate it.

Negotiating a Purchase

Before negotiating a price or sending a proposal out to bid, it's usually a good idea to do some price research. This can be tricky, however.

For example, if you or someone you know simply calls up a dealer and asks for a price, you're unlikely to be told the lower "institutional price" that you might ultimately get. Some dealers are reluctant to quote prices over the phone, or are prohibited by their suppliers from doing so. Others will refuse to quote a price if they know that the purchase will ultimately go out to bid.

Your institutional purchase may benefit the dealer or manufacturer in ways other than the profit from the sale. Therefore, when discussing your possible purchase, don't hesitate to mention:

- How prominently positioned the instruments will be in your institution or in the community
- How many students or audience members will come in contact with the instruments on a regular basis
- How often you or your institution is asked for purchase recommendations
- How musically influential your institution is in the surrounding community

The bottom line is this: You won't know what the final price will be until an official representative of your institution actually sits down with the dealer principal or until bids are awarded. Before you reach that point, however, and for planning purposes, you can make discreet inquiries and put together some estimates. As a rule of thumb, and only for the purposes of budgeting, if you subtract 10% to 15% from the dealer's "sale" price, you will likely come close to the institutional price.

If you represent a school that's required to send purchase requests out to bid, you may not have much of a role to play in negotiating a price. However, the way in which you word your bid will have a lot to do with the bids that you receive and the instruments that the bidding rules will compel you to purchase.

For example, if you really want Brand X with features A, B, and C, be sure to write your bid description so that it describes—within acceptable guidelines—the instrument that you wish to purchase, and rules out instruments that don't fit your needs. If your bid description is loosely written, you may receive low bids for instruments that don't meet your requirements.

Because pianos can last a very long time, any piano-buying decisions you make today for your institution can have consequences for a generation or more. Therefore, it pays to take the time to think carefully about your institution's present and future needs, to budget sufficient funds for purchase and maintenance, and to consult with individuals both within and outside your institution who may have special expertise or be affected by your decision. If you take the time to do this properly, then your constituents—be they students, faculty, worshippers, or concert-goers—will enjoy the fruits of your work for years to come. 🎹

George Litterst (www.georgelitterst .com) is a nationally known music educator, clinician, author, performer, and developer of music software. In the last role, Mr. Litterst is co-author of the intelligent accompaniment program *Home Concert Xtreme*, the electronic music-blackboard program *Classroom Maestro*, and the long-distance teaching program *Internet MIDI*, all from TimeWarp Technologies (www.timewarptech.com).

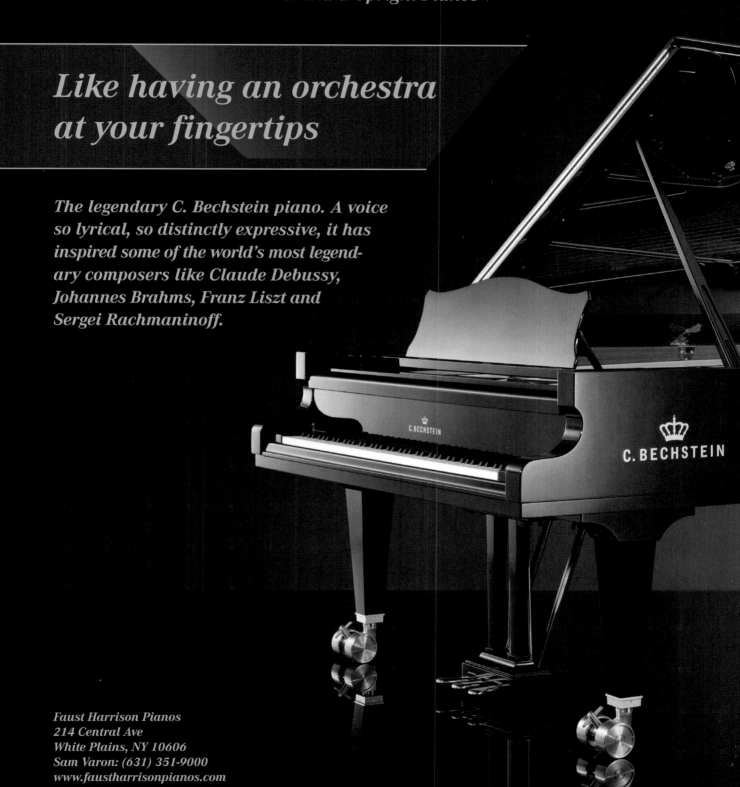

THE ADEQUATE AND EFFECTIVE MAINTENANCE of pianos in institutional settings differs from the typical service needs of the home environment in two major ways. Pianos in schools, churches, and colleges are, first of all, usually subjected to heavy use, and second, are very often situated in difficult climatic environments. These pianos will require more frequent service by technicians with special skills, and greater attention to climate control.

In college and university settings, pianos are frequently used eight to twelve hours a day by many different players. Some students have practice habits that involve a great deal of repetition, which causes greater wear to the actions and keys of the instrument in a way that reflects the patterns of their practice. This can easily be ten times more patterned repetition than a piano normally receives in your home. The parts of piano keys and actions that will show the greatest wear are made of felt, leather, and wood, and there are thousands of them in each piano. These materials are chosen, designed, and treated by manufacturers to maximize their working life, and considering the repetitive nature of their use, it's a wonder they last as long as they do.

No matter how well made, however, the nature of these materials dictates that when the piano is used for many hours, day after day, week after week, the wear and deterioration can be extensive. To maximize their longevity, it is very important to keep these pianos in good regulation so that the wear proceeds more evenly. Along with tuning, regular regulation of the action, pedals, and tone should be basic parts of any effective plan of piano maintenance. Without this, neglected instruments in such environments will quickly become impossible to regulate without extensive overhaul or replacement of parts.

At some point, of course, parts *will* have to be replaced, worthy instruments rebuilt, and unworthy ones replaced. But there is no need to hasten the inevitable by subjecting pianos to the worst form of abuse: neglect. Frequent and regular servicing of pianos is a requirement for any institution that hopes to maintain an adequate performance or learning situation that will not only meet the needs of its members, but serve as a vehicle for the recruitment of new students.

Depending on the security and rules established for using the pianos, abuse can also come in the form of vandalism or simple carelessness. Rules should be established that keep food and liquids away from pianos. Procedures for the safe moving of pianos should be established and strictly enforced to protect the instruments as well as those who do the moving. Untrained personnel should never move a piano anywhere.

The single largest factor affecting the need for piano maintenance, however, is a fluctuating climate. While an environment that is always too hot or too cold, or too wet or too dry, can cause deterioration, pianos can usually (within reason) be regulated to reliably perform in such an environment. However, many institutions provide interior climates of constant change. It's not unusual to find a school or church whose HVAC system produces 80°F and 8% relative humidity during the winter heating season, but 76°F and 80% relative humidity in the summer. These systems' air-exchange devices can also create drafts that

Guidelines for Effective Institutional Piano Maintenance

PIANO TECHNICIANS GUILD

Cline
Since 1889

Innovation is our tradition

For 134 years, Cline Pianos has combined innovation and tradition. Founded in the Pacific Northwest in 1889, Cline Pianos continues the North American philosophy of piano building. American engineers designed our pianos and each instrument is produced under careful supervision of our master craftsmen in select factories in the Far East.

DESIGNED IN THE USA USA PRODUCTION MANAGEMENT

MANUFACTURED IN CHINA

www.cline-pianos.com   509.946.8078

blow directly on the piano, further varying the temperature and relative humidity by a great deal. Often, the temperature settings on these systems are changed during vacation periods. A good target for any piano's environment is 68° F and 42% relative humidity. Installation of inconspicuously-located climate-control systems for the pianos is almost always necessary in institutional environments. A plan for the daily monitoring of these systems should also be considered. [*See the article,* "Caring For Your Piano," *for more information on climate-control systems for pianos.—Ed.*]

The most important factor in maintaining the utility and longevity of any institution's pianos is the choice of piano technician. An institutional technician should possess the advanced skills and experience required to prepare pianos for public concerts, organize and manage a large inventory of instruments, deal daily with high-level pianists and educators, and be familiar with the techniques necessary for the time-efficient maintenance of practice-room pianos. An underqualified technician can contribute to an accelerated rate of deterioration and shorten the lives of the instruments under his or her care. Some fully qualified technicians, mostly manufacturer-trained, have no formal credentials. However, hiring a Registered Piano Technician (RPT) member of the Piano Technicians Guild (PTG) ensures that at least a minimum standard of expertise has been tested for and achieved. A good way to begin planning any institution's piano-maintenance program is to read PTG's *Guidelines for Effective Institutional Piano Maintenance*, available in printed form or as a free download from **www.ptg.org**.

Chris Solliday, RPT, services the pianos at several institutions, including Lafayette College, Lehigh University, and East Stroudsburg University. He lives in Easton, Pennsylvania, and can be reached through his website at **www.csollidaypiano.com**.

TEN WAYS TO VOICE A ROOM

CHRISTOPHER STORCH

Have you noticed that your newly purchased piano doesn't sound quite the same as when you tried it in the showroom? The difference you notice between showroom and home may stem from the acoustics of the room in which the piano is placed. Not all problems with piano tone are best solved by voicing the instrument—it may be your *room* that needs voicing. Some of the factors that can significantly affect the sound of your piano room are: the size of the room, including ceiling height; the sound-absorbing and -reflecting materials in the room, which give it its reverberant character; and the number and orientation of objects in the room, which affect how sound is scattered or diffused.

Making the Distinction Between the Piano and the Room

It's important to distinguish between acoustical problems caused by the piano and those caused by the room. For instance, a problem of too much loudness is often caused by a piano that is too large for the room. This can be best addressed at or close to the piano, rather than by increasing the amount of sound-absorbing materials elsewhere in the room. On the other hand, such problems as harshness of tone, excess lingering sound, and hot and dead spots, can often be attributed to the room. Many of the following suggestions for loudness control or other acoustical adjustments are easily reversible; experiment with some of these before making more permanent changes to your piano or room.

Reverberation

Reverberation refers to the persistence of sound within a space after the source of the sound has stopped. Such prolongation of sound can help give music the qualities of blending, lushness, fullness, and breadth. Too much reverberation can make the music muddy and indistinct, and the buildup of reverberant sound can make the piano sound too loud. When there is too little reverberation, the room is said to sound "dry" or even "dead"; to compensate for this, the pianist might feel the need to overplay to achieve a lush, musical sound. In general, the larger the cubic volume of the space, the longer the reverberation time; the smaller the cubic volume, the shorter the reverberation time. The more sound-absorbing materials

in the space, the shorter the reverberation time; the fewer such materials, the longer the reverberation time. The length of reverberation is a matter of personal preference. Some pianists like having the room reverberation be part of the sound of their piano playing; others prefer keeping the sound of the room to a minimum, enjoying primarily the clear sound of the piano as modulated by their technique.

Hot or Dead Spots

Hot spots and dead spots are places in the room where certain frequencies or notes, though played with the same force, stand out more than other frequencies or notes. Problems of this type are best solved by installing sound-scattering objects: bookcases, furniture, wall

hangings, and so forth. Reorienting the piano or moving it slightly can also help.

Below are ten ways to mitigate problems in piano sound other than by voicing the instrument, beginning with some relatively simple things to do nearby the piano itself:

 Buy a piano that's the right size for the room.

The first and best way to avoid problems with room acoustics is to buy a piano that's the right size for the room. Too large a piano can overload a room with sound, while one that's too small may not be heard equally well in all parts of the space. A rule of thumb: Assuming a ceiling height of eight feet, the combined lengths of the four walls should be at least ten times the length of a grand piano or the height of a vertical. However, it's not always possible to follow this advice—in many cases, the purchase decision will be dictated more by musical needs or budget than by room size. A small piano, for example, may have performance problems inherent to the instrument's size, such as poor bass tone or an unresponsive action, even when it's the right size for the room. Or, if you're longing for a large grand's growling bass, be aware that, even though such a piano is perfectly capable of producing that sound, your room may not be able to support it.

When the piano's size is not a good match for the room, try voicing the piano, or experimenting with one of the following tips:

 Move or reorient the piano within the room.

Most rooms have three pairs of parallel surfaces: two sets of opposing walls, and the ceiling and floor. Parallel surfaces tend to produce standing waves—certain frequencies that sound much louder than others at some points in the room, but that are virtually inaudible at other points. Moving the piano away from room corners and partway along the length of a wall, and/or turning it at an angle this way or that, can sometimes mitigate this problem. You'll have to experiment, listening at different places within the room. Remember that the piano's sound when you sit at the keyboard will be different from its sound elsewhere in the room.

 Use a piano cover to directly reduce loudness.

Typical cloth string covers designed for grand pianos— that is, covers that lie directly on the strings—will only marginally reduce sound volume, especially if they have only a single layer of cloth. Most reports say that thin string covers are effective only for the highest notes, to take the edge off the sound. Thicker, sound-attenuating string covers, custom-made for a particular model of grand piano, work better. An even more effective mute for a grand would be a full-size, quilted cover that reaches the floor. However, this will require closing the lid completely and placing the music rack atop the cover—though unattractive, in some situations this is the only practical way to reduce excess loudness. For a vertical piano, a blanket or section of carpet can be attached to the piano's back.

 Place sound-absorbing material inside the piano, between the soundboard and the wooden structural support beams.

You may be able to drastically reduce a piano's loudness by inserting blankets or foam rubber blocks between a grand's soundboard and its wooden case beams, or between a vertical's soundboard and wooden posts. One possibility is to purchase the foam in sheets and cut shapes to fit. Your piano technician may have experience in doing this, and may also be able to help you avoid damaging the soundboard or creating the buzzes that can accompany this technique—ask for pointers. This method of loudness control won't be possible if you have a grand outfitted with a humidity-control system or an electronic player-piano system.

 Place a rug under a grand piano to absorb sound.

The sound of a grand piano is sent out into the room via the lid, which is propped up at an angle on the stick— and by a considerable reflection by the floor of sound emanating from the underside of the soundboard. If your floor covering is a sound-reflecting material such as wood, stone, or tile, the loudness can be greatly reduced by placing a rug under the piano. To absorb even more sound, place a thick pad under the rug. Experiment with the size of the rug or carpet and its orientation under the piano. Other, more temporary solutions: place a dog bed or a collection of throw pillows under the piano.

 Place objects under a grand piano to scatter sound.

Perhaps you don't want to absorb the sound coming out of the bottom of your grand piano, but just want to disperse it more evenly throughout the room. The space under a grand can be used for storage chests, plants, knickknacks, and the like.

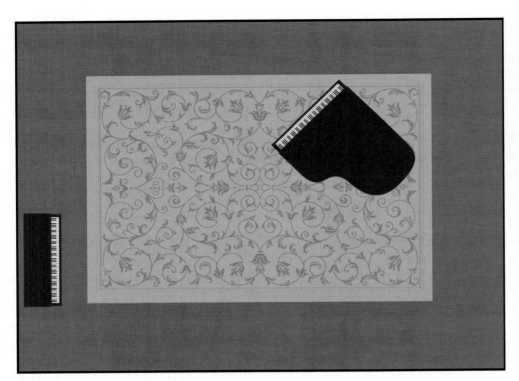

Moving the piano away from room corners and partway along the length of a wall, and/or turning it at an angle this way or that, can sometimes mitigate acoustic problems. Experiment and listen at different places within the room. If your floor is a sound-reflecting material, the loudness can be greatly reduced by placing a rug under the piano.

Let's say you've tried some or all of these steps; you've noticed some improvement, but not enough. Here are some more advanced treatments for the room itself.

 Cover or expose hard wall and/or window surfaces.

Glass tends to reflect high-frequency sound, while allowing lower frequencies to pass right through, never to return. A room with a lot of exposed glass will often sound harsh and bright, as it accentuates the treble notes. Covering these windows can help to absorb higher-frequency sound energy and thus restore the balance of bass and treble. Heavy fabric such as velour, sewn into gathers, works best to absorb sound. Sheer, semitransparent fabrics are much less effective, but can have subtle acoustical effects, if that's all that's required, and can be used to "fine-tune" the room.

Large areas of exposed bare walls and ceiling can produce a similar effect as glass, but are more effective at preserving bass energy. In a room that sounds too muddy—i.e., it makes music sound indistinct—sound-absorbing wall coverings such as tapestries, or hanging rugs, might be worth a try. Also available are fabric-wrapped, sound-absorbing panels that will work well in homes, though their "professional" look lacks the personal touch of one's own home furnishings.

In a space with high ceilings, hanging banners, flags, or other materials from the ceiling can cut down on reverberation.

Be aware that most household sound-absorbing materials do not work very well below about 200 Hz (about middle C). If your acoustical problem occurs below this frequency, look to other techniques or materials to solve it, including professional acoustical materials designed specifically to address low-frequency sound.

 Add or remove upholstered furniture and other sound-absorbing objects.

Adding sofas, pillows, upholstered chairs, carpets, and other sound-absorbing décor can reduce excess reverberation and loudness, and removing such objects will increase them. Even placing cloths over coffee and side tables will cut down the reflection of sound just a little bit. Plush, overstuffed furniture produces the greatest sound-absorbing effect. Upholstered furniture of leather, wood, or metal has less effect.

9 *Add or remove sound-scattering wall hangings, objects, and furniture.*

Be careful not to add *too* many sound-absorbing objects to the room—it's possible to go too far, making the room sound too dead, dry, or soft. Sometimes you don't want to absorb sound—you merely want to scatter or diffuse it more evenly about the room. The sound will then be more natural and less "hollow" without necessarily losing reverberation and loudness. In scattering sound, your goal is to use objects both large and small with complex shapes to break up large expanses of flat surfaces. Again, some experimentation is in order. Examples of sound-scattering objects are bookshelves (not too

full), tables, chandeliers, room-dividing screens, and sculpture. Designing a space with ceiling beams can also scatter sound.

You've tried everything! Below is one last word of advice.

10 *Hire a professional.*

Some of the acoustical phenomena described here can be confusing to the untrained. Even worse, some problematic combinations of piano and room may have more than one of these problems. If you've tried everything and still don't hear an improvement, consider seeking expert help from a piano technician or a room-acoustics consultant (acoustician). Such professionals may be able to help you design or furnish the space for the best sound,

suggest appropriate acoustical materials, and direct you to local suppliers for those materials. 🎹

Chris Storch, RPT, is an acoustician with 20 years' experience in the areas of architectural acoustics, noise and vibration control, and environmental noise abatement. Some of the more prominent projects on which he has consulted include Verizon Hall, in Philadelphia; Sibelius Hall, in Lahti, Finland; LG Arts Center, in Seoul, South Korea; and Fox Cities Performing Arts Center, in Appleton, Wisconsin. Storch is a 2009 graduate of the Piano Technology program at the North Bennet Street School, in Boston. He tunes and services pianos in the Boston area, and conducts research in piano acoustics in his spare time. He can be reached at chrisstor@aol.com.

A PIANO MAY LOOK large and imposing, but there is a great deal inside it that is delicate, and sensitive to both use and environmental changes. You have made a considerable investment in the instrument and now should protect that investment, as well as maximize your enjoyment of it, by properly caring for it. For most pianos in good condition receiving moderate use in the home, a budget of $300 to $500 per year should suffice for normal service.

If you bought the piano from a commercial seller, your first service will probably be a few weeks after delivery, by a technician associated with the seller. If you bought a used piano from a private seller and do not have a trustworthy recommendation to a technician, you can find the names of Registered Piano Technicians (RPT) in your area from the website of the Piano Technicians Guild (PTG), www.ptg.org. To become an RPT, one must pass a series of exams, assuring at least a minimum level of competence in piano servicing.

The following are the major types of service a piano needs on a regular or semi-regular basis. More information can be found in *The Piano Book*.

Tuning

Pianos go out of tune mostly because of seasonal changes in humidity that cause the soundboard and other parts to alternately swell and shrink. This happens regardless of whether or not the piano is played. Pianos vary in their responsiveness to fluctuations in humidity, but the variance is not always related to the quality of the instrument. People also differ in their sensitivity to tuning changes. New or newly restored pianos should be tuned three or four times the first year, until the strings are fully stretched out. After that, most pianos should be tuned between one and three times per year, depending on seasonal humidity changes, the player's sensitivity, and the amount of use. Pianos that receive professional levels of use (teaching, performance) are typically tuned more often, and major concert instruments are tuned before each performance. A regular home piano tuning typically costs between $100 and $200. However, if the piano has not been tuned regularly, or if it has undergone a large change in pitch, additional tuning work may be required at additional cost.

Regulation

Pianos also need other kinds of service. Due to settling and compacting of numerous cloth and felt parts, as well as seasonal changes in humidity, the piano's action (key and hammer mechanism) requires periodic adjustments to bring it back to the manufacturer's specifications. This process is called *regulation*. This should especially be done during the first six months to two years of a piano's life, depending on use. If it is not done, the piano may wear poorly for the rest of its life. After that, small amounts of regulating every few years will probably suffice for most pianos in home situations. Professional instruments need more complete service at more frequent intervals.

The thousands of parts in a piano action need periodic adjustment, or **regulation**, to compensate for wear and environmental changes.

A piano has over 200 strings, each of which must be individually tuned.

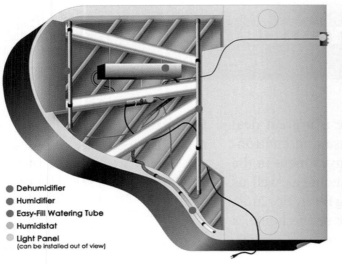

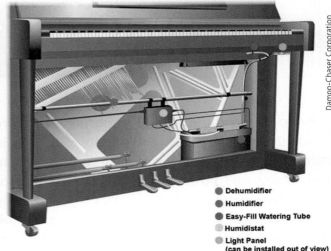

- ● Dehumidifier
- ● Humidifier
- ● Easy-Fill Watering Tube
- ○ Humidistat
- ○ Light Panel
  (can be installed out of view)

- ● Dehumidifier
- ● Humidifier
- ● Easy-Fill Watering Tube
- ○ Humidistat
- ○ Light Panel
  (can be installed out of view)

Voicing

Within limited parameters, the tone of a piano can be adjusted by hardening or softening the hammers, a process called *voicing*. Voicing is performed to compensate for the compacting and wear of hammer felt (which causes the tone to become too bright and harsh), or to accommodate the musical tastes of the player. Voicing should be done whenever the piano's tone is no longer to your liking. However, most piano owners will find that simply tuning the piano will greatly improve the tone, and that voicing may not be needed very often.

Cleaning and Polishing

The best way to clean dust and finger marks off the piano is with a soft, clean, lintless cloth, such as cheesecloth, slightly dampened with water and wrung out. Fold the cloth into a pad and rub lightly in the direction of the grain, or in the direction in which the wood was originally polished (obvious in the case of hand-rubbed finishes). Where this direction is not obvious, as might be the case with high-polish polyester finishes, rub in any one direction only, using long, straight strokes. Do not rub in a circular motion, as this will eventually make the finish lose its luster. Most piano manufacturers recommend against the use of commercially available furniture polish or wax. Polish specially made for pianos is available from some manufacturers, dealers, and technicians.

To clean the keys, use the same kind of soft, clean cloth as for the finish. Dampen the cloth slightly with water or a mild white soap solution, but don't let water run down the sides of the keys. If the keytops are made of ivory, be sure to dry them off right after cleaning—because ivory absorbs water, the keytops will curl up and fall off if water is allowed to stand on them. If the black keys are made of wood, use a separate cloth to clean them, in case any black stain comes off (not necessary for plastic keys).

Dust inevitably collects inside a piano no matter how good a housekeeper one is. A piano technician can safely vacuum up the dust or otherwise clean the interior of the piano when he or she comes to tune it.

Humidity Control

Because pianos are made primarily of wood, proper control of humidity will greatly increase both the life span of the piano and your enjoyment of it. A relative humidity of 42% is sometimes cited as ideal for a piano, but any humidity level that is relatively constant and moderate will suffice. Here are some common steps to take to protect your piano from fluctuations and extremes of humidity:

- Don't place the piano too near radiators, heating and cooling ducts, fireplaces, direct sunlight, and open windows.

- Avoid overheating the house during cold weather.

- Use air-conditioning during hot, humid weather.

- Add humidity to the air during dry weather with either a whole-house humidifier attached to a central air system or with a room humidifier. Room humidifiers, however, have to be cleaned and refilled frequently, and some make a lot of noise. If you use a room humidifier, don't place it too near the piano.

Instead of the above, or in addition to it, have a climate-control system installed in the piano. They make no noise, require very little maintenance, and cost $350 to $500 for a vertical piano or $400 to $600 for a grand, ordered and installed through your piano technician or piano dealer. The illustrations on the previous

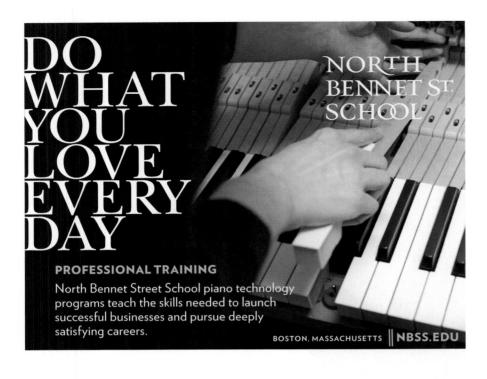
page of the Dampp-Chaser climate-control system show how the system's components are discreetly hidden inside the piano. For more information about these systems, see www.pianolifesaver.com.

Another solution to the humidity-control problem is **Music Sorb**, a non-toxic silica gel that naturally absorbs excess moisture from the air during humid times and releases it during times of dryness. It comes in packets or pouches sold through piano technicians. Enough for a single piano costs $65 to $70 and must be replaced once a year. Music Sorb probably won't control humidity changes in the piano quite as well as a Dampp-Chaser system, but may suffice in less severe climates, or in situations where plugging in and maintaining such a system is out of the question—or until the piano owner can afford the larger initial outlay of funds required for the system. ▥

WHEN SHOULD I HAVE MY PIANO TUNED?

When to tune your piano depends on your local climate. You should avoid times of rapid humidity change and seek times when the humidity will be stable for a reasonable length of time. Turning the heat on in the house in the fall, and then off again in the spring, causes major indoor humidity changes, and in each case it may take several months before the piano's soundboard fully restabilizes at the new humidity level.

In Boston, for example, the tuning cycle goes something like that shown in the graph. A piano tuned in April or May, when the heat is turned off, will probably be out of tune by late June. If it is tuned in late June or July, it may well hold its tune until October or later, depending on when the heat is turned on for the winter. If the piano is tuned *right* after the heat is turned on, however, say in October or November, it will almost certainly be out of tune by Christmas. But if you wait until after the holidays (and, of course, everyone wants it tuned *for* the holidays), it will probably hold pretty well until April or even May. In my experience, most problems with pianos in good condition that "don't hold their tune" are caused by poor timing of the tuning with the seasonal changes.

Note that those who live in a climate like Boston's and have their piano tuned twice a year will probably also notice two times during the year when the piano sounds out of tune but when, for the above reason, it should probably *not* be tuned. The only remedies for this dilemma are to have the piano tuned more frequently, or to more closely control the humidity.

The pitch of the piano in the tenor and low treble ranges closely follows the annual cycle of indoor humidity. The graph shows how a typical piano in Boston might behave. Most areas of the country that have cold winters will show a similar pattern.

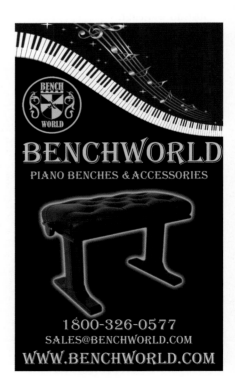

Benches

In all likelihood, your purchase of a new piano will include a matching bench. Benches for consumer-grade pianos are usually made by the piano manufacturer and come with the piano. Benches for performance-grade pianos are often provided separately by the dealer.

Benches come in two basic types: *fixed-height* or *adjustable*. Consumer-grade pianos usually come with fixed-height benches that have either a solid top that matches the piano's finish, or a padded top with sides and legs finished to match the piano. The legs on most benches will be miniatures of the piano's legs, particularly for decorative models. Most piano benches have music storage compartments. School and institutional-type vertical pianos often come with so-called "stretcher" benches—the legs are connected with wooden reinforcing struts to better endure heavy use.

Both solid-top and padded benches work well. The padded benches tend to be a little more comfortable, especially for those who have little natural padding of their own. They tend to wear more quickly, however, and are subject to tearing. Solid-top benches wear longer but are more easily scratched.

Adjustable benches are preferred by serious players who spend hours at the piano, and by children and adults who are shorter or taller than average. The standard height of a piano bench is 19" or 20". Adjustable benches typically can be set at anywhere from about 18" to 21". By adjusting the bench height and moving it slightly forward or backward, one can maintain the proper posture and wrist angle to the keyboard.

High-quality adjustable benches have a very heavy steel mechanism—so strong you could almost use it as a car jack! The duet-size bench (seats two) weighs well over 60 pounds. These benches are made of hard rock maple and come in most leg styles and finishes. The deeply tufted tops come in a heavy-duty vinyl and look like leather; tops of actual leather are available at additional cost. Both look great and wear well. The best ones, such as those made by Jansen, are expensive ($500 to $750) but are built to last a lifetime. Over the past few years, lesser-quality adjustable benches have come on the market. While these benches are adjustable within a similar range, the mechanisms aren't as hardy. They may be fine for light use, but most will not last nearly as long as the piano. A new style of adjustable bench, with steel legs, may be useful in high-use institutional settings.

A new type of adjustable bench on the market contains a hydraulic or pneumatic mechanism for raising or lowering the seat. There are different versions, but a typical one uses two nitrogen-gas cylinders, one on each side, and is good for 30,000 up-and-down cycles. The bench can be adjusted quickly and effortlessly by means of a handle on the side of

www.pljansen.com

Padded Bench

Wood Top Bench

Adjustable Artist Bench

Stretcher Bench

Adjustable Bench with Steel Legs

Hydraulic Bench

www.benchworld.com

Clip-On Lamp

Balance Arm Lamp

Floor Lamp

Desk Lamp

House of Troy

the bench. This can be an advantage to players whose wrists are easily fatigued by turning the knob of the traditional or standard type of adjustable bench, or for musicians who need to make height adjustments quickly and silently during a performance. These benches can also usually be set higher than the traditional kind. Most hydraulic or pneumatic benches are very stable, with metal legs (see photo), avoiding the wobbliness that can sometimes afflict four-legged wooden benches. Standard models range in price from $500 to $900; fancier versions, on which the metal is covered by wood, cost from $1,300 to $2,200.

Legs for both fixed-height and traditional adjustable benches are attached by a single bolt at the top of each leg. These bolts should be tightened anytime there is wobble in the bench. Don't over-tighten, however, as that might pull the bolt out of the leg.

Finally, if the piano you want doesn't come with the bench you desire, talk to your dealer. It's common for dealers to swap benches or bench tops to accommodate your preference, or to offer an upgrade to

a better bench in lieu of a discount on the piano.

Lamps

Having adequate lighting for the piano music is critical. It's hard enough to learn how to read music without having to deal with a lack of illumination, or with shadows on the sheet music. The ideal solution is track lighting in the ceiling just above the

player. In many homes and institutions, however, this is not feasible. In those instances, a piano lamp may well be the answer.

Piano lamps fall into two major groups: floor lamps and desk lamps. Floor lamps arch over the piano and hover over the music rack, while desk lamps sit directly on the piano or are attached to the music rack itself. Desk lamps are subdivided into three groups: a standard desk lamp that sits atop a vertical piano directly over the music rack; a "balance-arm" lamp that sits off to the side on a grand piano's music desk and has a long arm that hovers over the music rack; and a clip-on lamp that attaches directly to the music rack itself (see illustrations).

Piano lamps come in a variety of qualities, sizes, styles, finishes, and bulb types. The better ones are usually made of high-quality brass, while the least expensive are often made of very thin brass or are simply brass-plated. The light from incandescent-bulb lamps tends to be a tad harsh, but the bulbs are less expensive than those for fluorescent lamps, which, though pricier, emit a softer light.

Piano lamps are available through

most piano dealerships as well as at lighting stores. A limited selection can also be found at The Home Depot and Lowe's.

Accessories and Problem Solvers

Only a few accessories are used with pianos, and most are available at your local piano dealership. You might consider:

- **Caster Cups**. Caster cups are small cups that go under the wheels of vertical and grand pianos to protect the floor or carpet. They come in plastic or a variety of woods, and in clear acrylic that allows the carpet or hardwood floor to show through. If the caster cups have felt on the bottom, however, be careful, as the dye from the felt can bleed into carpeting, especially if it gets damp.

- **Piano Covers**. Used mostly in churches and schools (and homes with cats), piano covers are designed to protect the piano's finish from accidental damage, and are available to fit any size of piano. They come in vinyl or mackintosh (a very tight-weave fabric that is very water-resistant), brown or black on the outside, and a fleece-like material on the side that touches the piano. A thicker, quilted, cotton cover is available for use in locations where the piano is moved frequently or may get bumped.

Piano Covers

www.perfectlygrand.com

www.perfectlygrand.com

Bench Cushions

- **Bench Cushions**. Bench cushions are made in a variety of sizes, thicknesses (1" to 3"), fabrics, and colors. They are also available in tapestry designs, most with a musical motif, tufted or box-edged, and all have straps to secure them to the bench.

- **Pedal Extenders**. These extension devices are available for those whose feet do not comfortably reach the pedals. Some are nothing more than a brass pedal that bolts on to the existing pedal, while others are a box, finished to match the piano, that sits over the existing pedals and has pedals with rods to operate the piano's pedals.

- **Metronomes**. Many music teachers recommend using a metronome to improve students' timing. Any piano or musical-instrument dealership will generally have a wide selection, from the solid walnut, wind-up, oscillating metronome like the

one your grandmother had on her piano, to a new, beeping digital model.

- **Grand Piano String Covers**. Wool string covers are available in a variety of colors that complement the piano's finish. When in place, they provide a reduction in sound volume, and protection against dust (and cats). Thicker sound-reduction covers and baffles are also available.

- **Lid and Fallboard Slow-Close Systems.** Raising and lowering the lid of a grand piano is frequently difficult, and can be downright dangerous. This is due to the combination of its weight, which can exceed 50 pounds, and its position, which makes it hard to reach. Enter a new product that solves at least the weight problem: Safety-Ease Lid Assist.

Lucite

Wood

Caster Cups

www.perfectlygrand.com

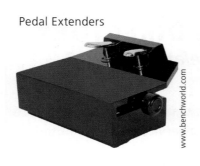
Pedal Extenders

www.benchworld.com

www.perfectlygrand.com

Metronomes

© Emre Yıldız

Safety-Ease consists of pneumatic cylinders that effectively counter-balance the weight of the lid and damp its movement so that it can be easily raised or lowered, even by a child. It mounts under the lid, between the lid hinges on the piano's rim, is finished in polished ebony to match most pianos, and requires no drilling or permanent installation. This unique system is sold and installed only by piano dealers or technicians. The installed price for small and mid-size grands is $500 to $600. More information is available at www.safety-ease.com.

The fallboard (keyboard cover) can also be a danger, not so much for its weight or position, but for the swiftness of its fall and because, when it falls, little fingers are likely to be in its path. Many new pianos today come with a pneumatically or hydraulically damped, slow-close fallboard. For those that don't, aftermarket devices are available from piano dealers or technicians.

- **Touch-Weight Adjustment Systems.** *Touch* or *touch weight* refers to the pressure required to press a piano key. Too little touch weight, or touch weight that is uneven from note to note, makes a piano action difficult to control; too much touch weight makes a

piano tiring to play, and can cause physical problems for the player over time. Touch-weight problems can be caused by poor action design, worn parts in older pianos, or incorrectly dimensioned replacement parts in restored pianos.

Historically, discussions, measurements, and adjustments in this area of piano technology have been about *static* touch weight—the force needed to make a piano key just begin to move slowly downward. Less well understood, and usually ignored, has been *dynamic* touch weight—the force required to press a key in actual normal, rapid playing. Here, the rapid movement of the key creates *inertia* (i.e., the tendency of a moving mass to keep moving in the same direction and at the same speed, and the tendency of a stationary mass to remain stationary.) Unlike static touch weight, which depends on the *relative* amount and positioning of mass on either side of the key's balance point, as well as on friction, dynamic touch weight depends on the *total* amount of mass in the system. Attempts to fix problems in static touch weight by adding mass to the front or rear of the key can cause problems with dynamic touch weight by creating excessive inertia.

Until fairly recently, technicians resorted to a patchwork quilt of homemade, trial-by-error remdies

for problems with static touch weight; dynamic touch weight wasn't even on their radar. More recently, a greater understanding of touch weight has emerged, and more sophisticated techniques for solving touch-weight problems are being developed. The gold standard among these techniques is that of David Stanwood, who developed the first system for mathematically describing, measuring, and solving problems related to dynamic touch weight. His system is applied by a network of specially trained technicians who, because of the comprehensive nature of the system and the remedies it suggests, tend to use it on higher-end instruments and those undergoing complete restoration. More information can be found at www.stanwoodpiano.com.

A simpler remedy, but only for heavy or uneven static touch weight on a grand piano, is a product called TouchRail, available through piano technicians. TouchRail is a rail with 88 individually adjustable springs that replaces a grand piano's key-stop rail. The springs press gently on the keys to the front of the balance point, enabling the technician to effectively "dial in" a desired touch weight and make it perfectly even from note to note. Because it's spring-based rather than mass-based, TouchRail won't add inertia to the action system, though of course it won't cure any pre-existing problems with excessive inertia, either. Installation requires no drilling, cutting, or other permanent modification of the piano, and the rail can be removed and replaced in seconds during routine piano service, just like a traditional key-stop rail. The installed price is around $795. See www.pitchlock.com for more information. 🎹

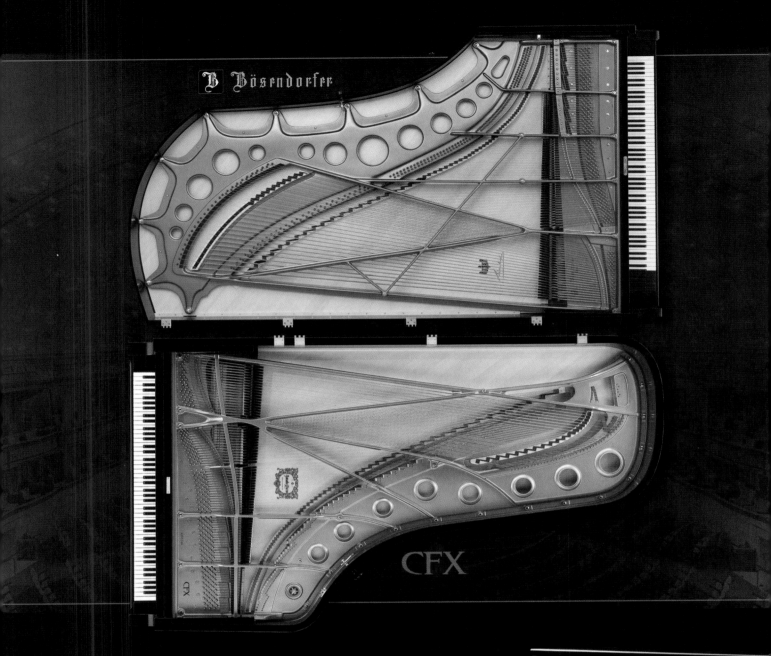

Two Legendary Concert Grands Are Coming Home.

Introducing the Clavinova CLP-500 Series

In addition to the powerful Yamaha CFX Grand, select CLP-500 models also include the warm Viennese sound of the legendary Bösendorfer Imperial Grand. With two world-renowned concert pianos available at the touch of a button, you get the luxury of choosing the right instrument for the music you wish to play. For the full list of exciting new CLP Clavinova features, visit www.yamaha.com/CLP. Find a Clavinova CLP-500 Series dealer near you by visiting: http://4wrd.it/CLP500adpb.

IF, AFTER HAVING READ "Acoustic or Digital: What's Best for Me?," you've decided on a digital piano, the next step is shopping for and selecting the right model for your needs. There are currently over 200 models of digital piano on the market. Narrowing the field requires exploring some basic issues. This article covers the needs of both entry-level shoppers and those interested in more sophisticated, feature-laden models. If you're looking for an entry-level instrument and are just interested in learning the basics, you can read "The Starter Digital Piano" below, then skip to "Shopping Options," toward the end of this article.

The Starter Digital Piano

If nothing else, a digital piano should be able to emulate an acoustic piano in basic ways. Fulfilling this function requires features found on most digital pianos today. Some first-time buyers, however, opt for an instrument with more than just the basics, and buy a model with additional sounds and "easy-play" features.

Matching the Player's Needs. Unless you expect to buy another piano in a year or so, you need to consider your long-term requirements. Who will be the primary player today? If it's for the family, how long will it be until the youngest child has the opportunity to learn? Does Mom or Dad harbor any musical interests? If so, it's likely that one family member or another will use the instrument for many years to come. This argues for getting a higher-quality instrument, whose advantages of better tone, touch, and features will be appreciated over time.

If multiple players will use the instrument, it needs to meet the expectations of the most advanced player. At the same time, a beginner in the family will benefit from educational features that are of no interest to the advanced player, and still another family member may just want to fool around with the instrument once in a while. Easy-play features and software will keep these players happy—and you might be surprised how many people are enticed into learning to play as a result of these easy first steps. So, obviously, an individual player may search among a very narrow range of instruments, while a family may have to balance the needs of several people. Fortunately, the wealth of available choices can easily accommodate any combination of individual and/or family needs.

Is a keyboard with fewer than 88 notes a viable alternative? In a word, no.

Voices and Expanded Capabilities. Most entry-level digitals have a few different piano voices, as well as a dozen or so other instrumental voices, such as harpsichord, church and jazz organ, vibes, and strings. These models, designed mainly to emulate the piano, are referred to as "standard" digital pianos. Many other,

slightly more expensive models, called "ensemble" digital pianos, come with expanded capabilities: all the instruments of the orchestra (and more), easy-play background accompaniments, rhythms, special effects, and much more. You might not think you need the additional capabilities of an ensemble digital, but having them can enable the beginner, as well as family members who don't take lessons, to have a lot more fun and sound like pros with minimal practice. For an advancing player, the opportunities for musical creativity are significantly enhanced.

If at all possible, you should try at least two or three instruments in your price and style range to determine which sounds best to *you*. If you plan to use headphones in your home (yes, parents—your children can practice silently using headphones), be sure to try out the pianos through headphones, as this can make a tremendous difference in sound. (For consistency of comparison, bring your own headphones.) Sometimes the instrument's weakest link is its built-in speaker system.

88-note Weighted Keyboard. Even entry-level digitals should feel much like an acoustic piano. If you have some playing experience, you'll want to try two or three competing models to see what feels best to *you*. None of the available models has an overly heavy touch. So-called semi-weighted keyboards, which depend on springs for their weight,

Slab type

Console type

Digital grand

should be avoided, as they don't feel enough like an acoustic piano. Is a keyboard with fewer than 88 notes a viable alternative? In a word, no. None have a decently weighted keyboard. In addition, students who use instruments with short keyboards tend to outgrow them quickly, and suffer some degree of disorientation when taking lessons on an 88-note keyboard.

Ease of Use. Make sure you understand how the instrument's controls work—additional features are of little use if you can't figure out how to use them. Ask to see the owner's manual (or download it from the manufacturer's website) and make sure that it's understandable.

Cabinet Type. Another factor that may shape your options is where the instrument will live. Is space at a premium? Are there limited placement options? If home is a dorm room or a small studio apartment and you need to make the most efficient use of every square inch, you may opt for a portable model (not a furniture-style cabinet) that can be placed on a stand for practice and

stuck in a closet when not in use. Bear in mind that this type of design, typically called a slab, doesn't necessarily limit the quality of instruments available to you—professional stage pianos also fit into this category. Slabs generally come with a single pedal, but many have optional stands that, like an acoustic piano, have three pedals. If you do go with a stand, don't get the cheapest one you can find. These are fine for 61-note portable keyboards, but tend to wobble when supporting the greater weight of a digital piano, and may not be able to be adjusted low enough to put the keyboard at the proper height from the floor (about 29 inches to the tops of the white keys). It should be noted that *portability* is a relative term: instruments in this category can range in weight from 25 to over 70 pounds, without stand.

Another option in the entry-level category is what is variously referred to as the vertical, upright, or console digital piano. The cabinetry of these models ranges from two flat side supports with a cross member for stability, to elegant designs that would look

at home in the most posh surroundings. It's common for individual models in this category to be available in multiple finish options, including synthetic wood grain, real-wood veneers, and, on some of the better models, the lustrous polished ebony often found on acoustic pianos. Most of these models have three pedals.

If space is no problem and you love the look of a grand piano, several digital pianos are available in "baby grand" cases. Remember that, most of the time, you pay a significant premium for this look, and that few of the digital grand models actually use the additional internal space to enhance the instrument beyond the non-grand model it's based on. There are two size classes of digital grands, one about five feet long and the other closer to three feet—just long enough for the tail to curve in a quasi-grand shape.

Additional Features. Virtually all models of digital piano include headphone connections for private practice, and MIDI and/or USB connections that allow you to connect the instrument to a Mac or

PC for use with a variety of music software. Other features included in many entry-level instruments are a built-in metronome, the ability to play more than one instrumental voice at a time (called *layering* or *splitting*; see "Digital Piano Basics"), and the ability to record and play back anything you play. While you may not be ready for a recording contract, the ability to listen to what you're practicing is a great learning tool.

Pricing. Slab models start at $500, console models at around $1,000. Digital grands begin at about $1,500, but the better-quality models start at around $5,000. In each category there are many options; spending more will usually get you some combination of better sound, features, touch, and appearance.

Those who are shopping for an entry-level digital and want to keep it simple can skip the next section and go directly to "Shopping Options."

Further Considerations for More Serious Shoppers

Before reading further about shopping, I suggest that you read the two "Digital Piano Basics" articles, and explore the brand profiles and the charts of features and specifications, all elsewhere in this issue. There you'll find detailed information about the features and benefits of both standard and ensemble digitals. Once you have a grasp of what these instruments can do and how they differ from one another, you'll be able to shop with a better idea of which features and level of quality you desire, which in turn will make your shopping efforts more efficiently focused and enjoyable.

Serious Listening

You've decided what type of instrument you're looking for and how much you're going to spend (unless, of course you hear something that just knocks your socks off, and your budget along with them). There are still a couple of last steps in preparation for the hunt.

If you don't already have a good set of headphones, this is the time to get them. Headphones are probably the most widely used accessory for digital pianos, and it's a sure bet that you, or another player in the house, will need them or wish the other player were using them—and they're an invaluable tool for auditioning digital pianos. Part of what you hear when you compare instruments is the speaker system, and this is a critical element; but headphones can also isolate you from noise in the store and give you a common baseline as you go from place to place trying different instruments. Most stores have headphones available, but they're typically low-end models, and never the same as the ones you listened to in the last store. I've always found it odd that people will agonize over the choice of a digital piano, spend hundreds—frequently thousands—of dollars on their choice, and then listen to it through $19.95 headphones. (See "Digital Piano Basics, Part 2" for a discussion of headphones.)

The final step is to "calibrate" your ears. Listen to recordings of solo piano. Listen to what you enjoy, be it jazz, classical, or ragtime—just listen a lot. For part of this listening, use the headphones you bought for your digital piano. This will embed in your head, as a benchmark, the sound of high-quality acoustic pianos. One of the great things about digital pianos is that if you love, say, honky-tonk piano, all you have to do is make sure the instruments you're considering have a Honky-Tonk setting. Then you can "change pianos" at will. But for the moment, listen to the best piano recordings you can get your ears on.

When you start to audition instruments, you'll become aware that some of what you're hearing isn't the instrument, or at least not what the instrument is supposed to do. Part of what you'll be hearing is the result of room acoustics and the instrument's placement in the showroom. If there are a lot of hard surfaces nearby—uncarpeted floors and large windows—the results will be different from what you'll hear in a "softer" environment, such as a carpeted living room with drapes, bookshelves, and upholstered furniture. Placement in the room will also affect the sound. If you're serious about buying a particular instrument, asking the dealer to move it to another part of the showroom isn't an unreasonable request. Another thing to be aware of is that the voice settings of most digital pianos include some degree of reverberation. This isn't a bad thing, but it's worthwhile to listen to the piano voice, and any other voices that are important to you, with the reverb and all other effects

turned off. This will allow you to judge those voices without any coloration or masking from the effects.

Evaluating Tonal Quality

Almost by definition, evaluating an instrument's tone is very subjective, and judging the tone of instruments that have a lot of voices can be overwhelming. Your best bet is to select the five or six instruments you think you'll use most and make them the standard for comparison as you shop. If you choose the piano on which those voices sound best to you, it's likely you'll find the others satisfying as well.

Digital pianos are really computers disguised as pianos, and the engineers who design them strive to develop a set of sounds and features unique to their brand. Like some features of a PC, many of the capabilities of digitals are hidden from view, accessible by pressing a sequence of buttons or through multi-screen menus. While the owner's manual will explain how to access these features or sounds, it's impractical for you to study the manuals of every instrument under consideration. Enter the salesperson! This is one of those instances where a well-trained salesperson can be invaluable.

Most manufacturers arrange trainings for their retailers' sales staffs, to enable them to demonstrate the relative advantages of that brand's features. Even if you're a proficient player, having a salesperson demonstrate and play while you listen can be a valuable part of the evaluation process. But remember that the salesperson is not going home with you! Don't be swayed by his or her talent—a really good player can make even a poor-sounding piano "sing." Focus your attention on the instrument itself.

You should make sure that you get the answers to a few key questions, either through the salesperson's demonstration or your own experimentation.

Generally, one of the instrument voices used most frequently is the piano. There is a great deal of variation in "good" piano tone. Many players like a bright, crisp sound, while others prefer a mellower tone. Some like a great deal of harmonic content, others a bell-like clarity with fewer harmonics. Whatever your preference, will you be satisfied with the piano sound of the model you're considering?

Many instruments sound slightly different as a note begins to play. For example, a flute takes a quarter of a second or so to build up enough air pressure to reach the pitch of the note, resulting in a "breathiness" to the sound. The same is true of many other wind instruments. Guitarists and other players of stringed instruments "bend" notes by varying their touch. Jazz organs often have a percussive "pop" at the beginning of the note. How well do the digital voices of the model you're evaluating emulate the actual instruments?

Even entry-level standard digitals include such effects as Reverb and Chorus. More sophisticated models have many other effects, as described in the "Digital Piano Basics" articles. Having heard them demonstrated, do you think these effects will be useful to you?

Take your time. Following the salesperson's demonstration, most dealers will let you spend time experimenting—although some may prefer that you use headphones.

Evaluating Touch

Aside from sound, the most important element in the selection of an instrument is likely to be the feel of the action. Unless you're considering only digital pianos that employ an actual acoustic action (see "Hybrid Pianos," elsewhere in this issue), you'll be selecting from a variety of actions that all try to emulate the feel of an acoustic action. The aspect of action feel that seems to generate the most discussion is whether the touch weight is light or heavy, and which is better. This is covered in more detail in "Digital Piano Basics, Part 1," but here's the bottom line: Just as there is no single correct piano sound, there is no single correct touch weight; rather, there is a range of acceptable touch weights. If you spend the majority of your playing time with a heavy action, when you encounter an instrument with a lighter action, be it acoustic or digital, you'll play too heavily—and vice versa. The only cure is to play as many instruments as possible, as often as possible. Listen to how each piano responds and adjust your touch accordingly. You've probably driven cars with light steering and cars with heavy steering, and generally managed to avoid hitting any trees with either of them. With varied experience, you learn to adapt.

Common to acoustic and digital actions is mechanical noise. Digitals are frequently accused of having noisier actions because their sound can be reduced to a whisper or played through headphones, leaving the action noise audible, whereas the sound of an acoustic piano tends to always mask its action noise. This is not to say that some digital actions aren't unusually noisy, but to honestly compare them, you have to play them with the volume turned off. In addition to letting you compare action noise, this prevents your mind from judging the *feel* of an action based on the *tone* of the instrument.

New or Used?

Because digital technology advances at a blistering pace relative to acoustic-piano technology, there is much less interest in used digitals than in used acoustics. Many of today's digital pianos eclipse the capabilities of the models of even five years ago. Combine this technological advancement with the fact that support of older instruments may be limited—after production of a particular model ceases, electronics manufacturers are required to maintain replacement parts for only seven years—and investing in older models becomes worthy of serious second thoughts.

Owner's manuals no longer accompany many used instruments. If you find an interesting used instrument, make sure that the manual is either still with it, or is readily available from the manufacturer or on the Internet. The manual is your best tool for ensuring that everything on the instrument still works correctly. It's not simply a matter of pressing every key, button, and pedal to see that they work; to thoroughly check the instrument, you also need to know what some of the less obvious controls are supposed to do. None of this is to say that used instruments should be avoided—I've played ten-year-old digital pianos that worked perfectly. But when considering an older digital piano, extra care should be exercised.

Shopping Options

Your shopping options depend on the type of digital piano you've decided to buy and the region you live in. In North America, different categories of instruments are available through different types of outlets. Furniture-style models, particularly the higher-end models manufactured by the largest suppliers, are available only through traditional bricks-and-mortar piano or full-line music retailers. The lower-priced furniture-style, slab, or stage models, and some of the less widely distributed brands, are available from a cross section of traditional bricks-and-mortar music retailers, club and warehouse chains such as Costco, consumer-electronics chains such as Best Buy, and online retailers.

PIANO ART

Coco Chanel
by Piano Solutions XXI
on a Steinway piano

"In order to be irreplaceable, one must always be different."
—*Coco Chanel*

This one-of-a-kind piano was designed in tribute to Coco Chanel, a legendary fashion designer and icon.

The airbrushed intertwined white lines on black canvas create various patterns that emulate fabric in fashion, covered with immense jewelry built from 48,500 brilliant-cut cubic zirconium, inlaid with various abstract lines and geometric pattern sequences illuminating infinite amount of imagery, giving it a multidimensional effect. The color for the piano plate was chosen in a beautiful and feminine "Candy Apple" deep red. A silhouette of Coco is painted on the inside of the lid and on the music leaf.

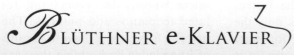

Perhaps the biggest difference between shopping for digital and acoustic pianos is that you usually want to make sure you get the specific acoustic piano you played on the showroom floor. But once you've decided on a model of digital piano, it doesn't matter if you get the one you actually tried or not. Every unit made of the same model will be identical to all other units.

Negotiating the price of a digital piano at a bricks-and-mortar retailer is no different from negotiating the price of an acoustic piano, which is discussed in "Piano Buying Basics," elsewhere in this issue. However, many of the simpler furniture-style digitals and nearly all portable or stage-piano models that are sold through a variety of local and online stores are virtually always sold at the same price, wherever you

shop. This is due to a pricing model called minimum advertised price, or MAP, used for many categories of products. A manufacturer's or distributor's MAP is the lowest price at which a dealer is allowed to *advertise* an item. Since prices are easily compared and all retailers want an even chance to win your business, everyone advertises at the MAP. And since the MAP is typically lower than the price at which the dealer might have preferred to sell the item, the price almost never drops below the MAP. Therefore, MAP has become the standard pricing for all non-piano-dealer models of digital piano.

You should find out how warranty service is handled for the instrument you've selected—not only the terms related to coverage for parts and labor, but where the service is performed. Like acoustic pianos,

most digital models available only through piano dealers have a warranty specifying in-home service; that is, the technician comes to you. Models sold outside of traditional piano stores must be brought to the technician's shop for warranty service. Ask your salesperson where the closest authorized service technician is located, or check the manufacturer's website.

You can see from the chart of digital piano specifications that it's not unusual for different models from the same manufacturer to have different warranty terms. It would be tempting to attribute this to differences in quality, but most often it's based on differences in anticipated use (home vs. commercial), and on marketing decisions for a given product segment. Unlike some warranties for acoustic pianos, I'm aware of no digital piano warranty that is transferable to a subsequent owner.

There are many decisions to be made when selecting a piano, digital or acoustic. But in the end, there is no substitute for playing and listening for yourself. The best anyone else can do is tell you what he or she would buy. But unless that person's requirements exactly match your own, all you'll end up with is a piano that's perfect for someone else.

Go out and try everything you can get your hands on— and enjoy the process! 🎹

For more information

If, after reading the articles in *Piano Buyer*, you still have questions about buying a digital piano, I recommend visiting the Digital Pianos—Synths & Keyboards Forum on Piano World (www.pianoworld.com), the premiere website for everything related to pianos and pianists. The helpful folks there have a wealth of knowledge and advice they are happy to share.

I found Yamaha's new Clavinova digital pianos to be a real pleasure to play. If I didn't already own a Yamaha C3 6' grand, I'd be writing a check for a CLP-575. I tried out these pianos at Music Exchange, a retail outlet in Dublin, California. I was impressed with their sound quality, solid construction, and user-friendly features.

Overview

The CLP-500 line ranges from the entry-level model 525 (MSRP: $2,199–2,599) up to the more full-featured 585 ($6,299–6,999). Music Exchange didn't have the 585 in stock, so I focused on the 575 ($4,999–5,699) and the less expensive 535 ($2,899–3,399). The differences between them were subtle, not glaring—the 535, though less expensive, sounded good and played well. [Yamaha also offers a version in a grand-piano–shaped cabinet, model CLP565GP ($5,999), not reviewed here.—*Ed.*]

Physically, these pianos resemble a traditional spinet. The body, extending from the keyboard area down to the floor, contains the speakers and the pedal mechanism. Yamaha's upscale CVP digital pianos have a broad front panel and a large display; the CLPs are more discreet in appearance. The control panel is set into the block at the left end of the keyboard, with a small LCD and 20 buttons. The labeling of the buttons is in small, dark gray lettering—elegant, but not easy to read in dim light.

The volume slider is at the right end of the keyboard. The speakers are tucked away out of sight in the body, and the connection jacks are in a block in the knee area, under the left side of the keyboard. The more expensive models have higher-wattage amplifiers and four or six speakers rather than two, which helps to create a more full-bodied piano tone. A standard lid slides out to cover the keyboard and to protect it from dust.

The CLPs are available in four finishes, including polished ebony. (My choice would be the handsome, matte dark rosewood.) From the 545 up, the music rack has flip-up music-book holders of brass. I wish I had these on my piano—having a music book fall shut while I'm playing is an annoyance. The holders angle upward rather than sticking up straight, making it easy to turn pages without tearing them.

Half-pedaling with the damper pedal worked properly. This is one of many features that added to the sensation that I was playing an acoustic piano. (I almost wrote, "that I was playing a real piano"—but these *are*

The Yamaha Clavinova CLP535

Models At a Glance

Shown here and on the next page are major features and specifications that differ from model to model, noting in which model each feature upgrade begins. Each model has many more features than are shown here. For a complete list of features and specifications, see http://usa.yamaha.com/products/musical-instruments/keyboards/digitalpianos/clp_series/

	CLP-525	CLP-535	CLP-545	CLP-565GP	CLP-575	CLP-585
VOICES						
Piano Sample	Yamaha CFIIIS	Yamaha CFX Bösendorfer Imperial	→	→	→	→
No. Voices	10	34	→	→	→	48+480XG
Key-Off Samples		Yes	→	→	→	→
Damper Resonance	Yes	→	→	→	Virtual Resonance Modeling (VRM)	→
String Resonance		Yes	→	→	Virtual Resonance Modeling (VRM)	→
CONTROL INTERFACE						
Graded Hammers (No. of weight zones)	4	→	→	→	88	→
Touch Sensitivity Levels	4	6	→	→	→	→
Key Counterweights						Yes
Wooden Naturals (White Keys)			Yes		Yes	→
Escapement		Yes	→	→	→	→
Enhanced (GP) Damper Pedal					Yes	→
LCD Display		Yes	→	→	→	→

Note: → indicates a value repeated from the previous column.

real pianos!) Unlike an upright acoustic, the CLP has three true pedals; the middle pedal is a sostenuto.

The 535 and 575 have 34 sounds: electric piano, double bass, harpsichord, and so on. The 585 also features Yamaha's General MIDI-compatible XG sound set. Sounds can be split or layered on the keyboard, so you can play walking bass with the left hand, for instance, or layer strings with the piano sound. Digital effects (concert-hall reverb and a shimmering chorus/celeste process) are included and can be adjusted to taste. All of the CLPs have a built-in metronome, but from the 545 up, you also get some drum loops to practice with, which is more fun.

Naturally, you can transpose the keyboard up or down in half-steps or octaves, or adjust the fine tuning to something other than A-440. A few non-equal temperaments (such as Werckmeister) can be selected.

The Piano Sound

The CLP-500 series models generate tones using samples (digital recordings) of an actual piano. All but the 525 have two acoustic piano multisamples: the 9' Yamaha CFX concert grand and the 9' 6" Bösendorfer Imperial. (Yamaha owns Bösendorfer.) The Bösendorfer has a richer, mellower tone; the CFX is brighter. The 34 available sounds include eight varieties of piano sound, such as Rock Grand and Mellow Grand.

Sampled pianos have come a long, long way in the past 30 years. Only an expert would be able to detect in the CLPs' tones the almost imperceptible sonic artifacts that arise from sampling. I could hear long, slow loops (repeating samples) in the bass register, for instance, but in normal playing these were completely undetectable. The quality of the samples was wonderful. The

Models At a Glance, *continued*

	CLP-525	CLP-535	CLP-545	CLP-565GP	CLP-575	CLP-585
EFFECTS, RHYTHMS						
Effects	Reverb	Reverb, Chorus, Brilliance, Master Effect	Reverb, Chorus, Brilliance, Master Effect, Stereophonic Optimizer	⟶	⟶	⟶
Split Keyboard		Yes	⟶	⟶	⟶	⟶
Preset Rhythms			20	⟶	⟶	⟶
RECORDING, MEMORY, STORAGE						
Recording (songs/tracks)	1/2	250/16	⟶	⟶	⟶	⟶
USB Audio Recorder (WAV)		Yes	⟶	⟶	⟶	⟶
Internal Memory	900KB	1.5MB	⟶	⟶	⟶	⟶
External Drives		USB Flash Memory	⟶	⟶	⟶	⟶
CONNECTIVITY						
Connectivity Options	Headphones, USB to Host	Headphones, USB to Host, MIDI, Aux In, Aux Out, USB to Device	⟶	⟶	⟶	Headphones, USB to Host, MIDI, Aux In, Aux Out, USB to Device, Aux Pedal
AMPLIFIER, SPEAKERS, POWER						
Amplifier (total watts)	40	60	100	70	160	180
No. Speakers	2	⟶	4	⟶	⟶	6
Speaker Box				Yes	⟶	⟶
Power Consumption	13W	20W	30W	30W	55W	60W
CABINET						
Style	Digital Console	Digital Console	Digital Console	Acoustic Grand	Digital Console	Acoustic Upright
PRICE						
MSRP	$2,199–2,599	$2,899–3,399	$3,699–4,299	$5,999	$4,999–5,699	$6,299–6,999
Est. Street Price or MAP	$1,700–2,000	$2,200–2,600	$2,900–3,400	$4,500	$3,900–4,500	$4,900–5,500

Note: ⟶ indicates a value repeated from the previous column.

amplitude envelopes—i.e., the decay of loudness as the note dies away—were perfect, as was the response to key velocity (harder and softer playing). Playing from the left end of the keyboard to the right end produced a good stereo sweep through the piano's speakers, though this sweep was less noticeable through headphones.

The high end had the breathy, undamped quality of an acoustic piano. Curiously, though, the high-register notes sustained longer when the damper pedal was down. This is not the case with an acoustic piano, in which this range *has* no dampers. I liked this effect; it could be musically useful.

The note release in these pianos was a bit soft. On a real grand, releasing the damper pedal suddenly will cause a distinct thump as the dampers drop back onto the strings—an effect that occasionally can be musically relevant. The CLP's damper pedal didn't do that. Letting it pop up just produced the normal sound of a smooth note release. In addition to half-pedaling, I could catch notes with the damper pedal before they died away completely, for a *sforzando-piano* effect. Notes held with the sostenuto pedal exhibited a bit of sympathetic resonance when I played staccato notes above or below them, but the effect was less prominent than in an acoustic grand.

The two top models in the CLP-500 line, the 575 and 585, include a built-in digital effect that Yamaha calls Virtual Resonance Modeling (VRM). This is supposed to create the kind of sympathetic interaction heard between groups of strings in an acoustic piano. It can be switched on or off, but I almost couldn't hear the difference. When I played open octave E's with both hands, the VRM seemed to make individual notes blend just a tiny bit. When it was switched off, the notes were perhaps a bit more distinct. But this is not a feature that I feel excited about.

The Keyboard

In an acoustic piano, the higher keys are actually lighter than the lower keys because of the difference in the hammers' weight. The feel of this difference is fairly successfully emulated in the CLP-500 models with what are known as graded-hammer actions. The lower-end models are graded into four weight zones, whereas in the 575 and 585, each of the 88 hammers is a different weight, just as in a good-quality acoustic grand. Yamaha calls this an 88-key Linear Graded Hammer action. In several of the higher-end CLP models, the white keys are also made of real wood. These differences subtly affect the realism of touch—I noticed that the 535's high keys felt just the slightest bit stiffer than the 575's (though this will be of no concern to most piano students). On the other hand, the high keys in the 575 felt a bit springy. This springiness was not objectionable, but I detect nothing like it in the action of a real grand.

The key dip was exactly what my fingers would have expected from a good-quality acoustic piano, as was the velocity response. I felt I was playing a piano, not a compromise. The keytops of all the models in the CLP-500 line are made of synthetic ivory, similar to what Yamaha uses on its acoustic pianos. I'm sure this contributed to the authentic feel.

Other Sounds

Five pad sounds (strings or choir) can be layered with the piano for a richer tone. The keyboard can also be split, allowing you to play a bass tone (acoustic, electric, or fretless electric) with the left hand and piano or organ with the right. The bass tones were excellent, as were the vibraphone and the nylon-string and steel-string guitars. The two pipe organs and the harpsichord were serviceable, but I didn't care for the two jazz organs.

The Rhodes electric piano is sampled at four key-velocity levels. While the transitions from one velocity level to the next were audible, the samples were well matched, and the result was playable—and definitely superior to some velocity cross-switched electric pianos I've heard. The DX7-style FM electric piano sample was less playable.

Electronic Features

The CLP-500 models have both MIDI and audio recording, which is very convenient for students—they can listen to their own playing and notice weak spots (a fairly brutal but useful process). Audio recording is done to an external USB memory device, but these pianos have their own internal memories for storing MIDI-based performances. You can record one part to the MIDI recorder, then play along with it using the same or a different sound. This would allow a teacher, for example, to record an accompaniment for a younger student to play over.

The auxiliary input jack (a stereo mini-jack suitable for connecting to your smartphone or tablet) both sends external sounds to the piano's speakers, and allows them to be recorded as new audio along with the piano performance. This is a super feature for advanced students, though it will require that you have access to recordings of "backing tracks" to play along with.

There are two ¼" headphone jacks. When you plug in headphones, the speakers are bypassed—perfect for practicing in an apartment. USB in and out jacks allow connection to a computer or to a memory device for audio recording. You can set the MIDI channel of the keyboard, but other than the keyboard itself and the pedals, the CLP has no MIDI performance hardware (no pitch-bend wheel, for instance).

Summary

Whether to buy a digital or an acoustic piano is a choice that players and families will have to make based on their own needs. It's still the case that a sampled digital piano doesn't sound quite as big or as full as an acoustic, for reasons having to do with string resonance and the soundboard. But compared to 20 years ago, these differences are likely to concern only the most discerning musicians. In many musical situations, you really won't be able to hear the difference.

For a family with a young piano student, or a pro who doesn't have space in a home studio for a grand, or an adult amateur who just loves playing the piano, the advantages of Yamaha's Clavinova CLP-500 models are jaw-dropping. The prices can't be beat, you never need to have them tuned, they're more portable than an acoustic piano, and you get the sound of a grand from a spinet-sized cabinet suitable for a small apartment—not to mention headphone jacks for practicing, a built-in recorder, and a variety of other sounds.

If your piano teacher tells you that only an acoustic piano will do, invite him or her down to the store to listen to one of the Clavinovas. Chances are, they'll change their tune in a hurry.

Jim Aikin (midiguru23@sbcglobal.net) has been reviewing synthesizers and other digital keyboards for *Keyboard, Electronic Musician,* and other magazines for more than 30 years. As an amateur pianist, he plays mostly Bach. He also teaches cello privately, plays in community orchestras, and composes and records in a computer-based home studio.

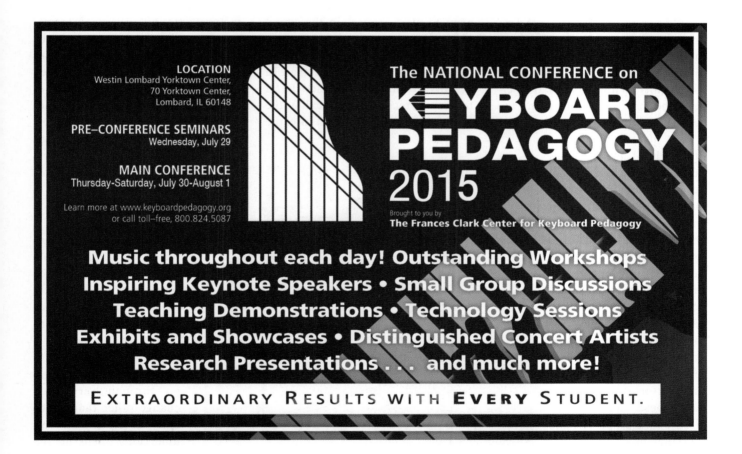

IN PART 1 OF THIS ARTICLE, we describe how a digital piano performs its most basic function—imitating the acoustic piano. We begin with tone production, then move on to controls—the keyboard and pedals—and conclude with the instrument's audio system. In Part 2, we explore all the ways that digital pianos can go beyond simply duplicating the functions of the acoustic piano.

Tone Production

Sample Rate and Bit Rate

The technology now used in most digital pianos to emulate the complex tonal behavior of the acoustic piano is called *sampling*. Sampling, in its simplest form, is the process of making a digital recording of a sound for later playback. A collection of samples, such as those needed to reproduce the tone of a piano, is called a *sample set*. There are many decisions to be made in compiling a sample set for an instrument as sonically complex as a piano, perhaps the most important being the *sample rate* and *bit rate*.

The *sample rate* determines how many times per second the sound will be measured. The sound must be sampled often enough to avoid missing changes that occur between sample times. This rate, in turn, depends on the frequency of the sound being sampled. The fundamental frequency of the highest note on the keyboard is 4,186 cycles per second, or hertz (Hz). But the overtones that accompany these fundamentals vibrate at multiples of the fundamental's

frequency, and must be properly recorded in order to accurately reproduce the tone. Fortunately, the inventors of the Compact Disc were well aware of this requirement, and long ago adopted the sampling rate of 44,100Hz for audio CD recordings.

The other decision is how finely to measure at each of those 44,100 times per second. Just as we don't want to miss changes in the sound that occur between the times we measured it, we also can't afford to miss the details of those changes. In digital recording, this is called the *bit rate*, or, as recording pros call it, the *bit depth*. The higher the bit rate, the

finer the detail that can be recorded. In computers, an 8-bit number represents up to 256 levels of detail, a 16-bit number can represent 65,536 levels, and a 24-bit number tops out at 16,777,216 levels. Once again, we will bow to the decision of the developers of the Compact Disc and go with the choice of a 16-bit number as our standard.

What all of this means is that, under the audio-CD standard, every second of sound sampled is measured 44,100 times at a degree of detail that can represent up to 65,536 individual levels. This one second of sample information takes up just over 86 kilobytes (KB) of memory space. Because digital piano manufacturers do not release information about their sampling standards, there's no basis for comparison with the audio-CD standard. However, the rates stated by developers of software pianos tend to be higher than this standard, so it's reasonable to assume that some digital piano manufacturers may exceed these rates as well.

Looping

One interesting characteristic of a piano note is that it can sustain for several seconds, but after the first couple of seconds much of the initial complexity of the sound is gone; the remaining seconds of sustained sound go through very little change other than gradually decreasing in volume. This opens up the

Bösendorfer mic'd for sampling

Vienna Symphonic Library

possibility to save some memory space, and thus some money, by introducing a process called *looping*. Looping involves selecting a short duration of the sound that remains essentially unchanged over a period of time, and repeating it over and over at gradually reduced volume levels. Done with care, the result is barely detectable when listening intently to the sustain of one note, and becomes completely lost in the commotion when playing normally.

Spatial Relations

The notes produced by an acoustic piano have a physical point of origin in the instrument's strings, and can be heard moving from left to right as you play a scale from the left (bass) end of the keyboard to the right (treble) end. To preserve this spatial relationship, the samples in a digital piano are recorded in two-channel stereo. This feature, often called "panning," adds to the realism by physically positioning the sounds in ways similar to what is heard from an acoustic piano.

Number of Notes Sampled

Now we must decide how many notes to sample. The obvious answer would seem to be "all of them," and some manufacturers take this route. But in the interest of keeping the cost of the digital piano under control, many manufacturers seek alternatives to sampling all 88 notes.

In an acoustic piano, the tonal behavior of the longer, bass strings is different from that of the shorter, treble strings. In fact, this tonal variation goes through several changes as you play up the keyboard from the bottom. Some of these changes are due to the differences in string length, others to differences in the types and numbers of strings associated with different ranges of notes. In the lowest bass, the hammers strike a single string per note. This

string is wrapped with heavy copper wire to slow its rate of vibration to produce the proper pitch. Depending on the piano's scale design, a couple of octaves up from the bottom of the keyboard it switches to two strings per note, each wound with a lighter copper wire. Finally, by mid-keyboard, three plain-wire strings are used for each note. (Each set of one, two, or three strings per note is known as a *unison* because all the strings in a given set are tuned at the same pitch to sound a single note.) The subtle changes brought about by these different string arrangements also figure in the tonal variations we hear as we move up and down the keyboard.

But the tonal changes from one note to the next are not always noticeable; sometimes, all that changes is the pitch. It turns out that it's a fairly simple matter for the digital piano to play back a sample at a different pitch. This makes it possible to save memory space by using one sample as the basis for two or three consecutive notes. Taken too far, this would result in obvious tonal problems. But if at least a third of the notes are sampled, with careful attention to areas of the keyboard where there are more noticeable changes, these shared samples can produce a convincing, if basic, tonal progression.

Sampling Dynamics

One more source of tonal variation—the effect of dynamics (variation in volume or loudness)—must be dealt with before we move on from our basic sample set. Striking a string harder results in a larger number and greater prominence of higher overtones, which, in addition to making the sound louder, give the tone more

"edge." Currently, in all but the least expensive instruments, digital pianos use from three to five dynamic samples. As you play with varying degrees of force, the digital piano selects the closest appropriate dynamic sample for playback. Entry-level pianos that use a single sample level for dynamics also use variable filtering of a note's overtones to simulate these tonal differences, sometimes with remarkable success.

Sampling Other Effects

Many digital pianos incorporate additional types of samples aimed at capturing more of the nuance of an acoustic piano. At this time, the two most common such samples are *string resonance* and *damper effect*. As with so many features, different manufacturers seldom use the same terms for the same effects. String resonance is related to the strings' overtones. Each of the overtones generated by a vibrating string are at, or close to, the fundamental frequencies of higher notes whose frequencies bear a mathematical relationship to the one played. This results in a weak sympathetic or resonant vibration of the strings of the related notes, and adds another dimension to the sound. (To hear this effect, slowly press the keys of a chord—for this discussion, let's make it a C chord—without actually sounding them. While holding these keys down, quickly strike and release the C an octave below the held chord and you'll hear, faintly, the sympathetic resonance of the C chord above.)

In an acoustic piano, a note's felt damper moves away from the string(s) when its key is depressed, and returns to stop their vibration when the key is released. The effect on the

> **Many digital pianos incorporate additional types of samples, capturing more of the nuance of an acoustic piano.**

OTHER METHODS OF VOICE PRODUCTION

Before sampling became commercially viable (i.e., affordable—when introduced, the first sampling instruments cost as much as a small house), various forms of "synthesis" were used to produce electronic music. Oscillators, filters, modulators, envelope generators, and other electronics worked together to make sounds never before heard, as well as sounds that vaguely mimicked those of familiar acoustic instruments. The classic model was Robert Moog's modular synthesizer of the late 1960s and '70s—the instrument that allowed Wendy Carlos to produce *Switched-On Bach*. Some of today's digital pianos retain the ability to modify their voices in much the same manner as these early synthesizers.

Looking at a currently emerging technology, we find a method called *physical modeling*. While modeling has been used before in software-based pianos, last year Roland released the V-Piano, the first digital piano to rely solely on this technology. More recently, Yamaha unveiled its new CP stage-piano line, which mixes modeling and sampling technologies. Modeling breaks down an instrument's sound into discrete elements that can be represented by mathematical equations, or algorithms. In the case of the acoustic piano, these algorithms represent the behavior of the primary elements that affect the tone—hammers, strings, soundboard, and dampers. Whereas in sampling, a preexisting sample is retrieved from the piano's memory, in modeling the tone is created in real time, based on a complex series of calculations. Sampling requires large amounts of memory for storing high-resolution sample sets, whereas modeling requires powerful processors to instantaneously make the many calculations needed to produce a given note.

sound is not instantaneous; it takes a fraction of a second for the strings' vibration to stop. During this time the tone is altered as its overtones rapidly decay. Damper-effect samples are triggered by releasing a key, and add another subtle dimension to the digital piano's sound.

Polyphony

Finally, we have to consider how many notes the instrument can play at once, which is expressed as its *polyphony*. A quick glance at your hands may suggest that 10 ought to be plenty. But consider what happens when you play a series of chords, or an arpeggio, while holding down the sustain pedal. Each note that continues to sustain takes up one note of polyphony. If you press the sustain pedal and play a three-note chord with both hands, then repeat those chords three more times in successively higher octaves, you will now be sustaining 24 notes. Played with layered voices (a combination of two different voices, such as piano and strings), that example would require 48 notes of polyphony. Some models of digital piano have 32 notes of polyphony, but most current models have 64 or more.

A cautionary note: As you delve into the specifications of digital pianos, the temptation to rank instruments based on numbers—how many notes were sampled, how much memory the sample set takes up, and so on—will be high. And the results would be highly unreliable. Designing a digital piano involves choices driven by economics (e.g., how much a model will sell for), by the intended customer's needs (beginner or professional), and, in no small part, by the engineering talent at the manufacturer's disposal. Engineering creativity, or lack of it, can turn the numerical specifications on their head, resulting in an instrument that sounds better—or worse—than its numbers would suggest.

Controlling Tone— The Keyboard

Just as in an acoustic piano, the role of the keyboard is to provide the player with intimate, reliable control of the instrument's tonal resources. But just as there is no single correct tone, there is no single correct feel; rather, there is an acceptable range of touch characteristics.

Touch Weight

As in an acoustic piano, the action of most digital pianos is primarily an arrangement of levers, but the digital action is far less complex and doesn't require regular adjustment. Players use a few definable criteria to judge an action. Some are easily measured, others are largely subjective. Among the most frequently debated by digital piano buyers is *touch weight*.

Touch weight is the amount of force, typically measured in grams, required to depress a key. A touch weight in the range of 50 to 55 grams is generally considered normal for an acoustic piano. The resistance offered by the key is a combination of friction and the mass of the parts being moved. Both of these factors behave slightly differently in acoustic pianos than in digital pianos. Measuring the touch weight of an acoustic piano is typically done with the sustain pedal fully depressed, which removes the weight of the dampers and reduces the force required to depress the key. The problem is, digitals don't *have* dampers, so the digital manufacturer has to decide between the higher weight the pianist will feel when the dampers are being lifted by the key, and the lighter weight when the dampers have been lifted by the sustain pedal. There is no single right answer—just design choices.

Friction is also a bigger factor in the action of an acoustic than in a digital piano. Most of the friction in an acoustic action is due to various hinge points and bearing surfaces, many of which have cloth or felt bushings. Over time, these bushings wear away or become compacted, reducing friction and the amount of force required to depress a key. Another factor is humidity. Felt and wood parts readily absorb and release moisture, effectively increasing or decreasing friction with changes in the amount of moisture in the air. Because digital actions contain far fewer felt parts and—with the exception of a few upper-end actions sporting wooden keys—no wooden parts at all, changes in friction due to wear and fluctuations in humidity are substantially reduced.

Yet another aspect of touch weight is that it varies from one end of the keyboard to the other. In an acoustic piano, the hammers are significantly heavier at the bass end of the keyboard than at the treble end, which results in heavier touch weight in the bass and lighter touch weight in the treble. Enter the *graded hammer action*: To replicate the touch weight of the acoustic piano keyboard, most digital piano actions employ in their designs the equivalent of graduated hammer weights. Rather than using 88 different weights across the span of the keyboard, which would be cost-prohibitive and of questionable value, it's common to use four different touch-weight values, each one used uniformly throughout one touch-weight zone.

Key Design

Some high-end digital pianos employ wooden keys to subtly move you closer to the feel of an acoustic action. The physical properties you may detect would be a slight flexing of the key, a difference in the mass of the key, and possibly a very slight difference in the shock absorption of wood vs. plastic when the key is depressed and bottoms out (although this is mostly masked by the felt pad under the key).

Another aspect of key design is the tactile property of the keytop material. Ivory is so prized (and missed) by acoustic piano players not for its appearance, but for the fact that it's porous, and thus offers a degree of "grip" that slick-surfaced plastic keytops don't. This grip is particularly valued when the playing gets serious and the pianist's fingers become sweaty, which typically occurs during demanding passages, when the pianist's accuracy and control are pushed to their limits. Ivory substitutes, such as Kawai's Neotex, Roland's Ivory Feel, and Yamaha's Ivorite, provide the positive properties of ivory without the discoloring, cracking, and chipping for which ivory is equally famous. Other manufacturers have since added this feature, and it's one worth considering when comparing instruments.

Dynamic (Velocity) Sensors

The final aspect of the digital piano action we'll explore is how it measures the force the player's fingers apply to the keys. This is typically done using two electrical contact switches that are closed in rapid succession as the key is depressed. Alternatively, some high-end digital hybrids use optical sensors to sense the key's motion—a small flag attached to the key breaks a beam of light as it descends. However, what these sensors actually measure is not force—that is, how hard the

> To replicate the touch weight of the acoustic piano keyboard, most digital piano actions use a graded hammer action.

key is depressed—but the speed or *velocity* with which it is depressed. This is why you'll sometimes see the term *velocity sensing* in the keyboard specifications. As the key moves to the bottom of its travel, the instrument measures how much time has elapsed between the signals received from the first and second sensors. A longer time indicates that the key was traveling slowly and tells the instrument to produce a softer tone; a shorter time means a faster, harder keystroke, and thus a louder tone—it's that straightforward. Some actions employ additional switches to trigger other sample types, such as the damper effect mentioned earlier.

Some digital pianos now employ three sensors ("Tri-Sensor" or "Triple-Sensor" keys) instead of the usual two. The additional sensor greatly improves the repetition speed by allowing the player to re-trigger a note without the key having to fully return to the top of its stroke. The third sensor also improves the instrument's response to legato passages.

The Pedals

Modern acoustic pianos have three pedals. Let's take a look at how they work, and how their functions translate to the digital piano.

In the common three-pedal arrangement of an acoustic piano, the pedal on the right is the *sustain pedal*. In the case of digital instruments having only one pedal, it is the sustain pedal. Some refer to this as the *damper pedal*, because its mechanical function on an acoustic piano is to lift the dampers away from the strings. On a digital piano, the sustain pedal is an electronic switch. When depressed, it tells the instrument to allow played notes to gradually decay as they would on an acoustic piano.

The most frequent question about a digital piano's sustain pedal is whether it can perform a function called *half pedaling*. The acoustic piano's sustain-pedal mechanism can move the dampers from a position of rest on the strings to a position completely clear of the strings—or anywhere in between. Between these two positions is the highly useful half-pedal position, which allows the player more control of tone and sustain. While half-pedal capability is now commonly found on upper-end digitals, it is not always present on lower-priced instruments, where the sustain pedal is more likely to be a simple on/off switch that allows full sustain or no sustain, but nothing in between. Some lower-priced digitals come with a separate square plastic or metal foot switch rather than something that looks like a piano pedal. However, even if the piano itself is capable of half-pedal control, the foot switch may provide only on/off sustain. The same may be true even with some pedals that have the appearance and movement of a piano pedal. It's always worth checking the specifications to be sure that both instrument *and* pedal are capable of half-pedal control.

At the left end of the three-pedal group is the *soft pedal*. The proper term for this in an acoustic grand piano—*una corda*, or "one string"—relates to its function. In an acoustic grand, this pedal, when depressed, laterally shifts the entire action—from keys to hammers—slightly to the right. Recall (from "**Tone Production**," above) that, on an acoustic piano, most notes have two or three strings associated with them. When the action is shifted to the right by the soft pedal, the hammer strikes only two of the three strings in each three-string unison. This has two effects: it reduces the volume of the sound, and it slightly alters the tonal quality.

As with the sustain pedal, the digital version of this pedal is simply

an electronic switch that activates an equivalent effect. Since the digital piano action can play at much lower volumes than the acoustic piano, the practical importance of this pedal for reducing sound volume is considerably lessened. However, its ability to alter tonal quality remains relevant—assuming it actually does so. Most do not.

The mysterious center pedal is the *sostenuto*. The easiest way to think of the sostenuto's function is as a selective sustain pedal. Play one or more keys anywhere on the keyboard and, while holding these keys down, press and hold the sostenuto pedal. The sostenuto mechanism will hold the dampers for these keys away from the strings, sustaining them even after you release the keys, but any subsequent keys played will not sustain when released (unless you also use the sustain pedal). Clear? The bottom line is that all three-pedal digital pianos incorporate this feature exactly as it works on an acoustic piano. In written music, the sostenuto pedal is called for in only a few pieces of classical music. If you need it, it's there, but chances are you never will. In digital pianos, the middle pedal is often assigned another function, **discussed in Part 2** of this article.

The Audio System

The final component of most digital pianos is the audio system—its amplifiers and speakers—which perform the same job as an acoustic piano's soundboard: making the piano's sound audible at useful volume levels. I say *most* digital pianos because some instruments designed specifically for stage use lack an onboard audio system, as they will always be connected to a sound-reinforcement, or public address (PA), system.

The digital pianos currently on the market offer anywhere from 12

dB	WATTS	DYNAMICS
64	0.015	ppp
67	0.03	
70	0.06	pp
73	0.12	
76	0.24	p
79	0.48	
82	0.96	mp/mf
85	1.92	
88	3.84	f
91	7.68	
94	15.36	ff
97	30.72	
100	61.44	fff
103	122.88	

to 360 watts (W) of output power, channeled through from two to twelve speakers. To understand why there is such a wide range of options, we need to look at how the system's power-output capability (and the type, number, and placement of speakers) relates to what we hear.

The smallest change in volume that most people can detect is 3 decibels (dB), and to achieve a 3dB increase in volume requires a doubling of the output power in watts. With these relationships in mind, let's look at some numbers.

Based on measurements of three of the most frequently encountered concert grand pianos—Bösendorfer model 290, Steinway & Sons model D, and Yamaha model CFIIIS—I arrived at a model dynamic range. This range extends from the softest note possible, at 64dB, to the loudest chord I could produce, at 103dB. Assigning a modest 0.015W—we're assuming a *very* efficient audio system—to produce the softest (64dB) note, the chart below traces the progression of amplifier power required to keep up with the increasing volume to the top of the piano's dynamic range. Different audio systems will have different starting points, depending on the size and number of speakers being powered, the efficiency of those speakers' use of power, and the notes played (bass requires more power to match the treble volume). Dynamic markings have been added to bring some musical perspective to the numbers.

If you've not seen this sort of table before, the results are startling. It's the last three or four steps of volume that really demand power from the amplifiers.

When the audio system attempts to reproduce a sound louder than it can accommodate, it goes into "clipping" and produces a distorted version of the sound. One thing to remember is that even the most powerful instruments can be driven into clipping if played loudly with the volume turned all the way up. Aside from distorting the sound, overdriving the system can damage the speakers and amplifiers. The key is to set the volume no higher than 75 to 80% of its maximum level.

If you've already peeked at the specification charts toward the end of this book, you know that only a few digital pianos produce 100-plus watts of output power per channel (left and right). Many of the models that do have that much power also separate the low-demand treble frequencies from the power-hog bass frequencies by providing each frequency range with its own amplifier and speaker(s). A very few go so far as to divide the audio system into three separate subsystems, for the bass, midrange, and highs. These designs, called "bi-amped" or "tri-amped," can make a noticeable difference in sound and power efficiency by using amplifiers and speakers optimized for specific frequency ranges rather than sending the entire frequency spectrum to a single full-range audio system.

Speakers

Because all of the digital pianos we'll consider in this publication have stereo audio systems, all discussions of speakers will assume matching left and right channels.

The least expensive digital pianos employ a single full-range speaker per side. While these speakers are typically described by the manufacturer as "full-range," they are in fact a compromise dictated by cost and, in the case of the most compact designs, space. While a full-range speaker may reproduce much of the 20Hz–20kHz frequency range required by the piano samples, those frequencies will not be treated equally. The frequency response of a speaker is judged not only by its range, but also by its "flatness," or accuracy. If we send to a speaker multiple signals at different frequencies but at the same volume level, then measure the speaker's output volume when producing those sounds, we will see the speaker's "frequency-response curve." The full-range speaker will usually be acceptably flat through the middle of the frequency range, but will fall off in volume at the upper and lower reaches of the spectrum. In other words, the speaker will not accurately reproduce the full range of the signal sent to it. This is not the result of poor speaker design. As a matter of fact, I'm frequently amazed at what the engineers can coax out of these speakers. But the fact remains that they are inaccurate, and in ways that color our perception of the instrument's sound. Even the best sample set is rendered unimpressive if the sparkling highs and thunderous lows are weak or missing.

For this reason, most upper-end models use three speakers, one of each optimized for the bass, midrange, or treble frequencies. Accurate reproduction of bass frequencies requires the movement of a great deal of air. This is accomplished by combining a relatively large surface area with a high degree of in-and-out movement. These bass speakers, or *woofers*, are largely responsible for our impression of an instrument's "guts."

At the opposite end of the frequency spectrum is the high-frequency speaker, or *tweeter*. The tweeter, which is physically quite small, is responsible for reproducing the nuances of the upper range of the instrument. Besides the obvious frequency difference between the outputs of the woofer and tweeter, they also differ in their placement requirements. Whereas low frequencies tend to radiate in all directions, the higher the frequency of the sound, the more directional it is, which means that the precise placement of the tweeter is much more important. Most of the low- and mid-frequency speakers on digital pianos are located below the keyboard because there's plenty of room there. The more directional nature of the high frequencies requires pointing the tweeters directly at the player's head, usually from somewhere on the instrument's control panel.

The newest twist in speaker systems—one that appears to be unique to digital pianos—is the *soundboard speaker*. This technology will be discussed in the article "Hybrid Pianos," elsewhere in this issue.

So we now have all the makings of a digital piano: a sound source, and the means to control and hear it. But none of the current crop of digital pianos stops there; all of them have additional capabilities. These extras range from a handful of additional voices to direct Internet access. Even if your current needs don't extend past the basics, you should understand the other features present on your instrument, and how they might surprise and lure you into musical adventures you've never contemplated. To continue, please read "Digital Piano Basics, Part 2: Beyond the Acoustic Piano." ▐▐▌▌

THE FIRST INSTRUMENTS we now call digital pianos were specialized versions of the synthesizers of the day (early 1980s). These synthesizers were capable of producing a staggering array of sounds, and allowed the player to exercise control over many details of those sounds. A standard feature of many synthesizers was the ability to produce the sounds of pianos and other conventional instruments, which led to the spin-off we now call the digital piano.

The first digital pianos retained some of the other capabilities of their parent instruments by including a few preset voices besides that of the acoustic piano. It wasn't long before subsequent models appeared with expanded voice capabilities, reverberation effects, background accompaniments, the ability to connect to other digital instruments and computers, and much more. In this article we'll look at each of these categories of "extras," what they do, and how they might enhance your musical experience.

Instrumental Voices

The designers of the first digital pianos correctly assumed that someone who needed the sound of an acoustic piano would probably benefit from a handful of related voices, such as the harpsichord, an organ sound or two, the very different but highly useful sounds of such electric pianos as the Fender Rhodes, and so on. To this day, even the most basic digital pianos feature voice lists very similar to those of the original models. What's changed over the years is the quality or authenticity of those voices, and the cost of producing them.

So far, in Part 1 of this article, I have discussed only samples of acoustic pianos. For most models of digital piano, the same sampling technology is used to reproduce the sound of other acoustic instruments. Typically, an expanded selection of high-quality instrumental samples is found in only the more expensive models. Remember that, depending on the sample rate used, samples may be more or less accurate representations of the original voice. Because manufacturers almost never reveal these sample rates, our ears must judge the relative quality of the voices of the digital piano models we're comparing.

Note that many manufacturers have trademarked their names for a particular sampling technology or other aspect of an instrument. The important thing to remember about trademarks is that while the trademarked name is unique, the underlying technology may be essentially the same as everyone else's. For instance, the generic term for digital sampling, discussed in Part 1, is Pulse Code Modulation, or PCM. But a manufacturer may call their PCM samples *UltraHyperDynoMorphic II Sampling*, and rightly claim to make the only product on the market using it. However, that makes it only a unique *name*, not necessarily a unique technology.

Layering and Splitting

Layering—the ability to have one key play two or more voices at the same time—is available on virtually all digital pianos. Some combinations, such as Piano and Strings, are commonly preset as a single voice selection. On many instruments, it's possible to select the voices you'd like to combine. This is frequently as simple as pressing the selection buttons for the two voices you want to layer. Once these are selected, many instruments then allow you to control the two voices' relative volumes. Using the popular Piano and Strings combination as an example, you may want the two voices to play with equal volume, or you may want the Piano voice to be the dominant sound, with just a hint of Strings. Other possible settings include the ability to set the apparent positions of the individual voices in the left-right stereo field—with Strings, say, predominantly on the left. The most advanced instruments make it possible to have only one voice's dynamics respond to your touch on the keyboard, while the other voice responds to a separate volume pedal (this is described in greater detail under "Other Controls").

The other commonly available voice option is *splitting*. Whereas layering provides the ability to play two voices with one key, splitting lets you play one voice on the right side of the keyboard, and a different voice on the left side—for instance, piano on the right and string bass on the left. This essentially lets the instrument behave as though it had two keyboards playing two different voices. The *split point* is the point in the keyboard where the right and left voices meet. While this split point has a default setting, it can also be moved to provide more playing room for one voice or the other. As with layered voices, there may be preset combinations, but you can also set up your own voice pairings; typically, additional options are available to vary relative volume levels and other settings between the two voices.

Effects

Digital *effects* electronically change a sound in ways the originally sampled source instrument typically could not. Effects can be loosely divided into those that mimic the acoustic properties of a performing space and those that modify the sound in non-acoustic and, in some cases, downright unnatural ways.

The most popular effect—in fact, the one most people never turn off— is Reverberation, or *Reverb*. The easiest way to understand reverb is to think of it as an echo. When reflective surfaces are close to the sound source and to you, the individual reflections of the original sound arrive at your ears from so many directions, and so closely spaced in time, that they merge into a single sound. But when the reflective surface is far away, there is a time lag between the original and reflected sounds that the ear recognizes as an echo, also known as "reverberant sound." The strength and duration of the echo depends on a number of factors, among them the volume and frequency of the original sound, and the hardness and distance of the reflective surfaces. Different amounts of Reverb lend themselves better to different types of music. Although you can just leave Reverb on the default setting, you also can broaden the instrument's tonal palette by exploring alternate settings.

The other common effect is *Chorus*. When a group of instruments play the same notes, the result is not simply a louder version of those notes. Even the best performers will be very slightly out of synchronization and out of tune with each other. This contributes to what's variously referred to as a "full," "fat," or "lush" sound. The Chorus effect is frequently built into ensemble voices like Strings and Brass and, of course, Choir.

Before we leave the subject of effects, there is one other application to be covered here: dedicated effects speakers. Some upper-end digital pianos now come with speakers whose role is not to produce the primary sound, but to add to the apparent ambience of the instrument and the room. These speakers and their associated effects can significantly alter the sound of instrument and room. When done well, these effects are not noticed until they're turned off, when the sound seems to "collapse" down to a smaller-sounding source.

Alternate (Historical) Tuning

One of the advantages offered by the digital piano is the fact that it never requires tuning. This does not, however, mean that it *cannot* be tuned. Just as we tend to think of the piano as something that has always sounded as it does today, we similarly tend to think that tuning is tuning, and has always been as it is now. In fact, our current practice of setting the A above Middle C at 440Hz, and the division of the octave into intervals of equal size for the purpose of tuning, are relatively recent developments.

Evidence suggests that international standard pitch, while a bit of a moving target depending on where, when, and for whom you were tuning, had pretty well settled down to A = 440 Hz by the mid-19th century. And by the late 19th century, following a few centuries of variation, we

had arrived at the tuning system of equal temperament.

Now that all that has been settled, why bother with alternate tunings? You may never use this capability, but for many it is a profound experience to hear firsthand how the music of J.S. Bach sounded to Bach himself, and thus to realize why he wrote the way he did. Instruments that include alternate tunings list in a menu the most common historical temperaments (tuning systems). Select an appropriate temperament, adjust the pitch control, and you have a time machine with keys. It's a simple and invaluable tool for those interested in music history, and some instruments allow you to create your own unique temperaments for the composition of experimental or modern music.

MIDI

Electronic musical instruments had been around for decades, but were unable to "talk" to each other until 1982 and the introduction of the Musical Instrument Digital Interface (MIDI) specification. Many musicians used two, three, or more synthesizers in their setups, each with a distinctive palette of sounds, to provide the widest possible range of voices. The problem was that the musicians couldn't combine sounds from different synths and control them from a single keyboard, because of differences in the electronic commands to which each synth responded. This ultimately led to a proposal for a common set of commands to which all digital musical instruments could respond.

In short, MIDI is not a sound source, but a set of digital commands—or, in the language of MIDI, *messages*—that can control a sound source. MIDI doesn't even refer to notes by their proper names; for example, middle C is note number 60. When you use the recording feature included in most digital pianos, what you're actually recording is a sequence of digital messages; hence the term *sequencer* for a MIDI recorder (some upper-end models now allow both MIDI and audio recording). These messages form a datastream that represents the musical actions you took. Some of the most common messages are listed in the table below.

There are *many* more message types, but this should give you an idea of how MIDI "thinks." Nothing is a sound—everything is a number. When recording or playing back a sequence of MIDI messages, timing—just as in a piece of music—is obviously a critical element, so MIDI uses a "synchronization clock" to control the timing of each message. MIDI can also direct different streams of messages to different channels. Each channel can be assigned to communicate with different devices; for instance, your computer and another keyboard.

While the MIDI specification of 1982 standardized commands for events such as note on, note off, control change, and program change, it didn't include a message type for instrumental voice. It was still necessary to manually set the voice that would play on each synth because there was no consistency between instruments from different manufacturers, or sometimes even within a single manufacturer's product line, as to which command would produce which voice. This changed with the adoption in 1991 of the General MIDI (GM) standard, updated in 1999 to General MIDI 2 (GM2).

Product specifications now frequently state that an instrument is General MIDI, or GM, compatible. Like MIDI, General MIDI specifies not a sound source but a standardized numbering scheme. Any digital instrument "thinks" of the different voices it produces not as Piano or Violin or Harpsichord, but as

BASIC MIDI MESSAGES	
Message	Action
Note On Event	The number of the note played and the key velocity (i.e., how fast the key went down)
Note Off Event	The number of the note released and the key's release velocity
Control Change	When the position of a control such as a pedal is changed, a message indicates the number assigned to that control and a value representing its new position
Program Change	When a new voice is selected, a message indicates the "patch" number of the new voice (the term patch goes back to the early days of the synthesizer, when different electronic elements were literally wired to each other with "patch cords")

Program Change numbers. General MIDI established a fixed list of Program Change Numbers for 128 "melodic instruments" and 1 "drum kit." GM2 later expanded this to 256 melodic voices and 9 drum kits. So all GM-compatible instruments use the same numbers to represent a given voice: Acoustic Grand Piano is always Program Change Number 1, Violin is always 41, and Harpsichord is always 7. A standardized numbering scheme of 256 melodic instrumental voices seems big enough to cover everything under the sun with room to spare, until you notice that some MIDI voices are actually combinations of instruments. For instance, Program Change Numbers 49 and 50 are String Ensemble 1 and 2, representing different combinations of string instruments playing in ensemble. Also, there are many Ethnic instruments (voices 105 through 112), and several Sound Effects, from chirping

birds to gunshots. If this has you feeling that perhaps 256 wasn't an unreasonably high number of voices after all, consider that many higher-end digital pianos have more than 500 voices, and some more than a thousand. This means that when you record using voices from the far end of the list on one manufacturer's "flagship" model, then play the recording back on someone else's top-of-the-line model, voice consistency once again flies out the window. Perhaps the most important thing to remember is that the GM standard doesn't specify the technology used to create the listed voices. One hint of the degree of variation possible under this system is the fact that your current cell phone is probably GM compatible.

In the 1990s, two proprietary extensions to the General MIDI standard were made, by Roland and Yamaha. Roland's GS extension was largely incorporated into the GM2 standard. Yamaha's XG extension defines far more voices than the other schemes, but hasn't been as widely adopted as General MIDI.

Connecting to a Computer

MIDI is now standard on all digital pianos. While it does allow your instrument to control or be controlled by other instruments, today it's most often used to connect the instrument to a computer. Connecting your instrument to a computer allows you to venture beyond the capacity of even the most capable and feature-packed digital piano.

MIDI-standard DIN connector

Connecting two instruments to each other requires two MIDI cables—one for each direction of data transmission between the two devices. Standard MIDI cables use a

5-pin DIN connector, shown here. Since personal computers don't use 5-pin DIN connectors, connecting a keyboard to a computer requires an adapter that has the MIDI-standard DIN connector on one end, and a computer-friendly connector on the other.

USB Connectors:
To Device (Type A),
To Host [Computer] (Type B)

In 1995, the USB standard was introduced to reduce the number of different connectors on personal computers. Subsequently, MIDI over USB has emerged as an alternative that replaces two MIDI cables with a single USB link. In addition to being a common connector on personal computers, USB's higher transmission speed increases MIDI's flexibility by allowing MIDI to control 32 channels instead of the 16 specified in the original MIDI standard. USB connectivity is now finding its way into the digital piano. All current digital instruments still have 5-pin DIN connectors for traditional MIDI, but many now sport USB connectors as well. One thing to be aware of is that there are two types of USB connections that can appear on instruments. One, "USB to Device," allows direct connection to a variety of external memory-storage devices. The other, "USB to Host," allows connection to computers. If you plan to use these connections, you need to check the type of USB connections available on the instruments you're considering. Simply stating "USB" in the specifications doesn't tell you the *type* of USB connectivity provided.

External Storage

External storage consists of any storage device that's connected to the instrument rather than being built into it. As instruments become more advanced, they can require greater amounts of space in which to store MIDI recordings, audio recordings, additional rhythm patterns and styles, even additional sounds. Because different users need different amounts of storage, it's becoming increasingly common for manufacturers to allow the user to attach external USB storage devices to augment onboard storage.

Floppy-disk drives were once popular in digital pianos, due to the large volume of MIDI files that were distributed using that format. These files run the gamut, from simple classical songs to complete orchestral arrangements, and even ones that use the special learning features of a particular instrument model to guide you through the process of learning a new piece of music. It's now possible to download these files from the Internet and store them on a USB flash drive (aka thumb drive). These drives are the ultimate in handy, portable storage, and can have as much as 64GB of memory. Not only are they unobtrusive when attached to the instrument; if your digital piano and computer are in different rooms, a flash drive can make file transfers quick and painless.

Some instruments give you the ability to play and record digital audio using a USB flash drive. These recordings are saved as uncompressed .WAV files, typically at the same bit depth (16) and sampling rate (44.1kHz), though not the same file format, used for commercial audio CDs: one five-minute song can consume up to 50MB of memory. Some instruments provide the option of recording your audio in the popular MP3 format, which can now offer good sound quality, and can be more convenient for listening and sending via e-mail. Either format can easily be transferred to a computer's hard drive, or a portable hard drive, for permanent storage.

Computer Software

As mentioned briefly in the discussion of MIDI, perhaps the most powerful option that accompanies the digital piano is the ability to connect your instrument to your personal computer and enhance your musical experience by using different types of music software. Software can expand capabilities your instrument may already have, such as recording and education, or it could add elements like music notation and additional voices. While it's beyond the scope of this article to describe music-software offerings in detail, we'll take a quick look here at the different categories: Recording and Sequencing, Virtual Instruments, Notation, and Educational.

Recording can take two forms on the digital piano: data and sound. All models that offer onboard recording (i.e., nearly all of them) record MIDI data. This means that all of the actions you take when you play a piece—both key presses and control actions—can be recorded by a MIDI sequencer. But remember that a MIDI sequence, or recording, is data, not sound. Recording the actual *sound* of your music is a different issue, and few digital pianos can do this.

Enter **recording software**. Recording software ranges from basic packages—even the most modest of which will exceed the recording capabilities of most digital pianos—to applications that can handle complete movie scores, including film synchronization. The higher-end applications are called Digital Audio Workstations (DAWs). These software applications cost more than many of the lower-priced digital pianos, and can be used to record, edit, and mix combinations of MIDI and audio tracks, limited only by the processing power and storage capacity of the computer. If you have an opportunity to look inside a modern recording studio, you'll find that computers running DAW software have replaced multi-track tape recorders.

Virtual instrument software can be controlled, or "played," by your digital piano via MIDI, and can also be played by recording software that resides on the computer. Virtual instruments can take the form of stand-alone software or plug-ins. Stand-alone instrumental software doesn't rely on other software, but plug-ins require a host application such as the DAW software described above, or other software developed specifically as a plug-in host. Virtual instruments can be sample sets for strings, horns, or even pianos, or they can accurately emulate the sonic textures and controls of popular electronic instruments that are no longer produced, such as certain legacy synthesizers. (A number of piano-specific virtual instruments are explored in the article "My Other Piano is a Computer," elsewhere in this issue.) While virtual instruments allow you to expand your sound palette beyond the onboard voices of your digital piano, they can place heavy demands on your computer's processor and memory. A mismatch of software demand and hardware capability can result in *latency*—audible delay between the time the key is played and the time the sound is heard. If both the digital piano's onboard voices and the virtual instrument's sounds are played simultaneously, there could be a time gap between the two outputs that would make the result unusable. Virtual instruments can be an exciting addition, but be prepared for the technical implications.

Notation applications are the word processors of music. If you have a tune in your head and want to share it, simply recording it will allow others to hear it. But in order for most people to *play* your music, it must be written out in standard notation. In the early days of notation software, it was necessary to place each note on the staff individually using the computer's keyboard and mouse. The advent of MIDI created the ability to play a note on a musical keyboard and have it appear on the computer screen. Today's notation programs virtually take musical dictation: you play it, and it appears on the screen.

But there's a slight hitch that must be addressed. The computer's capacity to accurately capture the timing of your playing, down to tiny fractions of a second, allows it to reproduce subtle nuances with great precision. In a recording, this is a great asset; in notation, it can be a complete disaster. If—in the computer's cold calculations—you've just played a passage involving dotted 128th-note triplets, the software will happily display them. Unless notation applications are told otherwise, they are perfectly capable of creating notation that is absolutely accurate *and* absolutely unreadable. This is where *quantization* comes in. Quantization—also applicable to the recording capabilities of higher-end digital pianos—allows you to specify, as a note value, the level of timing detail you desire. If the software is told to quantize at the eighth-note level, the printed music will contain no 16th notes—nothing shorter than an eighth note will be scored. If quantization is set at 16th notes, there will be more detail; if set to quarter notes, the music will be devoid of any timing detail beyond that value. This must be used judiciously; too much quantization and musical detail is lost, too little and the notation becomes an indecipherable pile of notes (for a good laugh, Google "Prelude and The Last Hope in C and C# Minor"). As with recording applications, there is a wide range of capabilities available, from programs that will let you capture simple melodies, to applications that will easily ingest the most complex symphonic works, transpose and separate the individual instrumental parts, and print them out.

The final category we'll discuss is **educational software**. Just as there are educational programs and games to assist in learning math or reading, there are applications that use the MIDI connection between your instrument and computer to help you learn different aspects of music. A music-reading program may display a note, chord, or passage on the screen; you play the displayed notes on the digital piano and the software keeps track of your accuracy and helps you improve. An ear-training application may play for you an interval that you then try to play yourself on the keyboard. The application will tell you what you did right or wrong and help you improve your ear. Other types teach music history and music theory. While many of these applications are geared to specific levels or ages, some can be set to multiple levels as you progress, or for use by multiple players.

Onboard Recording

Recording has been discussed above, in the "Computer Software" section. However, because nearly all digital pianos come with at least basic recording capability, it deserves a bit more attention. You may say that you have no intention of recording your music for others to hear, but in ignoring the instrument's ability to record what you've played, you may be overlooking one of the simplest ways of improving your playing. Whether you're just starting to play or are beginning to learn a new piece, being able to hear what you've just played is a learning accelerator.

I know what you're thinking: "I heard it while I was playing it." While most professional musicians have reached a level where they can effectively split their attention between the physical act of playing the instrument and the mental act of critically listening to what they're playing, few of the rest of us can do this. Recording and listening to yourself will reveal elements of your playing that you never noticed *while* you were playing, and will allow you to see where to make changes in your performance. This is even more useful when working with a teacher. Imagine listening with your teacher, music score in hand, and pausing the playback to discuss what you did in a particular measure. This is one of many reasons piano teachers are adding digital pianos to their studios; they're great learning tools.

One final thought on recording on the digital piano: Most manufacturers list recording capacity as a certain number of notes—typically in the thousands of notes. But not everyone is counting on the same number of fingers. Recall that MIDI records data "events," including note on, note velocity, note off, program change, control change, and a variety of others, many or all of which could have happened in conjunction with the playing of a single note. Each of these events consumes a certain amount of internal memory. Because this memory capacity is fixed, unless we know which events each manufacturer is counting as "notes," it's pointless to try to decide, based on these specifications, who offers more recording capacity. On the one hand, most instruments have more recording capacity than most owners will use. On the other hand, if recording capacity is important to you, this is another of the many areas in which simply buying the biggest numbers, or the most numbers for the dollar, is not a good strategy for selecting an instrument.

Automated Accompaniments, Chords, and Harmony— the Ensemble Piano

Some people, even some professional musicians, will tell you that using automated accompaniments—those rhythmic combinations of drums, bass lines, and chords—constitutes "cheating." This has never made sense to me. If I use a tool to do something that I couldn't possibly have done with my bare hands, am I cheating?

Whether or not a digital piano has these automatic features, frequently referred to as *styles*, is the primary factor that separates standard digital pianos from *ensemble* pianos. If your musical interest is focused solely on the classical piano repertoire, then this capability will probably be of no interest to you. If, however, you or someone in your household plays or plans to play a wide variety of musical styles, the ability to have backup instrumentalists at your beck and call is just entirely too much fun. No matter how good a player you may be, you can't be four people at once— or eight, or twelve, or an entire orchestra. These accompaniments are typically divided into groups by musical genre: Swing, Latin, Rock, World, and so on. The best of these styles are of a caliber that the best record producers would be proud of.

One thing to watch out for is the impact of automatic accompaniments on polyphony (see Part 1). Every bass line, drum beat, string sound, and guitar strum takes a toll on the number of simultaneous notes the instrument can produce. Thirty-two notes of polyphony can get used up in a big hurry when a complex style is playing in the background. If styles are important to you, look for higher polyphony numbers. Also, see if the instrument you're considering is capable of downloading additional styles, and how many styles are available for that model.

How do these styles "know" which key to use when playing all those chords and bass lines? In the simplest "single finger" settings, if the player needs an accompaniment style played in C, for example, she plays a C with the left hand. As chords change in the music, the player makes the appropriate change in the left hand to indicate what the accompaniment should play. Once the harmonies have been determined, the instrument can also apply them to the right hand by filling in the notes of the appropriate chord under the melody note. More sophisticated systems can decipher complex chords by evaluating all of the notes played on the keyboard, so that even advanced players can use the accompaniment styles without being held back from their normal style of playing.

All of this technology can make raw beginners sound as if they've been playing for years. While many players will progress beyond the simplest settings, other members of the family may continue using these playing aids for their own enjoyment.

Memory Presets

With the huge variety of voices, splits, layers, effects, and styles, it's handy to have a way to store favorite combinations. Many digital pianos come with a number of preprogrammed presets, and almost all of the more advanced models have programmable presets as well. These presets should be able to capture every possible setting on the instrument, from the obvious to the most obscure. Aside from the number of presets available, the placement of the preset buttons themselves can make a huge difference in their usefulness. Small, closely spaced, inconveniently placed presets might as well not be there—part of the pleasure of presets is not simply to instantly recall a setting that you've worked out in excruciating detail, but also to access that setting quickly and easily while playing. Even better is being able to assign preset changes to a seldom-used pedal (anything other than the sustain), so that each time you press the pedal, the instrument advances to the next preset. This can enable the creative player to step through sonic and rhythmic changes with ease while keeping his hands on the keyboard and distractions to a minimum.

Song Settings, Music Libraries, and Educational Tools

Many digital pianos are equipped with a list of *song presets*, a feature that goes by a variety of names depending on the brand of instrument. Like the memory presets described above, song presets incorporate all of the capabilities of that particular digital piano, but they work with particular songs. When you're new to the vast choices offered by some of the more advanced digital pianos, and unsure what sounds and styles to use for a song, these presets will set everything for you in a way suited to that song. Of course, this depends on the song you want to play being included in that instrument's song list in the first place. These lists range from a hundred or so built-in songs to downloadable databases containing thousands of songs, and the best of them accurately reflect the instrumentation, rhythms, and tempo (which you can slow down or speed up if necessary) of the original recordings. It's important to note that these song presets don't play the music for you; they just set up the instrument so that it will sound right when *you* play the music.

A related feature, but with a different purpose, is the *song library.*

Educational feature: A light indicates to the student which key should be pressed next.

Yamaha

A less expensive alternative is to use a keyboard display.

Casio

Once again, this feature goes by different names depending on the instrument's brand. Unlike the song presets, the song libraries *do* contain the actual music. In most cases these are from the classical piano repertoire and are recorded with the left- and right-hand parts on separate MIDI channels. They can be played with both hands turned on for listening or studying, or with only one hand turned on so the player can practice one hand's part while the instrument supplies the part for the other hand. In this way each part can be worked on separately, while both parts are heard. Although the tempo can be adjusted (for most of us, slowed way down), playing along with the other part keeps your tempo steady and your meter honest. Even without built-in libraries, an enormous amount of music has been recorded in this manner and can

be purchased—frequently with the printed notation—or downloaded free from the Internet.

Combinations of song libraries and computer-based educational software can be found on both entry-level and top-end instruments. These range from simple separation of left-hand/right-hand practice to complete lessons, tests, and tips on fingering. Some of the greatest aids to beginners are systems that combine the display of notation with visual cues as to which keys to play. Upper-end models use either lights aligned with each key, or movement of the key itself, to give the beginner a hand in correctly associating the note on the printed music with its key on the instrument. However, seeing which key to play, and actually playing it before the music has moved on, are two different things, and trying to do so can be a frustrating experience.

Some instruments make it easier to follow the light or key movements by waiting until the correct key is played before moving on to the next key. As a less expensive alternative, some lower-priced instruments show a small keyboard on the display with the required key indicated. While this still provides some guidance for the beginner, it's not nearly as easy to associate movements between the tiny keys in the display with the correct keys on the keyboard.

Other Controls

The ability to connect an accessory volume pedal is fairly common on upper-end and professional digital pianos. While the thought of a volume pedal attached to a piano may at first seem odd, it can actually add some interesting possibilities. Although it can be used to control the volume of the entire instrument, some models will allow you to select which aspects of the instrument are controlled by the pedal. One of my favorite ways to use the volume pedal is to layer an orchestral string voice with the piano voice and have the volume pedal control only the strings. This allows me to fade the strings in and out while the piano remains within its normal dynamic range.

While we're on the subject of pedals, it's worth noting that many instruments allow you to assign different functions to the standard piano pedals. As with the addition of the volume pedal above, this may initially strike you as a strange thing to do, but the presence of the non-piano voices can make sense of the situation. Some of the most common and handiest examples of

alternate functions for the less-used sostenuto and soft pedals are pitch bend, rotary-speaker speed control, and triggering rhythm breaks.

Pitch bend, as the name suggests, allows you to temporarily raise or lower the pitch of a note, then allow the note to slide back to its normal pitch. The most common setting is to have a pedal set to lower the pitch of a note by a half step (the very next note below), then allow the pitch to slide back up to normal when the pedal is released. Think of the opening clarinet line in Gershwin's *Rhapsody in Blue*—the trill leads to an ascending scale, and the player slides to the last note at the top of the scale. This effect is duplicated by depressing the pedal (set for pitch bend) and playing the upper note of the slide at the time you would have played the lower note. The pitch bend will cause the key for the upper note to instead play the lower note; then lift the pedal and you'll slide from the lower note to the upper one. It requires some practice, but isn't as difficult as it sounds.

Many instruments allow you to assign different functions to the standard piano pedals.

Setting a pedal for *rotary-speaker speed control* allows the digital piano player to duplicate the effect produced by the rotating baffle and horns of the classic Leslie speaker, typically used with "drawbar" or "jazz" organ sounds. One of the techniques used by players of this type of organ is switching between the slow Chorus rotation of the speaker and the fast Tremolo rotation. As this is done while playing, being able to tap a pedal to switch speeds makes the effect much easier to use.

One of the easiest and most useful pedal assignments is to trigger a *rhythm break*. The break is a brief variation in the rhythm or style in use

at the time. Once again, the ability to activate a feature without taking your hands off the keyboard makes use of that feature much more spontaneous.

Special controls usually found only on professional stage pianos are the *pitch bend* and *modulation wheels*. The pitch-bend wheel acts in the same way as the pitch bend described above, but with a dedicated control instead of a pedal. A number of different effects can be assigned to a modulation wheel, depending on the voice in use or the player's choice. The most common default setting is *vibrato*, a repeating pattern of up-and-down pitch variation around a note, such as the wavering sound in a singer's voice. The modulation wheel allows the player to control the amount of vibrato in real time while playing. This is particularly useful in creating additional realism with solo instrumental voices such as Saxophone, Violin, and Guitar.

Vocals

Many who love to play also love to sing, and the digital piano has something for vocalists as well. Many instruments now feature a microphone connection. In its most elementary form, this simply uses the digital piano's audio system as a PA for vocals. But some models throw the full weight of their considerable processing power behind the vocalist. Many vocal recordings and performances take advantage of effects processing to enhance the performer's voice. This can range from adding reverberation to effects that completely alter the performer's voice, making it sound like anything from Barry White to Betty Boop. Top-of-the-line digital pianos can even go beyond what some recording studios can do. Perhaps even more amazing is the ability of some instruments to combine the vocal input with their ability to harmonize, resulting in your voice coming out in four-part harmony. Display of karaoke lyrics is also common; the presence of a video output on some instruments allows the lyrics to be displayed on a TV or other monitor.

Moving Keys

When an acoustic player piano plays, the keys must move in order for the hammers to strike the strings and produce sound. The digital piano does not share this mechanical necessity, yet we now have digital pianos whose keys move when playing a recording. You'll recall from the section on recording that the digital piano can record and reproduce your playing, or can reproduce a MIDI file from another source. The sounds are produced by sending the playback data directly to the tone-production portion of the instrument, bypassing the keyboard. But since there is no dependency on moving keys, why go to the extra expense of making them move? Two reasons: First, it's one way for the instrument to direct beginners to the next melody note in the educational modes of some models, as described earlier under "Educational Tools." Second, it's just fun to watch. However, you should measure the value of this feature against the additional cost, and be mindful of the increased possibility of mechanical failure due to the additional moving parts of the key-drive mechanism.

Human Interface Design

The Man-Machine Interface, or MMI, as designers and engineers typically refer to it, defines how the player interacts with the instrument's controls. All of the amazing capabilities of the modern digital piano are of little value if the player can't figure out how to use them, or can't access them quickly while

playing. The considerations here are the location, spacing, grouping, size, shape, colors, and labeling of the controls. Take the example of the rhythm break discussed earlier. Its purpose is to alter the rhythm during playing. If the button that activates this feature is inconveniently located, small, and surrounded by closely spaced buttons of a similar size, shape, and/or color, its usefulness is severely limited. If, however, it's within easy reach of the keyboard, of decent size, and somewhat distinctive in appearance or markings, it becomes a useful tool.

In the case of instruments with displays, considerations include the size, resolution, and color capabilities of the screen and—more important—the logic behind its operation. Two types of screen interfaces are currently used on digital pianos: *touchscreens* and *softkeys*. Most readers are already familiar with touchscreens from ATMs and other modern institutional uses. The term *softkeys* doesn't refer to the feel of the keys, but to the fact that their functions are displayed on the adjacent screen, and change depending on the operation being displayed by the screen. This is as opposed to *hardkeys*, which have a single dedicated function. Each method has its proponents, but the interface type is less important than the MMI design. A smaller monochrome display that you can intuitively understand is better than a large color display that makes no sense to you.

Also worth considering is the placement of connections you'll use often. If you frequently switch back and forth between speakers and headphones, you'll want to make sure the headphone jack is easy to locate by sight or feel, and that the cord will be out of your way when plugged in. If you'll be using a USB memory device to transfer files between instruments or between the

instrument and a computer, make sure the USB port is easy to get to. In newer designs, a USB port is placed above the keyboard level for easy access, as opposed to earlier models in which the port was below the keyboard or on the instrument's rear panel.

We can't leave the subject of user interfaces without discussing the owner's manual. As with the MMI itself, a well-written manual can make it a pleasure to learn a new instrument, and a bad manual can be worse than useless. This is particularly important for higher-end instruments. Fortunately, many manufacturers allow you to download the manuals for their instruments. This lets you compare this critical aspect of the instruments you're considering. The manual should be thoroughly indexed, and clearly written and illustrated. Third-party tutorials are available for some instruments, especially the more complex models. These tutorials step you through the model's functions with audio or video instructions, and provide an alternative to sitting down with the manual.

Firmware Upgrades

The digital piano is, at heart, a highly specialized computer, and like all computers, its functions are dependent on its software. When we speak of the software that runs on the digital piano, we are typically talking about what is properly classified as *firmware*. Firmware is software that is embedded in a hardware device such as a microprocessor or associated memory chip. This can be done in two ways: the firmware can either be permanently burned into the chip, or it can be written in the chip's memory, which also means it can be rewritten if necessary. Just as computers occasionally need a software upgrade to fix

Sennheiser around-the-ear (circumaural) headphones

Shure in-ear, earbud-style headphones

Grado on-the-ear headphones

a previously undetected problem—a "bug patch"—the more complex digital pianos can benefit from the ability to accept firmware upgrades. This may never be necessary for a given model, or it may fix an obscure feature interaction or update the instrument's compatibility with external devices. In addition to checking on this capability, it's worth finding out how you would be notified of an update and what the actual update procedure involves. In most cases today, it's an easy, do-it-yourself procedure.

Headphones

Headphones are by far the most popular and frequently used digital-piano accessories. One of the advantages of digital pianos is the option to practice without disturbing others—or them disturbing you. Whether you're an occasional headphone user, or your instrument or situation dictates constant headphone use, selecting the right headphones will make a big difference in your playing comfort and enjoyment.

When I select headphones, I evaluate them using four criteria: fit, sound, isolation, and budget. Although it may seem that starting with sound is the obvious choice, my first priority is fit—it doesn't matter how great they sound if you can't stand to wear them for more than a few minutes. There are three basic styles of headphones: those that fit *around* the ear (circumaural) with the cushions resting on your head, those that rest directly *on* the ear, and those that fit *in* the ear. The style of headphone you choose will also determine the level of isolation. If isolation is critical for your situation, it should dictate the style of headphones.

There are a couple of variations on the circumaural and in-ear styles. Circumaural headphones can be open or sealed. Open designs don't cut you off from the outside world, and their output can be heard—very softly—by anyone nearby. Sealed designs offer more isolation but introduce some acoustic design problems that are difficult to get around until you get into the higher price ranges. In-ear headphones are available in the earbud style that sits in the outer ear, and the ear-canal type that fits inside the ear canal itself. The latter offers, by far, the best isolation in both directions, even when compared to headphones with active noise canceling.

Sound is very much a matter of personal preference and perception. One thing that can make the selection process easier is to bring a familiar CD with you when you audition headphones. While you may initially favor headphones that color the sound in some attractive way, this can become sonically tiring with extended listening. If you aim for a neutral sound, you'll end up with headphones that won't tire your ears over extended periods, and that will most accurately represent the sound produced by your digital piano or by the models you're considering.

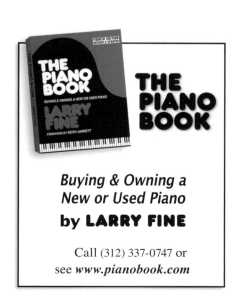

MENTION THE WORD *hybrid* today and most people think of cars that combine a traditional internal-combustion engine with an electric motor to improve gas mileage and reduce emissions. By definition, a hybrid—whether a rose, a breed of dog, or a car—results from the combination of two different backgrounds or technologies. Now the piano has joined the ranks of the hybrids.

A hybrid piano combines electronic, mechanical, and/or acoustical aspects of both acoustic and digital pianos, in order to improve or expand the capabilities of the instrument. While applying the term *hybrid* to piano designs is a recent development, the practice of combining elements from acoustic and digital pianos is more than 25 years old.

A hybrid piano can be created from either an acoustic or a digital piano, but we need to be clear about our definitions of *acoustic* and *digital*. The essential difference between acoustic and digital pianos is in how the sound is produced. In an acoustic piano, a sound is produced by the mechanical act of a hammer hitting strings, causing the strings to vibrate. In a digital piano, the sound is produced electronically, either from previously sampled acoustic pianos, or by physical modeling that employs a mathematical algorithm to produce sounds like those of an acoustic piano. (Here we're speaking only of that aspect of a digital piano that is designed to produce a piano-like sound. Digitals typically also can produce many other instrumental and non-instrumental sounds.)

Acoustic-based Hybrids: the MIDI Controller

On the acoustic side, the original hybrid instruments were not new pianos, but modifications of already existing pianos. In 1982, with the advent of Musical Instrument Digital Interface (MIDI), a computer language for musical instruments, instruments from different makers could "speak" to one another. Soon after, various kinds of mechanical contacts were invented for placement under the keys to sense keystroke information such as note, key velocity, and duration, and convert it into MIDI data. This MIDI information was then routed to synthesizers, which turned the information into whatever instrumental sounds the attached synthesizer was programmed to produce. When one instrument is used to control another in this manner through the transmission of MIDI information, the first instrument is called a MIDI controller. At the beginning, however, the sound of the acoustic piano could not be turned off, though it could be muffled in vertical pianos.

A hybrid results from the combination of two different technologies.

Early mechanical key contacts were subject to breakdown, or infiltration by dust, and their presence could sometimes be felt by sensitive players and interfere with their playing. The more advanced key contacts or sensors used today involve touch films or optical sensors that are more reliable and accurate, and add no significant weight to the touch. In time, also, mechanisms were invented for shutting off the acoustic piano sound entirely, either by blocking the hammers from hitting the strings, or by tripping (escaping) the action train of force earlier than normal, so that the hammers lacked the velocity needed to reach the strings. Headphones would block out any remaining mechanical noise, leaving only the sounds of the electronic instrument.

Not surprisingly, most makers of these MIDI controller/acoustic hybrid systems have been manufacturers of electronic player-piano systems. The same MIDI sensor strip used under the keys of these systems for their Record feature (which allows players to record their own playing for later playback) can also transmit the MIDI information to a digital sound source: either an internal source that comes with the piano (a *sound card*) or an external one, such as a synthesizer or a computer with appropriate software installed. All player-piano systems today allow, through MIDI control, for the accompaniment of the acoustic piano sound by digitally produced sound, be they other piano-like sounds, other instrumental sounds, or even entire orchestras.

In addition to the accompaniment function, it turns out that these hybrid systems in which the acoustic piano can be silenced potentially have another very practical function. If your playing is likely to meet with objections from neighbors or family, being able to silence the piano and then play as loudly as you want, while listening through headphones, can be very handy. Realizing this, the major player-piano manufacturers make the MIDI controller feature available—without the player piano—relatively inexpensively. These MIDI controllers include a MIDI sensor strip under the keys, or optical sensors for keys and hammers, but no hardware and electronics that would make the piano keys move on their own. Usually, these systems come with a "stop rail" or other mechanical device to prevent the hammers from hitting the strings, an internal digital sound source, and headphones. When you move a lever to stop the acoustic piano sound, you turn on the digital sound source, which is heard through the headphones. Yamaha calls this instrument Silent Piano; Kawai calls theirs AnyTime. PianoDisc calls their add-on system QuietTime; QRS's version is called SilentPNO.

Yamaha's **Silent Pianos** have sensors associated with their keys, hammers, and pedals that record their movements in MIDI format and output the information through a digital-piano sound chip to headphones or speakers, or to a computer for editing. With the addition of Yamaha's Silent System, the acoustic piano can be silenced and the instrument used as a digital piano with a real piano action.

Two new Silent Systems are now available. The SG2 system is available in the b1, b2, and b3 vertical models and the GB1K grand. This system offers a CFIIIS concert grand piano voice, nine additional voices, can record and playback MIDI files, and has USB capability to preserve recorded performances. The SH system, used in all other piano models, offers a piano voice that uses binaural sampling of the CFX concert grand, 18 additional voices, can record and play back MIDI and audio files, and has USB capability to preserve recorded performances. SH grand models also incorporate a QuickEscape mechanism that automatically adjusts the action when the Silent System is engaged so that the touch feels the same whether the piano is being played acoustically or in silent mode.

In 2014, Yamaha began offering its **TransAcoustic** piano series, with 48" vertical model U1TA and 5' 3" grand model GC1TA. Like the Silent Piano, the TransAcoustic (TA) is an acoustic piano that can also send digitally sampled sounds, including Yamaha's CFX Concert Grand samples, directly to headphones, sound systems, mixers, etc. The TransAcoustic differs from the Silent Piano in having two transducers attached to the piano's soundboard. The transducers convert the digital signal into an electromechanical impulse that sets the soundboard vibrating—literally turning the soundboard into a loudspeaker. The soundboard, strings, and case provide a natural acoustic resonance for the digital samples, which can be played at even the softest volumes without the use of headphones and, when combined with the piano's normal acoustic sound, can produce a more richly textured sound.

Kawai's silent/hybrid pianos, known as AnyTime (ATX), are part of its K series of vertical pianos. The K15-ATX2 (44") is a basic model; the more advanced K200-ATX2 (45") and K300-ATX2 (48") use the digital sound engine from Kawai's top-of-the-line CA-95 digital piano, as well as optical key and hammer sensors for the most sensitive control. The K300-AT2X also has a soundboard speaker system, similar in concept to that of Yamaha's TransAcoustic piano.

QuietTime, from PianoDisc, can mute an acoustic piano and let the user hear his or her performance through headphones via sampled sound. The **QuietTime MagicStar V5 S Series**, introduced in 2013, has a slimline control unit that includes a touchscreen and iDevice compatibility. It also supports all three pedals, has a port for a USB stick, and comes with 80 demo songs. The control-unit sound module contains 128 sampled instruments, including a full General MIDI (GM) sound set, as well as 11 popular instrument presets, such as piano with strings. It also includes a built-in, adjustable metronome. A MIDI key-sensor strip is installed under the keys, and a padded mute rail prevents the hammers from hitting the strings while retaining the motion and feel of the piano action. The mute rail is activated by moving a small lever under the keyboard, which also turns on the sampled sound. MagicStar comes with a control unit, power supply, MIDI cable, MIDI strip, pedal switches, headphones, and mute rail. When the piano is to be used as a MIDI controller only (i.e., with no sound module or with a separate sound module), the MIDI key-sensor strip can be purchased from PianoDisc separately as Pro-Scan, with or without the mute rail and headphones.

In late 2013, PianoDisc introduced another product in the Quiet-Time family: **ProRecord**. ProRecord uses fully optical, no-contact, high-speed key and pedal sensors to capture and record key and pedal movements. The system's sensitivity

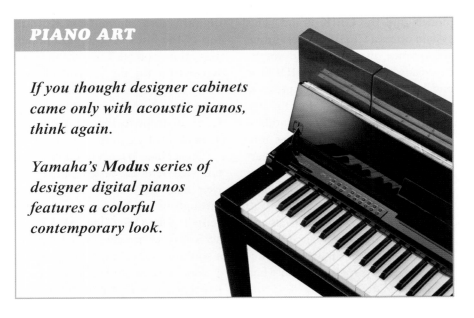
can be calibrated to a very fine level, allowing it to be customized to a particular piano action or player so that, for example, trills can be accurately reproduced when playing near the bottom or top of the key, even on a vertical piano. ProRecord comes with a tone generator with a GM2 128 + 100 instrument sound set and nine drum kits, including sympathetic string and damper resonance. The system is compatible with both Apple and Android smartphones, tablets, and apps, and with the PianoDisc iQ player-piano system. Like MagicStar, ProRecord comes with headphones, and a mute rail for muting the acoustic piano.

SilentPNO, from QRS, consists of the PNOscan record strip, a PNOmation II sound module, Wi-Fi adapter, and a stop rail for muting the acoustic piano. By muting the piano and turning on the soundcard, the pianist can play in privacy with headphones and enjoy the automatic recording features of PNOcloud and PNOmation, described in the article, "Buying an Electronic Player-Piano System."

But the accompaniment and "silent" functions of a hybrid MIDI controller/acoustic piano are only the beginning of what it can do. Just as the MIDI signal can be sent to a synthesizer or sound card, it can also be sent to a personal computer or transmitted over the Internet. Regardless of whether a MIDI controller originates in an acoustic or a digital piano, it enables the instrument to interact with music software to record, produce notation, control instrumental voices on a personal computer, or interact with other pianos in the same room or on different continents. The potential for hybrids in creating and teaching music is limited only by the imagination of the user. Notation softwares—from MakeMusic's Finale, Avid's Sibelius, GenieSoft's Overture, and others—allow the hybrid piano's key input (playing) to be converted to music notation. This notation can be edited, transposed, split into parts for different instruments, played back, and printed out. The possibilities for teaching are perhaps even more powerful.

Taking a lesson from a teacher in a different state or a master class from a performer in a different country becomes possible with hybrid technology, particularly when combined with the player-piano features. Exacting copies of performances can be sent to similarly equipped instruments for playback, and critiques—with musical examples—can be sent back to the student. Some systems enable this interaction in real time over broadband connections, complete with synchronized video.

As we've said, most of the activity in the field of acoustic hybrids has been among player-piano makers, whose offerings have been either specialized (Silent Piano) or add-ons (QuietTime, SilentPNO). However, MIDI capabilities are now standard in all acoustic pianos, vertical and grand, made by Story & Clark, a subsidiary of QRS, the only piano maker so far to have done this. If you add a stop rail to silence the piano (available from QRS) and a sound source, you could turn one of these instruments into a "silent" type of hybrid like those described above. But even without those additions, a Story & Clark piano can be used with a personal computer and music software for recording, notation, controlling computer-produced instrumental voices, or any of the myriad other uses possible with a MIDI controller.

All Story & Clark pianos come with a factory-installed PNOscan MIDI strip beneath the keys.

Digital-based Hybrids: Replicating the Acoustic Experience

Now, you may wonder: If you're just going to use a piano to interact with a computer, play piano sounds silently, or make other instrumental sounds, why bother with an acoustic piano at all? Why not just use a digital piano or keyboard of some kind? The reason is: the *experience*. Digital pianos are long on functionality but short on, shall we say, atmosphere. For those used to the looks, touch, tone, or other, less tangible aspects of acoustic pianos, digital pianos, in their "pure" form, just don't cut it—so digital piano makers have spent a great deal of time, energy, and money trying to mimic one or more of these aspects of acoustic pianos. The closer they get to duplicating the experience of playing an acoustic piano, the more they earn the right to the *hybrid* designation—because, when you get down to it, the function of an acoustic piano *is* the experience.

The first aspect of an acoustic piano that digital piano makers mimicked was, of course, the looks, and a large segment of the digital piano market consists of acoustic piano look-alikes. But that alone isn't enough to earn the title *hybrid*. Next, the mechanism of the acoustic piano found its way into the digital piano. Much engineering has gone into the numerous action designs in digitals, always in the attempt to make their feel and response as close as possible to that of a "real" piano. For example, Yamaha's GranTouch line of digital pianos uses a slightly modified acoustic piano action to trigger

> **Many digital piano actions these days have weighted and/or wooden keys, and other enhancements that do a reasonable job of emulating an acoustic piano action.**

the piano's sensors (the hammers are small and don't actually strike strings). With such an action, there's no need to simulate certain action processes, such as escapement, because it actually occurs mechanically. Many digital piano actions these days have weighted and/or wooden keys, and other enhancements that do a reasonable job of emulating an acoustic piano action; still, advanced pianists, especially classical ones, are unlikely to be satisfied by most of them.

Of course, digital piano makers have put more effort into copying the tone of the acoustic piano than any other aspect. How they've done this is beyond the scope of this article (see "Digital Piano Basics" for this information), but one interesting attempt is that of adding a soundboard to the digital. The Kawai CA-91, introduced in 2006, with its Soundboard Speaker System; and the Yamaha CGP-1000 Clavinova in 2007, with its Hybrid Active Soundboard System, both use an actual piano soundboard, set in motion by transducers, to augment the conventional speakers and impart a more natural tone to the instrument.

The latest entry in the hybrid arena is also the first instrument to be formally named a Hybrid Piano. Yamaha unveiled its Avant-Grand series in 2009. The Avant-Grand elevates the digital piano to a new level with a number of hybrid technologies, first of which is a real piano action. As mentioned above, this eliminates any discussion of whether or not it *feels* like an acoustic piano action—it *is* one. (However, whether or not the action feels *right* is still a legitimate topic of discussion.) This action controls the digital voices through the use of optical sensors, which measure the velocity of the keys and hammers without physically contacting any part of the action.

All three AvantGrand models have grand-piano actions, but whereas model N3 is also shaped like a grand, the cabinets of the lower-cost N1 and N2 are closer to that of a vertical piano (which brings up the interesting observation that the decision of whether to call a digital piano a "grand" or a "vertical" is not a simple one). In 2012, Yamaha introduced the model NU1 Hybrid Piano, the first digital piano with a real vertical-piano action.

One aspect of the traditional acoustic-vs.-digital argument that changes with the addition of a real action is the digital's advantage of rarely needing maintenance. While the AvantGrand and NU1 models will never need to be tuned, eventually their actions will require some degree of adjustment or regulation. (We'll bet the piano technician will be surprised when, on arriving to regulate an action, he or she finds the "piano" is a digital.)

But there's more to the feel of an acoustic piano than its action, and this brings us to the last attribute of acoustic pianos that designers of digitals have attempted to copy: the intangibles. With the AvantGrand, one "intangible"—the vibrations generated by the strings and transmitted throughout the instrument—has been made tangible. Yamaha has added this ingredient to the N2 and N3 by connecting transducers to the action to send the appropriate frequency and degree of vibration to the player's fingers. This is where the experience of playing becomes a bit . . . spooky. Not unlike an amusement-park ride that convinces your brain that you're dodging asteroids while hurtling through space when you are, in fact, fairly stationary, the AvantGrand's Tactile Response System quickly convinces you that you're feeling the vibrations of nonexistent strings.

The illusions don't stop there. When you depress a digital piano's sustain pedal, you're pressing a spring with constant tension. This is not how the sustain pedal feels on most acoustic pianos, in which the initial movement meets little resistance as the pedal takes up a bit of slack in the mechanism that lifts the dampers. Once the mechanism begins to lift the dampers, the resistance increases. Here again, the AvantGrand does a convincing job of conveying the feel and, perhaps more important, the degree of control available with an acoustic's sustain pedal, including half-pedaling and incremental control. The N3's four-channel sample set and 12-speaker audio system are also convincing, easily tricking the ears into thinking that considerably more than four feet of piano are in front of you. The AvantGrand and NU1 models all use samples from Yamaha concert grands for their sounds.

One area in which digital pianos are not intended to emulate acoustics is that of price. The Hybrid Pianos, with the sound and, in some cases, perhaps the experience, of a Yamaha concert grand, are priced similarly to some of the company's least expensive acoustic grands and verticals. Actually, such comparisons are barely possible—the acoustics lack many of the digitals' features, such as onboard recording, USB memory, transposition, and alternate tunings.

Which Side Are You On?

As the market for hybrid pianos heats up, buyers will increasingly have to choose between acoustic pianos with digital enhancements and digital pianos that try to create the acoustic experience. Decisions will be made by weighing the relative quality, and importance to the buyer, of action, tone, looks, price, and features. More advanced classical pianists whose digital needs are modest, and buyers who, among other things, are looking to fill up a living room with a large, impressive piece of furniture, will probably tend to stick with the acoustic-based hybrid for now. Those whose musical needs are more general, or who have a strong interest in digital features, may find digital-based hybrids more cost-effective.

Another factor that may come into play is that of life expectancy. A good acoustic piano will typically function well for 40 or 50 years, if not longer. Few digital pianos made 15 to 20 years ago are still in use, due either to technological obsolescence or to wear. True, the relevant technologies have evolved, as has the design of digital pianos and the quality of their construction. Realistically, however, if past experience is any guide, pianos that are largely acoustic with digital enhancement may well last for many decades, while those that are digitals enhanced with acoustic-like features are unlikely to last as long.

The piano has evolved a great deal since Bartolomeo Cristofori invented it in 1700, and that evolution continues. Today it is possible to buy a piano with an ABS-Carbon action (Kawai), a carbon-fiber soundboard (Steingraeber Phoenix), or one that looks as if it was made for the Starship *Enterprise*! The hybrid piano's blending of acoustic and digital technologies is just another step—or branch—in that evolution. 🎹

Yamaha AvantGrand model N3

BUYING AN ELECTRONIC PLAYER-PIANO SYSTEM

LARRY FINE

SOME OF YOU may have fond memories of gathering around Grandma's old upright player piano and pumping those huge pedals to make it play—until you could hardly walk! As with so many other devices, technology has revolutionized the player piano, replacing the pneumatic pressure and rolls of punched paper with electronics, CDs, and iPods. Today, nearly one out of every three new grand pianos is sold with an electronic player-piano system installed. The capabilities of these systems range from those that simply play the piano (often all that's desired for home use) all the way to those that allow composers to create, play, and print entire orchestral scores without ever leaving the piano bench. You can even watch a video of Billy Joel in concert on a screen built into your piano's music rack while, simultaneously, his "live" performance is faithfully reproduced on your piano! The features and technological capabilities are vast and still evolving.

Before you begin to wade through the possibilities, you should carefully consider your long-term needs. Since many of the features of the more sophisticated systems are related to recording one's performance, you should first decide whether or not you want the ability to record what you or others play on your piano. In many typical family situations, the piano, just like Grandma's, is primarily used for the children's lessons and for entertainment. If that's the case, one of the more basic systems, without recording capabilities, will likely be satisfactory. Most systems can be upgraded to add recording and other more advanced features, should you later find them desirable. However, as technologies advance, it may become increasingly difficult to upgrade your older system.

Some player systems can be added (retrofitted) to any new or used piano, while others are available only on a specific make of piano. When installed in a new piano, some must be installed by the piano manufacturer, while others can be installed by the dealer or at an intermediate distribution point. A factory-certified local installer of a retrofit can usually match the quality of a factory installation. Installation is messy and must be done in a shop, not in your home; but when done correctly, it won't harm the piano or void its warranty.

The player systems currently on the market can be described as falling into two categories: those intended primarily as home-entertainment systems or for lighter professional use (including commercial use in restaurants, hotels, etc.), and those whose play-back and recording functions are of "audiophile" quality and are intended for the most discriminating or high-level professional users. Generally speaking, the first category includes systems by PianoDisc, Pianoforce, QRS, and most Yamaha Disklaviers; the second category includes the Bösendorfer CEUS, Live Performance, and Disklavier Pro models. However, this classification scheme doesn't entirely do justice to "home entertainment" systems, which can be more sophisticated in other respects, such as versatility and functionality, than some "audiophile" systems.

The quality of a piano performance, either by a sophisticated electro-mechanical reproducing system or by a human being, greatly depends on the overall quality and condition of

The underside of a grand piano with solenoid rail (uncovered), power supply, and speaker installed.

QRS Music Technologies, Inc.

ELECTRONIC PLAYER SYSTEMS

HOW DO THESE THINGS MAKE THE PIANO PLAY?

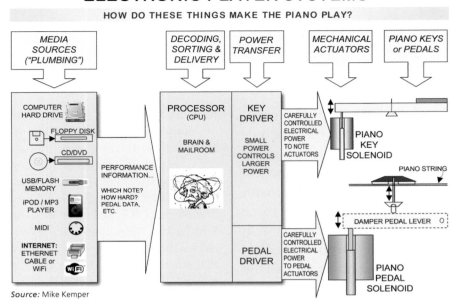

Source: Mike Kemper

the instrument being played. Thus, an out-of-tune and/or ill-voiced piano with a poorly regulated action would result in an unpleasant listening experience, whether played by human or machine. This, of course, emphasizes the importance of regular and proper maintenance of the instrument. With new pianos, the performance quality of the player-piano system is limited, to a large extent, by the performance quality of the piano itself. Don't scrimp on a piano to afford a player system.

How a Typical Electronic Player-Piano System Works

Basic player systems consist of:

- a solenoid (electromechanical actuator) rail installed in a slot cut in the piano keybed (the structural part of the piano that supports the keys and action)
- a processor unit and other electronics mounted under the piano
- a control box that plays floppy disks and/or CDs (depending on the model), and is either mounted under the keybed at the front of

the piano, or sits on or near the piano. In some models, the control box contains no disk drives and is hidden away under the piano, depending instead on your own CD player, MP3 player, or other device for the musical input.

- a remote-control device for operating the control box from a distance
- one or more amplified speakers, unless you choose a system config-uration that uses your own speakers

On the solenoid rail, there is one solenoid for each key. There is also a solenoid for the damper pedal and, sometimes, one for the una corda (soft) pedal. Each solenoid contains a mechanical plunger that, when activated by an electronic signal, pushes against a key or against the pedal trapwork. When playing compatible specialized software, one track contains the MIDI signal that drives the piano solenoids; the other tracks provide an instrumental and/or vocal accompaniment that plays through a stereo system or through

amplified speakers that come with the player system. The accompaniment may be in the form of synthesized or sampled sounds, or actual recordings of live musicians.

For recording, keystroke and pedaling information are recorded in MIDI format by a sensor strip installed beneath the keys and sensors attached to the pedals. Some systems also record hammer motion. This information can be stored for later playback on the same piano, stored on other media, or sent to other MIDI-compatible devices.

The same sensors used for recording can turn the piano into a MIDI controller. Add headphones, a device for mechanically silencing the acoustic piano, and a sound card or other tone generator, and you essentially have a hybrid acoustic/digital piano you can play late at night without disturbing anyone. Because this feature can be used independently of the player piano, most manufacturers of these systems make it available separately under such names as Silent Piano (Yamaha), Quiet-Time (PianoDisc), and SilentPNO (QRS). Of course, the MIDI controller can also be used with or without a tone generator to send a MIDI datastream to a computer for use with composing and editing software, among other applications. (See the article "Hybrid Pianos" in this issue for more information.)

Common Features

Basic player-piano systems share a number of features:

- playback of piano music with a good reproduction of the artist's performance
- playback of piano music with a full band, orchestral, and/or vocal accompaniment (yes, it will sing!)
- a repertoire of thousands of songs and the ability to download music from the Internet

- connectivity to home sound or home-theater systems
- remote control

Other capabilities, in a variety of applications, are considered valuable tools for composers, educators, and students, as well as performers. They include:

- a system of sensing key and pedal motions that can capture and record the nuances of a live performance for later playback or editing
- playing every instrument of the orchestra (and then some!), using the piano keyboard coupled with an onboard and/or outboard sound module
- the ability to import and export performances through a variety of wired/wireless connections, including MP3s, iPods, the Internet, etc.
- synchronizing a solo-piano performance on your piano with a commercially available CD or DVD of a famous performing artist
- Internet radio that streams data specifically formatted for the player system, for a virtually unlimited supply of musical input
- connectivity to a computer, facilitating music editing, enhancing, and printing
- connecting to teachers and other players anywhere in the world via the Internet

In addition to bundling some amount of music software with the purchase of their systems, most manufacturers record and separately sell software for their systems on floppies, CDs, or DVDs, or as downloads from a website. A significant caveat is that one manufacturer's software may—by design—not work unconditionally with another player's hardware.

Questions to Consider

To list and compare the wide variety of features and capabilities offered by each of the player systems would be beyond the scope of this article. However, the most significant concerns, aside from price, are the following. Ask your dealer or installer about the ones that interest or concern you.

- *Installation:* Can the system be installed in any piano (retrofit), or is it exclusive to a particular brand of piano? If exclusive, this will limit your options as to what brand of piano to buy.
- *Music Source:* Do you have a preference of source of music for the system: CDs, floppies, Internet downloads, iPod, MP3 player, etc.? This will influence your choice of system brand and configuration.
- *Recording:* Do you need recording capability, or the ability to use the system as a MIDI controller? This will also allow you to play silently with headphones, or to connect to a computer to edit and transcribe music, among other benefits.
- *Wireless:* Do you need to operate the system from a distance? Most systems have a wireless remote control available. Some can also be adapted for wireless transmission of music from the control box to the piano—for example, in a commercial establishment, where a CD player must be located some distance from the piano.
- *Visibility:* Is it important to you that the control unit not be visible or be very unobtrusive? Some models may be more suitable in this regard than others.
- *Equipment:* Do you need a system with a CD player, floppy disk drive, and/or iPod included, or will you be supplying your own? Do you need speakers or a video

monitor, or will you be connecting the system to your own stereo system or home theater?

- *Memory:* Do you need internal memory for data storage, or will you be using external data storage? Can external memory be connected?
- *Software Compatibility:* Can it play the music libraries of other manufacturers' systems? It's important to note, however, that because competitors sometimes change their formats and encryption, the ability to play the data format of a particular competitor's software may not be guaranteed.
- *Dynamic Resolution:* How many gradations of volume can the system record and play back? Most systems record and play back in 127 increments, which is more than sufficient for most uses. Some pre-recorded CDs play back with as little as 16 levels of expression—still probably enough for casual use, but you should test out the type of music you expect to listen to to see if it meets your musical expectations of dynamic range (gradations of loud and soft). A few systems can handle 1,000 or more increments. This may be desirable for high-level professional or recording applications, or for the most authentic playback of complex classical compositions. Likewise, some have higher processor speeds that scan the system a greater number of times per second for greater resolution. Some record by sensing only key movements, while others, for greater accuracy, also sense hammershank movements.
- *How many notes play back?* Some systems provide playback support for all 88 notes, while others come standard with as few as 80 solenoids (the highest and lowest

four notes are not supported), with 88 as an option. The reason for providing only 80 is that installing more than that number sometimes requires removing some wood from the top of the piano legs to accommodate the extra solenoids. This is not visible and doesn't harm the piano, but may not be desired by some customers. Most available music software will play just fine on 80 notes. But if you're planning to record yourself and use the notes at the extremes of the keyboard, or if you know you'll be playing back music recorded elsewhere that uses all 88 notes, you'll want the system to be able to play them. If that's the case, be sure to let the dealer or installer know.

- **Pedals:** Which pedals are played by hardware (solenoids) and which, if any, are mimicked by software? Hardware provides a more authentic piano performance, but duplication of pedal functions by software is simpler. Most important is hardware support for the sustain (damper) pedal, and all systems currently provide that. Only a few also provide hardware for the soft pedal (less important), and fewer still for the sostenuto (middle) pedal (unimportant).

- **Damper Pedal Performance:** Does it record multiple damper-pedal positions, allowing for pedaling techniques such as "half-pedaling," or does it simply record an "on" or "off" position? As with dynamic resolution, the recording and playback of multiple pedal positions is desirable for an authentic performance experience. The on/off mode is sufficient for very casual or simple uses.

- **Pedal Functionality:** Some add-on (retrofit) systems, when installed, may alter the functionality or feel of the pedals, especially the middle pedal. If possible, try playing a piano on which a similar player system is installed to see if the pedal operation is okay for you. If only the middle pedal is affected, it might not matter to you, because this pedal is rarely used.

- **Playing Softly:** How well does the system play softly without skipping notes and without excessive mechanical noise? This is especially important if you plan to use the player piano for soft background music. If so, be sure to try out the system at a low volume level to be sure it meets your expectations.

- **Music Software:** How well does the available music software satisfy your needs?

- **Options:** What special features, advantages, and benefits are included or are optionally available? Examples include the ability to synchronize the piano with commercially available CDs and DVDs, features used for teaching purposes, built-in video monitor, subscriptions to Internet music libraries or streaming radio that make available virtually unlimited input to your piano, bundled music software, and so forth.

- **Upgradability:** To what extent is the system upgradable? Most systems are highly upgradable, but the upgradability of some entry-level systems may be limited.

How Much Player-Piano Systems Cost

The cost of electronic player-piano systems varies enormously, not only from one system to the next, but even for the same system, depending on where it is installed and other factors.

A dealer has several ways of acquiring an add-on (retrofit) player system, which can affect the price at which the system is sold. Factory-installed systems—installed while the piano itself is being manufactured—are the least expensive for the dealer to acquire. Several large piano manufacturers are authorized to do this. In addition, the companies that make the player systems may factory-install them into brands that they own; for example, QRS Pianomation into the Story & Clark brand, and PianoDisc into the Mason & Hamlin brand. When installed this way, the difference in price between the piano alone and the piano plus player system may be quite moderate. The next more expensive options are when the player system is installed at an intermediate distribution point before reaching the dealer, or when a larger dealer, in his own shop, installs a system in a piano already on the showroom floor—with most brands of piano, either of these can be done. More expensive yet is when the smaller dealer must hire a local independent installer to install a system in a piano that is on the dealer's showroom floor. The most expensive option is to have a system installed in a piano you already own. In that situation you also incur the expense of having the piano moved to and from the installer's shop. The resulting retail price of the most expensive option can be double that of the least.

The cost can also vary because player systems are often used by dealers as an incentive to buy the piano. The dealer will charge well for an expensive piano, then "throw in" the player system at cost. Or vice versa—the dealer lets the piano go cheaply, then makes it up by charging list price for the system. The more modular systems can also vary in price, according to which options and accessories the dealer includes.

For all these reasons, quoting prices for player systems without knowing the context in which they're installed and sold is nearly futile. Nevertheless, as a rule of thumb, one of the more popular, typically configured, factory-installed QRS or PianoDisc systems with playback and accompaniment might add $5,000 to $6,000 to the street price of the piano, with recording capability adding another $1,500 or so. However, for the reasons given above, prices 30 percent lower or higher aren't unusual. A list of electronic player-piano add-on systems and their manufacturers' suggested retail prices follows the "Model & Pricing Guide" in this publication.

As for systems available only as factory installations, Yamaha Disklavier grands generally cost $8,000 to $20,000 (street price) more than the same Yamaha model without the player system. At the high end, a Bösendorfer CEUS will set you back $50,000 to $60,000 (street price). The retail prices of these systems are included under their companies' listings in the "Model & Pricing Guide."

THE SYSTEMS

BÖSENDORFER CEUS

Yamaha Corporation of America
P.O. Box 6600
Buena Park, California 90622
714-522-9415
info@boesendorferus.com
www.boesendorfer.com

Bösendorfer's SE Reproducer System, out of production for a number of years, has been replaced by an all-new design called CEUS (Create Emotions with Unique Sound), with updated electronics and solenoids. The visual display is discreetly located on the fallboard and is wireless, so the fallboard can be removed for servicing the piano without the need to disconnect any wires. Player controls for recording, playback, and data transfer are by means of a combination of keystrokes on the sharp keys aligned with the fallboard display, pedal movements, and four small, brass, touch-sensitive buttons on the left side of the fallboard. When the system is inactive, these four brass buttons are the only evidence that the CEUS system is installed in the piano. Optical sensors measure key and hammer movements at an extremely high sampling rate, for maximum accuracy and sensitivity to musical nuance. Bösendorfer has a library of recordings for CEUS, and the system will also play standard MIDI piano files. CEUS is available in every Bösendorfer grand model from 170 to 290 (but not 155), and adds about $95,000 to the piano's list price.

PIANODISC

PianoDisc
4111 North Freeway Blvd.
Sacramento, California 95834
916-567-9999
www.pianodisc.com

PianoDisc makes retrofit player-piano and performance-capturing systems, including a newly released optical recording system, that can be added to virtually any acoustic piano—grand or vertical, new or used—and even some digital pianos. Pianos fitted with PianoDisc systems maintain full functionality of all pedals, and playback (and optional record) of all 88 notes. Piano manufacturers offer factory-installed PianoDisc products, and piano dealers in over 60 countries have installations done at their locations by trained and certified PianoDisc technicians.

PianoDisc's principal player-piano system is called **iQ**. The core technology of the iQ system, hidden within the piano body, can play back PianoDisc music using, as a source, almost any media player. The most popular configuration is the iQ iPad Air bundled with an Apple iPad and Airport Express for wireless control. With iQ, customers can operate all functions of the system from a single, familiar source that also allows them to take advantage of hundreds of apps (offered through Apple's App Store and Google Play)

The black keys aligned with the fallboard display are among the controls used to operate the Bösendorfer CEUS.

for additional enhancement and enjoyment. Unique within the industry, iQ features a patented method of detecting adjustments made in the volume of the music player to automatically match the piano's volume to it. Each PianoDisc system includes a free package of music and video software valued at $1,400, and a set of five CDs of the customer's choice from the PianoDisc catalog.

PianoDisc's high-resolution solenoid system, **SilentDrive HD**, is standard equipment on all current PianoDisc player systems. Each key's solenoid recognizes 1,024 levels of expression. SilentDrive HD offers quiet playback of original piano performances, and features a faster processor and streamlined architecture that improve timing, velocity, and dynamics. The ProPedal proportional pedal feature, introduced in 2013, is a low-profile, invisible pedal-drive system that uses the piano's original pedal trapwork without any modification of the piano's profile or operation.

Also introduced in 2013 was the new YouTube channel **PianoTube LIVE**. It delivers, to the customer's home or commercial establishment, high-quality HD videos of live concerts, piano performances, and even multi-instrument/vocal recordings or albums synchronized to a customer's own piano. Using the PianoTube LIVE smartphone app, customers can easily record and upload their own video performances directly to YouTube, which can then stream and play PianoDisc-equipped pianos "live" all around the world without requiring the substantial bandwidth needed by some other systems. Compatible with player systems equipped with iQ technology, this exclusive PianoDisc channel is designed to enhance the PianoDisc experience by integrating it into social media and remote education networks.

Music Store, also introduced in 2013, has replaced MusiConnect as a simpler, more user-friendly way to buy and download music from the PianoDisc website. The new process includes a downloadable format that delivers compressed (Zipped) MP3 files directly to a computer. Other formats available for purchase include CD, floppy disk, and SD card. The new, streamlined process also includes pre-synced performances for the PianoDisc original-album genre PianoSync.

Beginning in the second quarter of 2014, PianoDisc customers will be able to use the latest Android technologies, in addition to Apple and other smart devices, to stream audio music and videos directly from PianoDisc's vast library to their pianos, using a custom PianoDisc app or a media player such as Avia or DoubleTwist. In addition, customers will be able to purchase and play digitally delivered content directly from a smart device in a simple one-step process. With Android integration, customers can also project the synchronized videos using Google's Chromecast.

PianoDisc's live, free, streaming piano radio network, available 24/7 to all iQ-based systems, can play a customer's piano directly. PianoDisc expects to soon add more stations with a greater variety of music programming. This service should be of special interest to hotels, restaurants, and other businesses that use PianoDisc to provide their customers with nonstop, royalty-free entertainment.

The **PianoDisc Remote** app is a utility for the iQ system with many custom features. Although piano and audio balance can be adjusted with the iQ Audio Balance Control, PianoDisc Remote lets users further customize the volume levels and balance of the piano and audio accompaniment, and to fine-tune their

iQ Flash, an entry-level system, is the latest addition to the PianoDisc line.

synchronization. Revamped with new features for 2014, this app is now available at a lower price ($24.99) through the Apple App Store.

iQ Flash, an entry-level system, is another addition to the PianoDisc line. Basic operation is accomplished by playing PianoDisc MP3 or MIDI files from USB, SD, or MMC flash memory. All functions can be accessed either from the included remote control or via a few multifunction buttons on the face of the iQ Flash control box. Audio and piano balance controls are easily adjusted with the wheel next to the SD slot. An easy-to-read, high-contrast, backlit LCD display allows the user to view and make song selections, and to use the Repeat and Shuffle features. Incorporating the Studio Performance package into iQ Flash allows players to capture performances as MP3 files on their preferred media-storage devices. With an additional mixer and a powered microphone, vocals can be added to the recording.

AlwaysPlay allows the user to import any MIDI file and play it back on the piano, even if the original recording contains no piano part. AlwaysPlay recognizes the lead instrument (guitar, organ, flute, etc.) and substitutes the piano for it.

For use with its systems, PianoDisc maintains a growing library of thousands of music titles available as digital downloads, CDs, DVDs, and high-definition Blu-ray discs. The library includes solo-piano performances by famous artists, piano with instrumental accompaniment (most of these are live recordings), and vocals in 28 different categories. PianoDisc has recently introduced over a dozen famous Chinese albums, including folk, popular, traditional, and classical Chinese music.

PianoSync is a MIDI-controlled piano performance that synchronizes with a commercially available audio CD of a major recording artist. PianoSync albums are purchased from PianoDisc's website as downloads or CDs. (The purchase includes the original artist's CD.) When the buyer plays the merged file on the PianoDisc system, the original CD recording is heard, along with its new, live piano accompaniment.

PianoVideo HD, the first high-definition video format created specifically for modern player-piano systems, combines MIDI, audio, and video. The PianoVideo HD technology gives PianoDisc owners the ultimate entertainment experience: as they watch a high-definition video, their piano will play along with it live, in sync with the pianist on screen. PianoVideo HD performances come on standard-definition DVD or Blu-ray discs.

PIANOFORCE

Pianoforce Inc., U.S.A.
115 South Ohio
Sedalia, Missouri 65301
877-542-8807
sales@pianoforce.us
www.pianoforce.com

Pianoforce is a relatively new entrant in the player-piano market under its own name, but the company that makes it—formerly Ncode Ltd., now Pianoforce EU, of Bratislava, Slovakia—has been developing and manufacturing front-end controllers for the player-piano systems of other companies, such as Baldwin and QRS, since 1995. In 2005, Pianoforce was first offered as a complete system in the pianos of selected piano makers. In 2006, it was introduced as a kit retrofittable to any piano, new or old. Designed and built by Pianoforce in Europe, the kit is ordered through a piano dealer, and is typically installed in a new piano at a distribution point or at the dealer location.

Pianoforce says that its system differs from those of its competitors in that the main rail component also contains all the controlling electronics, eliminating the need for a lot of complicated wiring and making for a neater, simpler installation. Also, a technician using the remote handset can customize the system to the piano and to the customer's preferences through the adjustment of many playing parameters, such as solenoid force, note release, and pedal release. These custom settings can then be saved in the controller. With the help of a small sensor mounted on the soundboard, the system automatically calibrates itself to the piano's sound. The combination of automatic calibration and manual setup ensures the best playback performance for each individual piano.

In 2007 Pianoforce introduced its latest controller, the Performance. Expanding on the company's past experience in supplying control components for other manufacturers, the new controller contains some of the newest, most advanced features available in a player piano, such as the ability to read the softwares of other systems—including Yamaha Disklavier, QRS (except SyncAlong), and Web Only Piano—plus standard MIDI files; and onboard connections to the Internet via an Ethernet or wireless hookup. There are three USB ports for greater versatility, such as plugging in flash drives or an external hard drive. There is an optical digital stereo output and a dedicated subwoofer output line. The system can now be controlled remotely, via WiFi, with the user's Android or Apple device, and Internet streaming radio is available 24/7 with piano accompanied by original audio tracks.

More recently, Pianoforce has introduced the Stealth Performer controller, which allows the controller to be hidden away, out of sight. With WiFi remote control, all of the functionality of the original Performance controller is available, but no hardware is visible on the front of the piano.

The system comes with 2GB of internal memory (expandable to 8GB), preloaded with approximately 20 hours of piano music.

KEESCAN, an optional recording feature, uses optical sensors to record key and sustain-pedal movements. Also available is the AMI box, which facilitates connection of a microphone, iPod, and other USB devices. In addition to the system's ability to play other makers' softwares, Pianoforce is building its own library of CDs.

SilentPlay, Pianoforce's newest feature, combines KEESCAN, the new SP1 sound module, and a special muting rail to permit silent play of the customer's vertical piano, while giving the performer unparalleled digital sound through headphones or speakers. Connection to a computer gives a composer complete control over his or her compositions, from editing individual notes to saving new music for later replay.

Pianoforce has offices in Europe (Pianoforce Europe) and the U.S. (Pianoforce Inc., U.S.A.); branches in Austria, Germany, Portugal, Spain, Switzerland, and the U.K.; and is represented in Australia, China, Hong Kong, and Macao.

QRS PNOmation

QRS Music Technologies, Inc.
269 Quaker Drive
Seneca, Pennsylvania 16346
800-247-6557
www.qrsmusic.com

PNOmation is an electronic player-piano system that can be installed in virtually any piano, grand or vertical, new or used. Most manufacturers endorse the PNOmation system, and will install it, at a dealer's request, at one of their manufacturing or distribution points. QRS installs the system in many major brands of piano at its own U.S. factory, and it can also be installed at a dealer location by a QRS-trained technician.

Traditionally, electronic player pianos have been defined by the type of control box at the front of the piano, or by the controller's capabilities. PNOmation differs in integrating the core features of every controller, including the music, into the PNOmation engine, thereby eliminating confusing options as well as the need to have a box hanging under the piano. Instead of offering a modular approach to the equipment required for various features, PNOmation offers all features standard, and a modular approach to their use. For example, the user can log in to the PNOmation system through any web-enabled device, pull up the system's embedded web-app user interface, and begin to play the piano; or, for those who are more comfortable with inserting their music selections into the device, music can be delivered via a USB thumb key; then you need only push Play on the system's remote control, or the Play button on the unit itself.

Key to PNOmation's flexibility is the fact that it is delivered in a stand-alone-network mode, with its own network serving its own user interface, or web app. The big advantage of this approach is that a web app gives the user full control of all parameters of the

The QRS PNOmation web app gives the user full control of all parameters of the system and how music is played.

QRS Music Technologies, Inc.

system and how music is played. Some customers are concerned only with whether a song is a solo performance or a performance with background music, which they can determine from the web-app screen. Other customers may want to manipulate a MIDI file to change the tempo or tuning, and some may want to upload a recorded performance to view or change. None of this is possible with an off-the-shelf MP3 playback engine, but all of it is easily done with QRS's PNOmation web app.

The web app also offers the customer several new control capabilities over the PNOmation engine, including controlled release of the sustain pedal, to give it a soft landing and eliminate the potential thump heard with the release of the damper tray. The same controlled-release technology has also been applied to the keys, improving the PNOmation's already quiet playback while adding much more lifelike fingering. Other features include trill timing compensation, delay compensation, pitch correction, and MIDI-output curve maps. While most customers will use the default settings, those who want to

dial in the perfect performance will be able to do so.

All of the data that controls the movements of the piano keys and pedals is in a non-compressed MIDI format (a high-definition MIDI format will soon be released). All music available for the new PNOmation—currently over 6,300 tracks and growing—can be purchased one song at a time or by the album, using a subscription or credits, giving listeners great flexibility in hearing what they want to hear.

While not required, connecting PNOmation to a home network is easy to do. As a device on a home network, a PNOmation-equipped piano can be updated and/or controlled remotely via the Internet by accessing the web-app user interface via iPhone, iPad, iTouch, Android, Mac, Google Chrome browser, Kindle Fire, or any other similar piece of technology.

SyncAlong is a patented means of delivering music, whereby a MIDI-controlled piano performance plays along with a commercially available audio MP3 of a major recording artist. SyncAlong allows the listener to hear the original artist's content while the piano plays along. **Qsync** is a DVD interface designed to implement QRS's patented DVD SyncAlong technology. With the addition of Qsync, a PNOmation player piano will be able to play along with selected popular, commercially available concert DVDs.

PNOmation can also be integrated with the **PNOscan** optical sensor strip, a leading technology for recording performances on an acoustic piano that is standard on all Story & Clark pianos. The PNOscan strip doesn't touch the keys, using only reflected light to continuously measure key and pedal movements. By integrating PNOscan with PNOmation in a one-time setup operation, one need only play the piano and the piece is recorded—no login, no need to push Record or Stop. Just pull up a bench and play, and your performance is saved both locally (named according to your preset preferences) and uploaded to your personal QRS PNOcloud account. The file can also be sent to your favorite editing program or e-mailed to a friend—all without boxes or wires.

YAMAHA DISKLAVIER

Yamaha Corporation of America
P.O. Box 6600
Buena Park, California 90622
714-522-9011
800-854-1569
infostation@yamaha.com
www.yamaha.com

Disklaviers are Yamaha (and now Bösendorfer) pianos that have been outfitted with an electronic player-piano system. These mechanisms are installed only in new Yamahas and the Bösendorfer model 200, and only at the Yamaha and Bösendorfer factories. They cannot be retrofitted into older Yamahas or any other brand.

Disklavier differs from most after-market systems in that Disklavier is not modular. Whatever Disklavier features come with a particular model of piano are what you get (although software upgrades are possible). The sophistication of the key, hammer, and pedal sensing also varies, depending on which Disklavier version is associated with that particular piano model. For a number of years, the Mark IV was the standard Disklavier version in the U.S. It has now been replaced by the E3.

Some of the highlights of the **E3 Disklavier** include:

- CD drive (floppy drive optional)
- flash memory
- infrared remote control
- built-in Ethernet for connecting to your network and downloading MIDI files
- grayscale (continuous) hammershank sensors for more

The control box on the Yamaha E3 Disklavier.

sensitive recording capabilities (except models DU1E3, DGB1KE3, and DGB1KE3C)
- XG tone generator with hundreds of synthesized and sampled sounds
- built-in speaker system (except model DU1E3)
- two-track recording capabilities
- Silent System (except models DU1E3, DGB1KE3, and DGB1KE3C): consists of Silent Mode (silences the acoustic piano for listening through headphones), Quiet Mode (silences the acoustic piano and directs the sound to speakers), Quick Escape Action (maintains correct action regulation when using Silent Mode or Quiet Mode), headphones, and a dedicated digital-piano sound chip.
- SmartKey: a teaching device
- CueTime: a smart accompaniment feature
- PianoSmart Audio Synchronization: the ability to link a piano track in MIDI format with selected popular CDs on the general market for synchronized playback
- Video Sync: videotape a piano performance and the Disklavier will play the performance perfectly on the piano whenever you play the video of the performance
- Disklavier Radio: a group of streaming MIDI music stations, available by subscription

- Disklavier TV: streaming performances (both live and on-demand) that include video, audio, and MIDI, all perfectly synchronized, available by subscription
- can be controlled via any Apple iDevice
- can play more softly than previous Disklavier systems without missing notes

The E3 Disklavier is available on the 48" U1 upright, and on all Yamaha grands except models CF4 and CF6. The version available for grands 6' 1" and larger is the E3PRO, which has higher internal recording resolution and a greater dynamic range than the regular E3.

As noted above, the version available on the U1 and on 5' grand model DGB1K has limited functionality—key sensors only, and no Silent System (and no speakers on the U1). In addition, a lower-cost, Classic version of the E3 is available only on the model GB1K. Although this model provides the same range of damper effects as a standard Disklavier, they are accomplished by acting directly on the damper action inside the piano, without physically moving the piano's pedals. This model also has only one MSP3 speaker (most other Disklavier models have two), and comes with a lower-cost bench.

(Note: No longer made, but still on dealers' showroom floors, the models DGC1ME3, DGC2E3, DC1E3, and DC2E3 have no hammer sensors and no Silent System.)

Owners of Mark IIXG and Mark III systems can access many of the advanced features found in the E3 system by purchasing replacement control unit DKC-850.

For simple playback, most player-piano systems now on the market are probably equally recommended. The Disklavier, however, has a slight edge in reliability, and its recording system is more sophisticated than most of the others, especially in the larger grands. For this reason, it is often the system of choice for professional applications such as performance and teaching, and much of Yamaha's marketing efforts are directed at that audience.

Two examples are especially noteworthy. Yamaha supports the Minnesota International e-Competition, in which contestants gather in several cities and play Disklavier concert grands. Their performances are recorded using Video Sync, then sent to judges in another location, who, rather than listen to recordings, watch and listen to the music reproduced perfectly on other Disklavier pianos.

A similar concept is a technology called Remote Lesson, which debuted in spring 2010 after years of development and testing. A student takes a lesson on one Disklavier while a teacher located far away teaches and critiques on a second Disklavier connected via the Internet, student and teacher communicating with each other in real time via video-conferencing. Initially, this feature will be made available only to selected universities and at additional cost. Details and timing regarding availability of this feature to individuals is still under discussion.

Yamaha's latest Disklavier offering is Disklavier TV, which uses RemoteLive technology. Disklavier TV makes it possible for Mark IV or E3 Disklavier owners to receive video, audio, and piano data in perfect sync, so they can receive concerts in their home with their Disklavier playing the piano part in sync with the rest of the concert. During the 2013 NAMM trade show, Yamaha used this technology to hold a major concert in which Elton John was broadcast live, playing Disklavier pianos in many different countries simultaneously, in perfect sync with program audio and video.

Yamaha maintains a large and growing library of music for the Disklavier, including piano solo, piano with recorded "live" accompaniment, piano with digital instrumental accompaniment, and PianoSmart arrangements. The system will also play standard MIDI files types 0 and 1. 🎹

Mike Kemper, a Los Angeles-based piano technician and expert on electronic player-piano systems, contributed to this article.

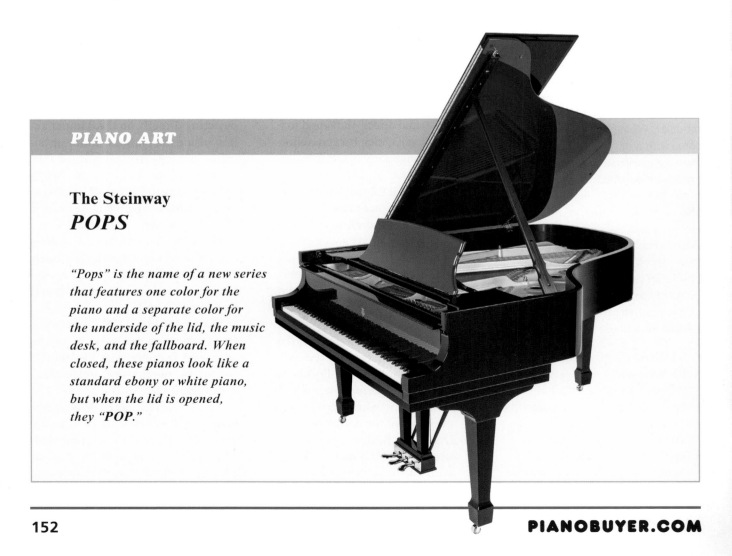

PIANO ART

The Steinway
POPS

"Pops" is the name of a new series that features one color for the piano and a separate color for the underside of the lid, the music desk, and the fallboard. When closed, these pianos look like a standard ebony or white piano, but when the lid is opened, they "POP."

Your Living Room Becomes the Artist's Stage!

One of the Disklavier's greatest features is the exclusive ability to transport you to the front row of concerts thousands of miles away without ever leaving your living room! DisklavierTV™ perfectly synchronizes video and audio with MIDI data streaming over the Internet so you can watch a musician perform **LIVE** on TV while actually playing YOUR piano!

Not only does DisklavierTV bring you live events, it also features hundreds of **ON DEMAND** single song selections that you can watch and listen to when it's convenient for you. Furthermore, Yamaha also offers frequent **WEEKEND ON DEMAND** broadcasts—available for weekends at a time, these include full length performances from major events and Yamaha artists.

Begin enjoying all the capabilities of your Disklavier by subscribing to DisklavierTV now! Simply visit www.4wrd.it/dtvadpb and sign up for a low-cost monthly or annual subscription!

Enjoy **LIVE** events, like the Monterey Jazz Festival.

Watch and listen to performers **ON DEMAND**.

See concerts each **WEEKEND ON DEMAND**.

 **YAMAHA**    disklavier ::::: T V :::::

THIS SECTION contains brief descriptions of most brands of new piano distributed nationwide in the United States. Brands that are associated with only a single dealer, or otherwise have marginal distribution, are omitted unless I believe them to be significant in some respect. These profiles contain, sometimes verbatim, material from the fourth edition of *The Piano Book* where still relevant and accurate, accumulated changes from past *Supplements*, and new material gleaned from interviews with manufacturers and industry professionals. The contact information listed for each brand is that of the brand's U.S. distributor, or of the manufacturer itself if there is no separate U.S. distributor. Most manufacturers had an opportunity to see, comment on, and correct for factual accuracy the descriptions of their products. To keep the size manageable, however, much historical and technical information was abbreviated or omitted, including information on older, discontinued models, and on problems and defects that have long since been rectified. Although the information in this publication will usually be sufficient to help guide you in purchasing a new piano, you may wish, at your leisure, to peruse *The Piano Book* for additional commentary on the brands you're considering. Just be aware that, particularly where it conflicts with information in this publication, *The Piano Book* may no longer be accurate. In most cases, brands included in *The Piano Book* but not here, are either out of business or no longer distributed in the United States.

As in *The Piano Book*, the articles here are a bit quirky—that is, they vary in length, and in the thoroughness with which they treat their subjects. Some companies have more interesting histories, some instruments have more unusual technical features, some brands have more controversial issues associated with them, and some manufacturers were more helpful than others in providing access to interesting material. The comments are more descriptive than evaluative. For a "road map" depicting how I think the piano industry views the different brands relative to one another, see the article "**The New-Piano Market Today.**"

Note: Electronic player-piano systems are covered in "**Buying an Electronic Player-Piano System**," elsewhere in this issue.

ALTENBURG, OTTO

Wyman Piano Company
P.O. Box 506
Colusa, California 95932
908-351-2000
info@wymanpiano.com
www.altenburgpiano.com

Pianos made by: Beijing Hsinghai Piano Group, Ltd., Beijing, China

This is the house brand of Altenburg Piano House, a New Jersey piano retailer in business for over 150 years, at one time as a manufacturer. This brand is sold via the Internet and through other dealers, in addition to the company's own stores. For many years, Otto Altenburg pianos have been made by Samick in Korea or Indonesia, though sometimes to musical and cabinet designs different from Samick's own. More recently, Altenburg has engaged the Beijing Hsinghai Piano Group in China to make a new line of pianos, some of which are exclusive to Altenburg, with individually hitched strings. The Beijing models are the ones shown in the Model & Pricing Guide of this issue. Grand models up to 5' 3" use a laminated soundboard, larger models use solid spruce.

Warranty: 12 years, parts and labor, transferable to future owners within the warranty period.

ASTIN-WEIGHT

Astin-Weight Piano Makers
P.O. Box 65281
Salt Lake City, Utah 84165
801-487-0641
astinweight@yahoo.com

Astin-Weight pianos have been made in Salt Lake City since 1959. The company continues to engage in limited production at several temporary locations due to storm damage at the factory. Most sales are made directly to consumers by the manufacturer at a steep discount.

Astin-Weight vertical pianos, 50" in height, are unusual from a technical standpoint because they have no backposts, instead relying on a massive full-perimeter plate; and also because the soundboard takes up the entire back of the piano, behind the pinblock, resulting in a much greater volume of sound than from a conventional piano (see *The Piano Book* for an illustration of this feature). Many of the cabinet finishes are simple, hand-rubbed oil finishes. The 41" console has been discontinued.

The Astin-Weight 5' 9" grand is produced in very limited quantities. It has an unusual symmetrical shape and is hinged on the treble side instead of the bass. The company says this shape allows for much longer strings and a greater soundboard area.

Warranty: 25 years, parts and labor.

BALDWIN

For current-model, new pianos:
North American Music, Inc.
11 Holt Drive
Stony Point, New York 10980
845-429-0106

For parts and warranty information on older pianos:
Baldwin Piano Company
309 Plus Park Boulevard
Nashville, Tennessee 37217
615-871-4500
870-483-6111 (parts)
800-444-2766 (Baldwin 24/7 consumer hotline)
www.baldwinpiano.com

Pianos made by: Baldwin (Zhongshan) Piano and Musical Instrument Co., Ltd., Zhongshan, Guangdong Province, China; Parsons Music Ltd., Yichang, Hubei Province, China

Baldwin Piano & Organ Co. was established in Cincinnati in 1862 as a retail enterprise and began manufacturing its own line of pianos in 1890. Throughout most of the 20th century, the company was considered one of the most successful and financially stable piano makers in the United States. Beginning in the 1980s, however, the quality declined, especially as a result of the relocation of action manufacturing to Mexico. In 2001, a combination of foreign competition and management problems resulted in bankruptcy, and purchase by Gibson Guitar Corporation.

Baldwin currently manufactures vertical pianos for the U.S. market in a factory it owns in Zhongshan, China, where it also maintains a major presence in the Chinese domestic, and other international, piano markets. It also contracts with Parsons Music, a large, well-respected manufacturer associated with a chain of music schools and stores in Hong Kong and China, to have grand pianos made under the Baldwin name. In 2007, Baldwin purchased a formerly government-owned piano factory in Dongbei, China, and for a while made grand pianos there, but due to a dispute with the Chinese government, production at that factory has been temporarily halted.

The company ceased regular piano production at its only remaining U.S. factory, in Trumann, Arkansas, at the end of 2008, though the facility remains open as a U.S. distribution and service center. Pianos sold in the U.S. now bear only the Baldwin name; all other piano names Baldwin owns and has recently used, such as Hamilton, Wurlitzer, Chickering, Howard, and D.H. Baldwin, have been retired, although some pianos bearing those names may remain on showroom floors for quite some time until sold.

Baldwin has re-created versions of most of its former U.S. vertical models at its facility in Zhongshan. In most instances, the cabinet styling of the former models, but not the scale designs, have been copied. Models B342 and B442 are 43" consoles, in attractive furniture styles similar to those of the former Acrosonic models 2096 and 2090, respectively. Model B243 is similar to the famous Baldwin Hamilton studio, the most popular school piano ever built, with toe-block construction. Model B252 is a nearly exact replica of the former 52" model 6000 upright, with Accu-just hitch pins, though with a bass sustain instead of a sostenuto pedal. In addition to re-creating versions of former U.S. vertical models, Baldwin has also created a number of new models to fill various price points and meet consumer demand.

The Baldwin grands made by Parsons Music have some similarities to the former U.S.-made Artist grands in terms of cabinet styling and material specifications, but the scale designs have been changed. Premium features include a maple rim, sand-cast plate, solid Alaskan Sitka spruce soundboard, duplex scaling, real ebony-wood sharps, German Röslau music wire, German Abel hammers, and a slow-close fallboard. All grand models are now available in a hand-rubbed, satin ebony finish.

Baldwin has licensed the Magic-Lid (formerly known as Safety-Ease) slow-close grand lid system, which is now standard on the 5' 10" model BP178 and the 6' 3" model BP190.

Baldwin sells an electronic player-piano system called ConcertMaster, available only on Baldwin pianos.

Warranty: 10 years, parts and labor, to the original purchaser.

BECHSTEIN, C.

including W. Hoffmann

Bechstein America

212-581-5550

info@bechstein-america.com

www.bechstein.de

Pianos made by: C. Bechstein Pianoforte Fabrik GmbH, Berlin and Seifhennersdorf, Germany; and C. Bechstein Europe Ltd. (former Bohemia Piano Ltd.), Hradec Králové, Czech Republic

Bechstein was founded in 1853 by Carl Bechstein, a young German piano maker who, in the exploding world of piano technology of his day, had visions of building an instrument that the tradition-bound piano-making shops of Berlin were not interested in. Through fine workmanship and the endorsement of famous pianists, Bechstein soon became one of the leading piano makers in Europe, producing over 5,000 pianos annually by 1900. The two World Wars and the Depression virtually destroyed the company, but it was successfully rebuilt. In 1963 it was acquired by Baldwin, and in 1986 Baldwin sold it to Karl Schulze, a leading West German piano retailer and master piano technician, who undertook a complete technical and financial reorganization of the company. In the early 1990s, Bechstein acquired the names and factories of Euterpe, W. Hoffmann, and Zimmermann. Pianos with these names are currently being sold in Europe, but only W. Hoffmann is sold in North America. In 2006 Bechstein purchased a controlling interest in the Czech piano maker Bohemia, and integrated it into a new entity called C. Bechstein Europe Ltd.

Bechstein says that all Bechstein-branded pianos are manufactured in Seifhennersdorf, Germany, and that W. Hoffmann pianos are made in the Czech Republic. Bechstein recently announced a technical-cooperation agreement with the Chinese piano maker Hailun, and it is widely believed in the industry that major components for some Bechstein and/or W. Hoffmann models are made

outside Europe. With few exceptions, Bechstein prefers not to divulge where the components for its instruments are made, a policy that frustrates some industry observers who seek transparency. However, the company says that, whatever the origin, all parts are inspected and made to conform to its rigid standards; in my experience, all models, including the less expensive ones, continue to receive praise for their high quality.

Bechstein-branded pianos use Abel or Renner hammers, solid European spruce soundboards, beech or beech and mahogany for grand rims and some structural parts, and maple pinblocks. Three pedals are standard on all pianos, the grands with sostenuto and the verticals with practice pedal (sostenuto optional). Over the past decade, all Bechstein grands have been redesigned with a capo bar (eliminating the agraffes in the treble), higher tension scale, and front and rear duplex scales for better tonal projection and tonal color. Also, unlike older Bechsteins, which had an open pinblock design, in the redesigned grands the plate covers the pinblock area. For better tuning control, the higher-level pianos are without tuning-pin bushings.

Bechstein pianos are available in two levels of quality. The regular verticals and partially redesigned versions of the old grand models now comprise a lower-priced "B" series, and say only "Bechstein" on the fallboard. They were previously named the Academy series. The 51½" Concert 8 (one of my all-time favorite verticals), several smaller verticals, and the fully redesigned grands (models D, C, B, M/P, and L), are the higher-priced line and say "C. Bechstein" on the fallboard. The company says that both lines are made in Germany, though for cost-effectiveness some parts and components may originate in the Czech Republic.

The differences between the B series and C. Bechstein lines appear to be primarily in tonal philosophy and cabinetry. C. Bechstein grands were designed with a higher tension scale for better projection, and with various components that the company believed would result in the greatest usable palette of tonal color: tapered soundboard, vertically laminated bridges, hornbeam hammer shanks, solid keybed, thicker rim, and hammers with walnut moldings and AAA felt. The grand soundboard is installed after the inner and outer rims are joined. The ribs are tapered after being glued to the soundboard, and the heavy-duty rim posts are dovetailed and embedded in the rim.

The less-expensive, traditional, B-series grands have an untapered soundboard, solid beech bridge with beech cap, maple hammer shanks, expansion-type keybed, and hammers with mahogany moldings and AA felt. The same quality wood and strings are used in both. The rim parts are joined, and the soundboard and ribs installed, in a more efficient, less time-consuming manner than with the C. Bechstein models. C. Bechstein keys still use leather key bushings, whereas the B-series keys use the more conventional cloth bushings. Bone keytops are an option on the C. Bechstein pianos, and genuine ebony sharps are used on both series.

The company uses its own Silver Line action in the Bechstein series and, in the C. Bechstein series, its Gold Line action, which is made to slightly stricter tolerances. As part of its global strategy, the company uses multiple suppliers for nearly all parts; parts for the Gold Line action come from Renner in Germany, while Silver Line parts are sourced from several countries, including China. Both actions appear to be well made, and both are of the Renner design, with the smooth, responsive touch characteristic of that design. Of course, the parts from Renner are more time-tested than the others.

The C. Bechstein cabinetry is much sleeker and more sophisticated than the plain B series, though both cabinets are finished to the same standard. The C. Bechstein plates receive the royal hand-rubbed finish; the other plates are just spray-finished in the conventional manner.

When the two lines are compared side by side, there are differences in their finished quality and performance level. Although the B-series pianos are, generally speaking, very good instruments with a slightly warmer default tone quality, the C. Bechstein models clearly outperform this less expensive line, and are free of the small tonal inconsistencies and minor flaws we have observed in the B series. It's possible that the comparative shortcomings of the B-series instruments could be remedied by further technical work, but it's apparent that they are not prepped at the factory to the same standard as the C. Bechstein pianos.

C. Bechstein grands are impeccably made in Europe and are "orchestrally" voiced, a concept that the company says is related to the change of timbre at different velocities of touch. According to Bechstein, customers who do not explore this feature of tonal design often prematurely assume that the piano is voiced too bright for the American musical taste. (However, several of my colleagues had high praise for the wide dynamic range, tonal color, and responsive action of the redesigned 7' 8" model C grand.) The company maintains that since voicing is a matter of overall piano design, their pianos are voiced at the factory to their tonal standard and should not be significantly altered. Some customers may still prefer the slightly warmer sound of the B-series grands, which are also about half the price of the C. Bechstein models.

Bechstein engineers oversee production of the Bechstein-designed W. Hoffmann line of pianos in the company's Czech facility. This is a mid-priced line intended to compete with other mid-priced pianos from Eastern Europe and Japan. Currently it consists of five grand and four vertical models in two series. The Tradition-series instruments are entirely made in the Czech Republic. The Vision-series pianos are assembled in the Czech Republic, but their strung backs (the instruments' structural and acoustical parts) are imported from China.

Warranty: 5 years, parts and labor, to original purchaser.

BEIJING HSINGHAI

Beijing Hsinghai Piano Group, Ltd., part of the Beijing Hsinghai Musical Instruments Co., has been producing pianos in Beijing, China, since 1949. It manufactures more than 50,000 vertical and grand pianos annually, mostly for domestic Chinese consumption. In 2005 the company consolidated its three older plants into a new facility of 1.2 million square feet. The pianos are available throughout the world under the Otto Meister and Hsinghai (or Xinghai) labels, as well as under various other labels as joint ventures with other manufacturers and distributors, including Wyman and Altenburg. Kawai also has a joint venture with Beijing, though the pianos (formerly under the name Linden) are distributed only in Canada and Europe.

BLÜTHNER

including Haessler and Rönisch. See also Irmler.

Blüthner USA LLC
5660 W. Grand River
Lansing, Michigan 48906
517-886-6000
800-954-3200
info@bluthnerpiano.com
www.bluthnerpiano.com
www.roenisch-pianos.de/en/
In Canada, contact Bluethner Piano Canada Inc.
604-264-1138
rrgarvin@telus.net
www.bluethner.ca

Pianos made by: Julius Blüthner Pianofortefabrik GmbH, Leipzig, Germany

Blüthner has been making pianos of the highest quality in Leipzig, in the eastern part of Germany, since 1853, and though nationalized in 1972, always remained under the management of the Blüthner family. Until 1900, Blüthner was Europe's largest piano factory. During World War II, the factory was bombed, but after the war the East German government allowed the Blüthner family and workers to rebuild it because the Blüthner piano was considered a national treasure (and because the Soviet Union needed quality pianos). With the liberation of Eastern Europe, Blüthner is again privately owned by the Blüthner family.

Blüthner pianos have beech rims (grands), solid spruce soundboards, Delignit pinblocks, Renner actions, Abel hammers, and polyester finishes. Pianos for export have three pedals, including sostenuto on the grands, and celeste (practice) on the verticals. Blüthner builds about 100 verticals a year in four sizes, and 500 grands a year in six sizes.

In addition to numerous specialized furniture styles and finishes, Blüthner has two recently issued special editions. In honor of the company's 150th anniversary, Blüthner introduced a Jubilee model with a commemorative cast-iron plate in the style of the special-edition pianos of a century ago. It is available in several sizes, in any style or finish. A Julius Blüthner edition honoring the founder of the company, now operated by the fifth generation of his family, is available in most grand sizes, and features, among other embellishments, brass inlays in the lid, round Victorian legs, and a very fancy, elaborately carved music desk in the styling designed by the founder.

Blüthner pianos incorporate several unique technical features. With aliquot stringing, the notes in the highest treble section (about the top two octaves) have four strings each instead of three. The extra string is raised slightly above the others and vibrates only sympathetically. The effect, heard mainly in medium to forte playing, is similar to that of a duplex scale, adding tonal color to the treble and aiding the singing tone. Another feature concerns the angled hammers, which may at first look odd, though the reason may not be readily apparent. It turns out that the angled hammers are actually cut at an angle to match the string line and mounted straight on the shanks instead of being cut straight and mounted at an angle like other brands. The company says that the effect is to more evenly distribute the force of the blow across both the strings and the hammers, and to make a firmer connection with the backchecks, which are also positioned in a straight line. Visually, the effect is an even, rather than a staggered, hammer line.

In what is perhaps a world's first, Blüthner has designed and built a piano for left-handed pianists. This is a completely backward piano, with the treble keys, hammers, and strings on the left and the bass on the right. When it was introduced, a pianist gave a concert on it after only a couple of hours of practice! It is currently available in the 6' 10" and 9' 2" sizes by special order (price not available).

With voicing, Blüthner pianos have a very full sound that is warm, romantic, and lyrical, generally deeper and darker than some of their German counterparts. Sustain is good, but at a low level of volume, giving the tone a refined, delicate character. The action is a little light, but responsive. The pianos are built of superb materials, and are favorably priced compared to some of their competitors.

In the 1990s a Haessler line of pianos was added to the Blüthner line. (Haessler is a Blüthner family name.) Created to better compete in the American market, Haessler pianos have more conventional technical and cosmetic features than Blüthner pianos and cost about 25 percent less. For example, the grands are loop-strung instead of single-strung, there is no aliquot stringing, and the hammers are cut and mounted in the conventional way. Case and plate cosmetics are simpler. The pianos are made in the Blüthner factory in Germany to similarly high quality standards.

Blüthner now also owns the Rönisch brand, established by Carl Rönisch in Dresden in 1845. In his day, Rönisch was a pioneer in piano building, and his instruments were sold throughout the world. Rönisch's son sold the company after World War I, and production was moved to Leipzig after the Dresden factory was bombed in 1945. During the Communist era, the company was taken over by the state and combined with other piano factories, becoming privately owned again in the 1990s. In 2009, Blüthner purchased Rönisch and integrated the manufacturing of Rönisch pianos into its own factory. The pianos were redesigned, and are now offered in three vertical and three grand sizes, in more than 100 cabinet styles, woods, and finishes.

Warranty: Blüthner and Haessler—10 years, parts and labor, to original purchaser.

BÖSENDORFER

Yamaha Corporation of America
P.O. Box 6600
Buena Park, California 90622
714-522-9415
info@boesendorferus.com
www.boesendorfer.com

Pianos made by: L. Bösendorfer Klavierfabrik GmbH, Vienna, Austria

Bösendorfer was founded in 1828 in Vienna, Austria, by Ignaz Bösendorfer. The young piano maker rose to fame when Franz Liszt endorsed his concert grand after being unable to destroy it in playing, as he had every other piano set before him. Ignaz died in 1858 and the company was taken over by his son, Ludwig. Under Ludwig's direction, the firm greatly prospered and the pianos became even more famous throughout Europe and the world. Ludwig, having no direct descendants, sold the firm to a friend, Carl Hutterstrasser, in 1909. Carl's sons, Wolfgang and Alexander, became partners in 1931. Bösendorfer was sold to Kimball International, a U.S. manufacturer of low- and medium-priced pianos, in 1966. In 2002 Kimball, having left the piano business, sold Bösendorfer to BAWAG Bank, Austria's third largest financial institution. The bank encountered financial troubles unrelated to Bösendorfer and sold the piano company to Yamaha in 2008. Yamaha says it will not be making any changes to Bösendorfer's location or methods of production, and that its sales network will continue to be separate from Yamaha's. Bösendorfer manufactures fewer than 500 pianos a year, with close to half of them sold in the U.S.

Bösendorfer makes a 52" upright and eight models of grand piano, from 5' 1" to the 9' 6" Imperial Concert Grand, one of the world's largest pianos. The 5' 1" grand, new in 2012 and unusually small for a Bösendorfer, has the same keyboard as the 5' 8" grand, ensuring a good touch despite the instrument's small size. The company also makes slightly less expensive versions of four grand models known as the Conservatory Series (CS). Conservatory Series grands are like the regular grands except that the case receives a satin finish instead of a high polish, and some cabinet details are simpler. Previously, the CS models also had a satin-finished plate, and were loop-strung instead of single-strung, but in 2009, regarding these features, the specifications of the regular models were restored. All Bösendorfer grand pianos have three pedals, the middle pedal being a sostenuto.

One of the most distinctive features of the grands is that a couple of models have more than 88 keys. The 7' 4" model has 92 keys and the 9' 6" model has 97 keys. The lowest strings vibrate so slowly that it's actually possible to hear the individual beats of the vibration. Piano technicians say that it is next to impossible to tune these strings by ear, although electronic tuning aids can help accomplish this. Of course, these notes are rarely used, but their presence, and the presence of the extra-long bridge and larger soundboard to accommodate them, add extra power, resonance, and clarity to the lower regular notes of the piano. In order not to confuse pianists, who rely on the normal keyboard configuration for spatial orientation while playing, the keys for these extra notes are usually covered with a black ivorine material.

The rim of the Bösendorfer grand is built quite differently from those of all other grands. Instead of veneers bent around a form, the inner rim is made in solid sections of spruce and beech that are joined together. The outer rim has a solid core of quartersawn spruce that is grooved by Bösendorfer craftsmen so that it can be bent around the inner rim; after bending, the grooved sections are filled with spruce inserts. Because spruce is better at transmitting than reflecting sound, the extensive use of spruce in the rim has the effect of making the rim an acoustical extension of the soundboard, causing the entire body of the piano to resonate. This, along with the scale design, may be why Bösendorfers tend to have a more delicate treble, and a bass that features the fundamental tone more than the higher harmonics. Although the stereotype that "Bösendorfers are better for Mozart than Rachmaninoff" may be an exaggeration (as evidenced by the number of performing artists who successfully use the piano in concert for a wide variety of music), the piano's not-so-"in-your-face" sound is certainly ideally suited for the classical repertoire, in addition to whatever else it can do. In recent years Bösendorfer has made some refinements to its designs to increase tonal projection. The relatively newer 6' 1", 7', and 9' 2" models have been designed specifically to appeal to pianists looking for a more familiar sound. In all models, however, the distinctive Bösendorfer difference is still readily apparent.

In the past few years, Bösendorfer has introduced a number of interesting instruments in new cabinet styles. These include a Porsche-designed modern piano in aluminum and polished ebony (it can be special-ordered in any standard Porsche finish color); the Liszt, Vienna, and Chopin models of Victorian-styled pianos; and limited-edition models, such as the Liszt Anniversary, Beethoven, Mozart, Hummingbird, and Schönbrunn. Perhaps not to be outdone by Porsche, in 2009 Bösendorfer produced a model commissioned and designed by Audi on the occasion of that automaker's 100th anniversary.

Bösendorfer makes a unique electronic player-piano system called CEUS. See "**Buying an Electronic Player-Piano System,**" elsewhere in this issue, for more information. The Bösendorfer model 200 is optionally available with a Yamaha Disklavier E3 installed.

Perhaps the world's most expensive piano inch for inch, Bösendorfer grands make an eloquent case for their prices. They are distinctive in both appearance and sound, and are considered to be among the finest pianos in the world.

Warranty: 10 years, parts and labor, transferable to future owners within the warranty period.

BOSTON

Steinway & Sons
One Steinway Place
Long Island City, New York 11105
718-721-2600
800-366-1853
boston@steinway.com
www.steinway.com/boston

Pianos made by: Kawai Musical Instrument Mfg. Co., Ltd., Hamamatsu, Japan and Karawan, Indonesia

In 1992 Steinway launched its Boston line of pianos, designed by Steinway & Sons and built by Kawai. Steinway's stated purpose in creating this line was to supply Steinway dealers with a quality, mid-priced piano containing some Steinway-like design features for those customers "who were not yet ready for a Steinway." In choosing to have a piano of its own design made in Japan, Steinway sought to take advantage of the efficient high-technology manufacturing methods of the Japanese while utilizing its own design skills to make a more musical piano than is usually available from that part of the world. In 2009, Steinway launched the Performance Edition of the Boston piano with enhancements to the instruments' design and specifications, including a grand inner rim of maple for increased structural integrity and improved tone, the patented Octagrip® pinblock for smoother tuning and more consistent torque, and improvements to hardware and keytop material, among other things. Performance Edition models have model numbers ending in PE. Sold only through select Steinway dealers, Boston pianos are currently available in three sizes of vertical and five sizes of grand. All are made in Japan, except the model UP-118S PE, which is made in Kawai's Indonesian factory.

Boston pianos are used by a number of prestigious music schools and festivals, including Aspen, Bowdoin, Brevard, Ravinia, and Tanglewood.

The most obvious visible feature of the Boston grand piano's design (and one of the biggest differences from Kawai pianos) is its wide tail. Steinway says this allows the bridges to be positioned closer to the more lively central part of the soundboard, smoothing out the break between bass and treble. This, plus a thinner, tapered, solid-spruce soundboard and other scaling differences, may give the Boston grands a longer sustain though less initial power. The wide-tail design may also endow some of the grands with the soundboard size normally associated with a slightly larger piano. The verticals are said to have a greater overstringing angle, for the same purpose. Over the last few years, the Boston verticals have been redesigned for greater tuning stability and musical refinement.

A number of features in the Boston piano are similar to those in the Steinway, including the above-mentioned maple inner rim, vertically laminated bridges for better tonal transmission, duplex scaling for additional tonal color, rosette-shaped hammer flanges to preserve hammer spacing, and radial rim bracing for greater structural stability. The Boston grand action is said to incorporate some of the latest refinements of the Steinway action. Cabinet detailing on the Boston grands is similar to that on the Steinway. Boston hammers are made differently from both Kawai and Steinway hammers, and voicers in the Kawai factory receive special instruction in voicing them. All Boston grand models come with a sostenuto pedal; all verticals have a practice (mute) pedal, except for the model UP-118S PE, which has a bass sustain.

Boston grands also have certain things in common with Kawai RX-series grands: tuning pins, grand leg and lyre assemblies, radial rim bracing, sostenuto pedal, and the level of quality control in their manufacture. The same workers build the two brands in the same factories. One important way they differ is that Kawai uses carbon-fiber–reinforced ABS Styran plastic for most of its action parts, whereas Boston uses only traditional wooden parts. Although similarly priced at the wholesale level, Kawai pianos tend to be a little less expensive to the retail customer than comparably sized Bostons due to the larger discounts typically given by Kawai dealers.

Steinway guarantees full trade-in value for a Boston piano at any time a purchaser wishes to upgrade to a Steinway grand.

Piano technicians are favorably inclined toward Boston pianos. Some find them to have a little better sustain and more tonal color than Kawais, while being otherwise similar in quality. When comparing the two brands, I would advise making a choice based primarily on one's own musical perceptions of tone and touch, as well as the trade-up guarantee, if applicable.

Warranty: 10 years, parts and labor, to original purchaser.

BRODMANN

Piano Marketing Group, LLC
752 East 21st Street
Ferdinand, Indiana 47532
812-630-0978
gtrafton222@gmail.com
www.brodmann-pianos.com

Pianos made by: Parsons Music, Hong Kong

Joseph Brodmann was a well-known piano maker in Vienna in the late 18th and early 19th centuries. Ignaz Bösendorfer apprenticed in Brodmann's workshop and eventually took it over, producing the first Bösendorfer pianos there. The modern-day Brodmann company was founded in 2004 by two former Bösendorfer executives, pursuing a direction they say was planned a number of years ago as a possible second line for Bösendorfer, but was eventually abandoned. In 2014 this company was dissolved; the trademark and distribution rights to the Brodmann name are being sold off to distributors in different parts of the world.

Brodmann says its mission is to produce a piano with high-end performance characteristics at an affordable price by using European components in key areas, strict quality control, and manufacturing in countries with favorable labor rates.

There are three lines of Brodmann piano. The Professional Edition (PE) pianos, made in China, are designed in Vienna and use European components such as Strunz soundboards, Abel hammers, Röslau strings, and Langer-designed actions (Renner in the model 228, a Chinese action in the verticals). Several vertical models use carbon-fiber action parts, for greater uniformity and dimensional stability. For quality control, Brodmann has its own employees from Europe in the factory. The scale design of the 6' 2" model PE 187 is said to be similar to that of a Steinway model A and is often singled out for praise.

The Conservatory Edition (CE), for the more price-conscious buyer, is also made in China, and comprises all Chinese parts (except for Japanese hammer felt), and receives Brodmann quality control.

The Artist Series (AS), introduced in 2011 and available only in the larger grand sizes (including a concert grand) and the largest upright size, is partially made in China and then shipped to Germany, where the German strings and action are installed and all musical finishing work is performed. The rim is made of maple; the soundboard, ribs, and pinblock are from Bolduc, in Canada; and the piano uses a Renner action, Kluge keyboard, and Abel or Renner hammers.

Brodmann has discontinued its entry-level piano line, Taylor London.

Warranty: 12 years, parts and labor, transferable to future owners within the warranty period.

BURGER & JACOBI

Ciampi USA
1520 Appian Way
Montebello, California 90640
323-236-2446
g.ciampi@ciampi.it
www.burgerjacobi.com/en

Pianos made by: Burger & Jacobi, Hradec Králové, Czech Republic

In 1872, Christian Burger began making pianos in his workshop in Burgdorf, Switzerland, later moving to larger quarters in Biel. He was joined in 1879 by his son-in-law, Herman Jacobi. For more than a century, aided by good workmanship, thousands of satisfied customers, and the endorsement of Johannes Brahms, Burger, Jacobi, and four generations of their descendants continued making pianos in Switzerland. In 1990, the company was purchased by the Ciampi Group, of Rome, Italy, a leading European distributor of musical instruments, whose founder had once worked at Burger & Jacobi. Ciampi moved production to the Petrof factory in the Czech Republic, where their pianos continued to be produced until recently, with distribution primarily limited to Europe. In 2010, Ciampi purchased its own factory in the same town as Petrof's, and is now expanding distribution to North America.

For North American distribution, Burger & Jacobi is starting with three vertical and four grand models, with prices and features aimed at the middle to upper level of the piano market. The pianos are manufactured at their factory in the Czech Republic, and contain a "Made in Europe" certification. Czech-made Detoa actions and keyboards are used in all models except the two largest grands, which have Renner actions. All models contain a solid spruce soundboard, Röslau strings, and Abel or Renner hammers. The 50" upright has a true sostenuto pedal.

Warranty: 5 years, parts and labor.

CABLE, HOBART M. — See Schumann.

CABLE-NELSON — See Yamaha.

CHASE, A.B. — See Everett.

CHERNOBIEFF

Chernobieff Pianos & Harpsichords
Lenoir City, Tennessee
865-986-7720
mammothpiano@gmail.com
www.chernobieff.com

Reminiscent of some piano designs attempted 200 years ago, Chernobieff's Mammoth is one of the most unusual pianos being built today. Dubbed a Vertical Concert Grand, Mammoth's model VCG stands 7' 2" tall, weighs 1,200 pounds, and has the scale design and sound of a 9' concert grand.

The piano's immense structure includes six laminated wooden back posts and a welded steel frame, yet despite its bulk, the instrument appears quite attractive in its custom-made cabinet of Brazilian cherry. The soundboard and ribs are of Sitka spruce. The action, invented specifically for this piano, appears superficially to be like that of a vertical, but actually contains the double-escapement feature of a grand piano action.

Inventor-builder Chris Chernobieff got his start assembling dulcimer and harpsichord kits, and branched out into piano service and rebuilding about 15 years ago. Inspired by other technicians who built their own pianos, Chernobieff asked, "Why not me?" Having spent the last several years designing and building the Mammoth, he now has plans for a 6' vertical and some innovative grand models.

Mammoth model VCG retails for $98,000.

CLINE — See Hailun.

CONCERTMASTER — See Baldwin.

CONOVER CABLE — See Samick.

CRISTOFORI

Jordan Kitt's Music
12303 Twinbrook Parkway
Rockville, Maryland 20852

Schmitt Music
2400 Freeway Blvd.
Brooklyn Center,
Minnesota 55430

301-770-9081
(Chris Syllaba)
info@cristoforipianos.com

763-566-4560 x5075
(Wayne Reinhardt)
www.cristoforipianos.com

Pianos made by: Guangzhou Pearl River Piano Group Ltd., Guangzhou, Guangdong Province, China

Originally issued under the name Opus II, the Cristofori and Lyrica brands are a joint undertaking by Jordan Kitt's Music, which owns and operates four piano dealerships in the D.C. and Atlanta markets; and Schmitt Music, which has more than a dozen locations throughout the Midwest and in Denver. Nearly ten years ago, wanting to improve their entry-level product offerings, the two companies combined forces to negotiate upgrades of product features and quality control directly with the factory. Today, although the brands are identical, Cristofori is sold only in Jordan Kitt's stores, Lyrica in Schmitt Music stores. Bartolomeo Cristofori (1655–1731) was, of course, the inventor of the piano.

The Cristofori and Lyrica lines are manufactured by China's largest piano manufacturer, Guangzhou Pearl River Piano Group. The uprights come in numerous sizes, styles, and finishes, including 42½" continental consoles and 43" decorator consoles in traditional and French cherry cabinets. The 48" professional upright, appropriate for home or institutional use, has front legs with toe blocks for strength, a large soundboard and long strings for bigger sound, and—new in 2012—a slow-close fallboard. Grands come in lengths of 4' 10", 5' 3", 5' 7", and 6' 2". The 5' 3" and 5' 7" sizes are wide-tail designs, which gives these mid-sized grands a larger soundboard area and, thus, a bigger sound.

The Cristofori and Lyrica pianos are differentiated from Pearl River's own line of pianos by upgraded specifications such as the use of highest-quality Mapes strings from the U.S.; all-spruce veneered soundboards of premium Siberian spruce; a different selection of cabinet styles; and a full, transferable warranty. U.S. technicians inspect every Cristofori and Lyrica piano at the Pearl River factory prior to crating and shipping.

Warranty: 12 years, parts and labor, transferable to future owners within the warranty period.

CUNNINGHAM

Cunningham Piano Company
5427 Germantown Avenue
Philadelphia, Pennsylvania 19144
800-394-1117
215-438-3200
www.cunninghampiano.com

Pianos made by: Ningbo Hailun Musical Instruments Co. Ltd., Ningbo, Zhejiang Province, China; with Cunningham Piano Company, Philadelphia, Pennsylvania

Cunningham Piano Company began manufacturing pianos in 1891 and, in its time, was the largest piano maker in Philadelphia. The original Cunningham factory ceased production in December 1943. The company was reopened in December 1945 as a piano rebuilder and retailer. Today, Cunningham specializes in the restoration of high-quality American and European pianos, and produces the new Matchless Cunningham.

Designed by Frank Emerson, the Matchless Cunningham is based on the original Cunningham scale designs. "Matchless" is used in reference to an offer made by Patrick Cunningham over a century ago: that he would pay $10,000 to anyone who could build a better piano. Because no one ever took him up on his offer, Cunningham labeled his piano the Matchless. Today, Matchless also refers to a unique combination of high-quality parts and a successful American scale design, assembled in China at the world-class Hailun factory, and with quality control overseen by Cunningham in Philadelphia. The line consists of grands from 5' to 9' and two verticals, 44" and 50".

Cunningham grands have maple rims (arguably necessary for best sound), custom-designed German Abel Hammers, German music wire, agraffes, duplex scaling, and slow-close mechanisms on both the fallboard and lid. Cunningham regularly sends technical staff to the Ningbo Hailun factory to oversee production, and each piano undergoes a thorough final preparation by Cunningham in Philadelphia.

The special Heritage Series incorporates art cases that reflect late Victorian styling. Handcrafted cabinet parts are made and installed in Cunningham's Philadelphia facility, making each instrument unique. Customers have the option of customizing certain aspects of the cabinetry based on their personal preferences.

Warranty: 10 years, parts and labor.

DONGBEI

The Dongbei Piano Company in China is owned by Baldwin Piano Company, a subsidiary of Gibson Guitar Corporation, and until fairly recently made pianos that were sold in North America by various distributors and under a variety of names, including Baldwin, Everett, and Hallet, Davis & Co. (see listings under those names). Pianos made under the names Nordiska and Weinbach are no longer distributed in the U.S.

Dongbei is Chinese for "northeast." In 1952, Dongbei was formed by splitting off from a government-owned piano factory in Shanghai and establishing a new government-owned factory in the northeastern part of the country. Dongbei began a process of modernization in 1988 when it purchased the designs and manufacturing equipment for a vertical piano model from the Swedish company Nordiska when that company went out of business. The Swedish-designed model 116 vertical was strikingly more advanced than Dongbei's own Prince and Princess lines. (At that time, Dongbei made only vertical pianos.)

In 1991 Dongbei entered into an agreement with Korean piano maker Daewoo whereby Daewoo would assist Dongbei in improving its production of vertical pianos. In 1996 that relationship was extended to the design and production of grands. In 1997, when Daewoo decided to leave the piano business, Dongbei purchased nearly all of Daewoo's grand-piano manufacturing equipment and began making grands. Export to the U.S. began in 1994 under the brand name Sagenhaft, at first only of vertical pianos. When the export of grands began in 1998, other brand names, such as Nordiska, Everett, and Story & Clark, began to become available, and over the next 10 years production for both domestic use and for export grew enormously.

When Daewoo left the piano business in 1997, some of the technicians and designers sent by Daewoo to advise Dongbei stayed on with Dongbei for many years, during which they designed numerous new piano models. Some of these technicians had trained in both Korea and Germany. In the opinion of many technicians who have examined a variety of pianos from China, the Dongbei grand-piano designs are musically among the best and most successful.

In early 2007 Gibson Musical Instruments, parent of Baldwin Piano Company, acquired Dongbei Piano and renamed it Baldwin Dongbei (Yingkou) Piano and Musical Instrument Co., Ltd., thus creating a major piano-manufacturing power in China with two plants. (The other plant, Baldwin [Zhongshan] Piano and Musical Instrument Co., Ltd., is in southern China.) To make the formerly government-owned operation more efficient and profitable, Baldwin had to reduce the size of Dongbei's workforce and production output. Due to a dispute with the Chinese government over these issues, however, piano production at Dongbei was discontinued, and Baldwin is contracting with Parsons Music, another Chinese piano maker, to manufacture Baldwin grand pianos.

ESSEX

Steinway & Sons
One Steinway Place
Long Island City, New York 11105
718-721-2600
800-366-1853
essex@steinway.com
www.steinway.com/essex

Pianos made by: Guangzhou Pearl River Piano Group Ltd., Guangzhou, Guangdong Province, China

Essex pianos are designed by Steinway & Sons engineers and are made in China by Pearl River. Steinway introduced its Essex line of pianos in early 2001 with a limited offering of models made by Young Chang, and the brand kept an unusually low profile in the piano market for a number of years. In 2006, a major relaunch of Essex included a new and very complete line comprising 35 grand and 31 vertical models and finishes.

Today, two grand sizes and three vertical scales are made. The 42" model EUP-108 is a continental-style version of the 44" model EUP-111 console. The 46" model EUP-116 studio is available in 10 different and striking cabinets designed by Steinway & Sons and renowned furniture designer William Faber. Styles include: Classic, Queen Anne, Italian Provincial, French Country, Formal French, English Country, English Traditional, Contemporary, and Sheraton Traditional. These models incorporate various leg designs (including cabriole leg, spoon leg, and canopy-styled tapered leg and arm designs) and hand-carved trim (such as Acanthus leaf and tulip designs, and vertical bead molding), highly molded top lids, picture-frame front panels, and stylized, decorative music desks. The 48" model EUP-123 upright comes in a traditional style in four finishes, along with Empire and French styles; an all-new school model, the EUP-123S, is offered in ebony polish only.

The Essex grands are available in 5' 1" (EGP-155) and 5' 8" (EGP-173) sizes in Classic and French Provincial styles. They come in a variety of regular and exotic veneers in high polish polyester and satin luster (semigloss) finishes.

Like Steinway's Boston pianos, the Essex line was designed with a lower tension scale and incorporates many Steinway-designed refinements. Included in these are a wide tail design that allows the bridges to be positioned closer to the more lively, central part of the soundboard, smoothing out the break between bass and treble. This and a thinner, tapered solid-spruce soundboard, and other scaling differences, produce a tone with a longer sustain. Other Steinway-designed features include an all-wood action with Steinway geometry, and with rosette-shaped hammer flanges, like those used in Steinway grands, to preserve hammer spacing; pear-shaped hammers with reinforced shoulders and metal fasteners; vertically laminated bridges with a solid maple cap; duplex scale; radial bracing (in grands); and staggered backposts (in verticals).

Steinway has put an immense amount of time and effort into the relaunch of Essex. The pianos are entirely new designs by Steinway engineers, not warmed-over designs from other companies. Steinway has a permanent office in Shanghai, China, and full-time employees who inspect the pianos made in the Asian factory. I expect that the quality of the Essex pianos will be toward the upper end of what these factories are capable of producing. So far, feedback from piano technicians confirms this expectation.

Steinway guarantees full trade-in value for an Essex piano toward the purchase of a Steinway grand within 10 years.

Warranty: 10 years, parts and labor, to original purchaser.

ESTONIA

Laul Estonia Piano Factory Ltd.
7 Fillmore Drive
Stony Point, New York 10980
845-947-7763
laulestoniapiano@aol.com
www.estoniapiano.com

Pianos made by: Estonia Klaverivabrik AS, Tallinn, Estonia

Estonia is a small republic in northern Europe on the Baltic Sea, near Scandinavia. For centuries it was under Danish, Swedish, German, or Russian domination, and finally gained its independence in 1918, only to lose it again to the Soviet Union in 1940. Estonia became free again in 1991 with the collapse of the Soviet Union.

Piano-making in Estonia goes back over 200 years under German influence, and from 1850 to 1940 there were nearly 20 piano manufacturers operating in the country. The most famous of these was Ernst Hiis-Ihse, who studied piano making in the Steinway Hamburg and Blüthner factories and established his own company in 1893. His piano designs gained international recognition. In 1950 the Communist-dominated Estonian government consolidated many smaller Estonian piano makers into a factory managed by Hiis, making pianos under the Estonia name for the first time. The instruments became prominent on concert stages throughout Eastern Europe and, amazingly, more than 7,400 concert grands were made. However, after Hiis's death, in 1964, the quality of the pianos gradually declined, partly due to the fact that high-quality parts and materials were hard to come by during the Communist occupation of the country. After Estonia regained its independence in 1991, the factory struggled to maintain production. In 1994 Estonia pianos were introduced to the U.S. market.

In 1994 the company was privatized under the Estonia name, with the managers and employees as owners. During the following years, Indrek Laul, an Estonian recording artist with a doctorate in piano performance from the Juilliard School of Music, gradually bought shares of the company from the stockholders until, in 2001, he became sole owner. Dr. Laul lives in the U.S. and represents the company here. In 2005, at its 100th-anniversary celebration, the Juilliard School named him one of the school's top 100 graduates; and in 2015, the President of Estonia awarded Laul the Presidential Medal, in recognition of the contribution Estonia pianos have made to awareness of that country. Estonia makes 200 to 300 pianos a year, all grands, mostly for sale in the U.S.

Estonia pianos have rims of laminated birch, sand-cast plates, Renner actions and hammers, laminated red beech pinblocks, and European solid spruce soundboards. They come in 5' 6", 6' 3", 6' 10" (new in 2013), 7' 4" (introduced in 2011), and 9' sizes. All have three pedals, including sostenuto, and come with a slow-close fallboard and an adjustable artist bench.

When I reported on Estonia pianos for the fourth edition of *The Piano Book* (2001), it was a good piano with much potential; but in the decade that followed, Dr. Laul introduced so many improvements to the piano that it became practically a different, much higher-level instrument. In 2010, Estonia began investing in designing new models, and the knowledge gained from designing the 6' 10" model L210, introduced in 2013, was used the following year to implement changes to most of the other models. These modifications included a complete soundboard redesign, new support beams of resonant spruce with improved doweled connection to the rim, and new specifications for hammer density. The model L190 also has a new, focused beam structure.

The Estonia factory makes a custom line of piano, offering exotic veneers such as rosewood, bubinga, pyramid mahogany, and Makassar ebony, and is willing to finish instruments to fit the desires of individual customers.

In the short time Estonia pianos have been sold here, they have gathered an unusually loyal and devoted following. Groups of owners of Estonia pianos, independent of the company, frequently hold musical get-togethers at different locations around the country.

The pianos have a rich, warm, singing tone and a wide dynamic range; are very well constructed and well prepared at the factory; and there is hardly a detail that the company has not examined and impressively perfected. The price has risen over the years, but they are still an unusually good value among higher-end instruments.

Warranty: 10 years, parts and labor, to original purchaser.

EVERETT

including A.B. Chase and Vose & Sons

Wrightwood Enterprises, Inc.
717 St. Joseph Drive
St. Joseph, Michigan 49085
616-828-0618
www.everett-piano.com

Pianos made by: Dongbei Piano Company, Ltd., Yingkou,
Liaoning Province, China

The Everett Piano Company originated in Boston in 1883 and moved to South Haven, Michigan, in 1926. It was acquired by Yamaha in 1973. Until mid-1986, Yamaha made a line of Everett vertical pianos in the Michigan factory alongside its U.S.-made Yamaha pianos. When Yamaha moved its U.S. piano manufacturing to Thomaston, Georgia, in 1986, it contracted with Baldwin to continue making Everett pianos. The contract terminated in 1989, and Yamaha dropped the line permanently. See the entry for Everett in *The Piano Book* for more information about pianos from that era.

The Everett name has been used by Wrightwood Enterprises, Inc. since 1995. The pianos are made in China by the Dongbei Piano Company (see Dongbei). The grands have duplex scaling and a bass scale that is custom made for the Everett brand, the company says. The same pianos are also sold under the A.B. Chase and Vose & Sons labels.

Warranty: 10 years, parts and labor, to original purchaser.

FALCONE — See Schumann.

FANDRICH & SONS

Fandrich & Sons Pianos
7411 Silvana Terrace Road
Stanwood, Washington 98292
360-652-8980
877-737-1422
fandrich@fandrich.com
www.fandrich.com

Pianos made by: Pearl River

In the late 1980s, Darrell Fandrich, RPT, an engineer, pianist, and piano technician, developed a vertical piano action designed to play like a grand, for which 10 patents were issued. In July 2013, a new patent application was filed in the U.S. (along with an application for future international patents) on an improved version of the action. The improvement features use of a grand-piano knuckle, and results in improved touch and repetition, and the feel of aftertouch at the bottom of the keystroke.

You can see an illustration of the original Fandrich Vertical Action™, an explanation of how it works, and some history of its development in the third and fourth editions of *The Piano Book* and on the Fandrich & Sons website. Since 1994, Fandrich and his wife, Heather, have been installing Renner-made Fandrich actions in selected new pianos, selling them under the Fandrich & Sons label. They also sell some grands (with regular grand actions) under that name.

Over the years, the Fandrichs have installed their actions in over 300 instruments, including ones from Bohemia, Feurich, Klima, Pearl River, Wilh. Steinberg, and Steingraeber. At present, the action is being installed in 51½" Pearl River uprights featuring Lothar Thomma scale designs (under the Fandrich & Sons label), and, by special order, in 51" Steingraeber uprights (under the Steingraeber & Söhne label). The converted pianos are available directly from the Fandrichs, as well as from their Canadian representative, in Montreal (contact the Fandrichs for information).

Playing a piano outfitted with a Fandrich Vertical Action is a very interesting experience. The action easily outperforms that of most other vertical pianos on the market, and some grands as well. The Fandrichs have now had 25 years of experience in refining and servicing the action, and reports suggest that customers are very satisfied with them.

Fandrich & Sons grand pianos are manufactured in China by the Pearl River Piano Group. These pianos feature Lothar Thomma scale designs, and are remanufactured at the Fandrich & Sons facility in Stanwood, Washington. The company offers three sizes of grand piano—models 170 (5' 7"), 188 (6' 2"), and 212 (7')—in two configurations: Standard (S) and Enhanced (E), the latter with Heller bass strings from Germany and/or Abel hammers, depending on customer preference. The tone of the S model is said to be powerful, dark, and sonorous; the E model, in contrast, is more brilliant and transparent. All models feature precision touchweighting using the Fandrich-Rhodes Weightbench™ system, which enables precise control of action inertia as well as traditional up- and downweight; redesigned pedal-lyre and trapwork systems; and a very extensive high-end preparation. All Fandrich & Sons pianos come with an adjustable matching bench.

The Fandrichs are passionate about their craft and choose the brands they work with carefully for musical potential. In addition to making standard modifications and refinements to remedy perceived shortcomings in the original Chinese-made instruments, the Fandrichs are inveterate tinkerers always searching for ways to make additional improvements, however subtle. As a result, many who play the pianos find them to be considerably more musical than their price and origin would suggest.

Warranty: 12 years, parts and labor, to original purchaser.

Note: Do not confuse the Fandrich & Sons pianos with the 48" Fandrich upright that was once manufactured with a Fandrich Vertical Action by Darrell Fandrich's brother, Delwin Fandrich. That piano has not been made since 1994.

FAZIOLI

Fazioli Pianoforti S.p.A.
Via Ronche 47
33077 Sacile (Pn), Italy
+39-0434-72026
info@fazioli.com
www.fazioli.com

In 1978, musician and engineer Paolo Fazioli of Rome, Italy, began designing and building pianos, with the object of making the finest-quality instruments possible. Now even the most famous piano makers of Western Europe are recognizing his accomplishment, and artists throughout the world are using the instruments successfully on the concert stage and elsewhere.

As a youth, Fazioli studied music and engineering, receiving advanced degrees in both subjects. He briefly attempted to make a living as a concert pianist, but instead joined his family's furniture company, rising to the position of factory manager in the Rome, Sacile, and Turin factories. But his creative ambitions, combined with his personal search for the perfect piano, finally led him to conclude that he needed to build his own piano. With advice and financial backing from his family, in 1977 Fazioli assembled a group of experts in woodworking, acoustics, and piano technology to study and scientifically analyze every aspect of piano design and construction. The following year, prototypes of his new instruments in hand, he began building pianos commercially in a factory housed at one end of the family's Sacile furniture factory, a top supplier in Italy of high-end office furniture.

In 2001, Fazioli built a new, expanded, modern piano-production facility, and in 2005 opened an adjoining 198-seat concert hall with a stage large enough for a chamber orchestra, where he maintains a regular concert schedule of well-known musicians who perform there. The concert hall is designed so that it can be adjusted acoustically with movable panels and sound reflectors to optimize the acoustics for performing, recording, or testing, and for different kinds of music, musical ensembles, and size of audience. The hall is used for the research and testing of pianos—every instrument Fazioli makes is tested here. In addition to these activities in the concert hall, the new factory also contains a department for ongoing research in piano design in cooperation with a number of educational institutions.

Fazioli builds only grands, about 150 per year, in six sizes from 5' 2" to 10' 2", the last one of the largest pianos in the world, with the further distinction of having four pedals. Three are the usual sustain, sostenuto, and una corda. The fourth is a "soft" pedal that brings the hammers closer to the strings—similar to the function in verticals and some older grands—to soften the sound without altering the tonal quality, as the una corda often does. A unique compensating device corrects for the action irregularity that would otherwise occur when the hammers are moved in this manner. The fourth pedal is available as an option on the other models. Fazioli also offers two actions and two pedal lyres as options on all models. Having two actions allows for more voicing possibilities without having to constantly revoice the hammers. A second pedal lyre containing only three pedals can be a welcome alternative for some pianists who might be confused by the presence of a fourth pedal.

All Fazioli pianos have inner and outer rims of maple, and seven-ply maple pinblocks from Bolduc, in Canada. The pianos have Renner actions and hammers and Kluge keyboards. The bronze capo d'astro bar is adjustable in the factory for setting the strike point and treble string length for best high-treble tone quality, and is removable for servicing if necessary; and the front and rear duplex scales can be tuned to maximize tonal color. The company says that a critical factor in the sound of its pianos is the scientific selection of its woods, such as the "resonant spruce" obtained from the Val di Fiemme, where Stradivari reportedly sought woods for his violins. Each piece of wood is said to be carefully tested for certain resonant properties before being used in the pianos. Similarly, three different types of wood are used for the bridge caps, each chosen for the most efficient transmission of tonal energy for a particular register.

An incredible level of detail has gone into the design and construction of these pianos. For instance, in one small portion of the soundboard where additional stiffness is required, the grain of the wood runs perpendicular to that of the rest of the soundboard, cleverly disguised so as to be almost unnoticeable. The pianos are impeccably prepared at the factory, including very fine voicing—even perfect tuning of the duplex scales.

A series of stunning art-case pianos is a testament to the ability of the Fazioli artisans to execute virtually any custom-ordered artistic variation on the six Fazioli models.

Many artists, and others most familiar with Fazioli pianos, describe them as sources of inspiration with a wide color palette and dynamic range, and combining great power with great warmth in a way that causes music played on them to "make sense" in a way made possible by few other pianos.

Each Fazioli piano is built saving one ton of carbon dioxide, thanks to the use of electricity produced by a new photovoltaic system installed on the roof of the Fazioli factory.

Warranty: 10 years, parts and labor, transferable to future owners within the warranty period.

FEURICH

Feurich USA
1771 Post Road East
Suite 239
Westport, Connecticut 06880
203-858-5979
eric@perarts.com
www.feurich.com

Pianos made by: Ningbo Hailun Musical Instruments Co. Ltd., Ningbo, Zhejiang Province, China

This German piano manufacturer was founded in Leipzig in 1851 by Julius Feurich. At its height in the early part of the 20th century, the company employed 360 people, annually producing 1,200 upright and 600 grand pianos. Like many German manufacturers, however, Feurich lost its factory during World War II. Following the war, the fourth generation of the Feurich family rebuilt in Langlau, in what became West Germany.

In 1991, Bechstein purchased Feurich and closed the Langlau factory, but in 1993 the name was sold back to the Feurich family. For a time, production was contracted out to other German manufacturers, including Schimmel, while the Feurich family marketed and distributed the pianos. In 1995, Feurich opened a new factory in Gunzenhausen, Germany. Under the direction of Julius Feurich, the fifth generation, the family-owned company once again began building its own high-quality pianos.

In 2011, Feurich was acquired by Wendl & Lung, headquartered in Vienna, Austria, which distributed a line of pianos under that name made to their specifications by Hailun in China. The Wendl & Lung pianos were rebranded as Feurich, and distributed along with Feurich pianos made under license by Julius Feurich in Gunzenhausen.

In 2012, Julius Feurich terminated his licensing agreement with Wendl & Lung, choosing instead to manufacture pianos independently under another name. Wendl & Lung continues to make and distribute Feurich pianos, utilizing a separate assembly line within the Hailun factory. In addition, a new line of German-made Feurichs is under development, to be manufactured near Cologne.

Ernest Bittner, founder and Managing Director of Wendl & Lung, has continued to develop the Feurich line, introducing a new model 115 vertical, designed by Rolf Ibach. The popular model 178 grand has undergone many changes, including refinements of action ratios and the implementation of a completely new cast-iron frame. This piano is becoming the model 179, to further differentiate it from the Hailun-branded model 178.

For its U.S. distribution, Feurich is following its European business model of using distribution centers to complete the musical preparation of the instruments—every piano entering the country is unboxed and completely prepped. In fact, Feurich pianos entering this country have received no voicing at the Hailun factory, which allows the distribution centers to control the critical final hammer preparation and voicing. Currently, Feurich has very limited distribution in the U.S.

Feurich offers an optional Harmonic Pedal on its grand pianos. This fourth pedal is essentially the inverse of a sostenuto—instead of holding up the dampers of notes pressed prior to depressing the pedal, it holds up all but those notes. The effect, known as "remanence harmony," is to allow the overtones of the depressed notes to sing out in a sustained fashion.

Warranty: 5 years, parts and labor, to original purchaser.

FÖRSTER, AUGUST

German American Trading Co., Inc.
P.O. Box 17789
Tampa, Florida 33682
813-961-8405
germanamer@msn.com
www.august-foerster.de

Pianos made by: August Förster GmbH, Löbau, Germany

The August Förster factory was founded by Friedrich August Förster in 1859 in Löbau, Germany, after Förster studied the art of piano building. During the years of control by the government of East Germany, the factory was managed by the fourth-generation piano builder, Wolfgang Förster. After the reunification of Germany and privatization, Wolfgang and his family once again owned their company. August Förster GmbH is now managed in the fifth generation by Wolfgang's daughter, Annekatrin Förster.

With a workforce of 40 using a great deal of hand labor, Förster makes about 120 grands a year in four sizes, and 150 verticals a year in three sizes. The pianos are very well built structurally, and the cabinets are elegant. Rims and pinblocks are of beech, soundboards of solid mountain-grown spruce, and bridges are of hardrock maple (without graphite). Each string is individually terminated (single-strung). The actions are made by Renner with Renner hammers. A sostenuto pedal is standard on all grand models.

The tone of August Förster grands is unique, with a remarkable bass: dark, deep, yet clear. As delivered from the factory, the treble is often quite bright, and for some American tastes might be considered a bit thin—it is a less complex sound that emphasizes clarity. This, however, can be modified somewhat with voicing and a good dealer preparation. The instruments are quite versatile, at home with Mozart or Prokofiev, classical or jazz. The 6' 4" model is often said to have an especially good scale. The concert-quality 7' 2" and 9' 1" models are well balanced tonally, and over the years have been endorsed by many famous artists. The Renner actions are very responsive and arrive in exacting regulation. The new 53" model 134K anniversary upright, intended for pianists who don't have space for a grand, has such grand-piano–like features as a full sostenuto; a large, adjustable music desk; and black keys of real ebony.

Most of the comments regarding the quality of materials and workmanship of the Förster grands also apply to the verticals. The cabinet of the vertical is of exceptional width, with extra-thick side panels of solid-core stock. Counter bridges are used on the outside of the soundboard to increase its mass. The verticals have a full set of agraffes, and all the hardware and handmade wood parts are of elegant quality. The actions are built by Renner. The verticals possess the same warm, rich, deep bass tone as the grands.

Warranty: 5 years, parts and labor, to original purchaser.

FRIDOLIN— See Young Chang.

GEYER, A.

Piano Marketing Group, LLC
752 East 21st Street
Ferdinand, Indiana 47532
812-630-0978
g.trafton@psci.net
www.geyer-pianos.com
Company Headquarters: Steffes & Schulz GmbH
Mühlgasse 11-13, D-65183 Wiesbaden, Germany
Phone: +49-611-992240
colintaylor@btconnect.com
Pianos made by: A piano factory in Zhejiang Province, China

The A. Geyer brand and factory were established by the Geyer family in 1877, in Eisenberg, Thuringia, Germany, and the brand was well known in the late 19th and early 20th centuries, when Eisenberg was a significant center for piano building. Also produced in the Geyer factory over the years were the brands of Fuchs & Mohr, Sassmann, Steinberg, and Weisbrod. In time, the Geyer factory became the Wilh. Steinberg factory, which continues to produce pianos today.

Today, A. Geyer is a new company, with headquarters in Wiesbaden, Germany. The company's founders are Christoph Schulz, a fourth-generation German piano maker; Frederik Steffes, the former owner of the Wilh. Steinberg factory; and Colin Taylor, formerly with Bösendorfer and Brodmann. Although the company is new, the three founders bring to it decades of combined experience in piano manufacturing, and a vision, they say, to create a piano wonderful in sound, touch, and style, with outstanding value for the money.

Although the pianos are designed in Germany, A. Geyer production is located near Hangzhou, in Zhejiang Province, China, a region just outside of Shanghai that has become a center of piano manufacturing. The company founders believe that their knowledge and experience of traditional German methods of piano making, combined with local Chinese resources, can result in a better piano at lower cost.

Currently, A. Geyer makes three upright pianos and five grands. All pianos use carefully selected Chinese parts that are subject to strict quality controls. German Wurzen felt is used for the upright hammers, and Abel hammers for the grands. All pianos have a solid-spruce-core veneered soundboard and Japanese Suzuki strings. The actions and keyboards have been designed by the company's German master piano builder. All pianos are inspected by the company's technicians before leaving the factory.

Warranty: 5 years, parts and labor, to original purchaser.

GROTRIAN

Grotrian Piano Company GmbH
P.O. Box 5833
D-38049 Braunschweig, Germany
+49-531-210100
+49-531-2101040 (fax)
contact@grotrian.de
www.grotrian.de

Don Glasgow
Director of Sales North America
251-967-2431
don.glasgow@gmail.com

Friedrich Grotrian was born in 1803 in Schöningen, Germany, and as a young man lived in Moscow, where he ran a music business and was associated with piano manufacturing. Later in his life he teamed up with C.F. Theodor Steinweg, son of Heinrich Steinweg, to build pianos. Heinrich had emigrated to the U.S. about 1850, soon to establish the firm of Steinway & Sons. Theodor followed in 1865, selling his share in the partnership to Wilhelm Grotrian, son of Friedrich, who had died in 1860. Thereafter, the firm became known as Grotrian-Steinweg. (In a legal settlement with Steinway & Sons, Grotrian-Steinweg agreed to use only the name Grotrian on pianos sold in North America.)

Even as early as the 1860s, Grotrian pianos were well known and highly respected throughout Europe. Each successive generation of the Grotrian family maintained the company's high standards and furthered the technical development of the instrument. Today the company is owned by the sixth generation of Grotrians. In 2015, the company will celebrate its 180th anniversary with special, limited-edition versions of the Friedrich Grotrian upright and the Grotrian 6' 3" grand.

Grotrian grands have beech rims, solid spruce soundboards, laminated beech pinblocks, Renner actions, and are single-strung. Grotrian prides itself on what it calls its "homogeneous soundboard," in which each piece of wood is specially chosen for its contribution to the tone of the soundboard. The cast-iron plate is attached with screws along the outer edges of the rim, instead of on top of the rim, which the company says allows the soundboard to vibrate more freely. The vertical pianos have a unique star-shaped wooden back structure and a full-perimeter plate. Grotrian makes five sizes of grand and six sizes of vertical piano. New "studio" versions of grand models 192 (6' 3") and 208 (6' 10"), made for institutions, have scratch-resistant cabinet finishes, wider music desks, and more impervious soundboard finishes.

Grotrian also makes a lower-cost line, called Friedrich Grotrian, with a beech back frame but no back posts, and a simpler cabinet. It's available in a 43½" model in polished ebony with legs, and in 43½" and 45" models for institutional use, with satin finishes but without legs. The Friedrich Grotrian models are also completely made at the Grotrian factory in Braunschweig, Germany.

The treble of Grotrian pianos has extraordinary sustaining characteristics. It also has a pronounced sound of attack, subtle and delicate. The tenor is darker than many other brands. The bass can be powerful, but without stridency. Overall, Grotrian pianos have a unique, expressive sound and are a pleasure to play. Over the years, many well-known pianists have endorsed or expressed appreciation for Grotrian pianos.

Warranty: 5 years, parts and labor, transferable to future owners.

HAESSLER — See Blüthner.

HAILUN

including Cline and Emerson

Hailun America
P.O. Box 1130
Richland, Washington 99352
509-946-8078
877-946-8078
info@hailun-pianos.com
www.hailun-pianos.com

Pianos made by: Ningbo Hailun Musical Instruments Co. Ltd., Ningbo, Zhejiang Province, China

Ningbo Hailun began making piano parts and components in 1986 under the Ningbo Piano Parts Factory name, and began assembling entire pianos in 1995. Its assembly facility converted to a full-scale piano manufacturing facility in 2000. Today, the Hailun factory has over 400,000 square feet of production capacity and 800 employees. A 200,000-square-foot expansion project is underway to accommodate distribution in the U.S. market. Additionally, a new cabinet factory is now complete and began production in 2008. In addition to making pianos under the Hailun name, the company also makes the Feurich brand (formerly Wendl & Lung—see Feurich). Hailun also makes pianos or components under contract for several other manufacturers and distributors. Hailun recently conducted an Initial Public Offering of stock on the Shenzen Stock Exchange.

Currently, the Hailun line consists of four vertical sizes (mostly larger uprights) and five grand sizes. In 2010, the company introduced the 52" model HU7-P, with a duplex scale, agraffes, and a steel capo bar for, the company says, a "lush and powerful sound in the American tradition." This model also has a middle pedal that operates a true sostenuto mechanism.

(Note: Model designations on the cast-iron plates of some Hailun pianos may differ from those in Hailun marketing materials and in this publication because the models may have different names in the Chinese and U.S. markets. In each such case, the scale designs are the same, but, according to Hailun, the U.S. models contain the higher-quality parts and materials advertised in U.S. marketing materials and on the Hailun America web page.)

Hailun America is in the process of introducing several new grand and vertical models under the Emerson brand name (formerly the Hailun Vienna Series). The W.P. Emerson Co. was founded in 1849 by William P. Emerson, later changing its name to the Emerson Piano Co. Located in Boston, the company became a meeting place of old-world artisans and new-world technology, and grew into one of the largest and most reputable piano manufacturers of its time, selling its pianos throughout the world. The distributor of today's Emerson piano says that it seeks to continue the tradition of bringing together the new and old worlds, combining European, American, and Asian resources to address the need for an exacting, quality instrument that "reflects the Western tradition of piano building" at a more favorable price, and to "create a warm tonal experience in the tradition of the Viennese sound."

Emerson pianos are designed by an international team of piano designers close to the Hailun factory, and are manufactured by Hailun. The wood for its soundboards is sourced from the North Austrian Alps. The grands are designed with a wide tail, vertically laminated maple bridges, a slightly firmer touch, and faster action speed. The vertical has a patented TriGon duplex scale, agraffes, a full-perimeter plate, and an enhanced soundboard design. Each purchaser of an Emerson may, within 18 months of purchase, request that a special highly qualified technician, known as a Vienna Concert Technician, spend a full day of concert-level regulation and voicing on the piano at the customer's home.

In 2011, Hailun introduced a slow-close piano lid in all its grand piano models. Graphically named the Hailun Limb Protection System (HLPS), this is a version of the Safety-Ease retrofit system, described elsewhere in this publication, built into the piano at the factory. HLPS allows even a child to easily lift the otherwise heavy lid of a grand piano without danger, and prevents a falling lid from crashing down onto arms and hands. A version of HLPS, called HLPS Plus, and available only in the Vienna models, allows the user to adjust a grand piano lid to any position without the need for a lid propstick. Apart from the safety benefit, HLPS Plus allows the user to modulate sound projection by adjusting the lid position.

Hailun is a little different from most of the other Chinese companies selling pianos in the U.S.: Its founder and owner, Chen Hailun, is an entrepreneur in the Western style, and deeply involved in every aspect of the business. Originally a maker of molds for industrial use, Chen got into the piano business when piano manufacturers started to use his services to make piano parts. In 1998 he bought out the government's position in his company to better control quality and hiring decisions.

While modern manufacturing methods are fully utilized, the factory also uses a large amount of skilled manual labor. Chen seeks out the best workers by paying considerably higher wages than other piano makers in China, he says, and provides an in-depth training program for his workers, conducted by piano builders and technicians from the U.S. and Europe. He also assists in the training of future piano technicians through an association with a local university. His greatest aspiration, Chen says, is to make the best piano in Asia.

Over the years, much of Chen's technical efforts have gone into maximizing the precision and stability of the pianos and parts his company makes. This is evidenced by the substantial investment in computer-controlled machinery used for precision cutting; the design of keys, keybeds, and other parts to resist warping; and the fact that grand piano actions are actually interchangeable between instruments of the same model (this requires an unusually high level of precision). The pianos themselves exhibit good quality control and intelligence in design. In terms of materials, the company uses maple in grand piano rims, a feature indicative of higher quality and arguably necessary for the best sound. In 2011, the company began sourcing its own supply of the highest-quality Austrian spruce, and plans to make its own soundboards with this spruce for select piano models. *Piano Buyer*'s reviewers have tried out several Hailun grands (see reviews in the Fall 2009, Fall 2010, and Fall 2011 issues) and have been impressed with their musicality.

To help it reach the highest quality standards, Hailun has also hired an impressive group of experts from Japan (Ema Shigeru), Europe (Stephen Paulello, Claire Trichet, Sibin Zlatkovic, Peter Veletzky), and the U.S. (Frank Emerson). In 2009, to oversee and assist with quality control, Hailun hired Rolf Ibach, owner of Rud. Ibach Sohn, one of the oldest and most reputable European piano companies, which closed its doors in 2008 after more than 200 years in business.

Hailun USA has initiated several support programs designed to increase the speed at which service requests are handled, and to measure customer satisfaction. It has also introduced the Hailun Dream Assurance Program, in which the company guarantees, subject to certain limitations, that the sound of any purchased Hailun piano will be to the customer's liking or, within 90 days of purchase, the company will exchange the piano for another of the same model. Under the company's Gold Service Program, Hailun dealers are obligated to provide each customer with one free service call between 60 and 180 days after purchase of a piano.

Hailun America is reintroducing the Cline brand to the U.S. market in the form of entry-level models made by Hailun. Chester L. Cline began selling pianos in Tacoma, Washington, in the 1880s, and produced pianos under his own name beginning in 1889. He eventually expanded his retail chain throughout the Northwest and, in the 1920s, into California, becoming one of the largest piano dealers in the West. In the 1980s and '90s, pianos bearing the Cline name were made by several manufacturers of entry-level pianos.

Today, Cline makes 46½" and 48" verticals and a 4' 11" grand. The grand comes with the HLPS lid-support system. Both the 48" vertical and the grand are optionally available with the MG Silent System, which can turn the acoustic piano into a digital one that can be played with headphones at any time of day or night. It also features a metronome, and allows performances to be recorded and exported in MIDI format to share with others. (See the chapter on **Hybrid Pianos** for more information about silent systems.) Owners of Cline pianos in North America are entitled to receive a trade-in credit of the full amount paid for the instrument toward the purchase of a new grand made by Hailun, Emerson, Petrof, or Sauter (all of whom share a common distributor).

Warranty: Hailun— 15 years, parts and labor, to the original owner, transferable to the second owner within the warranty period. Cline—10 years, parts and labor, to original purchaser. Emerson—5 years, parts and labor, to original purchaser. Electronics—1 year, parts and labor, to original purchaser. See also the Dream Assurance Program, described above.

HALLET, DAVIS & CO.

Hallet Davis Pianos
11 Holt Drive
Stony Point, New York 10980
845-429-0106
usapianos@yahoo.com
www.halletdavispianos.com

Pianos made by: various makers (see text)

This famous old American piano brand dates back to at least 1843 in Boston, and has changed hands many times over the years. It eventually became part of the Aeolian group of piano brands, and instruments bearing the name were manufactured at Aeolian's Memphis plant until that company went out of business in 1985. Subsequently, North American Music began producing Hallet, Davis, & Co. pianos, first in Korea, and now in China.

The Heritage and Signature Collections are made by the Beijing Hsinghai Piano Group, Ltd. (see Beijing Hsinghai), and by the Silbermann Piano Co. The upper-level pianos, known as the Imperial Collection II, are manufactured by Parsons Music, a factory associated with a large chain of music stores in China and Hong Kong, and the third-largest producer of pianos in China.

HARDMAN, PECK & CO.

Hardman Pianos
11 Holt Drive
Stony Point, New York 10980
845-429-0106
info@hardmanpiano.com
www.hardmanpiano.com

Pianos made by: Beijing Hsinghai Piano Group, Ltd., Beijing, China

Hugh Hardman established the Hardman Piano Company in New York City in 1842. Leopold Peck joined the company in 1880, and became a partner in 1890, at which time the company was renamed Hardman, Peck & Company. In the early 20th century, Hardman, Peck was sold to the Aeolian Corporation, which eventually moved to Memphis, where it remained until it went out of business in 1985. Today's Hardman, Peck & Company pianos are manufactured in China by the Beijing Hsinghai Piano Group (see Beijing Hsinghai). The piano line offers a selection of vertical and grand pianos in a variety of styles and finishes to meet the needs of entry-level and mid-level pianists.

HEINTZMAN & CO.

including Gerhard Heintzman

Heintzman Distributor Ltd.
210-2106 Main Street
Vancouver, British Columbia V5T 3C5
Canada
U.S.: 303-765-5775
pianopop3@msn.com
Canada: 604-801-5393
info@hzmpiano.com
www.hzmpiano.com

Pianos made by: Heintzman Piano Company, Ltd., Beijing, China

Heintzman & Co. Ltd. was founded by Theodore August Heintzman in Toronto in 1866. By 1900, Heintzman was one of Toronto's larger manufacturing concerns, building 3,000 pianos per year and selling them throughout Canada and abroad through a network of company stores and other distributors. The pianos received high praise and won prizes at exhibitions. Even today, technicians frequently encounter old Heintzman pianos built in the early part of the 20th century and consider them to be of high quality. In the latter decades of the century, Heintzman, like other North American brands, struggled to compete with cheaper foreign imports. The factory finally closed its doors in 1986 and relocated to China. (For a few years thereafter, some pianos continued to be sold in Canada under the Heintzman and Gerhard Heintzman names.) At first the company was a joint venture with the Beijing Hsinghai Piano Group (see **Beijing Hsinghai**), but when the Chinese government began allowing foreign ownership of manufacturing concerns, the Canadian partner bought back majority ownership and took control.

The new company, known as Heintzman Piano Company, Ltd., is Canadian owned and managed and has a private, independent factory dedicated to producing Heintzman-brand pianos. Heintzman makes pianos to the original Canadian Heintzman designs and scales using some of the equipment from Canada. James Moffat, plant manager of the Canadian Heintzman factory for 40 years, has been retained as a consultant and visits the factory in China several times a year. The company even uses some components from Canada, such as Bolduc soundboards, in grands and larger verticals. The factory makes about 5,000 pianos per year.

The smallest vertical made under the Heintzman name is 43½" tall, but pianos for export to North America typically start at 48" and contain a mixture of Chinese and imported parts, such as pinblocks and treble strings from Germany and Mapes bass strings from the U.S. Verticals 48½" and taller use Renner Blue or Abel Blue hammers, and the largest two sizes have Canadian Bolduc soundboards of solid Eastern white spruce. All verticals 50" and taller have a middle pedal that operates a bass-sustain mechanism, as well as a Silent Switch that operates a mute bar for silent practice.

The grands—5', 5' 6", 6' 1", 6' 8", and 9' long—also use German pinblocks and strings, Mapes bass strings, Renner Blue or Abel Blue hammers, and Canadian Bolduc or German Strunz soundboards of solid spruce.. The 9' concert grand comes with a full Renner action and Kluge keys from Germany. A Renner action is a higher-priced option on the other models. All grands come with a sostenuto pedal. A 6' 1" model patterned on the old Heintzman model D was introduced in 2007.

New in 2013, and aimed at a slightly more upscale audience, is the Royal series of verticals and grands, with two-tone cabinet trim and inlays on the inside of the lid, as well as a Bolduc or Strunz soundboard, Abel or Renner Blue hammers, and Mapes bass strings.

Heintzman Piano Company also makes the slightly less expensive Gerhard Heintzman brand. This line uses less expensive materials and components, such as Japanese hammers and a veneer-laminated spruce soundboard in the verticals (a Bolduc soundboard in some of the grands). The polished ebony grands have a silver plate and trim.

Warranty: Heintzman and Gerhard Heintzman—10 years, parts and labor, from the factory, transferable to future owners within the warranty period.

HOFFMANN, W. — See Bechstein, C.

HSINGHAI — See Beijing Hsinghai.

IRMLER

including Schiller

Blüthner USA LLC
5660 W. Grand River
Lansing, Michigan 48906
517-886-6000
800-954-3200
916-337-1086
info@irmler-piano.com
www.irmler-piano.com
In Canada, contact Bluethner Piano Canada Inc.
604-264-1138
rrgarvin@telus.net
www.bluethner.ca

Pianos made by: Irmler Piano GmbH, Leipzig, Germany, and other factories (see text)

Irmler is a sister company of Blüthner, and Irmler pianos are distributed through the Blüthner dealer network. The brand has recently been reintroduced to the market in two series: Studio and Professional.

The Studio series is largely made in a factory in China owned by Irmler. The pianos are then shipped to the Blüthner factory in Germany, where Abel hammers are installed and the pianos are inspected and adjusted as needed, prior to shipping to dealers. The pianos have Delignit pinblocks and veneer-laminated spruce soundboards. The grand rims are of Chinese oak and the grand actions are made with Renner parts. The Studio-series verticals include a number of models with interesting, modern cabinet designs.

The Professional series, also known as Irmler Europe, is assembled in Germany using strung backs (structural and acoustical elements) from Samick in Indonesia and cabinets from Poland (suppliers are subject to change). The pianos have Delignit pinblocks and solid spruce soundboards. Grands have rims of maple and beech, action parts by Renner (U.S. distribution only), and duplex scaling. Vertical actions are by Detoa.

The Irmler Studio series is also available from some dealers under the Schiller brand name, with a slightly modified cabinet; prices are comparable to those for Irmler.

Warranty: 10 years, parts and labor, to original purchaser.

KAWAI

including Shigeru Kawai

Kawai America Corporation
2055 East University Drive
Rancho Dominguez, California 90220
310-631-1771
800-421-2177
310-223-0900 (Shigeru Kawai)
acoustic@kawaius.com
www.kawaius.com
www.shigerukawai.com

Pianos made by: Kawai Musical Instrument Mfg. Co., Ltd.; Hamamatsu, Japan, and Karawan, Indonesia

Kawai was founded in 1927 by Koichi Kawai, an inventor and former Yamaha employee who was the first person in Japan to design and build a piano action. While Kawai is second in size to Yamaha among Japanese piano manufacturers, it has a well-deserved reputation all its own for quality and innovation. Nearly all Kawai grands and taller uprights are made in Japan; most consoles and studios are made in Indonesia. The company closed its North Carolina factory in 2005.

One of Kawai's most important innovations is the use of ABS Styran plastic in the manufacture of action parts. More than 40 years of use and scientific testing have shown this material to be superior to wood for this purpose. ABS does not swell and shrink with changes in humidity, so actions made with it are likely to maintain proper regulation better than wood actions. The parts are stronger and without glue joints, so breakage is rare. These parts are present in every Kawai piano. In the current Millennium III action found in some models, the ABS is reinforced with carbon fiber so it can be stronger with less mass. Having less mass to move (that is, less inertia), the action can be more responsive to the player's intentions, including faster repetition. Certain contact surfaces on the action parts are also micro-engineered for ideal shape and texture, resulting in a more consistent touch. Although it took a number of years to overcome the idea that plastic parts must be inferior, there is essentially no dispute anymore among piano technicians on this subject.

Kawai's vertical piano offerings change frequently and are sometimes confusing. At present there are three basic series of Kawai verticals. The console series begins with the 44½" model 506N, a basic entry-level console in an institutional-style cabinet (legs with toe blocks). Model K-15 is a 44" version of this in a continental-style cabinet (no legs), and model 508 is a 44½" version in a simple furniture-style cabinet (freestanding legs). Model 607 is the same piano in a fancier furniture-style cabinet. All have the same internal workings. The action in this series is slightly smaller than a full-size action, so it will be slightly less responsive. However, it is more than sufficient for beginner or casual use.

Kawai has replaced both of its former studio models, the UST-7 and UST-8, with the 46" model UST-9, made in Indonesia. This model has the stronger back of the UST-7, rather than that of the UST-8, which was not known for its tuning stability. The UST-9 also contains the Millennium III action; an angled, leather-lined music desk to better hold music; and a stylish, reinforced bench. The 46½" model 907 is essentially the UST-9 in a fancy, furniture-style cabinet.

Kawai's K series of upright models has been updated in 2014, and the model names have been changed. The former K-2, K-3, K-5, K-6, and K-8, all sold in North America, have become the new K-200 (45"), K-300 (48"), K-400 (48"), K-500 (51"), and K-800 (53"). The K-400 is internally the same as the K-300, but its cabinet includes a grand-piano–style music desk (formerly available only with the K-8) and a folding, low-profile fallboard. The K-500—at 51", two inches taller than the old K-5—has been extensively redesigned internally, with longer bass strings, a larger soundboard, and a redesigned cast-iron plate. Several of the new K-series models are available in the AnyTime (ATX) series as silent/hybrid pianos. See the article on **Hybrid Pianos** for details.

As before, all K-series models include Kawai's Millennium III actions, made with carbon-fiber composites. The hammers in all models are now made with underfelt and mahogany moldings, which Kawai says improves the responsiveness of the action and the tonal sustain. All models have redesigned, tapered soundboards for improved tonal response; double-braced and steel-reinforced keybeds to prevent warping and flex; and come with slow-close fallboards and adjustable benches. The K-500 and K-800 both feature Kawai's Neotex ivory-substitute key material, and the K-800 comes with a sostenuto pedal. The K-series cabinets have been redesigned for a sleeker, more modern appearance.

Kawai makes three series of grand pianos: GX, GE, and GM. The GX line (formerly RX; see below), which is sold in North America in a version known as the BLAK series, is the most expensive and has the best features. It is designed for the best performance, whereas the GE and GM series are designed more for efficiency in manufacturing, with fewer refinements. The GX/RX pianos are the only Kawai grands with a radial beam structure, focused and connected to the plate using a cast-iron bracket at the tenor break. This system makes for a more rigid structure, which translates into better tone projection. The soundboard of the GX/RX

models is tapered for better tonal response, and the rim is thicker and stronger than in the GE and GM models. The BLAK pianos use a new version of the Millennium III action with hammer-shank stabilizers, designed to retain power by keeping the shank from wavering under a heavy blow; have agraffes, duplex scaling, lighter hammers (less inertia), and Neotex synthetic ivory keptops; and come with a slow-close fallboard. The GX/RX grands get more precise key weighting, plus more tuning, regulating, and voicing at the factory. The cabinetry is nicer looking and of better quality than that of the GE and GM series pianos, with the polished ebony models in the new BLAK series receiving a UV-cured, scratch-resistant coating on the music rack.

In 2013, the RX series was changed to GX—see our **review** in the Spring 2014 issue. The pinblock is more securely attached to the case for better tuning stability, and the front stretcher has been made thicker, stiffening the structure, and thus both conserving tonal energy and contributing to tuning stability. The rim now uses alternating layers of two different hardwoods, one chosen for tonal power, the other for warmth. There have also been some changes to the scale designs and soundboard taper.

Some of the GX/RX features are also found in the GM and GE pianos, but this varies with the model. The GM-10K is the only Kawai grand made in Indonesia. It has Kawai's standard ABS action, no agraffes or duplex scaling, standard keytops, and a regular fallboard. The GM-11, new in 2013 and also made in Indonesia, is the same as the GM-10K, except that it has agraffes and a different plate. The model GM-12, made in Japan, has the regular Millennium III action (without hammer-shank stabilizers), no agraffes or duplex scaling, standard keytops, and a slow-close fallboard. The GE models, also made in Japan, have the regular Millennium III action, agraffes, duplex scaling, Neotex keytops, and a slow-close fallboard.

Kawai's quality control is excellent, especially in its Japanese-made pianos. Major problems are rare, and other than normal maintenance, after-sale service is usually limited to fixing the occasional minor buzz or squeak. Kawai's warranty service is also excellent, and the warranty is transferable to future owners within the warranty period (a benefit that is not common these days). The tone of most Kawai pianos, in my opinion, is not as ideal for classical music as some more expensive instruments, but when expertly voiced, it is not far off, and in any case is quite versatile musically. In part because the touch is so good, Kawai grands are often sought by classical pianists as a less-expensive alternative to a

Steinway or other high-end piano. Kawai dealers tend to be a little more aggressive about discounting than their competition (Yamaha). There is also a thriving market for used Kawais. (If you're considering buying a used Kawai, please read "Should I Buy a Used 'Gray Market' Yamaha or Kawai Piano?" on pages 176–177 of *The Piano Book*, or the shorter version in "Buying a Used or Restored Piano" in this publication.)

The Shigeru Kawai line of grands represents Kawai's ultimate effort to produce a world-class piano. Named after Kawai's former chairman (and son of company founder Koichi Kawai), the limited-edition (fewer than 300 per year) Shigeru Kawai grands are made at the separate facility where Kawai's EX concert grands are built.

Although based on the Kawai RX designs, the Shigeru Kawai models are "hand made" in the extreme. Very high-grade soundboard spruce is air-dried for multiple years, then planed by hand by a worker who knocks on the wood and listens for the optimum tonal response. Ribs are also hand-planed for correct stiffness. String bearing is set in the traditional manner by planing the bridges by hand instead of having pre-cut bridges pinned by machine. Bass strings are wound by hand instead of by machine. Hammers are hand-pressed without heat for a wider voicing range, and the hammer weights are carefully controlled for even touch. Hammer shanks are thinned along the bottom so that their stiffness is matched to the hammer mass. These procedures represent a level of detail relatively few manufacturers indulge in.

In 2012, Kawai updated the Shigeru Kawai grands, changing the cabinet styling and some of the pianos' construction features. The inside of the rim is now finished with bird's-eye maple veneer, and the round legs have been changed to straight legs with brass trim. The rim itself is now made of alternating layers of rock maple and mahogany, which Kawai says provides more power without losing warmth in the tone. The structure at the front of the piano has been made stronger, and the beams underneath are now made from spruce instead of the laminated mahogany Kawai uses in its other models. The keys have been lengthened for a better touch, especially on the smaller models.

Each buyer of a Shigeru Kawai piano receives a visit within the first year by a Kawai master technician from the factory in Japan. These are the same factory technicians who do the final installation of actions in pianos, as well as the final voicing and regulation. According to those who have watched them work, these Japanese master technicians are amazingly skilled. Because the Shigeru Kawai pianos have been on the market only since 2000 and in very limited quantities, many piano technicians

have yet to service one. Those who have, however, tend to rank them among the world's finest instruments, and Shigeru Kawai pianos are often chosen by pianists participating in international piano competitions.

Warranty: Kawai and Shigeru Kawai—10 years, parts and labor, transferable to future owners within the warranty period.

KAYSERBURG — See Pearl River

KIMBALL

Kimball Piano USA, Inc.
1819 North Major Avenue
Chicago, Illinois 60639
312-212-3635
kimballpiano@gmail.com
www.kimballpianousa.com

Kimball, a name with a long history in the piano world (see *The Piano Book* for details), is now being produced by Kimball Piano USA, Inc., which acquired the rights to the Kimball name in 2005. Kimball International, which previously owned the Kimball brand and produced Kimball pianos from 1959 to 1996, was primarily a furniture maker that mass-produced a very average piano.

In contrast, Kimball is now controlled by a Registered Piano Technician (RPT) who has returned Kimball to its historical roots in Chicago and says he is placing the company's focus on the musical instrument and on technical details of American piano design and construction. The result of this focus is two new collections of Kimball pianos: Classic and Artist.

The Kimball Classic Collection consists of the 5' 1" model K1 and 6' 2" model K3 grands. Parts and components for these models are being sourced primarily from China and Europe. They include a rim made of maple and oak (grands); full-length back posts (vertical); bridges planed and notched by hand in the traditional manner; a wet-sand cast plate; Herrburger Brooks keys, action, and hammers; Röslau strings; Delignit pinblock; and a solid spruce soundboard.

The Kimball Artist Collection includes the 5' 8" model A2 grand and the 49" model A49 vertical. The company says that the Artist Collection embodies its commitment to producing high-quality performance pianos by paying great attention to the design of the scale, soundboard, and action, and to proper execution and attention to details. High-end components, primarily from Germany, include a rim of European beech (grand), Renner action (grand), Strunz premium solid spruce soundboard and ribs, Delignit pinblock, Röslau strings, Klinke agraffes, and Abel hammers. The vertical has full-length spruce back posts and a Herrburger Brooks action; cabinets are from China.

In the U.S., Kimball is doing final assembly and detailing of the instruments, with a major focus on proper action, hammer, and key installation to ensure superb playability. At its facility in Chicago, Kimball now has a showroom where, by appointment, both individual customers and dealers are welcome to see and play the new pianos.

Warranty: 10 years, parts and labor, to original purchaser.

KINGSBURG

Doremi USA Inc.
5036 Dr. Phillips Boulevard, Suite 288
Orlando, Florida 32819
866-322-5986
info@kingsburgusa.com
www.kingsburgusa.com

Pianos made by: Yantai Kingsburg Piano Co., Ltd., Yantai, Shandong Province, China

+86-535-6932912
kingsburgpiano@163.com
www.kingsburgpiano.com.cn

Yantai Kingsburg, formerly known as Yantai Longfeng, was established in 1988, and at various times made pianos under the Steigerman and Perzina brand names. It is located in a temperate area of northern China that, the company says, is ideal for piano making because of its moderate humidity level.

All Kingsburg pianos have been designed by well-known piano designer Klaus Fenner, and scales are currently undergoing adjustment by Italian piano builder Luigi Borgato. Components are sourced from around the world: from Germany, Röslau piano wire, Abel hammers, and Dehonit pinblocks; from the Czech Republic, Detoa actions; and from Japan, tuning pins and mineral (ivory-like) keytops. All pianos now feature keys of real ebony wood and come with a slow-close fallboard. Interesting design features include longer keys on upright models for more grand-like performance, brass-bar duplex scale, and the company's exclusive Tri Board solid spruce soundboard, which, in the taller vertical models, is unattached to the piano back at the bottom, for better bass tone and improved tuning stability.

At present, the Kingsburg line comprises larger uprights and two sizes of grand, with plans to possibly expand into the market for home console pianos. Custom styles and finishes are also available.

A key focus of Yantai Kingsburg is that the final factory preparation of the pianos be done in such a manner that the dealer can deliver the instrument to the customer's home with very little additional work being required. To that end, the U.S. distributor's Japanese affiliate sends highly trained technicians to the factory to fully tune, voice, and regulate each Kingsburg piano to their high standards before it is crated for shipment.

Warranty: 12 years, parts and labor, to original purchaser.

KNABE, WM.

See also Samick.

Samick Music Corp. (SMC)
1329 Gateway Drive
Gallatin, Tennessee 37066
615-206-0077
info@smcmusic.com
www.knabepianos.com

Pianos made by: Samick Musical Instrument Mfg. Co. Ltd., Inchon, South Korea; and Bogor, West Java, Indonesia

Founded in Baltimore in 1837 by Wilhelm (William) Knabe, a German immigrant, Wm. Knabe & Co. established itself in the 19th and early 20th centuries as one of the finest piano makers in America. Over the years, Knabe pianos have left an important mark on the music field, including over 40 years as the official piano of the Metropolitan Opera, sponsoring Tchaikovsky's appearance at the opening of Carnegie Hall, and their places inside the White House and Graceland. Today, Knabe is the official piano of the American Ballet Theatre at the Met. 2012 marks the company's 175th anniversary.

As part of the consolidation of the American piano industry in the early 20th century, Knabe eventually became part of the Aeolian family of brands. Following Aeolian's demise in 1985, the Knabe name became part of Mason & Hamlin, which was purchased out of bankruptcy in 1996 by the owners of PianoDisc. For a time, a line of Knabe pianos was made for PianoDisc by Young Chang in Korea and China. When the line was discontinued, Samick acquired the Wm. Knabe & Co. name. (Note: "Knabe" is pronounced using the hard K sound followed by "nobby.")

SMC (Samick's U.S. distribution subsidiary) began by using the Wm. Knabe name on some of the pianos formerly sold as the World Piano premium line of Samick instruments. In 2002, SMC developed the

Concert Artist series for the Knabe name. Highlighting this series are the 5' 8" and 6' 4" grand models, which have been redesigned, based on the original 19th- and early 20th-century Knabe scale designs and cabinet styles in use when the company was based in Baltimore. Features include sand-cast plates, lacquer semigloss wood finishes, Renner actions on larger grands, German hammers, and rims of maple and oak. The company has added 5' 3", 7' 6", and 9' 2" models for the American market. The verticals feature unique cabinet designs with bird's-eye maple and mahogany inlays, rosewood key inserts, and tone escapement. The 52" upright includes a full sostenuto, hand-activated mute rail, and agraffes throughout the bass section of the piano.

For two years, SMC completed assembly of Concert Artist grands at its Tennessee facility, with strung backs made in Indonesia or Korea. Now, most Knabe pianos are made in their entirety in Indonesia but are still uncrated in the U.S., where they are inspected, tuned, regulated, and voiced before being shipped to dealers.

In 2011, SMC unveiled two additional product lines within the Knabe family: the Academy and Baltimore series. The Academy series has many of the same features and specifications as the popular, upper-end, Kohler & Campbell Millennium brand, also made by Samick: a maple or beech inner rim (grands); a premium soundboard of solid white spruce; German hammers; a Samick Premium Action; satin lacquer semigloss wood finishes; and a Samick-made hornbeam action rail (larger verticals). (See **Samick** for more about Kohler & Campbell.) The Academy series also boasts two institutional studio uprights, the WMV245 and WMV247, both with full-length music racks, the WMV247 also with agraffes through the bass section.

The Baltimore series offers a more modestly priced alternative to the institutional Academy series or upper-end Concert Artist series. This line features an all-spruce "surface tension" (veneered) soundboard. The grands provide a full sostenuto pedal, slow-close fallboard, fully adjustable music desk and rack, multiple finishes in both satin ebony and wood tones, and, recently, a new designer grand with accents of Bubinga or African Pommele. The verticals showcase a wide range of sizes and cabinet styles, including wood tones in French cherry, traditional mahogany, and Renaissance walnut.

Warranty: 10 years, parts and labor, transferable to future owners within the warranty period.

KOHLER & CAMPBELL — See Samick.

LOMENCE

J.D. Grandt Piano Supply Co.
181 King Road
Richmond Hill, Ontario L4E 2W1
Canada
905-773-0087
info@jdgrandt.com
www.jdgrandt.com
Pianos made by: Lomence Modern Crystal Piano Co., Ltd., Foshan, Guangdong Province, China

The Lomence factory is located in Foshan, China, approximately one hour north of Guangzhou, in the southern region of China. A manufacturer of traditional pianos since 1998, Lomence discovered great success in its local market after experimenting with more modern-looking cabinet designs. The distinguishing feature of Lomence pianos is that many of the cabinet parts, including the top lid, front panel, fallboard, and side gables, are made of clear acrylic. The sharps on the tallest vertical are also of clear acrylic, creating an interesting effect in which they appear black from above but clear from the side.

Lomence pianos are available in three vertical sizes, 47.5", 48.5", and 50.5", and a 6' grand. Material specifications include German Röslau music wire, Siberian spruce soundboard, laminated Austrian spruce keys, nickel-plated hardware, and a slow-close fallboard.

Warranty: 10 years, parts and labor, to the original purchaser.

MASON & HAMLIN

Mason & Hamlin Piano Company
35 Duncan Street
Haverhill, Massachusetts 01830
916-567-9999
www.masonhamlin.com
Pianos made by: Mason & Hamlin Piano Co., Haverhill, Massachusetts

Mason & Hamlin was founded in 1854 by Henry Mason and Emmons Hamlin. Mason was a musician and businessman and Hamlin was an inventor working with reed organs. Within a few years, Mason & Hamlin was one of the largest makers of reed organs in the U.S. The company began making pianos in 1881 in Boston, and soon became among the most prestigious of the Boston piano makers. By 1910, Mason & Hamlin was considered Steinway's chief competitor. Over the next 85 years, Mason & Hamlin changed hands many times. (You can read the somewhat lengthy and interesting history in *The*

Piano Book.) In 1996 the Burgett brothers, owners of PianoDisc, purchased Mason & Hamlin out of bankruptcy and set about reestablishing manufacturing at the six-story factory in Haverhill, Massachusetts. The company emphasizes limited-quantity, handbuilt production, and currently manufactures from 200 to 350 pianos per year. Daily tours are offered to visitors.

Since acquiring the company, the Burgetts have brought back most of the piano models from the company's golden Boston era (1881–1932) that originally made the company famous. Refinements have been made to the original scale designs and other core design features. First came the 5' 8" model A and 7' model BB, both of which had been manufactured by the previous owner. Then, in fairly rapid succession, came the 6' 4" model AA, the 9' 4" model CC concert grand, and the 5' 4" model B. The development of these three models was an especially interesting and costly project: in the process, the engineering staff resurrected the original design of each model, constructed new rim presses, standardized certain features, refined manufacturing processes, and modernized jigs, fixtures, templates, and machinery, improvements that afterward were applied to the company's other models. The 50" model 50 vertical piano has also been reintroduced and redesigned, with longer keys for a more grand-like touch, and improved pedal leverage. Internal parts for the verticals are made in Haverhill, then assembled in the company's Sacramento factory, where it also installs PianoDisc systems.

All Mason & Hamlin grands have certain features in common, including a wide-tail design; a full-perimeter plate; an extremely thick and heavy maple rim; a solid spruce soundboard; a seven-ply, quartersawn maple pinblock; and the patented tension-resonator Crown Retention System. The tension resonator (illustrated in *The Piano Book*), invented by Richard Gertz in 1900, consists of a series of turnbuckles that connect to specific points on the inner rim. This system of turnbuckles is said to lock the rim in place so that it cannot expand with stress and age, thereby preserving the soundboard crown (curvature). (The soundboard is glued to the inner rim and would collapse if the rim expanded.) While there is no modern-day experimental evidence to confirm or deny this theory, anecdotal evidence and observations by piano technicians tend to validate it because, unlike most older pianos, the soundboards of old Mason & Hamlins almost always have plenty of crown.

In the early part of the 20th century, Wessell, Nickel & Gross was a major supplier of actions to American piano manufacturers, including Mason & Hamlin. Over the years, the name fell into disuse. In 2004 Mason & Hamlin revived the name by registering the trademark, which now refers to the design and specifications of Mason & Hamlin actions. The company manufactures a new line of carbon-fiber action parts of strikingly innovative design, which the company makes available to its dealers and to rebuilders as a high-performance upgrade to the traditional wood action. The company explained that it has moved to using composite parts because of the inherent shortcomings of wood: it's prone to breakage under constant pounding, the parts vary in strength and mass from one piece of wood to the next, and wood shrinks and swells with changing temperature and humidity. Composite parts, on the other hand, are more than ten times as strong as wood; are built to microscopic tolerances, so they are virtually identical; and are impervious to weather. According to the company, material scientists predict that in the benign environment of a piano, the minimum life expectancy of composite parts is 100 years. The Wessell, Nickel & Gross composite action is now standard on all new Mason & Hamlin pianos.

Mason & Hamlin grands are available in ebony and several standard and exotic wood finishes, in both satin and high polish. Satin finishes are lacquer, the high-polish finishes are polyester. Most sizes are also available in a stylized case design called Monticello, which has fluted, conical legs, similar to Hepplewhite style, with matching lyre and bench. In 2009 Mason & Hamlin introduced the Chrome art-case design, in polished ebony with chrome and stainless-steel case hardware replacing the traditional brass hardware. This design also has art-deco case styling, a silver plate, and a new fallboard logo in a modern font. This modern-font logo, along with a new slow-close fallboard, is standard on all new Mason & Hamlin grands.

In 2014, to commemorate the company's 160th anniversary, Mason & Hamlin introduced the Cambridge Collection. Model designs in this series feature two-toned cabinets in hand-rubbed finishes of polished ebony and either bubinga or Makassar ebony. On the grands, the hand-selected exotic veneers appear on the fallboard, the music desk, the lid underside, and the inner rim; on the verticals, they appear on the upper and lower front panels.

The tone of Mason & Hamlin pianos is typically American—lush, singing, and powerful, not unlike the Steinway in basic character, but with an even more powerful bass and a clearer treble. The designers have done a good job of making a recognizable Mason & Hamlin sound that is consistent throughout the model line. The 5' 8" model A has a particularly powerful bass for a piano of its size. The treble, notably weak in prior versions, has been beefed up, but the bass is still the showpiece of the piano. The new 5' 4" model B also has a large-sounding bass for its size. The "growling" power of the Mason & Hamlin bass is most apparent in the 7' model BB. The 6' 4" model AA is a little better balanced between bass and treble, one reason why it is a favorite of mine.

The basic musical design of Mason & Hamlin pianos is very good, as is most of the workmanship. As with other American-made pianos, musical and cabinet detailing, such as factory voicing and regulation and plate and cabinet cosmetics, are reasonable but lag somewhat behind the company's European competitors in finesse. The company says it is standard procedure for final voicing and regulation to be finished off by thorough and competent dealer prep.

In recent years many companies have turned to China and other international sources for parts and materials, for several reasons: a domestic source is no longer available, to save money, to increase the security of supply, and, in some cases, to increase quality. Among makers of high-end pianos, Mason & Hamlin has been pioneering in this regard, though it is not the only company to do so. The company's worldwide sourcing of parts and materials, along with its investment in modernized equipment, has made the Mason & Hamlin a better instrument while keeping the piano's price at a reasonable level. It's a very good value among high-end instruments.

Warranty: 5 years, parts and labor, transferable to future owners within the warranty period.

MAY BERLIN — See Schimmel.

PALATINO
The Music Link
P.O. Box 57100
Hayward, California 94545
888-552-5465
piano@palatinousa.com
www.palatinousa.com

Pianos made by: AXL Musical Instrument Co., Ltd. Corp., Shanghai, China

Although Palatino may be a relatively new name to the piano world, it is not a newcomer to the music business. For almost 20 years, parent company AXL has been manufacturing a full range of musical instruments under its own name and under a variety of other, recognizable brand names. The company has a highly automated factory, employing CNC routers from Japan and Germany, and importing high-quality materials and components for its pianos from around the world.

Palatino makes about 7,000 pianos annually in three categories: Classic, Professional, and Concert. The Classic series includes a 48½" vertical and a 5' grand; the Professional series, a 50" vertical and 5' 9" and 6' 2" grands; and the Concert series, featuring Renner actions and hammers, 5' 9" and 6' 2" grands. Features common to all Palatino pianos include a solid spruce soundboard, high-quality German-felt hammers, hard rock-maple bridges and pinblock, German Röslau strings, wet-sand–cast plate, Renner-style action, slow-close fallboard, solid brass hardware, and adjustable artist bench. In addition, Professional- and Concert-series pianos have soundboards of solid, AAA-grade Canadian white spruce, and German hammers (Renner hammers for the Concert series).

Based on personal observation and dealer reports, Palatino pianos appear to have good quality control and are prepared well at the factory before being shipped to dealers. Our own reviewer tested a couple of the grand models and found them to be very musical and a pleasure to play (see review in the Fall 2009 issue).

Warranty: 10 years, parts and labor, transferable to future owners within the warranty period. Benches and slow-close fallboard mechanisms are warranted for one year.

PARSONS MUSIC
Parsons Music Corporation
8/F, Railway Plaza
39 Chatham Road South
Tsim Sha Tsui, Kowloon
Hong Kong
+852 2333 1863
mailto@parsonsmusic.com
www.parsonsmusic.com
www.parsonsmusic.com.cn

Parsons Music Corporation, headquartered in Hong Kong, was founded in 1986 by Terence and Arling Ng as a small music-lesson studio. Since then it has become China's largest music retailer, with more than 100 retail locations and 80 music schools throughout China and Hong Kong. In 1997, the company expanded into manufacturing pianos and other musical instruments, and is now the third largest piano maker in China.

At present, all of the pianos Parsons makes for sale in this part of the world are made for and distributed by other companies under those companies' own brand names. However, Parsons manufactures and sells, in China and Hong Kong, its own house brands, Yangtze

River, Toyama, and Schönbrunn; manufactures the brand Barrate & Robinson, which it licenses the right to sell in China; has a strategic alliance with Kawai, in which Parsons distributes Kawai pianos in China, and manufactures select Kawai models for sale only in Parsons Music's stores in China; owns the German piano maker Wilh. Steinberg and manufactures some of its models in China; and cooperates in the manufacture of the Pianoforce electronic player-piano system, and distributes it in China and Hong Kong. Parsons Music's commitment to piano manufacturing is also demonstrated by its ownership of an iron-plate foundry, a wood-processing facility, and even the forests in which the wood for its instruments is grown. In recent years, Parsons has become known within the piano-manufacturing community as the source of some of the best-made pianos from China.

PEARL RIVER

including Ritmüller and Kayserburg

GW Distribution, LLC
P.O. Box 329
Mahwah, New Jersey 07430
845-429-3712
www.pearlriverusa.com
www.ritmullerusa.com
www.kayserburgusa.com
info@pearlriverusa.com

Pianos made by: Guangzhou Pearl River Piano Group Ltd., Guangzhou, China

Established in 1956, Pearl River Piano Group has become the largest piano manufacturer in the world, with a production of over 125,000 pianos annually by more than 2,500 workers. The company builds pianos under the Pearl River, Ritmüller, and Kayserburg names, as well as under a few other names for OEM contracts with distributors such as **Cristofori** (with Jordan Kitt's Music) and **Essex** (with Steinway). (See separate listings under those names.) Pearl River is the best-selling piano brand in China, and is exported to more than 100 countries. After a successful IPO in 2012, the formerly government-owned company completed construction of a new, state-of-the-art, 1.2-million-sq.-ft. factory, to which it will transition over the next five years. The factory combines traditional craftsmanship with advanced CNC digital machinery, and complies with European high-level technology and process standards.

In recent years, Pearl River has revised and streamlined its model line with the assistance of Lothar Thomma, a well-respected Swiss scale designer, and his colleague Stephen Mohler, who is now head of Pearl River's quality control. Many new models have been introduced, while older models have been reviewed and modified. Currently, Pearl River verticals begin with the 42½" console model UP108 in continental style (no legs), and the 43" console model EU111 (new in 2015) in several traditional American furniture styles. They continue with a series of studio models, including the 45" model UP115M5 in a traditional institutional style (legs with toe blocks), and the 45" model UP115E in a school-friendly institutional style with special casters and a full-length music desk. Finally, there are the upright models, including the 46½" model EU118 (new in 2015), and the relatively new 48" model EU122 and 51½" model EU131 concert upright, both designed by Lothar Thomma.

Pearl River grands come in six sizes, from 4' 11" to 9', and have been redesigned by Thomma over the last two years to include features such as vertically laminated bridges with solid maple caps, lighter touchweights, German hammer felt, and new scale designs.

Pearl River also makes pianos under the Ritmüller name, a brand that originated in Germany in 1795. Lothar Thomma was engaged in 2007 to design, from the ground up, a line of higher-end pianos that would be distinct from the Pearl River line. These instruments were introduced in North America in 2009 under the Ritmüller name. In most other parts of the world, these pianos are branded Kayserburg.

Ritmüller pianos come in three distinct price categories: Premium, Performance, and Classic. The Premium models feature solid spruce soundboards, Renner hammers, hornbeam and maplewood actions, and real ebony sharps, among other higher-quality features. Piano Buyer's reviewers have auditioned several of the new grand models and have been very impressed. See reviews in the **Fall 2009** issue of the grand models GH-160, 170, and 188; in the **Fall 2010** issue of the GH-148R; and in the **Fall 2011** issue of the GH-188R. In addition, the 48" model UH-121R vertical and the 4' 10" model GH-148R grand have been chosen as "Staff Picks." The Performance models, introduced in 2014, are all designed by Lothar Thomma and feature unique scales, offset backposts, ebony sharps, high-quality German Abel hammers, and a veneered and tapered all-spruce soundboard. The Classic series, introduced in 2011, is a line of lower-cost instruments currently comprising three vertical models. Also designed by Thomma, they feature a veneered all-spruce soundboard and German Röslau strings.

In 2013, Pearl River brought to North America the upper-level Kayserburg Artists series. These instruments are handmade by two dozen of Pearl River's most experienced craftsmen, personally managed by Stephen Mohler in what can be described only as a small "German" piano workshop inside a large Chinese piano factory. The Kayserburg Artists craftsmen have all completed a rigorous training that includes studying the world's finest pianos and working side by side with visiting European craftsmen. The Kayserburg Artists pianos contain such high-end features as soundboards of tight-grained, solid European spruce, Renner hammers, Laoureux (French) damper felt, German Röslau strings, vertically laminated maple bridges with rosewood cores and solid beech caps, German IvoryLeit natural keytops, and genuine ebony sharps.

Warranty: 10 years, parts and labor, to original purchaser.

PERZINA, GEBR.

including G. Steinberg

Perzina Pianos America LLC
70 SW Century Drive, Suite 100-278
Bend, Oregon 97702
541-639-3093
844-PER-ZINA
888-754-0654 (fax)
marti@bolpianos.nl
www.perzina-america.com

Pianos made by: Yantai Perzina Piano Manufacturing Co., Ltd., Yantai, Shandong Province, China

The Gebr. Perzina (Perzina Brothers) piano company was established in the German town of Schwerin in 1871, and was a prominent piano maker until World War I, after which its fortunes declined. In more recent times, the factory was moved to the nearby city of Lenzen and the company became known as Pianofabrik Lenzen GmbH. In the early 1990s the company was purchased by Music Brokers International B.V. in the Netherlands. Eventually it was decided that making pianos in Germany was not economically viable, so manufacturing was moved to Yantai, China, where both verticals and grands were made for a number of years by the Yantai Longfeng Piano Co. under the Perzina name. In 2003 Music Brokers International established its own factory in Yantai, called Yantai-Perzina, where it now builds Perzina pianos.

Perzina verticals have several interesting features rarely found in other pianos, including a "floating" soundboard that is unattached to the back at certain points for freer vibration, and a reverse, or concave soundboard crown. (There may be something to this; the Perzina verticals sound very good, their bass being particularly notable.) Soundboards are of solid Austrian white spruce.

A new line of Perzina grand pianos was introduced in 2011, designed and manufactured by Perzina in cooperation with a major European manufacturer. All contain solid Austrian white spruce soundboards, duplex scaling, and Renner AA or Abel hammers, among other high-quality components. A Perzina action is standard, with Detoa and Renner actions optionally available at additional cost. All models come with a slow-close fallboard, and most come with an adjustable artist bench. The distributor says that each grand is unpacked in the U.S., and inspected, polished, regulated, and voiced to the dealer's specifications before being shipped to the dealer.

The company's European headquarters says it ships many European materials to Yantai, including Degen copper-wound strings, Röslau strings, Delignit pinblocks, Renner hammers, English felts, European veneers, and Austrian white spruce soundboards. New machinery is from Germany, Japan, and Italy. According to the company, all the piano designs are the original German scales. The Renner actions used by Perzina are ordered complete from Germany, not assembled from parts.

The Perzina factory also manufactures G. Steinberg (formerly called Gerh. Steinberg) pianos for distribution in the U.S. Gerhard Steinberg began making pianos in Berlin in 1908. The firm he established changed hands many times during the 20th century, the most recent being its acquisition by Music Brokers International B.V., in 1993. G. Steinberg grands are lower-cost versions of Perzina grands; the verticals, also a lower-cost alternative, are of an entirely different design from that of Perzina verticals.

Warranty: 10 years, parts and labor, to original purchaser.

PETROF

Piano Royale Prague LLC
P.O. Box 1130
Richland, Washington 99352
509-946-8078
877-946-8078
www.petrof.com

Pianos made by: Petrof, spol. s.r.o., Hradec Králové, Czech Republic

The Petrof piano factory was founded in 1864 by Antonin Petrof in Hradec Králové, an old, historic town 100 kilometers east of Prague, in the present Czech Republic. Five generations of the Petrof family owned and managed the business, during which time the company kept pace with technical developments and earned prizes for its pianos at international exhibitions. The Czechs have long been known for their vibrant musical-instrument industry, which also includes makers of brass, woodwind, and stringed instruments.

In 1947, when all businesses in the Czech Republic were nationalized by the state, the Petrof family was forced out of the business. In 1965 Petrof, along with other piano manufacturers, was forced to join Musicexport, the state-controlled import-export company for musical instruments. Since the fall of the Soviet Union and the liberation of Eastern Europe, the various factories that were part of Musicexport have been spun off as private businesses, including Petrof, which is once again owned and controlled by the Petrof family. Currently Petrof manufactures 5,000 vertical pianos and 900 grands annually.

Petrof recently introduced a series of six new grand piano models, named (in size order) Bora, Breeze, Storm, Pasat, Monsoon, and Mistral, from 5' 2" to 9' 2" in length. Most component parts are produced by Petrof or other Czech factories, including the hardware, plates, and cabinetry. Soundboards are of solid Bohemian spruce, grand rims are of laminated beech and birch, pinblocks are of compressed beech, plates are cast in wet sand, and hammers are from Renner or Abel. These pianos also boast several interesting features: The soundboard is custom-tapered and asymmetrically crowned for optimal resonance; the treble bridge is capped with genuine ebony for better transmission of treble tone; front and rear duplexes are tuned for tonal color; pianos are single-strung for tuning stability; an adjustable bolt has been added from the plate to the wooden cross block for additional tuning stability; and a decorative veneer has been added to the inner rim. The earlier series of Petrof grands with model numbers containing roman numerals will coexist with the new models as long as supplies last.

Actions in Petrof pianos are standard Detoa on the smaller verticals, Renner on the larger grands and larger verticals, and either Renner parts on a Petrof action frame or Petrof Original Actions made by Detoa on mid-size instruments.

Petrof has also invented and patented a version of its new grand action that uses tiny opposing magnets on the wippens and wippen rail. These magnets allow for the removal of the usual lead counterweights in the keys and, according to the company, significantly alter the action's dynamic properties. The new action also furthers the European Union's stated environmental goal of phasing out the use of lead in pianos. The action is adjusted in the factory for a standard touchweight and is serviced in exactly the same way as a standard action. The Magnetic Accelerated Action, as it is known, is a special-order option on the grands. Petrof also offers as an option the Magnetic Balanced Action, which allows the player to quickly and easily change the touchweight in the range of ±4–5 grams simply by turning a knob.

Petrofs are known for their warm, rich, singing tone, full of color. The pianos are solidly built and workmanship is good. After careful preparation, the pianos can sound and feel quite beautiful and hold their own against other European brands. Wages in the Czech Republic have risen in recent years, and with it the price of Petrof pianos, but the company has placed a greater emphasis on quality control and enhanced features in the new models in order to meet the higher expectations that come with higher prices.

Note: For years, Weinbach pianos were made by the Petrof company and were virtually identical to Petrof brand pianos. The Weinbach name is no longer being used in North America.

Warranty: 10 years, parts and labor, to original purchaser, from the manufacturer.

PRAMBERGER

See also Samick.

Samick Music Corp. (SMC)
1329 Gateway Drive
Gallatin, Tennessee 37066
615-206-0077
info@smcmusic.com
www.smcmusic.com

Pianos made by: Samick Musical Instrument Mfg. Co. Ltd., Bogor, West Java, Indonesia

The Pramberger name was used by Young Chang for its premium-level pianos under license from the late piano engineer Joseph Pramberger, who at one time was head of manufacturing at Steinway & Sons. When Pramberger died, in 2003, his estate terminated its relationship with Young Chang and signed up with Samick. However, since Young Chang still holds the rights to its piano designs, Samick has designed new pianos to go with the name.

The J.P. Pramberger Platinum piano is a higher-end instrument, formerly made in Korea, and now made in Indonesia under Korean supervision using the CNC equipment acquired by Samick during its partnership with Bechstein. It is then shipped to the U.S. for inspection, tuning, regulating, and voicing before being shipped to dealers. Several American technicians who had known and worked with Joe Pramberger went to Korea at Samick's request to design this piano. Benefiting by work previously done by Bechstein engineers at the Samick factory, they began with a modified Bechstein scale, then added several features found on current or older Steinways, such as an all-maple (or beech) rim, an asymmetrically tapered white spruce soundboard, vertically laminated and tunneled maple and mahogany bridges with maple cap, duplex scaling, a Renner/Pramberger action, and Renner or Abel hammers. One of the technicians told me that the group feels its design is an advancement of Pramberger's work that he would have approved of.

The Pramberger Signature (formerly known as J. Pramberger) is a more modestly priced instrument from Indonesia whose design is based on the former Korean-built Young Chang version. This line uses Samick's Pratt-Reed Premium action, Renner or Abel hammers, and a Bolduc (Canadian) solid spruce soundboard. The institutional verticals in this line have all-wood cabinet construction and agraffes in the bass section, and the decorator versions include Renner hammers and a slow-close fallboard.

The Pramberger Legacy, the newest addition to the Pramberger line, has a veneer-laminated "surface tension" soundboard, and provides a reasonably priced option for the budget-minded consumer. These models were formerly sold under the Remington label. (The Remington brand is no longer a regular part of the Pramberger lineup, but is available to dealers on special order.)

[Note: Samick's Pratt-Reed Premium action should not be confused with the Pratt-*Read* action used in many American-made pianos in the mid to late 20th century and eventually acquired by Baldwin. Samick says its Pratt-Reed action, designed by its research and development team and based on the German Renner action, is made in Korea.]

See **Samick** for more information.

Warranty: 10 years, parts and labor, transferable to future owners within the warranty period.

RAVENSCROFT

Spreeman Piano Innovations, LLC
7898 East Acoma Drive, Suite 105
Scottsdale, Arizona 85260
480-664-3702
info@RavenscroftPianos.com
www.RavenscroftPianos.com

Handcrafted in Scottsdale, Arizona by piano builder Michael Spreeman, the Ravenscroft piano entered the market for high-end performance pianos in 2006. Two models are available, the 7' 3" model 220 and the 9' model 275. The 220 made its debut in 2007 in the Manufacturers' Showcase of the 50th Annual Convention of the Piano Technicians Guild. A custom-built model 275 is currently the official piano at the Tempe Center for the Arts.

While the general trend in the industry seems to be toward outsourcing to less expensive suppliers, Spreeman says his concept is the exact opposite. Appealing to the niche market of high-end consumers, Spreeman's approach is more along the lines of the early European small-shop builders, with an emphasis on quality and exclusivity.

The case and iron frame of the Ravenscroft piano are constructed in Germany by Sauter to Ravenscroft specifications and shipped to the Arizona facility. The Renner action and Kluge keys of each piano are computer-designed to optimize performance. The rib scale, soundboard, bridges, and string scale are designed by Spreeman, who meticulously hand-builds each instrument with his three-person team.

Currently, only four to six pianos are produced yearly, with pricing beginning at $230,000 for a model 220, and up to $550,000 for a model 275 with "all the extras," including titanium string terminations, exotic veneers, intarsia, artwork, and inlays of precious stones. Most instruments are custom ordered and can take up to a year to complete.

RITMÜLLER — See Pearl River.

RÖNISCH — See Blüthner.

SAMICK

including Kohler & Campbell.
See separate listings for Wm. Knabe, Pramberger, and Seiler.
Samick Music Corp. (SMC)
1329 Gateway Drive
Gallatin, Tennessee 37066
615-206-0077
info@smcmusic.com
www.smcmusic.com

Pianos made by: Samick Musical Instrument Mfg. Co. Ltd., Inchon, South Korea; and Bogor, West Java, Indonesia

Samick was founded by Hyo Ick Lee in 1958 as a Baldwin distributor in South Korea. Facing an immense challenge in an impoverished and war-torn country, in the early 1960s Lee began to build and sell a very limited quantity of vertical pianos using largely imported parts. As the economy improved, Lee expanded his operation, and in 1964 began exporting to other parts of the world, eventually becoming one of the world's largest piano manufacturers, now making most parts in-house. Over the next several decades, Samick expanded into manufacturing guitars and other instruments and opened factories in China and Indonesia, where it shifted much of its production as Korean wages rose. The Asian economic crisis of the late 1990s forced Samick into bankruptcy, but the company emerged from bankruptcy in 2002 and is now on a sound financial footing.

The company says that "Samick" means "three benefits" in Korean, symbolizing the wish that the activities of the company benefit not only the company itself, but also the customers and the Korean economy.

Samick Music Corporation (SMC), the North American sales and marketing arm of the Korean company, distributes Samick, Kohler & Campbell, Pramberger, Wm. Knabe, and Seiler pianos in North America (see separate listings for **Wm. Knabe, Pramberger,** and **Seiler**). Samick no longer distributes pianos under the Bernhard Steiner, Conover Cable, Hazelton Bros., Remington, and Sohmer & Co. names. SMC has a manufacturing, warehousing, and office facility in Tennessee, at which it uncrates, inspects, tunes, regulates, and voices its upper-level Wm. Knabe, J.P. Pramberger, and Kohler & Campbell Millennium-series pianos before shipping them to dealers. While Samick says it will continue to make some pianos in Korea, it is gradually moving most of its production to Indonesia.

Until just a few years ago, Samick primarily made pianos under the Samick and Kohler & Campbell brand names. (For historical information about the original Kohler & Campbell piano company, see *The Piano Book*.) In the 1980s Klaus Fenner, a German piano designer, was hired to revise the Samick scale designs and make them more "European." Most of the Samick and Kohler & Campbell pianos now being made are based on these designs.

Although in most respects the Samick and Kohler & Campbell pianos are similar in quality, so as not to compete with one another the grands are available in different sizes and have some different features. The two lines are primarily differentiated by the fact that Kohler & Campbell grands (except the smallest model) have solid spruce soundboards and individually hitched stringing (also known as single stringing), whereas the Samick grands have veneer-laminated soundboards and conventional loop stringing. A veneer-laminated soundboard (which Samick calls a "surface tension soundboard") is essentially a solid spruce soundboard surrounded by two very thin veneers. Samick pioneered the use of this soundboard with Klaus Fenner's technical advice in early 1980, and it is now used by others as well. Tonally, it behaves much more like a solid spruce soundboard than the old kind of laminated soundboard, which was essentially plywood. Like the old kind, however, it won't crack or lose its crown. The solid spruce soundboard may have a slight tonal advantage, but the laminated one will last longer, so take your pick.

Likewise, single stringing is more elegant to those who know pianos, but otherwise offers little or no advantage over loop stringing. The two brands' vertical pianos are more alike: They have the same difference in soundboards as the grands, but are all loop-strung and come more or less in the same sizes.

Kohler & Campbell's upper-level Millennium pianos have higher-quality features than the regular series, now called New Yorker. The Millennium grands have a maple rim, premium Canadian Bolduc tapered solid spruce soundboard, Renner action and hammers, and satin wood finishes available in lacquer semigloss. The verticals have Renner parts on a Samick-made Pratt-Reed hornbeam action rail, Bolduc solid spruce soundboard, Renner hammers, lacquer semigloss wood finishes, and a sostenuto pedal on the 52" model. All Samick and New Yorker–series Kohler & Campbell pianos are made in Indonesia for the U.S. market. Smaller Millennium verticals and grands are made in Indonesia, larger ones in Korea. However, all Millennium-series pianos are shipped to the U.S. for inspection and tone and action regulation before being shipped to dealers.

[Note: Samick's Pratt-Reed Premium action should not be confused with the Pratt-*Read* action used in many American-made pianos in the mid to late 20th century and eventually acquired by Baldwin. Samick says its Pratt-Reed action is made in Korea and designed after the German Renner action.]

In the Kohler & Campbell price list, KC models are Indonesian-made, New Yorker–series verticals; KM are Indonesian-made Millennium-series verticals; KMV are Korean-made Millennium-series verticals; KCG and KIG are Indonesian-made New Yorker–series grands; KCM are Indonesian-made Millennium-series grands; and KFM are Korean-made Millennium-series grands.

Quality control in Samick's Korean and Indonesian factories has steadily improved, especially in the last few years, and the Indonesian product is said to be almost as good as the Korean. Many large-scale issues have been addressed and engineers are now working on smaller refinements. The company says that new CNC machinery installed in 2007 has revolutionized the consistency and accuracy of its manufacturing. Climate control in the tropically situated Indonesian factory, and issues of action geometry, are also among the areas that have recently seen improvement. Samick's upper-level pianos—Kohler & Campbell Millennium series, J.P. Pramberger, and Wm. Knabe—have met with a very positive response from technicians as to their musical design and performance, exceeding comparably priced pianos from Japan in those regards. Workmanship is good, although still not quite as consistent as in the Japanese pianos. Many of Samick's Indonesian pianos are priced similarly to low-cost pianos from China, and technicians often report finding the Samicks to be more consistent than some of the Chinese. With dealer prep, Samick-made pianos are a good value for most typical uses.

[Note: Samick-made pianos have an odd system of serial numbers consisting of a series of letters and numbers. The system appears to vary from factory to factory. Please contact SMC for information on the date of manufacture of a Samick-made piano.]

Warranty: 10 years, parts and labor, transferable to future owners within the warranty period.

SAUTER

Sauter USA
P.O. Box 1130
Richland, Washington 99354
509-946-8078
877-946-8078
+49-7424-94820 (factory)
info@sauteramerica.com
info@sauter-pianos.de
www.sauter-pianos.de
www.sauterpiano.com

Pianos made by: Carl Sauter Pianofortemanufaktur GmbH & Co. KG, Max-Planck-Strasse 20, 78549 Spaichingen, Germany

---

The Sauter piano firm was founded in 1819 by Johann Grimm, stepfather to Carl Sauter I, and has been owned and managed by members of the Sauter family for six generations, currently by Ulrich Sauter. The factory produces about 800 vertical pianos and 120 grand pianos a year in its factory in the extreme south of Germany, at the foot of the Alps. Structural and acoustical parts are made of high-quality woods, including solid Bavarian spruce soundboards and beech pinblocks. Actions are made by Renner, and Sauter makes its own keys. The keybed is reinforced with steel to prevent warping, and all pianos are fully tropicalized for humid climates. The larger verticals use an action, designed and patented by Sauter, that contains an auxiliary jack spring to aid in faster repetition. Sauter calls this the R2 Double Escapement action. (Although the term *double escapement* does not apply here as it has historically been used, the mechanism has some of the same effects.)

Sauter pianos are especially known for the variety of finishes and styles in which they are available, many with intricate detail and inlay work. It is common to find such rare woods as yew, burl walnut, pyramid mahogany, and genuine ebony in the cabinets of Sauter

pianos, as well as special engravings, which can be customized to any customer's desires. Sauter's M Line of vertical pianos features exclusive cabinet detailing and built-in features such as a hygrometer to measure relative humidity. New Masterline institutional uprights, sold directly to institutions and not through dealers, include protective sidebars, industrial-grade casters, and locking mechanisms. Amadeus is a special-edition 6' 1" grand honoring the 250th anniversary of Mozart's birth, with styling reminiscent of that in Mozart's time. The natural keytops are of polished bone, the sharps of rosewood with ebony caps. Only 36 are to be made, one for each year of Mozart's life.

The company also has introduced versions of its 48" upright and 6' 11" and 7' 6" grands with cabinets designed by the famous European designer Peter Maly. Some recent designs include the 48" upright Vitrea, after the Latin word for glass, with a veneer of greenish glass covering the front of the cabinet; and Ambiente, a 7' 6" grand that is asymmetrically curved on both the bass and treble sides. In the recent past, Sauter has won several prestigious design awards for its Peter Maly–designed pianos.

A couple of extremely unusual models bear mentioning. The 7' 3" model 220 has colored lines painted on the soundboard and white inlays on the tops of the dampers as guides for musicians performing music for "prepared piano," ultramodern music requiring the insertion of foreign objects between the strings, or the plucking or striking of strings directly by the performer. The 1/16-tone microtonal piano is an upright with 97 keys that has a total pitch range, from its lowest to its highest note, of only one octave, the pitch difference from key to key being only 1/16 of a tone (1/8 of a semitone). You can read more about these strange instruments in *The Piano Book*.

Sauter pianos are high-quality instruments with a lush, full, singing tone, closer to an "American" sound than most other European pianos.

Warranty: 5 years, parts and labor, to original purchaser.

SCHILLER — See Irmler.

SCHIMMEL

including Vogel, May Berlin, Wilhelm Schimmel

Schimmel Piano Corporation
329 North New Street
Lititz, Pennsylvania 17543
800-426-3205
schimmel@ptd.net
www.schimmel-piano.de

Pianos made by: Wilhelm Schimmel Pianofortefabrik GmbH, Braunschweig, Germany (Schimmel) and Kalisz, Poland (Vogel and Wilhelm Schimmel); unspecified factory in China (May Berlin)

Wilhelm Schimmel began making pianos in Leipzig in 1885, and his company enjoyed steady growth through the late 19th and early 20th centuries. The two World Wars and the Depression disrupted production several times, but the company has gradually rebuilt itself over the past 60 years with a strong reputation for quality. Today, Schimmel is managed by Hannes Schimmel-Vogel, the husband of Viola Schimmel. Schimmel makes about 2,500 verticals and 500 grands per year and is one of Europe's most prolific piano makers.

Among European piano manufacturers, Schimmel has been a pioneer in the use of computer-aided design and manufacturing. The company has used its Computer Assisted Piano Engineering (CAPE) software to research, design, and implement virtually every aspect of making a piano, from keyboard layout and action geometry to soundboard acoustics and scale design. According to Schimmel, the combination of CNC machinery and handcraftsmanship leads to better results than handwork alone. Schimmel also believes that precision is aided by controlling as much of the production process as possible. For that reason, Schimmel produces its own piano-cabinet components and its own keyboards, which it also supplies to other German piano makers.

For a number of years, Schimmel has organized its model lineup into two principal categories: Schimmel Konzert (model names beginning with K) and Schimmel Classic (model names beginning with C). The Konzert series consists of some of the more recently designed and larger vertical models, and six grand models. The company says that the purpose of the Konzert series is to expand the Schimmel line upward to a higher level of quality than it had previously attained. The Classic series consists of the rest of the verticals, the 6' model 182 grand, and the 6' 10" model 208 grand. This series represents models that have been tested over time and are solid, traditional, high-quality instruments, but without all the latest refinements.

The Konzert series uprights—48" model K122, 49" model K125, and 52" model K132—are based on a more sophisticated philosophy of construction than the Classics. These models also incorporate triplex scaling and other advanced design features. Schimmel's philosophy for these uprights was to design them to be as much like the grands as possible. The treble scales, in fact, are exactly the same as in the Konzert grands. All uprights have adjustable gliders (to adjust to unevenness in the floor) and come with a matching adjustable bench.

In all Konzert grand models, the case sides are angled slightly to obtain a larger soundboard, and all have tunable front and rear duplex ("triplex") scales for greater tonal color, real ebony sharps, and mineral white keytops to mimic the feel of ivory, among other advanced features. The largest grands have reinforced keys for optimal energy transmission.

In 2013, Schimmel announced a major change to its model lineup: An updated, more upscale Konzert series of grand pianos. Notable changes include the use of the model 280's concert-grand action in all Konzert grand sizes, requiring a redesign of each model; selection of improved soundboard and bridge materials; and more time spent voicing the instruments at the factory. Schimmel will continue to produce the previous Konzert grand models entirely in Germany, under the Classic name. Other lines just released to dealers include Schimmel International (built in Germany, with parts sourced internationally) and Wilhelm Schimmel (to be assembled in the company's factory in Kalisz, Poland). These last two lines represent new production concepts and will serve as replacements for the older Classic instruments and the Vogel brand.

Schimmel grand pianos have historically had a tone that was very bright and clear, but a bit thin and lacking in color in the treble. The grands were redesigned, in part, to add color to the tone, and the result is definitely more interesting than before. Sustain is also very good. The pianos are being delivered to U.S. dealers voiced less bright than previously, as this is what the American ear tends to prefer. As for the verticals, the smaller models tend to have a very big bass for their size, with a tone that emphasizes the fundamental, giving the bass a warmer character. The 52" model K132, which features a grand-shaped soundboard, has a very big sound; listening to it, one might think one was in the presence of a grand.

In 2002, Schimmel acquired the PianoEurope factory in Kalisz, Poland, a piano restoration and manufacturing facility. Schimmel at first used this factory to manufacture its Vogel brand, a moderately priced line named after the company's president. This line has now been replaced by the Wilhelm Schimmel brand. Schimmel says that although the skill level of the employees is high, lower wages and other lower costs result in a piano approximately 30 percent less costly than the Schimmel. Wilhelm Schimmel grand pianos feature full Renner actions, with other parts mainly made by Schimmel in Braunschweig, or by the Kalisz factory. The Wilhelm Schimmel pianos, though designed by Schimmel, don't have all the refinements and advanced features of the latest Schimmel models. Nevertheless, under the Vogel name, which can still be found in dealer inventories, they have received praise from many quarters for their high-quality workmanship and sound.

Until 2012, Schimmel imported an entry-level series of pianos from China under the name May Berlin. The pianos were made by an unspecified supplier. The company says it sent soundboard wood and hammer felt for grand pianos to the supplier's factory. When completed, the pianos were inspected in the factory by a top Schimmel technician.

Warranty: Schimmel, Vogel, Wilhelm Schimmel, May Berlin—10 years, parts and labor, to original purchaser.

SCHULZE POLLMANN

North American Music Inc.
11 Holt Drive
Stony Point, New York 10980
845-429-0106
www.schulzepollmann.com
www.namusic.com
Pianos made by: Schulze Pollmann s.r.l., Borgo Maggiore, San Marino

Schulze Pollmann was formed in 1928 by the merger of two German piano builders who had moved to Italy. Paul Pollmann had worked first with Ibach, then with Steinway & Sons (Hamburg), before opening his own piano factory in Germany. He later moved to Italy, where he met Albert Schulze, another relocated German piano builder. Pollmann managed the combined firms until 1942, and was followed by his son Hans, who had managed the piano maker Schimmel before returning to his father's firm. Recently, the company relocated a short distance to San Marino, a tiny city-state entirely surrounded by Italy.

In North America, Schulze Pollmann offers two series of pianos: Masterpiece (grands) and Studio (verticals). The Masterpiece Series pianos, available only by special order, are made entirely in Italy and San Marino, and contain Delignit pinblocks, Renner actions and hammers from Germany, and Ciresa solid red-spruce soundboards from the Val di Fiemme, in Italy.

The company uses both sophisticated technology and handwork in its manufacturing. All soundboards have finger-jointed construction to optimize stability and prevent cracking. Many of the cabinets have beautiful designs and inlays. The Studio series is partially made in Asia and finished off, including deluxe cabinetwork, in San Marino.

The uprights are well built and have a warm, colorful sound with a good amount of sustain. The treble is not nearly as brittle sounding as in some other European uprights. Schulze Pollmann grands are likewise very nicely crafted and arrive at the dealer in good condition, needing only solid preparation to sound their best.

In 2005, Italian auto manufacturer Ferrari Motor Car selected Schulze Pollmann as a partner in the launch of its new Ferrari 612 Scaglietti series of automobiles. For the occasion, Schulze Pollmann crafted a limited-edition version of its 6' 7" model 197/G5 grand piano, still available, with a case that sports Ferrari's racing red and a cast-iron plate in Ferrari gray carbon, the same color as the Scaglietti's engine. The car and the piano have been exhibited together in cities around the world.

Warranty: 10 years, parts and labor.

SCHUMANN

including Falcone, Geo. Steck, Hobart M. Cable,
Welkin Sound
1609 South Grove Avenue #103
Ontario, California 91761
909-484-7498
866-473-5864
estherk@welkinsound.com
estherk@sejungusa.com
www.welkinsound.com
Pianos made by: Nanjing Moutrie Piano Company, Ltd., Nanjing, Jiangsu Province, China

From 2001 to 2012, the Falcone, Geo. Steck, and Hobart M. Cable brands were manufactured by the Korean-based company Sejung at its factory in Qingdao, China. In 2012, this factory was acquired by Parsons Music, and manufacture of these brand names was terminated. Beginning in the summer of 2013, these brands are being made for the North American market by Nanjing Moutrie Piano Company, in Nanjing, Jiangsu Province, China. Nanjing Moutrie's Schumann brand is also being imported here. The Geo. Steck name is no longer being used.

Nanjing Moutrie was established in 1991, and sells the Moutrie and Schumann brands, among others, internationally. The company uses modern CNC machinery to manufacture more than 10,000 pianos per year. The eight vertical sizes and four grand sizes available in the U.S. market use laminated Tibetan spruce soundboards, German strings and pinblocks, agraffes, bubinga inner rims on the grands, and slow-close fallboards, among other modern and advanced features.

SEILER

including Johannes Seiler

Samick Music Corp. (SMC)
1329 Gateway Drive
Gallatin, Tennessee 37066
800-592-9393
615-206-0077
info@smcmusic.com
www.seilerpianousa.com

Pianos made by: Ed. Seiler Pianofortefabrik, Kitzingen, Germany; with Samick Musical Instrument Mfg. Co. Ltd., Bogor, West Java, Indonesia

---

Eduard Seiler, the company's founder, began making pianos in 1849, in Liegnitz, Silesia, then part of Prussia. By 1923 the company had grown to over 435 employees, was producing up to 3,000 pianos per year, and was the largest piano manufacturer in Eastern Europe. In 1945 and after World War II, when Liegnitz (now Legnica) became part of Poland, the plant was nationalized by the Polish Communist government, and the Seiler family left their native homeland with millions of other refugees. In 1954, Steffan Seiler reestablished the company in Copenhagen under the fourth generation of family ownership, and began making pianos again. In 1962 he moved the company to Kitzingen, in Bavaria, Germany, where it resides today. Steffan Seiler died in 1999; the company was managed by his widow, Ursula, until its sale to Samick in 2008. Seiler now produces about 1,000 pianos annually. Samick continues Seiler's tradition of making high-quality pianos, while diversifying the product lineup to suit a wider range of buyers.

Seiler uses a combination of traditional methods and modern technology. The scale designs are of relatively high tension, producing a balanced tone that is quite consistent from one Seiler piano to the next. Although brilliant, the tone also sings well, due to, the company says, a unique, patented soundboard feature called the Membrator system, used in Seiler's SE and ED lines: The perimeter of the soundboard is sculpted to be thicker and heavier in mass than the central portion of the board, forming an internal frame within the soundboard itself. The lighter, inner area becomes the vibrating membrane—a diaphragm on its own—unimpeded by the larger soundboard's attachment to the inner rim. Seiler says that its use of the Membrator system, as well as effective rib positioning, improves the soundboard's efficiency in radiating sound. It's easy to identify the Membrator by the tapered groove around the perimeter of the board.

The grands have wide tails, for greater soundboard area and string length. The German Seiler pianos feature Bavarian spruce soundboards, multi-laminated Delignit pinblocks, quartersawn beech bridges, full Renner actions, and slow-close fallboards. A few years ago, the grands were redesigned with a duplex scale for greater treble tonal color, and with longer keys and a lighter touch. Musically, these redesigns were very successful; they retained the typical Seiler clarity, but had longer sustain and a more even-feeling touch.

In 2010, Samick expanded the Seiler line to cover three price points. The top-level, SE-series instruments continue to be handcrafted at the Seiler factory in Kitzingen, Germany, just as they have been for many years. These come in two styles, Classic and Trend. The construction and specifications of the two styles are the same, but the Trends look a bit more modern, and sport a silver-colored plate and chrome hardware, whereas the Classics have the traditional gold- or bronze-colored plate and brass hardware. Both are available in dozens of special furniture styles with beautiful, exotic woods and inlays.

The mid-level Seiler pianos, the ED models, are also known as the Eduard Seiler line. The pianos are manufactured entirely at Samick's Indonesian factory, using German CNC machinery, to the exact scales and specifications of the hand-built German models. The actions include Renner wippen assemblies and an action rail of Delignit or hornbeam, with keys made by Samick.

Still found in some dealer inventories, the recently discontinued ES models use the same strung backs and cabinets as the ED series. These components were then shipped to Kitzingen, where assembly was completed, full Renner actions and German hammers installed, and the final musical finishing of the instruments performed.

In July 2013, the new Johannes Seiler line was introduced. Though it features cabinetry as beautiful as that of its more expensive brethren, this lower-cost line has its own scale design not shared by other Samick-owned brands, and is produced entirely in the company's Indonesian facility, using Samick's premium action and hammers from Abel. These three grand and three vertical models can be identified by the "Johannes Seiler" label on the fallboard.

At both the German and Indonesian factories, strung backs are inspected and cabinet parts carefully fitted to ensure that all specifications have been met to precise tolerances. Soundboard mass distribution and rib positioning are under strict quality control, to achieve consistency in the soundboard's acoustical properties. Pre-stretching of the strings is done several times, followed by multiple tunings, to ensure maximum stability. Hammer alignment, voicing, and key weighting and balancing are all carefully performed by experienced Seiler technicians, both at the factory and at the company's Tennessee distribution facility, before shipment to dealers.

Seiler's 52" upright is available by special order with the optional Super Magnet Repetition (SMR) action, a patented feature that uses magnets to increase repetition speed. During play, tiny magnets attached to certain action parts of each note repel each other, forcing the parts to return to their rest position faster, ready for the next keystroke.

Warranty: 10 years, parts and labor, to original purchaser.

Sejung — See Schumann.

SOHMER

Persis International, Inc.
2647 N. Western Ave. #8030
Chicago, Illinois 60647
773-342-4212
www.sohmerpianos.com

Founded by German immigrant Hugo Sohmer in 1872, Sohmer & Co. was owned and managed by the Sohmer family in New York City for 110 years. Having no descendants to take over the business, the founder's grandsons sold the company in 1982. As the company changed hands several times over the following decade, limited production of Sohmer pianos took place in Connecticut and Pennsylvania, finally ceasing in 1994 (see the Sohmer entry in *The Piano Book* for a more detailed recent history).

Pianos are once again being made under this venerable name, once considered among the finest of American-built instruments. Sohmer pianos from Persis International are manufactured by Royale, a Korean firm descended from a former joint venture between the German manufacturer Ibach and the Korean manufacturer Daewoo, neither of which any longer makes pianos. During the German-Korean joint venture, the string scales, bridges, soundboards, rib dimensions, actions, keys, and hammers were redesigned by Ibach to German standards. Models include a 50" vertical and 5' 3", 5' 10", and 7' 2" grands. The pianos have high-quality European components, such as Renner actions, Abel hammers, Delignit pinblocks, Röslau strings, and Ciresa solid spruce soundboards.

In the past, there was a legal dispute over the ownership of the Sohmer trademark, and for a short time, Sohmer-branded pianos were distributed by both Persis International and Samick Music Corporation (SMC). That dispute was settled in favor of Persis, and SMC stopped selling Sohmer pianos in 2010, relinquishing all rights to the Sohmer brand. (Note: Persis's pianos are labeled "Sohmer," and SMC's were labeled "Sohmer & Co.")

Warranty: 10 years, parts and labor, to original purchaser.

STECK, GEO. — See Schumann.

STEINBERG, G. — See Perzina, Gebr.

STEINBERG, WILH.

including Eisenberg
Thüringer Pianoforte GmbH
Mozartstr. 3
07607 Eisenberg, Germany
+49 (0) 36691 / 595-0
+49 (0) 36691 / 595-40 (fax)
sales@wilh-steinberg.com
www.Wilh-Steinberg.com

Pianos made by: Thüringer Pianoforte GmbH, Eisenberg, Germany; some models made by, or in partnership with, Parsons Music Ltd., China.

This company, formerly known as Wilh. Steinberg Pianofortefabrik, was formed after the reunification of Germany by the merger of several East German piano companies that collectively trace their origins back to 1877. Since July 2013, the company has been owned by Parsons Music Ltd. in China. In addition to its own pianos, Thüringer Pianoforte makes several other European piano brands under OEM agreements. The company also specializes in custom cabinets and finishes. Piano production is about 700 verticals and 50 grands per year.

Thüringer Pianoforte makes pianos under the names Wilh. Steinberg and Eisenberg, in three levels of quality. The highest-quality level is the Wilh. Steinberg Signature series. These pianos are made in Germany, with actions by Renner and keyboards by Kluge. Cabinets for the verticals are made by Thüringen in its own facilities; grand cabinets are made by Parsons Music in China.

"Amadeus" and "Passione" are models in this series with special cabinet styles.

The second level of quality is represented by the Wilh. Steinberg Nomos series, and contains only vertical pianos. These models use components manufactured in China, but the instruments are assembled, regulated, and voiced in Germany.

The third level, represented by the Eisenberg line, is entirely made in China using Thüringer designs, but at an affordable price point. New in 2013, and available through Atlantic Music Center, is 5' 5" Eisenberg model E-165, with a Phoenix System bass bridge using bridge agraffes, which, the manufacturer says, provides much greater resonance in the bass (see **www.hurst woodfarmpianos.co.uk** for more information on the Phoenix system).

Warranty: 5 years, parts and labor, to original purchaser.

STEINGRAEBER & SÖHNE

Steingraeber & Söhne
Steingraeberpassage 1
95444 Bayreuth, Germany
+49-921-64049
+49-921-58272 (fax)
steingraeber@steingraeber.de
www.steingraeber.de

Bayreuth is famous the world over for its annual summer Wagner festival. But tucked away in the old part of town is a second center of Bayreuth musical excellence and one of the world's best-kept secrets: Steingraeber & Söhne. The company was founded in 1852 by Eduard Steingraeber, though its roots date back to the 1820s, when Eduard's father and uncle opened a workshop for square pianos and organs in the city of Neustadt. Eduard was an innovative piano designer, exhibiting his first full-size cast-iron frame at the world exhibition in Paris in 1867. From 1872 on, Steingraeber was associated with, and built pianos for, Franz Liszt and Richard Wagner, and in 1873 opened its first concert hall in Bayreuth.

Steingraeber has worked with furniture designers since 1904, when it collaborated with Bruno Paul on his Art Nouveau furniture for the St. Louis World's Fair. More recently, the company built a piano designed by Jørn Utzon, architect of the Sydney Opera House, with features reminiscent of that building. The Steingraeber engineering department offers consulting services on the technical development of pianos. This service was created in 1991, after reunification, to assist piano manufacturers of the former East Germany, and has designed and manufactured prototypes of new piano models for a number of European piano manufacturers. These designs are different from Steingraeber's own current models. In 2012, Steingraeber entered into a cooperative agreement with Pearl River, in China, to help that company design and manufacture a new line of premium pianos.

Steingraeber is one of the smaller piano manufacturers in the world, producing fewer than 80 grands and 60 verticals per year for the top end of the market. It is owned and operated by sixth-generation family member Udo Schmidt-Steingraeber, who still makes pianos using the traditional methods of his forebears at the company's present factory, which it has occupied since 1872.

Steingraeber makes three sizes of vertical piano: 48", 51", and 54". An interesting option on the vertical models is their "twist and change" panels: two-sided top and bottom panels, one side finished in polished ebony, the other in a two-toned combination of a wood veneer and ebony. The panels can be reversed as desired by the piano owner to match room décor, or just for a change of scenery.

The company also makes five sizes of grand piano: 5' 7", 6' 3", 7', 7' 7", and 8' 11". The 5' 7" model A-170 grand has an unusually wide tail, allowing for a larger soundboard area and longer bass strings than are customary for an instrument of its size. The 7' model C-212, known as the Chamber Concert Grand, and recently redesigned from the model 205, was intended to embody the tone quality of the Steingraeber Liszt grand piano of circa 1873, but with more volume in the bass register. The 8' 11" model E-272 concert grand was introduced in 2002 for Steingraeber's 150th anniversary. Unique features include a drilled capo bar for more sustain in the treble, unusually shaped rim bracing, and a smaller soundboard resonating area in the treble to better match string length. In 2007, Steingraeber introduced the 7' 7" D-232 concert grand to provide an additional smaller, concert-size instrument. Its design includes many of the innovations of the E-272. New in 2012 is the 6' 3" model B-192, which follows the design enhancements of the D-232 and C-212 in a size more comfortable for homes and smaller concert halls.

Steingraeber pianos have a unique sound, with an extensive tonal palette derived from a mixture of clarity and warmth.

Steingraeber is known for its many innovative technical improvements to the piano, one of which is a new action for uprights, available in all three vertical-piano models. This SFM action, as it is called, contains no jack spring, instead using magnets to return the jack more quickly under the hammer butt for faster repetition. Another innovation, introduced in 2013, is the optional sordino pedal, which inserts a thin strip of felt between hammers and strings. Popular in early

19th-century grand pianos, the purpose of this feature is not, as in most modern pianos, to damp the sound almost completely, but rather to create a distant, ethereal sound, and thus to expand the instrument's expressive possibilities. On a Steingraeber piano, the sordino can either replace the sostenuto as the middle pedal or, be operated by a fourth pedal or a knee lever. A knee lever can also be employed to activate the so-called Mozart Rail, which reduces both the hammer-blow distance and the key-touch depth to simulate the sound and touch of the pianos of Mozart's day. In 2014, Steingraeber introduced the world's lightest grand piano lid, made of modern aircraft material with a honeycomb interior, which makes the lid nearly 50% lighter than conventional lids. The company says that the new material also projects sound better. Steingraeber also specializes in so-called ecological or biological finishes, available as an option on most models. This involves the use of only organic materials in the piano, such as natural paints and glues in the case, and white keytops made from cattle bone.

Steingraeber pianos can also be special-ordered with a carbon-fiber soundboard, and with the Phoenix system of bridge agraffes (see **www.hurstwoodfarmpianos .co.uk** for more information on the Phoenix system).

In addition to its regular line of pianos, Steingraeber makes a piano that can be used by physically handicapped players who lack the use of their legs for pedaling. A wireless (Bluetooth) pedal actuator is operated by biting on a special denture.

Warranty: 5 years, parts and labor, transferable to future owners within the warranty period.

STEINWAY & SONS

Steinway & Sons
One Steinway Place
Long Island City, New York 11105
718-721-2600
800-366-1853
www.steinway.com

Heinrich Engelhardt Steinweg, a cabinetmaker and piano maker from Seesen, Germany, emigrated with his family to the United States in 1850, and established Steinway & Sons in 1853. Within a relatively short time, the Steinways were granted patents that revolutionized the piano, and which were eventually adopted or imitated by other makers. Many of these patents concerned the quest for a stronger frame, a richer, more powerful sound, and a more sensitive action. By the 1880s, the Steinway piano was in most ways the modern piano we have today, and in the next generation the standards set by the founder were strictly adhered to. (The early history of Steinway & Sons is fascinating, and is intimately connected to the history of New York City and the piano industry in general. You can read a summary of it in *The Piano Book;* there are also several excellent books devoted to the subject.)

In the 1960s the fourth generation of Steinways found themselves without any heirs willing or able to take over the business, and without enough capital to finance much-needed equipment modernization; eventually, in 1972, they sold their company to CBS. CBS left the musical instrument business in 1985, selling Steinway to an investment group. In 1995 the company was sold again, this time to Conn-Selmer, Inc., a major manufacturer of brass and woodwind instruments, and the combined company (called Steinway Musical Instruments, Inc.) was taken public on the New York Stock Exchange. In 2013, Paulson & Company, a private-equity firm led by Queens native John Paulson, purchased the public company and took it private once again. Paulson has said that he is committed to continuing the quality-first approach on which Steinway has built its reputation. Steinway also owns a branch factory in Hamburg, Germany, which serves the world market outside of the Americas, and two major suppliers: the Herman Kluge company, Europe's largest maker of piano keys; and the O.S. Kelly company, the only remaining piano plate foundry in the U.S.

Steinway makes two types of vertical piano in three sizes: a 45" model 4510 studio, a 46½" model 1098 studio, and a 52" model K-52 upright. Models 4510 and 1098 are technically identical, with differences only in the cabinets: the former is in a period style for home use, the latter in an institutional cabinet for school use or less furniture-conscious home use. In all three models, the middle pedal operates a sostenuto mechanism. All Steinway verticals use a solid spruce soundboard, have no particleboard, and in many other ways are similar in design, materials, and quality of workmanship to Steinway grands. Actions are made by Renner. Model K-52 in ebony, and model 1098 in ebony, mahogany, and walnut, come with an adjustable artist bench, the others with a regular bench.

Technicians have always liked the performance of Steinway verticals, but used to complain that the studio models in particular were among the most difficult pianos to tune and would unexpectedly jump out of tune. In recent years, Steinway has made small design changes to alleviate this problem. The pianos are now mechanically more normal to tune and are stable, but an excess of false beats (tonal irregularities) still make the pianos at times difficult to tune.

Steinway makes six sizes of grand piano, two of which are new within the last several years. All ebony, mahogany, and walnut grand models come with an adjustable artist bench, the others with a regular bench.

The 5' 1" model S is very good for a small grand, but has the usual limitations of any small piano and so is recommended only where space considerations are paramount. The 5' 7" model M is a full six inches longer, but costs little more than the S. Historically one of Steinway's more popular models, it is found in living rooms across the country. Its medium size makes the tone in certain areas slightly less than perfect, but it's an excellent home instrument.

The 5' 10½" model L has been replaced with the model O of the same size. Model O was first produced in 1902, but discontinued in 1924 in favor of the model L. Changes over time in both engineering and musical taste, as well as a desire to better synchronize the offerings of the New York factory with Hamburg (where the model O was never abandoned), seemed to dictate a return to the O. The main difference between the two models is in the shape of the tail—the L has a squared-off tail, the O a round tail—but this can also affect the soundboard and bridges and therefore the tone.

Reintroduction of the model O followed by one year the reintroduction of the legendary 6' 2" model A. First offered in 1878 and discontinued in New York in 1945, the model A revolutionized piano making by featuring, for the first time, the radial rim bracing and one-piece bent rim construction now used in all Steinway grands. Over the years the model A has gone through several makeovers, each of slightly different size and scaling. The version being reintroduced was made in New York from 1896 to 1914 and is the same size as the model A that has been made at the Hamburg factory for more than a century. Models O and A are suitable for larger living rooms, and for many school and teaching situations.

The 6' 10½" model B is the favorite of many piano technicians. It is the best choice for the serious pianist, recording or teaching studio, or small recital hall. Small design changes and other refinements to this model in recent years have brought a steady stream of accolades. The 8' 11¾" model D, the concert grand, is the flagship of the Steinway line and the piano of choice for the overwhelming majority of concert pianists. It's too large for most places other than the concert stage.

Steinway uses excellent materials and construction techniques in the manufacture of its grands. The rims, both inner and outer, are made in one continuous bend from layers of maple, and the beams are of solid spruce. The keybed is of quartersawn spruce planks freely mortised together, and the keys are of Bavarian spruce. The pinblock consists of seven laminations of maple with successive grain orientations of 45 and 90 degrees. The soundboard is of solid Sitka spruce, the bridges are vertically laminated of maple with a solid maple cap, and all models have duplex scaling.

It is well known that Steinway's principal competition comes from used and rebuilt Steinways, many of which come in exotic veneers or have elaborately carved or customized "art cases." The company has responded by expanding its product line to include modern-day versions of these collector's items. The Crown Jewel Collection consists of the regular models in natural (non-ebonized) wood veneers, many of them exotic. They are finished in a semigloss that Steinway calls Satin Lustre. In addition to satin and semigloss finishes, all regular Steinway grands are also now available in polyester high-polish ebony, lacquer high-polish ebony, and polyester high-polish white.

Limited Edition models, issued at irregular intervals, are reproductions of turn-of-the-century designs, or pianos with artistic elements that make them unique. The newest Limited Edition model, honoring the 70th anniversary of the birth of John Lennon, is the Imagine Series, a white piano that incorporates artwork by Lennon, along with other design elements.

During the early 1900s, ownership of art-case Steinways became a symbol of wealth and culture. Steinway has resumed this tradition by regularly commissioning noted furniture designers to create new art-case designs, usually around a theme. For example, in 1999 Frank Pollaro designed an art case called Rhapsody to commemorate the 100th anniversary of the birth of George Gershwin. The piano featured a blue-dyed maple veneer adorned with more than 400 hand-cut mother-of-pearl stars and a gilded silver plate. Each year sees new art-case pianos from Steinway, and they are truly stunning.

As another way of capitalizing on the popularity of older Steinways, the company also operates at its factory the world's largest piano rebuilding facility for the restoration of older Steinways. *The Piano Book* contains a great deal of additional information on the purchase of older or restored Steinways. See also "Buying a Used or Restored Piano" in this publication.

The underlying excellence of the Steinway musical designs and the integrity of the construction process are the hallmarks of the Steinway piano. Steinway pianos at their best have the quintessential American piano sound: a powerful bass, a resonant midrange, and a singing treble with plenty of tonal color. Although other brands have some of these characteristics, it is perhaps the particular combination of harmonics that comprise the Steinway's tonal coloration that, more than anything else, distinguishes it from other brands and gives it its richness, depth, and power. The construction process creates a very durable and rigid framework that also contributes to the power of its sound.

Musical and cabinet detailing, such as factory voicing and regulation, and plate and cabinet cosmetics, are reasonable, but have traditionally lagged somewhat behind the company's European competitors in finesse. Over the last couple of years, however, the company has been making a determined effort to remedy this by paying close attention to many small details, and by applying lessons learned from its European operations. Examples include: rounding the edges and corners of satin ebony models so they will better hold the finish and not prematurely wear through; more careful woodworking on the bottom of the piano, and applying a clear coat of lacquer to the bottom instead of painting it to cover imperfections; protecting the case and plate during stringing and other manufacturing operations so they don't have to be touched up, often imperfectly, later on; additional time spent playing-in pianos during manufacture in order to naturally harden the hammers so they don't need quite so much chemical hardening and voicing in the field; and other improvements too numerous to mention here. (See discussion and photo essay on this subject in the **Spring 2011 issue** of *Piano Buyer*.)

Steinway pianos require more preparation by the dealer than most pianos in their class, but, as mentioned above, the factory preparation has greatly improved, so the work required by the dealer is no longer excessive. Still, some dealers are more conscientious than others, and I occasionally hear of piano buyers who "can't find a good Steinway." How much of this is due to inherent weaknesses in some pianos, how much to lack of dealer preparation, and how much to customer bias or groundless complaining is hard to tell. I suspect it is a little of each. Piano technicians who work on these pianos do sometimes remark that some seem to have more potential than others. Many dealers do just enough regulating and voicing to make the instruments acceptable to the average customer, but reserve the highest level of work for those situations where a fussy customer for one of the larger models is trying to decide between a few particular instruments. Most customers for a Steinway will probably find one they like on the sales floor. However, if you are a discriminating buyer who has had trouble finding a Steinway that suits your preferences, I recommend letting the salesperson know, as precisely as you can, what you're looking for. Give the salesperson some time to have a few instruments prepared for you before making a decision. It may also help to tactfully let the salesperson know that you are aware

that other options are available to you in the market for high-end pianos. By the way, customers seeking to purchase a model B or D Steinway who have not found the piano they are looking for at their local dealer can make arrangements with that dealer to visit the Steinway factory in New York, where a selection of the larger models is kept on hand for this purpose.

As mentioned earlier, Steinway owns a branch factory in Hamburg, Germany, established in 1880. The "fit and finish" (detailing) of the pianos at this factory is reputed to be better than at the one in New York, although pianists sometimes prefer the sound of the New York Steinway. Traditionally, the Hamburg factory has operated somewhat autonomously, but more recently the company has been synchronizing the two plants through technical exchanges, model changes, jointly built models, and materials that are shipped from New York to Hamburg. It's possible to special-order a Hamburg Steinway through an American Steinway dealer; or an enterprising American customer could travel to Europe, buy one there, and have it shipped back home.

In 2008 Steinway underwent a change in management, the first in 23 years. For the first time, the company's top executives were recruited from its European operations rather than from America. It is speculated that this may have signaled a subtle change of direction with regard to quality issues, and may be one of the reasons that European quality standards are appearing to be more strictly applied to the American-made instruments.

Warranty: 5 years, parts and labor, to original purchaser.

STORY & CLARK

Story & Clark Piano Co.
269 Quaker Drive
Seneca, Pennsylvania 16346
800-247-6557
814-676-6683
www.qrsmusic.com

Owned by: QRS Music Technologies, Inc.

Pianos made by: various Asian manufacturers

Hampton Story began making pianos in 1857 and was joined by Melville Clark in 1884. The business settled in Grand Rapids, Michigan, in 1901, where it remained, under various owners, until about 1986. Around 1990, a new owner moved the company to its present location in Seneca, Pennsylvania. Over the years, pianos were manufactured under a number of different names, including, in recent years, Story & Clark, Hobart M. Cable, Hampton, and Classic. In 1993 QRS Piano Rolls, Inc., now QRS Music Technologies, Inc., purchased Story & Clark. (Ironically, QRS itself was founded in 1900 by Melville Clark, of the Story & Clark Piano Co. of old.) QRS, historically the nation's major source of music rolls for traditional player pianos, now manufactures an electronic player-piano system, called PNOmation, that can be retrofitted into any piano (see "Buying an Electronic Player-Piano System").

Story & Clark offers two series of vertical and grand pianos, which are made to its specifications by various Asian manufacturers. The Heritage Series is a popularly priced line of verticals and grands with a Storytone II soundboard—Story & Clark's name for a veneer-laminated, all-spruce soundboard.

The Signature Series also comes in both vertical and grand models. These pianos feature premium Renner hammers, Röslau strings, maple and mahogany rims, solid brass hardware, Bolduc tapered soundboards of solid spruce, sand-cast plates, and advanced low-tension scales. The pianos have cabinet designs that offer lots of detail for the money and coordinate with major furniture trends. In spite of their beauty, the company says, these pianos are also appropriate for school and commercial applications.

In keeping with the tradition, begun by Hampton Story and Melville Clark, of integrating the latest technology into pianos, all Story & Clark grand pianos now come equipped with both the PNOmation electronic player-piano system, and a package of SilentPNO features, including PNOscan™. Vertical pianos are equipped with only PNOscan. PNOscan is an optical sensor strip attached to the key frame directly under the keys. It senses the entire movement of each key so that it can precisely re-create every detail of an original performance, including the force, speed, and duration of each note played, without affecting the touch or response of the keyboard. The data captured by PNOscan is then transmitted through either a USB connection or MIDI output to a computer, general MIDI sound module, or other digital device. PNOscan and PNOmation are both HD MIDI ready. The addition of PNOscan to every Story & Clark acoustic piano gives customers the potential to have all the features of a digital piano. When combined with various accessories, PNOscan gives users the ability to learn, record, compose, practice in silence, and more. In addition, the ability of PNOscan to interface seamlessly with an iPad, tablet, or other computing device allows for their integration with the web-enabled PNOmation system recently introduced, with SilentPNO (a hybrid digital/acoustic piano), and with programs such as Music Minus One.

Beginning in 2013, the PNOmation system factory-installed in Story & Clark grands will be fully concealed, with no solenoid-rail cover visible, requiring no cutting of the legs to fit the entire 88-note system, and allowing full use of the original pedals and trapwork.

Warranty: 15 years, parts, and 5 years, labor, to original purchaser.

VOSE & SONS — See Everett.

WALTER, CHARLES R.

Walter Piano Company, Inc.
25416 CR 6
Elkhart, Indiana 46514
574-266-0615
www.walterpiano.com

Charles Walter, an engineer, was head of Piano Design and Developmental Engineering at C.G. Conn in the 1960s, when Conn was doing important research in musical acoustics. In 1969 Walter bought the Janssen piano name from Conn, and continued to make Janssen pianos until 1981. In 1975 he brought out the Charles R. Walter line of consoles and studios, based on his continuing research in piano design. Walter began making grands in 1997.

The Walter Piano Company is fairly unique among U.S. piano manufacturers in that it is a family business, staffed by Charles and his wife, several of their grownup children, and various in-laws, in addition to unrelated production employees. The Walters say that each piano is inspected and signed by a member of their family before being shipped. Dealers and technicians report that doing business with the Walters is a pleasure in itself.

The Charles R. Walter line consists of 43" and 45" studio pianos in various decorator and institutional styles, and 5' 9" and 6' 4" grands. Note that both vertical models have full-size actions and therefore are studio pianos, not consoles, as I define those terms. In fact, they are identical pianos inside different cabinets. Walter calls the 43" model a console because of its furniture styling, but due to its larger action, it will outplay most real consoles on the market.

Although Mr. Walter is not oblivious to marketing concerns, his vertical piano bears the mark of being designed by an engineer who understands pianos and strives for quality. The pianos are built in a traditional manner, with heavy-duty, full-length spruce backposts; a solid spruce soundboard; and Delignit pinblock. Exceptionally long, thick keys that are individually lead-weighted provide a very even feel across the keyboard. The scale design is well thought out and the bass sounds good most of the way to the bottom. The cabinetry is substantial, contains no particleboard, and is beautifully finished. Some of the fancy consoles in particular, such as the Queen Anne models, are strikingly beautiful. The pianos are well prepared at the factory and so need minimal preparation by the dealer.

The vertical pianos now use Renner actions, but a Chinese-made action is available as a lower-cost option, reducing the price of the piano by about $1,500. The Chinese parts are virtually indistinguishable from the Renner parts, but they make the action feel just slightly lighter due to differing spring tensions.

The Walter 5' 9" and 6' 4" grands were designed by Del Fandrich, one of the nation's most respected piano-design engineers. Both models have high-quality features such as a maple rim, Renner action, Kluge keys, Delignit pinblock, tapered solid spruce soundboard, and Abel hammers (Ronsen hammers in the 5' 9" model). The 5' 9" grand also has a number of innovative features: A portion of the inner rim and soundboard at the bass end of the piano are separated from the rest of the rim and allowed to "float." Less restricted in its movement, the soundboard can reproduce the fundamental frequencies of the lower bass notes more as a larger piano does. A special extension of the tenor bridge creates a smoother transition from bass to treble. Eight plate nosebolts increase plate stability, helping to reduce energy loss to the plate and thus increase sustain. Inverted half-agraffes embedded in the capo bar maintain string alignment and reduce unwanted string noise. The Walter grands are competently built and play very well.

Warranty: 12 years, parts and labor, transferable to future owners within the warranty period.

WEBER — See Young Chang.

WEINBACH — See Petrof.

WENDL & LUNG — See Feurich.

WERTHEIM

Wertheim Piano
51 Park Street
South Melbourne, Victoria
3205 Australia
+61 (3) 9690 5566
+61 (0) 418 350124 (mobile)
info@wertheimpiano.com
www.wertheimpianousa.com

Pianos made by: Huzhou J.sder Piano Co., Ltd., Deqing County, Zhejiang, China

Wertheim pianos were first produced in Germany from 1875 to 1908, and then in Richmond, Australia, a suburb of Melbourne, from 1908 to 1935. Approximately 18,000 uprights were made during the Richmond period. They were popular, all-purpose pianos with a good reputation for easy maintenance, and were used in a wide range of settings, including schools and public halls. The most famous exponent of the Wertheim brand was Dame Nellie Melba, who frequently requested Wertheim pianos for her performances. The business was very successful, and the Wertheim family achieved celebrity status in Australia during the 1920s. However, the Depression, coupled with the rise of the radio as the dominant form of entertainment, led to a decline in piano sales, and the factory closed in 1935.

The Wertheim brand is currently owned and distributed by John Martin, who revived it in 2002. In his more than 44 years in the music industry, Martin has owned full-line music retail stores, managed a buying group for music-store retailers, and manufactured and distributed Wertheim pianos.

Wertheim pianos are currently manufactured by the J.sder Piano Co., in Deqing County, Zhejiang, China. The pianos include parts such as Röslau strings, Strunz soundboards, and Abel hammers, all from Germany; as well as agraffe construction, sharps of real ebony, and a soft-close fallboard—features that, among pianos made in Asia, are found only in the higher-quality brands. The company says that the pianos are voiced to European standards and tastes. Wertheim says that its aim is to make the best-value, top-class pianos, using the best designs, materials, and workmanship. To that end, it has affiliated with Australian quality-control specialist Christopher Whelan.

Currently, the Wertheim Euro line of pianos is being introduced in North America, with 48½" and 52½" uprights, and 4' 10", 5' 7", and 6' 1" grands, each available in several popular finishes.

Warranty: 5 years, parts and labor, to original purchaser.

WYMAN

Wyman Piano Company
P.O. Box 506
Colusa, California 95932
513-543-0909
206-350-7912 (fax)
info@wymanpiano.com
www.wymanpiano.com

Pianos made by: Beijing Hsinghai Piano Group, Ltd., Beijing, China

Wyman Piano Company was created by experienced former Baldwin executives with more than 60 years of combined piano industry experience. Although a relatively new company, Wyman distribution has grown to include the U.K., Germany, and Japan, as well as the U.S.

The regular Wyman line consists of six vertical piano sizes and four grand models in a variety of cabinet styles and finishes. All are based on German scale designs and are manufactured in China by the Beijing Hsinghai Piano Group (see **Beijing Hsinghai**) at that company's new 1.2-million-square-foot factory.

Wyman offers the model CD2 player-piano system by Pianoforce, a new entrant in the field of player-piano systems (see **Pianoforce** in the **article on electronic player-piano systems**). The optional CD system features a unique stamped rail designed specifically for these pianos that, according to the company, allows a much lower profile than other player systems that use universal rails to fit any piano. These are installed at the Beijing factory.

Wyman says that its executives make frequent trips to the factory in Beijing to monitor manufacturing and inspect finished instruments.

Warranty: 10 years, parts and labor, transferable to future owners within the warranty period. Lifetime warranty on the soundboard.

XINGHAI — See Beijing Xinghai.

YAMAHA

including Cable-Nelson. See separate listing for Disklavier in "Buying an Electronic Player-Piano System."

Yamaha Corporation of America
P.O. Box 6600
Buena Park, California 90622
714-522-9011
800-854-1569
infostation@yamaha.com
www.yamaha.com

Pianos made by: Yamaha Corporation, Hamamatsu, Japan and other locations (see text)

Torakusu Yamaha, a watchmaker, developed Japan's first reed organ, and founded Yamaha Reed Organ Manufacturing in 1887. In 1899, Yamaha visited the U.S. to learn how to build pianos. Within a couple of years he began making grand and vertical pianos under the name Nippon Gakki, Ltd. Beginning in the 1930s, Yamaha expanded its operations, first into other musical instruments, then into other products and services, such as sporting goods and furniture, and finally internationally.

Export of pianos to the U.S. began in earnest about 1960. In 1973, Yamaha acquired the Everett Piano Co., in South Haven, Michigan, and made both Yamaha and Everett pianos there until 1986. In that year, the company moved its piano manufacturing to a plant in Thomaston, Georgia, where it made Yamaha consoles, studios, and some grands until 2007, when a depressed piano market and foreign competition forced it to close its doors. Since then, the company has introduced new models, made in other Yamaha factories, to replace those formerly made in Thomaston.

Yamaha is probably the most international of the piano manufacturers. In addition to its factories in Japan, Yamaha has plants in Mexico, China, and Indonesia. Yamaha pianos sold in the U.S. are made in Japan, China, and Indonesia. In 2009, Yamaha closed its factories in England (with Kemble) and Taiwan. Models formerly made in those factories are now being produced in Yamaha's other Asian plants. Yamaha also owns the renowned Austrian piano maker, Bösendorfer.

Yamaha's console line consists of the 43" model b1, in continental style, with a laminated soundboard; and the 44" models M460 and M560 in furniture style (free-standing legs), representing two levels of cabinet sophistication and price. All are internally similar (except for the soundboard) and have a compressed action typical of a console, which means that the action will not be quite as responsive as in larger models.

The studio line consists of the popular 45" model P22 in institutional style (legs with toe blocks) with school-friendly cabinet; the furniture-style version P660; and the 45" model b2, with a less-expensive institutional-style cabinet. The b2 replaces the Chinese-made model T118. All studio models are internally similar, with a full-size action. All Yamaha verticals under 48" tall are now made in the company's Indonesian factory, which has been making pianos for more than 30 years and, according to Yamaha, adheres to the same quality standards as its Japanese plant.

The uprights are the very popular 48" model U1; the 48" model b3, which is made in Indonesia, has the same scale design as the U1, and replaces the Chinese-made model T121SC; and the 52" model U3. The U3 joins the YUS5 (see below) in having a "floating" soundboard—the soundboard is not completely attached to the back at the top, allowing it to vibrate a little more freely to enhance the tonal performance. A new Super U series of uprights (YUS1, YUS3, and YUS5) have different hammers and get additional tuning and voicing at the factory, including voicing by machine to create a more consistent, more mellow tone. The YUS5 has German Röslau music wire instead of Yamaha wire, also for a mellower tone. This top-of-the-line 52" upright also has agraffes, duplex scaling, and a sostenuto pedal (all other Yamaha verticals have a practice/mute pedal). The U- and YU-series uprights are all made in Japan and come with soft-close fallboards.

Yamaha verticals are very well made for mass-produced pianos. The taller uprights in particular are considered a "dream" to service by technicians, and are very much enjoyed by musicians. Sometimes the pianos can sound quite bright, though much less so now than in previous years. The current version of the model P22 school studio is said to have been redesigned to sound less bright and to have a broader spectrum of tonal color. Double-striking of the hammer in the low tenor on a soft or incomplete keystroke is a problem occasionally mentioned in regard to Yamaha verticals by those who play with an especially soft touch. This tendency is a characteristic of the action design, the trade-off being better-than-normal repetition for a vertical piano. If necessary, it's possible that a technician can lessen this problem with careful adjustment, but at the risk of sacrificing some speed of repetition.

Yamaha grands come in several levels of sophistication and size. The Classic Collection consists of the 5' model GB1K, the 5' 3" model GC1M, and the 5' 8" model GC2. The GB1K has simplified case construction and cabinetry, no duplex scale, and the middle pedal operates a bass-sustain mechanism. It does have a soft-close fallboard. It is currently the only Yamaha grand sold in the U.S. that is made in Indonesia. The GC1M and GC2 have regular case construction, duplex scale, soft-close fallboard, and sostenuto pedal.

The Conservatory Classic and Conservatory Concert Collections of C-series grands were replaced in 2012 with the CX series, consisting of the 5' 3" model C1X, the 5' 8" model C2X, the 6' 1" model C3X, the 6' 7" model C5X, the 7' model C6X, and the 7' 6" model C7X. The new CX series incorporates some of the design elements of the limited-production CF series (see below) into the higher-production C-series pianos to create a sound more like that of a high-end American or European instrument—see our **review** in the Spring 2014 issue. Features include a European spruce soundboard crowned using CF-series technology, a thicker rim and bracing, German music wire, additional time spent voicing, regulating, and tuning by very skilled craftsmen, and some changes in cabinet design.

Both the C and CX models have the advanced construction, scaling, and cabinetry mentioned earlier, including a true sostenuto pedal and a soft-close fallboard. Both also have vertically laminated bridges with maple or boxwood cap. The vertically laminated design is similar to that found in Steinways and other fine pianos, and is considered to give the bridges greater strength and resistance to cracking and better transmission of vibrational energy. All C and CX grands have keytops of Ivorite™, Yamaha's ivory alternative.

Finally, the new CF Series Concert Grand Pianos consist of the 9' model CFX (replacing the model CFIIIS), and the 6' 3" model CF4 and 7' model CF6 (respectively replacing, in the U.S., the models S4B and S6B, which will remain available by special order only). The pianos in this collection are made in a separate factory to much higher standards and with some different materials: e.g., maple and mahogany in the rim, which is made more rigid, for greater tonal power, than in the other collections; higher-grade soundboard material; a treble "bell" (as in the larger Steinways) to enhance treble tone; German strings, and hammer and scaling changes, for a more mellow tone; as well as the more advanced features of the other collections. The result is an instrument capable of greater dynamic range, tonal color, and sustain than the regular Yamahas. The new CF-series pianos have a thicker rim and more substantial structure than their predecessors, for greater strength and tonal projection, and the method for developing the soundboard crown has been changed to allow the soundboard to vibrate more freely and with greater resonance. The models CF4 and CF6 have an open pinblock design reminiscent of some European pianos, which gives the tuner slightly greater control over the tuning pins. Yamaha says that the CF series represents 19 years of research and development by its craftsmen, designers, and engineers. The Yamaha concert grand is endorsed and used by a number of notable musicians, including Olga Kern, Michael Tilson Thomas, Chick Corea, and Elton John.

Other than the special grands just described, Yamaha grands have historically been a little on the percussive side and have been said not to "sing" as well as some more expensive pianos. The tone has been very clear and often bright, especially in the smaller grands, although the excessive brightness that once characterized Yamaha has seems to be a thing of the past. The clarity and percussiveness are very attractive, but are sometimes said to be less well suited for classical music, which tends to require a singing tone and lush harmonic color. On the other hand, Yamaha is the piano of choice for jazz and popular music, which may value clarity and brightness more than the other qualities mentioned. More recently, however, Yamaha has been trying to move away from this image of a "bright" piano whose sound is limited to jazz. First with its larger grands, and more recently with the smaller ones, Yamaha has changed the bridge construction and hammer density, and provided more custom voicing at the factory, to bring out a broader spectrum of tonal color.

Both Yamaha's quality control and its warranty and technical service are legendary in the piano business. They are the standard against which every other company is measured. For general home and school use, piano technicians probably recommend Yamaha pianos more often than any other brand. Their precision, reliability, and performance make them a very good value for a consumer product.

Yamaha also makes a piano under the name Cable-Nelson. The verticals are made in Yamaha's factory in Hangzhou, Zhejiang Province, China, southwest of Shanghai, where the company also makes guitars. The 45" model CN116 is an institutional-style vertical with a laminated soundboard. The model CN216 is a furniture-style version of the 116. The 5' Cable-Nelson grand model CN151 is made in Indonesia alongside the Yamaha grand model GB1K.

Cable-Nelson is the name of an old American piano maker whose roots can be traced back to 1903. Yamaha acquired the name when it bought the Everett Piano Company, in 1973, and used the name in conjunction with Everett pianos until 1981.

There is a thriving market for used Yamahas. If you're considering buying a used Yamaha, please read "Should I Buy a Used, 'Gray Market' Yamaha or Kawai Piano?" on pages 176–177 of *The Piano Book*, and "Buying a Used or Restored Piano" in this publication.

Yamaha also makes electronic player pianos called Disklaviers, as well as a variety of hybrid acoustic/ digital instruments—including Silent Piano (formerly called MIDIPiano), the AvantGrand series, and the model NU1, that account for a substantial percentage of the company's sales. These products are separately reviewed in the articles "Buying an Electronic Player-Piano System" and "Hybrid Pianos."

Warranty: Yamaha and Cable-Nelson—10 years, parts and labor, to original purchaser.

YOUNG CHANG
including Weber, Albert Weber, and Fridolin

Young Chang North America, Inc.
6000 Phyllis Drive
Cypress, California 90630
657-200-3470
800-874-2880
www.youngchang.com
www.weberpiano.com

Pianos made by: Young Chang Co., Ltd., Incheon, South Korea; and Tianjin, China

In 1956, three brothers—Jai-Young, Jai-Chang, and Jai-Sup Kim—founded Young Chang and began selling Yamaha pianos in Korea under an agreement with that Japanese firm. Korea was recovering from a devastating war, and only the wealthy could afford pianos. But the prospects were bright for economic development, and as a symbol of cultural refinement the piano was much coveted. In 1962 the brothers incorporated as Young Chang Akki Co., Ltd.

In 1964 Yamaha and Young Chang entered into an agreement in which Yamaha helped Young Chang set up a full-fledged manufacturing operation. Yamaha shipped partially completed pianos from Japan to the Young Chang factory in Incheon, South Korea, where Young Chang would perform final assembly work such as cabinet assembly, stringing, and action installation. This arrangement reduced high import duties. As time went by, Young Chang built more of the components, to the point where they were making virtually the entire piano. In 1975 the arrangement ended when Young Chang decided to expand domestically and internationally under its own brand name, thus becoming a competitor. Young Chang began exporting to the U.S. in the late 1970s, and established a North American distribution office in California in 1984. In addition to making pianos under its own name, Young Chang also made pianos for a time for Baldwin under the Wurlitzer name, for Samsung under the Weber name, and private-label names for large dealer chains and distributors worldwide.

Weber & Co. was established in 1852 by Albert Weber, a German immigrant, and was one of the most prominent and highly respected American piano brands of the late 19th and early 20th centuries. During the consolidation of the American piano industry in the early 20th century, Weber became part of the Aeolian family of brands. Following Aeolian's demise in 1985, Young Chang acquired the Weber name.

In 1995, in response to rising Korean wages and to supply a growing Chinese domestic market, Young Chang built a 750,000-square-foot factory in Tianjin, China, and gradually began to move manufacturing operations there for some of its models. Today, the Tianjin facility produces Young Chang and Weber pianos, and components for the Albert Weber line, which is assembled in South Korea.

Hyundai Development Company, a Korean civil-engineering and construction firm, acquired Young Chang in 2006. The company says that Hyundai Development has brought the necessary capital for factory renovations and has instituted new advanced industrial quality-control systems.

In 2008 Young Chang hired noted American piano designer Delwin D. Fandrich to undertake a redesign of the entire Young Chang and Weber piano line. Highlights include extensively redesigned cast-iron plates, new string scales, and new rib designs. New directly-coupled bass bridges, along with unique "floating soundboard" configurations, improve soundboard mobility around the bass bridge for better bass tonal response. At the same time, a revised hammer-making process, in which the hammers are cold-pressed with less felt compression, provides for greater hammer resilience and improved tone, with less voicing required. Fandrich says that all of these features and processes contribute to his goal of building instruments with improved tonal balance and musicality, and provide opportunities to standardize manufacturing processes for better quality control. The new designs were phased in gradually from 2011 to 2013.

Along with being redesigned by Delwin Fandrich, former multiple piano lines were consolidated into just three lines: the Young Chang (Y) and Weber (W) series are entry- and mid-level instruments made in China, and the Albert Weber (AW) line comprises upper-level models made in Korea. The AW grands have lower-tension scales, maple rims, and Renner actions, and higher-quality hammer felt, soundboard material, and veneers (on wood-veneered models). The Y and W grands have lauan rims and Young Chang actions. The AW verticals use slightly better materials than the other verticals for the cabinets, hardware, music wire, and keys, though in general the differences are smaller than with the grands.

The Young Chang and Weber pianos distinctly differ from one another: the Weber models have a low-tension scale and softer, cold-pressed hammers, and the greater warmth and romantic tonal characteristics that often accompany that type of scale; the Young Chang models have a higher-tension scale and firmer cold-pressed hammers, and the greater brightness and stronger projection of a more modern sound. The Weber line, also known as the Premium Edition, also has agraffes in the bass section of the verticals, and beveled lids on the grands. Beginning in 2015, Weber grands will be optionally available with Wessell, Nickel & Gross composite actions.

For Schimmel dealers, Young Chang now makes the Fridolin brand as a lower-cost alternative to the Schimmel piano. Fridolin is named after Fridolin Schimmel, younger brother of Wilhelm Schimmel, who founded the Schimmel Piano Company in Germany in 1885. Fridolin emigrated to America in 1890 and established his own piano-manufacturing business in Faribault, Minnesota, in 1893. Today's Fridolin-branded pianos are similar to Young Chang's Weber line, except that the Fridolins have upgraded hammers, and receive deluxe preparation in the factory before being shipped to dealers. The Fridolin line is warranted by Young Chang.

Quality control in Young Chang's Korean factory has improved little by little over the years, and is now nearly as good as that in Japan. Most of the problems currently encountered are minor ones that can be cured by a good dealer make-ready and a little follow-up service, and the pianos hold up well in the field, even in institutions. The Albert Weber pianos, in particular, have great musical potential and respond well to expert voicing. Pianos from the factory in China, like other pianos from that country, have been uneven in quality, but in recent years have greatly improved. Young Chang says that Hyundai Development Group has upgraded the factories in both countries, and that the pianos made at the Tianjin factory are now on a par with those made in Korea.

Young Chang also owns Kurzweil Music Systems, a manufacturer of professional keyboards and home digital pianos, which it acquired in 1990.

Warranty: Young Chang and Weber—10 years, parts and labor, to the original purchaser; Albert Weber—15 years, parts and labor, transferable to future owners during the warranty period, plus a lifetime warranty on parts to the original owner. ▦

[*Online Edition readers*: After reading the following introduction, please click below to access the free searchable database of acoustic piano models and prices.]

[Acoustic Piano Database]

This guide contains price information for nearly every brand, model, style, and finish of new piano that has regular distribution in the United States and, for the most part, Canada. Omitted are some marginal, local, or "stencil" brands (brands sold only by a single dealership). Prices are in U.S. dollars and are subject to change. Prices include an allowance for the approximate cost of freight from the U.S. warehouse to the dealer, and for a minimal amount of make-ready by the dealer. The prices cited in this edition were compiled in February 2015 and apply only to piano sales in the U.S. Prices in Canada are often very different due to differences in duty, freight, sales practices, and competition.

Note that the prices of European pianos vary with the value of the dollar against the euro. For this edition, the exchange rate used by most manufacturers was approximately €1 = $1.20–1.30. Prices of European pianos include import duties and estimated costs of airfreight (where applicable) to the dealer. However, actual costs will vary depending on the shipping method used, the port of entry, and other variables. Also keep in mind that the dealer may have purchased the piano at an exchange rate different from the current one.

Unless otherwise indicated, cabinet styles are assumed to be traditional in nature, with minimal embellishment and straight legs. Recognizable furniture styles are noted, and the manufacturer's own trademarked style name is used when an appropriate generic name could not be determined. Please see the section on "Furniture Style and Finish" in the article "Piano-Buying Basics" for descriptions or definitions of terms relating to style and finish.

"Size" refers to the height of a vertical or the length of a grand. These are the only dimensions that vary significantly and relate to the quality of the instrument. The height of a vertical piano is measured from the floor to the top of the piano. The length of a grand piano is measured from the very front (keyboard end) to the very back (tail end) with the lid closed.

About Prices

The subject of piano pricing is difficult, complicated, and controversial. One of the major problems is that piano dealers tend to prefer that list prices be as high as possible so they can still make a profit while appearing to give very generous discounts. Honesty about pricing is resisted.

But even knowing what is "honest" is a slippery business because many factors can have a dramatic effect on piano pricing. For one thing, different dealerships can pay very different wholesale prices for the same merchandise, depending on:

- the size of the dealership and how many pianos it agrees to purchase at one time or over a period of time
- whether the dealer pays cash or finances the purchase
- the degree to which the dealer buys manufacturer overstocks at bargain prices
- any special terms the dealership negotiates with the manufacturer or distributor.

In addition to these variations at the wholesale level, retail conditions also vary from dealer to dealer or from one geographic area to another, including:

- the general cost of doing business in the dealer's area
- the level of pre- and post-sale service the dealer provides
- the level of professionalism of the sales staff and the degree to which they are trained and compensated
- the ease of local comparison shopping by the consumer for a particular type of piano or at a particular price level.

Besides the variations between dealerships, the circumstances of each sale at any particular dealership can vary tremendously due to such things as:

- how long a particular piano has been sitting around unsold, racking up finance charges for the dealer
- the dealer's financial condition and need for cash at the moment

- competing sales events going on at other dealerships in the area
- whether or not the customer is trading in a used piano.

As difficult as it might be to come up with accurate price information, confusion and ignorance about pricing for such a high-ticket item is intolerable to the consumer, and can cause decision-making paralysis. I strongly believe that a reasonable amount of price information actually greases the wheels of commerce by giving the customer the peace of mind that allows him or her to make a purchase. In this guide I've tried to give a level of information about price that reasonably respects the interests of both buyer and seller, given the range of prices that can exist for any particular model.

Prices include a bench except where noted. (Even where a price doesn't include a bench, the dealer will almost always provide one and quote a price that includes it.) Most dealers will also include delivery and one or two tunings in the home, but these are optional and a matter of agreement between you and the dealer. Prices do not include sales tax.

In this guide, two prices are given for each model: Manufacturer's Suggested Retail Price (MSRP) and Suggested Maximum Price (SMP).

Manufacturer's Suggested Retail Price (MSRP)

The MSRP is a price provided by the manufacturer or distributor and designed as a starting point from which dealers are expected to discount. I include it here for reference purposes—only rarely does a customer pay this price. The MSRP is usually figured as a multiple of the wholesale price, but the specific multiple used differs from company to company. **For that reason, it's fruitless to compare prices of different brands by comparing discounts from the MSRP.** To see why, consider the following scenario:

Manufacturer A sells brand A through its dealer A. The wholesale price to the dealer is $1,000, but for the purpose of setting the MSRP, the manufacturer doubles the wholesale price and sets the MSRP at $2,000. Dealer A offers a 25 percent discount off the MSRP, for a "street price" of $1,500.

Manufacturer B sells brand B through its dealer B. The wholesale price to the dealer is also $1,000, but manufacturer B triples the wholesale price and sets the MSRP at $3,000. Dealer B offers a generous 50 percent discount, for a street price of, again, $1,500.

Although the street price is the same for both pianos, a customer shopping at both stores and knowing nothing about the wholesale price or how the MSRPs are computed, is likely to come away with the impression that brand B, with a discount of 50 percent off $3,000, is a more "valuable" piano and a better deal than brand A, with a discount of 25 percent off $2,000. Other factors aside, which dealer do you think will get the sale? It's important to note that there is nothing about brand B that makes it deserving of a higher MSRP than brand A—how to compute the MSRP is essentially a marketing decision on the part of the manufacturer.

Because of the deceptive manner in which MSRPs are so often used, some manufacturers no longer provide them. In those cases, I've left the MSRP column blank.

Suggested Maximum Price (SMP)

The Suggested Maximum Price (SMP) is a price I've created, based on a profit margin that I've uniformly applied to published wholesale prices. (Where the published wholesale price is believed to be bogus, as is sometimes the case, I've made a reasonable attempt to find out what a typical small dealer actually pays for the piano, and use that price in place of the published one.) Because in the SMP, unlike in the MSRP, the same profit margin is applied to all brands, the SMP can be used as a "benchmark" price for the purpose of comparing brands and offers. The specific profit margin I've chosen for the SMP is one that dealers often try—but rarely manage—to attain. Also included in the SMP, in most cases, are allowances for duty (where applicable), freight charges, and a minimal amount of make-ready by the dealer. Although the SMP is my creation, it's a reasonable estimate of the **maximum** price you should realistically expect to pay. However, **most sales actually take place at a discount to the SMP**, as discussed below.

Actual Selling or "Street" Price

As you should know by now from reading this publication, most dealers of new pianos are willing—and expect—to negotiate. Only a handful of dealers have non-negotiable prices. For more information on negotiating, please see **"Negotiating Price and Trade-Ins"** in the article **"Piano Buying Basics."** *The Piano Book* also gives advice about negotiating tactics.

How good a deal you can negotiate will vary, depending on the many factors listed earlier. But in order to make a budget, or to know which pianos are within your budget, or just to feel comfortable enough to actually make a purchase, you need some idea of what is considered normal in the industry. In most cases, discounts from the Suggested Maximum Price range from 10 to 30 percent. This does *not* mean that if you try hard enough, you can talk the salesperson into giving you a 30 percent discount. Rather, it reflects the wide range of prices possible in the marketplace due to the many factors discussed earlier. For budgeting purposes only, I suggest figuring a discount of about 15 or 20 percent. This will probably bring you within about 10 percent, one way or the other, of the final negotiated price. Important exception: Discounts on Steinway pianos generally range from 0 to 10 percent. For your convenience in figuring the effects of various discounts,

a discount calculator is included in the model and price database, accessible through the electronic edition of this publication.

There is no single "fair" or "right" price that can be applied to every purchase. The only fair price is that which the buyer and seller agree on. It's understandable that you would like to pay as little as possible, but remember that piano shopping is not just about chasing the lowest price. Be sure you are getting the instrument

that best suits your needs and preferences, and that the dealer is committed to providing the appropriate level of pre- and post-sale service.

For more information about shopping for a new piano and how to save money, please see pages 60–75 in *The Piano Book, Fourth Edition.*

[*Online Edition readers:* Click below to access the free searchable database of acoustic piano models and prices.]

[Acoustic Piano Database]

Model	Feet	Inches	Description	MSRP*	SMP*
ALTENBURG					
Verticals					
AV108		42.5	Continental Polished Ebony	5,000	3,690
AV108		42.5	Continental Polished Cherry/Mahogany	5,075	3,750
AV110		43	Classic Polished Ebony	5,500	4,090
AV110		43	Classic Polished Cherry/Mahogany	5,575	4,150
AV110		43	American Country Oak/Sable Brown Mahogany	6,300	4,690
AV110		43	French Provincial Cherry/Country French Oak	6,425	4,790
AV115		45	Polished Ebony	5,763	4,290
AV115		45	Polished Cherry/Mahogany	5,735	4,350
AV118		46	Institutional Polished Ebony	6,576	4,890
AV118		46	Institutional Satin Walnut	6,635	5,190
AV120		48	Polished Ebony	6,300	4,890
AV120		48	Polished Mahogany	6,375	4,950
AV132		52	Classic Polished Ebony	7,750	5,990
Grands					
AG145	4	9	Polished Ebony	11,563	8,790
AG145	4	9	Polished Mahogany/Cherry/White	12,088	9,190
AG160	5	3	Polished Ebony	13,975	10,780
AG160	5	3	Polished Mahogany/Cherry/White	14,475	11,180
AG170	5	7	Polished Ebony	15,550	11,990
AG170	5	7	Polished Mahogany/Cherry/White	16,075	12,390
AG185	6	1	Polished Ebony	18,188	13,790
AG185	6	1	Polished Mahogany/Cherry/White	18,725	14,190
			With Round or Curved Legs, add		1,000
			Satin Ebony/Mahogany/Cherry, add		800
ASTIN-WEIGHT					
Verticals					
U-500		50	Oiled Oak	17,180	16,180
U-500		50	Santa Fe Oiled Oak	18,580	17,580
U-500		50	Lacquer Oak	17,580	16,580
U-500		50	Oiled Walnut	17,780	16,780
U-500		50	Lacquer Walnut	18,180	17,180
Grands					
	5	9	Satin Ebony	39,500	38,500

*See pricing explanation on page 201.

Model	Feet	Inches	Description	MSRP*	SMP*
BALDWIN					
Verticals					
B342		43	French Provincial Satin Cherry	9,265	6,790
B442		43	Satin Mahogany	9,265	6,790
BJ120		47	Polished Ebony	7,985	5,990
BJ120		47	Polished Rosewood	8,295	6,190
BP1		47	Polished Ebony	7,985	5,990
B243		47	Satin Ebony/Walnut (school piano)	9,265	6,790
B247		47	Polished Ebony	9,265	6,790
BH122		48	Polished Ebony	8,625	6,390
BJ124		48	French Provincial Polished Ebony/Rosewood	9,265	6,790
BP3		48	French Provincial Polished Ebony/Rosewood	9,265	6,790
BP5		49	Polished Ebony	9,585	6,990
BP5		49	Polished Rosewood	9,895	7,190
B252		52	Satin Ebony	11,495	8,190
Grands					
BP148	4	10	Satin Ebony	21,095	14,190
BP148	4	10	Polished Ebony	20,145	13,590
BP148	4	10	Polished Mahogany/Walnut/White	21,095	14,190
BP152	5		Satin Ebony	23,595	15,790
BP152	5		Polished Ebony	22,695	15,190
BP152	5		Polished Mahogany/Walnut/White	23,695	15,790
BP165	5	5	Satin Ebony	25,595	16,990
BP165	5	5	Polished Ebony	24,595	16,390
BP165	5	5	Polished Mahogany/Walnut/White	25,595	16,990
BP178	5	10	Satin Ebony	35,195	22,990
BP178	5	10	Polished Ebony	33,595	21,990
BP178	5	10	Polished Mahogany/Walnut/White	35,195	22,990
BP190	6	3	Satin Ebony	42,195	27,390
BP190	6	3	Polished Ebony	40,295	26,190
BP190	6	3	Polished Mahogany/Walnut/White	42,195	27,390

BECHSTEIN, (C.)

Models beginning with "B" say only "Bechstein" on the fallboard. Others say "C. Bechstein."

Bechstein Verticals

Model	Feet	Inches	Description	MSRP*	SMP*
B112		44	Polished Ebony	24,000	24,000
B112		44	Polished White	25,200	25,200
B116		45.5	Polished Ebony	24,800	24,800
B116		45.5	Satin Mahogany/Walnut/Cherry	29,600	29,600
B116		45.5	Polished White	27,600	27,600
B120 Select		47.5	Polished Ebony	26,200	26,200
B120 Select		47.5	Satin Mahogany/Walnut/Cherry	31,200	31,200
B120 Select		47.5	Polished Mahogany/Walnut/Cherry	31,200	31,200
B120 Select		47.5	Polished White	29,000	29,000
B124 Imposant		49	Polished Ebony	27,200	27,200
B124 Imposant		49	Polished White	28,800	28,800
B124 Style		49.5	Polished Ebony	28,200	28,200
B124 Style		49.5	Satin Mahogany/Walnut/Cherry	33,000	33,000
B124 Style		49.5	Polished Mahogany/Walnut/Cherry	33,000	33,000
B124 Style		49.5	Polished White	30,000	30,000

C. Bechstein Verticals

Model	Feet	Inches	Description	MSRP*	SMP*
M116K		45.5	Polished Ebony	33,200	33,200
Classic 124		49	Polished Ebony	42,000	42,000
Classic 124		49	Satin Walnut/Mahogany/Cherry	47,800	47,800
Classic 124		49	Polished Walnut/Mahogany/Cherry	47,800	47,800
Elegance 124		49	Polished Ebony	43,800	43,800

*See pricing explanation on page 201.

Model	Feet	Inches	Description	MSRP*	SMP*
BECHSTEIN, (C.) *(continued)*					
Elegance 124		49	Satin Walnut/Cherry	50,800	50,800
Elegance 124		49	Polished Walnut/Mahogany/Cherry	50,800	50,800
Concert 8		51.5	Polished Ebony	70,600	70,600
Concert 8		51.5	Satin Walnut/Mahogany/Cherry	80,800	80,800
Concert 8		51.5	Polished Walnut/Mahogany	81,600	81,600
Concert 8		51.5	Special Woods	82,000	82,000
Bechstein Grands					
B160	5	3	Polished Ebony	62,000	62,000
B160	5	3	Polished Mahogany/Walnut	79,800	79,800
B160	5	3	Polished White	75,400	75,400
B160	5	3	Satin and Polished Special Woods	84,000	84,000
B175	5	8	Polished Ebony	68,600	68,600
B175	5	8	Polished Walnut/Mahogany	86,200	86,200
B175	5	8	Polished White	82,000	82,000
B175	5	8	Satin and Polished Special Woods	90,600	90,600
B190	6	3	Polished Ebony	73,000	73,000
B190	6	3	Polished Mahogany/Walnut	93,000	93,000
B190	6	3	Polished White	88,600	88,600
B190	6	3	Satin and Polished Special Woods	97,400	97,400
B208	6	8	Polished Ebony	84,200	84,200
B208	6	8	Polished Mahogany/Walnut	102,000	102,000
B208	6	8	Polished White	97,600	97,600
B228	7	5	Polished Ebony	95,200	95,200
C. Bechstein Grands					
L167	5	6	Satin and Polished Ebony	112,400	112,400
L167	5	6	Satin Mahogany/Walnut/Cherry	134,400	134,400
L167	5	6	Polished Mahogany/Walnut/Cherry/White	134,400	134,400
L167	5	6	Special Woods	141,800	141,800
MP192	6	4	Satin and Polished Ebony	132,000	132,000
MP192	6	4	Satin Mahogany/Walnut/Cherry	154,000	154,000
MP192	6	4	Polished Mahogany/Walnut/Cherry/White	154,000	154,000
MP192	6	4	Special Woods	161,400	161,400
B212	7		Satin and Polished Ebony	164,600	164,600
C234	7	7	Polished Ebony	199,400	199,400
D282	9	2	Polished Ebony	253,200	253,200
BLÜTHNER					
Prices do not include bench.					
Verticals					
D		45	Satin and Polished Ebony	31,713	29,542
D		45	Satin and Polished Walnut/Mahogany	34,250	31,825
D		45	Satin and Polished Cherry	34,408	31,967
D		45	Satin and Polished White	33,933	31,540
D		45	Satin and Polished Bubinga/Yew/Rosewood/Macassar	35,201	32,681
C		46	Satin and Polished Ebony	35,237	32,713
C		46	Satin and Polished Mahogany/Walnut	38,055	35,250
C		46	Satin and Polished Cherry	38,232	35,409
C		46	Satin and Polished White	37,703	34,933
C		46	Satin and Polished Bubinga/Yew/Rosewood/Macassar	39,113	36,202
C		46	Saxony Polished Pyramid Mahogany	44,750	41,275
C		46	Polished Burl Walnut/Camphor	47,569	43,812
A		49	Satin and Polished Ebony	40,599	37,539
A		49	Satin and Polished Mahogany/Walnut	43,846	40,461
A		49	Satin and Polished Cherry	44,049	40,644
A		49	Satin and Polished White	43,440	40,096
A		49	Satin and Polished Bubinga/Yew/Rosewood/Macassar	45,064	41,558

*See pricing explanation on page 201.

Model	Feet	Inches	Description	MSRP*	SMP*
BLÜTHNER (continued)					
A		49	Saxony Polished Pyramid Mahogany	51,560	47,404
A		49	Polished Burl Walnut/Camphor	54,808	50,327
B		52	Satin and Polished Ebony	45,961	42,365
B		52	Satin and Polished Mahogany/Walnut	49,638	45,674
B		52	Satin and Polished Cherry	49,867	45,880
B		52	Satin and Polished White	49,178	45,260
B		52	Satin and Polished Bubinga/Yew/Rosewood/Macassar	51,016	46,914
B		52	Saxony Polished Pyramid Mahogany	58,370	53,533
B		52	Polished Burl Walnut/Camphor	62,047	56,842
S		57.5	Satin and Polished Ebony	61,762	56,586
S		57.5	Satin and Polished Mahogany/Walnut	66,703	61,033
S		57.5	Satin and Polished Cherry	67,012	61,311
S		57.5	Satin and Polished White	66,086	60,477
S		57.5	Satin and Polished Bubinga/Yew/Rosewood/Macassar	68,556	62,700
S		57.5	Saxony Polished Pyramid Mahogany	78,438	71,594
S		57.5	Polished Burl Walnut/Camphor	83,379	76,041
Verticals			Sostenuto pedal, add	3,400	3,060
Grands					
11	5	1	Satin and Polished Ebony	80,621	73,559
11	5	1	Satin and Polished Mahogany/Walnut	87,071	79,364
11	5	1	Satin and Polished Cherry	87,474	79,727
11	5	1	Satin and Polished White	86,265	78,639
11	5	1	Satin and Polished Bubinga/Yew/Rosewood/Macassar	89,489	81,540
11	5	1	Saxony Polished Pyramid Mahogany	103,195	93,876
11	5	1	Polished Burl Walnut/Camphor	103,195	93,876
11	5	1	President Polished Ebony	91,810	83,629
11	5	1	President Polished Mahogany/Walnut	98,260	89,434
11	5	1	President Polished Bubinga	100,676	91,608
11	5	1	President Burl Walnut	114,384	103,946
11	5	1	Wilhelm II Satin and Polished Ebony	94,327	85,894
11	5	1	Wilhelm II Polished Mahogany/Walnut	101,873	92,686
11	5	1	Wilhelm II Polished Pyramid Mahogany	120,600	109,540
11	5	1	Wilhelm II Polished Burl Walnut	120,600	109,540
11	5	1	Ambassador Santos Rosewood	116,336	105,702
11	5	1	Ambassador Walnut	113,192	102,873
11	5	1	Nicolas II Satin Walnut with Burl Inlay	115,578	105,020
11	5	1	Louis XIV Rococo Satin White with Gold	124,776	113,298
11	5	1	Jubilee Polished Ebony	98,026	89,223
11	5	1	Jubilee Polished Mahogany/Walnut	104,476	95,028
11	5	1	Jubilee Burl Walnut	120,600	109,540
11	5	1	Julius Bluthner Edition	104,118	94,706
10	5	5	Satin and Polished Ebony	92,938	84,644
10	5	5	Satin and Polished Mahogany/Walnut	100,373	91,336
10	5	5	Satin and Polished Cherry	100,838	91,754
10	5	5	Satin and Polished White	99,444	90,500
10	5	5	Satin and Polished Bubinga/Yew/Rosewood/Macassar	103,161	93,845
10	5	5	Saxony Polished Pyramid Mahogany	117,102	106,392
10	5	5	Polished Burl Walnut/Camphor	117,102	106,392
10	5	5	President Polished Ebony	104,127	94,714
10	5	5	President Polished Mahogany/Walnut	111,562	101,406
10	5	5	President Polished Bubinga	114,350	103,915
10	5	5	President Burl Walnut	128,291	116,462
10	5	5	Senator Walnut w/Leather	111,888	101,699
10	5	5	Senator Jacaranda Satin Rosewood w/Leather	121,212	110,091
10	5	5	Wilhelm II Satin and Polished Ebony	108,738	98,864
10	5	5	Wilhelm II Polished Mahogany/Walnut	117,437	106,693
10	5	5	Wilhelm II Polished Pyramid Mahogany	134,507	122,056

*See pricing explanation on page 201.

Model	Feet	Inches	Description	MSRP*	SMP*
BLÜTHNER (continued)					
10	5	5	Wilhelm II Polished Burl Walnut	134,507	122,056
10	5	5	Ambassador Santos Rosewood	134,110	121,699
10	5	5	Ambassador Walnut	130,485	118,437
10	5	5	Nicolas II Satin Walnut with Burl Inlay	128,812	116,931
10	5	5	Louis XIV Rococo Satin White with Gold	143,839	130,455
10	5	5	Jubilee Polished Ebony	110,343	100,309
10	5	5	Jubilee Polished Mahogany/Walnut	117,778	107,000
10	5	5	Jubilee Burl Walnut	134,507	122,056
10	5	5	Julius Bluthner Edition	114,996	104,496
6	6	3	Satin and Polished Ebony	101,364	92,228
6	6	3	Satin and Polished Mahogany/Walnut	109,473	99,526
6	6	3	Satin and Polished Cherry	109,979	99,981
6	6	3	Satin and Polished White	108,459	98,613
6	6	3	Satin and Polished Bubinga/Yew/Rosewood/Macassar	112,514	102,263
6	6	3	Saxony Polished Pyramid Mahogany	127,718	115,946
6	6	3	Polished Burl Walnut/Camphor	127,718	115,946
6	6	3	President Polished Ebony	112,552	102,297
6	6	3	President Polished Mahogany/Walnut	120,661	109,595
6	6	3	President Polished Bubinga	123,702	112,332
6	6	3	President Burl Walnut	138,907	126,016
6	6	3	Senator Walnut w/Leather	124,320	112,888
6	6	3	Senator Jacaranda Satin Rosewood w/Leather	133,644	121,280
6	6	3	Wilhelm II Satin and Polished Ebony	118,595	107,736
6	6	3	Wilhelm II Polished Mahogany/Walnut	128,083	116,275
6	6	3	Wilhelm II Polished Pyramid Mahogany	145,123	131,611
6	6	3	Wilhelm II Polished Burl Walnut	145,123	131,611
6	6	3	Ambassador Santos Rosewood	139,517	126,565
6	6	3	Ambassador Walnut	136,841	124,157
6	6	3	Nicolas II Satin Walnut with Burl Inlay	140,490	127,441
6	6	3	Louis XIV Rococo Satin White with Gold	156,878	142,190
6	6	3	Jubilee Polished Ebony	118,768	107,891
6	6	3	Jubilee Polished Mahogany/Walnut	126,877	115,189
6	6	3	Jubilee Burl Walnut	145,123	131,611
6	6	3	Julius Bluthner Edition	125,874	114,287
6	6	3	Jubilee Plate, add	5,594	5,035
4	6	10	Satin and Polished Ebony	120,222	109,200
4	6	10	Satin and Polished Mahogany/Walnut	129,839	117,855
4	6	10	Satin and Polished Cherry	130,440	118,396
4	6	10	Satin and Polished White	128,637	116,773
4	6	10	Satin and Polished Bubinga/Yew/Rosewood/Macassar	133,446	121,101
4	6	10	Saxony Polished Pyramid Mahogany	151,479	137,331
4	6	10	Polished Burl Walnut/Camphor	151,479	137,331
4	6	10	President Polished Ebony	131,410	119,269
4	6	10	President Polished Mahogany/Walnut	141,028	127,925
4	6	10	President Polished Bubinga	144,635	131,172
4	6	10	President Burl Walnut	162,668	147,401
4	6	10	Senator Walnut w/Leather	142,968	129,671
4	6	10	Senator Jacaranda Satin Rosewood w/Leather	152,292	138,063
4	6	10	Wilhelm II Satin and Polished Ebony	140,659	127,593
4	6	10	Wilhelm II Polished Mahogany/Walnut	151,912	137,721
4	6	10	Wilhelm II Polished Pyramid Mahogany	168,884	152,996
4	6	10	Wilhelm II Polished Burl Walnut	168,884	152,996
4	6	10	Ambassador Santos Rosewood	162,804	147,524
4	6	10	Ambassador Walnut	158,404	143,564
4	6	10	Nicolas II Satin Walnut with Burl Inlay	166,627	150,964
4	6	10	Louis XIV Rococo Satin White with Gold	186,064	168,458
4	6	10	Jubilee Polished Ebony	137,626	124,863
4	6	10	Jubilee Polished Mahogany/Walnut	147,244	133,520

*See pricing explanation on page 201.

Model	Feet	Inches	Description	MSRP*	SMP*
BLÜTHNER (continued)					
4	6	10	Jubilee Burl Walnut	168,884	152,996
4	6	10	Julius Bluthner Edition	147,630	133,867
4	6	10	Queen Victoria JB Edition Polished Rosewood	176,690	160,021
2	7	8	Satin and Polished Ebony	134,369	121,932
2	7	8	Satin and Polished Mahogany/Walnut	145,118	131,606
2	7	8	Satin and Polished Cherry	145,790	132,211
2	7	8	Satin and Polished White	143,774	130,397
2	7	8	Satin and Polished Bubinga/Yew/Rosewood/Macassar	149,149	135,234
2	7	8	Saxony Polished Pyramid Mahogany	170,648	154,583
2	7	8	Polished Burl Walnut/Camphor	170,648	154,583
2	7	8	President Polished Ebony	145,557	132,001
2	7	8	President Polished Mahogany/Walnut	156,307	141,676
2	7	8	President Polished Bubinga	160,338	145,304
2	7	8	President Burl Walnut	181,837	164,653
2	7	8	Senator Walnut w/Leather	155,400	140,860
2	7	8	Senator Jacaranda Satin Rosewood w/Leather	164,724	149,252
2	7	8	Wilhelm II Satin and Polished Ebony	157,211	142,490
2	7	8	Wilhelm II Polished Mahogany/Walnut	169,788	153,809
2	7	8	Wilhelm II Polished Pyramid Mahogany	188,053	170,248
2	7	8	Wilhelm II Polished Burl Walnut	188,053	170,248
2	7	8	Ambassador Santos Rosewood	181,962	164,766
2	7	8	Ambassador Walnut	177,044	160,340
2	7	8	Nicolas II Satin Walnut with Burl Inlay	187,713	169,942
2	7	8	Louis XIV Rococo Satin White with Gold	207,959	188,163
2	7	8	Jubilee Polished Ebony	151,773	137,596
2	7	8	Jubilee Polished Mahogany/Walnut	162,523	147,271
2	7	8	Jubilee Burl Walnut	188,053	170,248
2	7	8	Julius Bluthner Edition	170,940	154,846
2	7	8	Queen Victoria JB Edition Polished Rosewood	195,475	176,928
1	9	2	Satin and Polished Ebony	171,750	155,575
1	9	2	Satin and Polished Mahogany/Walnut	185,490	167,941
1	9	2	Satin and Polished Cherry	186,349	168,714
1	9	2	Satin and Polished White	183,773	166,396
1	9	2	Satin and Polished Bubinga/Yew/Rosewood/Macassar	190,643	172,579
1	9	2	Saxony Polished Pyramid Mahogany	218,123	197,311
1	9	2	Polished Burl Walnut/Camphor	223,275	201,948
1	9	2	President Polished Ebony	183,738	166,364
1	9	2	President Polished Mahogany/Walnut	197,478	178,730
1	9	2	President Polished Bubinga	202,631	183,368
1	9	2	President Burl Walnut	219,579	198,621
1	9	2	Wilhelm II Satin and Polished Ebony	200,948	181,853
1	9	2	Wilhelm II Polished Mahogany/Walnut	217,024	196,322
1	9	2	Wilhelm II Polished Pyramid Mahogany	236,771	214,094
1	9	2	Wilhelm II Polished Burl Walnut	241,923	218,731
1	9	2	Ambassador Santos Rosewood	236,397	213,757
1	9	2	Ambassador Walnut	231,863	209,677
1	9	2	Nicolas II Satin Walnut with Burl Inlay	245,603	222,043
1	9	2	Jubilee Polished Ebony	190,398	172,358
1	9	2	Jubilee Polished Mahogany/Walnut	204,138	184,724
1	9	2	Jubilee Burl Walnut	241,923	218,731
1	9	2	Julius Bluthner Edition	216,373	195,736
1	9	2	Queen Victoria JB Edition Polished Rosewood	244,938	221,444

*See pricing explanation on page 201.

Model	Feet	Inches	Description	MSRP*	SMP*
BÖSENDORFER					
Verticals					
130		52	Satin and Polished Ebony	68,999	65,998
130		52	Satin and Polished White, other colors	76,599	72,998
130		52	Polished, Satin, Open-pore: Walnut, Cherry, Mahogany, Pomele	80,999	77,198
130		52	Polished , Satin, Open-pore: Bubinga, Pyramid Mahogany, Santos Rosewood, Burl Walnut, Birdseye Maple, Macassar, Madronna, Vavona, Wenge	87,399	82,998
Grands					
155	5	1	Satin and Polished Ebony	109,999	104,998
155	5	1	Satin and Polished White, other colors	123,799	116,998
155	5	1	Polished, Satin, Open-pore: Walnut, Cherry, Mahogany, Pomele	129,999	124,998
155	5	1	Polished , Satin, Open-pore: Bubinga, Pyramid Mahogany, Santos Rosewood, Burl Walnut, Birdseye Maple, Macassar, Madronna, Vavona, Wenge	142,999	124,198
155	5	1	Chrome: Satin and Polished Ebony	124,999	118,198
170CS	5	8	Conservatory Satin Ebony	99,999	96,398
170	5	8	Satin and Polished Ebony	117,999	112,398
170	5	8	Satin and Polished White, other colors	131,999	124,998
170	5	8	Polished, Satin, Open-pore: Walnut, Cherry, Mahogany, Pomele	139,799	132,198
170	5	8	Polished , Satin, Open-pore: Bubinga, Pyramid Mahogany, Santos Rosewood, Burl Walnut, Birdseye Maple, Macassar, Madronna, Vavona, Wenge	151,299	142,998
170	5	8	Chrome: Satin and Polished Ebony	129,999	123,998
170	5	8	Johann Strauss: Satin and Polished Ebony w/Maple	142,999	134,998
170	5	8	Johann Strauss: Satin Cherry	164,999	155,998
170	5	8	Liszt: Polished Vavona	169,999	159,998
170	5	8	Chopin, Louis XVI: Satin Pommele	193,999	183,398
170	5	8	Baroque: Light Satin Ivory; Vienna: Polished Amboyna	209,999	197,998
170	5	8	Artisan Satin and Polished	274,999	258,998
185CS	6	1	Conservatory Satin Ebony	108,999	102,998
185	6	1	Satin and Polished Ebony	123,999	116,998
185	6	1	Satin and Polished White, other colors	135,999	128,998
185	6	1	Polished, Satin, Open-pore: Walnut, Cherry, Mahogany, Pomele	144,999	136,998
185	6	1	Polished , Satin, Open-pore: Bubinga, Pyramid Mahogany, Santos Rosewood, Burl Walnut, Birdseye Maple, Macassar, Madronna, Vavona, Wenge	155,999	147,998
185	6	1	Chrome: Satin and Polished Ebony	135,999	128,998
185	6	1	Johann Strauss: Satin and Polished Ebony w/Maple	145,999	138,198
185	6	1	Johann Strauss: Satin Cherry	169,999	160,998
185	6	1	Liszt: Polished Vavona	175,999	165,998
185	6	1	Edge: Satin and Polished Ebony	195,999	184,998
185	6	1	Chopin, Louis XVI: Satin Pommele	199,999	188,598
185	6	1	Baroque: Satin Light Ivory; Vienna: Polished Amboyna	213,999	200,998
185	6	1	Porsche Design: Diamond Black Metallic Gloss	229,999	216,998
185	6	1	Artisan Satin and Polished	282,999	266,998
200CS	6	7	Conservatory Satin Ebony	113,999	108,198
200	6	7	Satin and Polished Ebony	132,999	125,798
200	6	7	Satin and Polished White, other colors	147,999	139,998
200	6	7	Polished, Satin, Open-pore: Walnut, Cherry, Mahogany, Pomele	157,599	148,998
200	6	7	Polished , Satin, Open-pore: Bubinga, Pyramid Mahogany, Santos Rosewood, Burl Walnut, Birdseye Maple, Macassar, Madronna, Vavona, Wenge	169,999	161,198
200	6	7	Chrome Satin and Polished Ebony	145,596	120,744
200	6	7	Chrome: Satin and Polished Ebony	146,999	138,998
200	6	7	Johann Strauss: Satin and Polished Ebony w/Maple	156,599	147,998
200	6	7	Johann Strauss: Satin Cherry	187,999	176,998
200	6	7	Liszt: Polished Vavona	189,999	178,998

*See pricing explanation on page 201.

BÖSENDORFER (continued)

Model	Feet	Inches	Description	MSRP*	SMP*
200	6	7	Beethoven Polished Ebony	161,999	152,998
200	6	7	Edge: Satin and Polished Ebony	212,999	200,998
200	6	7	Schönbrunn: Polished Ebony and Maple	198,999	179,998
200	6	7	Chopin, Louis XVI: Satin Pommele	218,899	204,998
200	6	7	Baroque: Satin Light Ivory; Vienna: Polished Amboyna	234,999	220,998
200	6	7	Artisan Satin and Polished	304,999	284,998
214CS	7		Conservatory Satin Ebony	124,999	116,998
214	7		Satin and Polished Ebony	149,999	140,998
214	7		Satin and Polished White, other colors	164,999	154,998
214	7		Polished, Satin, Open-pore: Walnut, Cherry, Mahogany, Pomele	177,599	166,998
214	7		Polished , Satin, Open-pore: Bubinga, Pyramid Mahogany, Santos Rosewood, Burl Walnut, Birdseye Maple, Macassar, Madronna, Vavona, Wenge	192,499	180,998
214	7		Chrome: Satin and Polished Ebony	164,999	154,998
214	7		Johann Strauss: Satin and Polished Ebony w/Maple	173,999	162,998
214	7		Johann Strauss: Satin Cherry	207,999	194,998
214	7		Liszt: Polished Vavona	212,999	200,998
214	7		Beethoven: Polished Ebony	177,999	166,998
214	7		Edge: Satin and Polished Ebony	238,999	224,998
214	7		Chopin, Louis XVI: Satin Pommele	239,999	227,998
214	7		Baroque: Satin Light Ivory; Vienna: Polished Amboyna	259,999	244,998
214	7		Porsche Design: Diamond Black Metallic Gloss	276,999	260,998
214	7		Audi Design Polished Ebony	339,999	320,998
214	7		Artisan Satin and Polished	339,999	320,998
225	7	4	Satin and Polished Ebony	165,999	156,998
225	7	4	Satin and Polished White, other colors	182,999	172,998
225	7	4	Polished, Satin, Open-pore: Walnut, Cherry, Mahogany, Pomele	195,999	184,998
225	7	4	Polished , Satin, Open-pore: Bubinga, Pyramid Mahogany, Santos Rosewood, Burl Walnut, Birdseye Maple, Macassar, Madronna, Vavona, Wenge	212,999	200,998
225	7	4	Chrome: Satin and Polished Ebony	181,999	170,998
225	7	4	Johann Strauss: Satin and Polished Ebony w/Maple	189,999	178,998
225	7	4	Johann Strauss: Satin Cherry	229,999	216,998
225	7	4	Liszt: Polished Vavona	237,999	223,998
225	7	4	Chopin, Louis XVI: Satin Pommele	269,999	254,998
225	7	4	Baroque: Satin Light Ivory; Vienna: Polished Amboyna	289,999	272,798
225	7	4	Artisan Satin and Polished	369,999	348,998
280	9	2	Satin and Polished Ebony	219,999	206,998
280	9	2	Satin and Polished White, other colors	239,999	225,198
280	9	2	Polished, Satin, Open-pore: Walnut, Cherry, Mahogany, Pomele	258,999	242,998
280	9	2	Polished , Satin, Open-pore: Bubinga, Pyramid Mahogany, Santos Rosewood, Burl Walnut, Birdseye Maple, Macassar, Madronna, Vavona, Wenge	279,999	262,998
280	9	2	Johann Strauss: Satin and Polished Ebony w/Maple	252,999	237,998
280	9	2	Johann Strauss: Satin Cherry	302,999	284,998
280	9	2	Liszt: Polished Vavona	309,999	291,198
280	9	2	Chopin, Louis XVI: Satin Pommele	355,999	332,998
280	9	2	Baroque: Satin Light Ivory; Vienna: Polished Amboyna	379,999	356,798
280	9	2	Porsche Design: Diamond Black Metallic Gloss	409,999	385,998
280	9	2	Artisan Satin and Polished	443,999	415,998
290	9	6	Satin and Polished Ebony	249,999	232,998
290	9	6	Satin and Polished White, other colors	273,999	256,998
290	9	6	Polished, Satin, Open-pore: Walnut, Cherry, Mahogany, Pomele	293,999	275,998
290	9	6	Polished , Satin, Open-pore: Bubinga, Pyramid Mahogany, Santos Rosewood, Burl Walnut, Birdseye Maple, Macassar, Madronna, Vavona, Wenge	317,999	298,998
290	9	6	Johann Strauss: Satin and Polished Ebony w/Maple	282,999	266,998
290	9	6	Johann Strauss: Satin Cherry	345,999	323,998

*See pricing explanation on page 201.

Model	Feet	Inches	Description	MSRP*	SMP*
BÖSENDORFER (continued)					
290	9	6	Liszt: Polished Vavona	353,999	332,998
290	9	6	Chopin, Louis XVI: Satin Pommele	403,999	379,998
290	9	6	Baroque: Satin Light Ivory; Vienna: Polished Amboyna	431,999	405,998
290	9	6	Artisan Satin and Polished	499,999	472,998
170-280			CEUS, add	94,999	94,999
290			CEUS, add	99,999	99,999
200			Disklavier E3, add	24,999	24,999

BOSTON

Boston MSRP is the price at the New York retail store.

Verticals

Model	Feet	Inches	Description	MSRP*	SMP*
UP-118E PE		46	Satin and Polished Ebony	11,600	11,600
UP-118E PE		46	Polished Mahogany	13,400	13,400
UP-118E PE		46	Satin and Polished Walnut	13,400	13,400
UP-118S PE		46	Satin Black Oak/Honey Oak	7,600	7,600
UP-118S PE		46	Satin Mahogany	9,100	9,100
UP-126E PE		50	Polished Ebony	13,900	13,900
UP-126E PE		50	Polished Mahogany	16,100	16,100
UP-132E PE		52	Polished Ebony	15,400	15,400

Grands

Model	Feet	Inches	Description	MSRP*	SMP*
GP-156 PE	5	1	Satin and Polished Ebony	21,100	21,100
GP-163 PE	5	4	Satin and Polished Ebony	25,800	25,800
GP-163 PE	5	4	Satin and Polished Mahogany	28,200	28,200
GP-163 PE	5	4	Satin and Polished Walnut	28,600	28,600
GP-163 PE	5	4	Polished White	31,800	31,800
GP-178 PE	5	10	Satin and Polished Ebony	30,200	30,200
GP-178 PE	5	10	Satin and Polished Mahogany	32,600	32,600
GP-178 PE	5	10	Satin and Polished Walnut	33,100	33,100
GP-193 PE	6	4	Satin and Polished Ebony	39,200	39,200
GP-215 PE	7	1	Satin and Polished Ebony	51,400	51,400

BRODMANN

Verticals

Model	Feet	Inches	Description	MSRP*	SMP*
CE 118		46	Polished Ebony	6,890	5,580
PE 116		45	Polished Ebony	7,770	6,180
PE 121		47	Polished Ebony	8,670	6,780
PE 121		47	Polished Mahogany/Walnut	9,570	7,380
PE 121		47	Polished White	9,870	7,580
PE 123C		48	Italian Provincial Satin Walnut	9,870	7,580
PE 123M/W		48	French Provincial Polished Mahogany/Walnut	9,870	7,580
PE 125		48	Polished Ebony	9,570	7,380
PE 130		52	Polished Ebony	11,375	10,100
AS 132		52	Polished Ebony	19,975	16,980

Grands

Model	Feet	Inches	Description	MSRP*	SMP*
CE 148	4	11	Polished Ebony	16,500	12,000
CE 175	5	9	Polished Ebony	19,500	14,000
PE 150	4	11	Polished Ebony	20,070	14,380
PE 162	5	4	Polished Ebony	23,070	16,380
PE 162	5	4	Polished Mahogany/Walnut	25,770	18,180
PE 162	5	4	Polished White	24,870	17,580
PE 162	5	4	Polished Bubinga	26,070	18,380
PE 162	5	4	Polished Two Tone (Ebony/Bubinga)	26,070	18,380
PE 162	5	4	Strauss Polished Ebony	25,470	17,980
PE 162	5	4	Strauss Polished Two Tone (Ebony/Bubinga)	26,070	18,380

*See pricing explanation on page 201.

Model	Feet	Inches	Description	MSRP*	SMP*
BRODMANN *(continued)*					
PE 187	6	2	Polished Ebony	26,370	18,580
PE 187	6	2	Polished Mahogany/Walnut	29,070	20,380
PE 187	6	2	Polished White	28,470	19,980
PE 187	6	2	Polished Bubinga	29,970	20,980
PE 187	6	2	Polished Two Tone (Ebony/Bubinga)	27,270	19,180
PE 187	6	2	Strauss Polished Ebony	28,470	19,980
PE 187	6	2	Strauss Polished White	32,970	22,980
PE 187	6	2	Strauss Polished Two Tone (Ebony/Bubinga)	29,370	20,580
PE 187C	6	2	Senator Walnut	35,970	24,980
PE 212	7		Polished Ebony	41,970	28,980
PE 228	7	5	Polished Ebony	53,970	36,980
AS 188	6	2	Polished Ebony	53,970	36,980
AS 211	6	11	Polished Ebony	68,970	46,980
AS 227	7	4	Polished Ebony	77,970	52,980
AS 275	9		Polished Ebony	107,475	86,980
BURGER & JACOBI					
Verticals					
BJ-U118		44	Polished Ebony	11,255	11,255
BJ-U118		44	Polished Mahogany/Walnut	12,170	12,170
BJ-U118		44	Polished White	12,737	12,737
BJ-U125		49	Polished Ebony	14,500	14,500
BJ-U131		50	Polished Ebony	19,250	19,250
Grands					
BJ-G1S	5	5	Polished Ebony	32,645	32,645
BJ-G1S	5	5	Polished White	34,500	34,500
BJ-G2S	6	1	Polished Ebony	39,695	39,695
BJ-G3S	6	8	Polished Ebony	74,800	74,800
BJ-G3 Majestic	9		Polished Ebony	109,700	109,700
CABLE, HOBART M. *— see Schumann*					
CABLE-NELSON					
Verticals					
CN 116		45	Polished Ebony	4,399	4,399
CN 216		45	Satin Walnut	4,499	4,499
Grands					
CN 151	5		Polished Ebony	9,399	9,399
CHASE, A.B. *— see Everett*					
CLINE					
Verticals					
CL118		46.5	Polished Ebony		6,300
CL118		46.5	Polished Ebony w/Nickel		6,500
CL118		46.5	Polished Walnut/Mahogany		6,500
CL121/123		48	Polished Ebony		7,390
CL121/123		48	Polished Ebony w/Nickel		7,590
CL121/123		48	Polished Mahogany/Walnut		7,590
CL121/123		48	Polished Mahogany/Walnut w/Detail Trim		7,590
Grands					
CL 150	4	11	Polished Ebony		12,300
CL 150	4	11	Polished Mahogany/Walnut		12,500

*See pricing explanation on page 201.

Model	Feet	Inches	Description	MSRP*	SMP*
CRISTOFORI					
Verticals					
CRV425		42.5	Continental Polished Ebony	3,569	3,569
CRV430		43	French Provincial Satin Cherry	4,715	4,715
CRV430		43	Mediterranean Satin Oak	4,409	4,409
CRV450S		45	Satin Ebony	5,765	5,093
CRV450S		45	Satin Walnut	5,765	4,988
CRV450S		45	Satin Oak	5,765	5,093
CRV480		48	Polished Ebony	6,605	6,038
CRV480		48	Polished Mahogany	6,815	6,248
Grands					
CRG48	4	8	Polished Ebony	7,865	7,865
CRG48	4	8	Polished Mahogany	8,390	8,390
CRG410	4	10	Satin Ebony	9,965	9,083
CRG410	4	10	Polished Ebony	9,965	8,768
CRG410	4	10	Polished Mahogany	10,490	9,188
CRG410	4	10	French Provincial Satin Cherry	11,015	9,608
CRG53	5	3	Satin Ebony	12,590	10,973
CRG53	5	3	Polished Ebony	12,590	10,658
CRG53	5	3	Satin Walnut/Mahogany	13,115	11,078
CRG53	5	3	Polished Walnut/Mahogany	13,115	11,078
CRG53	5	3	French Provincial Satin Cherry	14,165	11,498
CRG53	5	3	Polished Bubinga	14,375	11,498
CRG53	5	3	Polished White	13,115	11,078
CRG57	5	7	Satin Ebony	15,215	11,813
CRG57	5	7	Polished Ebony	15,215	11,498
CRG57	5	7	Satin Walnut/Mahogany	15,740	11,918
CRG57	5	7	Polished Walnut/Mahogany	15,740	11,918
CRG57	5	7	French Provincial Satin Cherry	16,790	12,338
CRG57	5	7	Polished Bubinga	17,105	12,338
CRG57	5	7	Polished White	15,740	11,918
CRG62	6	2	Satin Ebony	17,315	13,283
CRG62	6	2	Polished Ebony	17,315	12,968
CRG62	6	2	Polished Mahogany	18,155	13,388
CUNNINGHAM					
Verticals					
Liberty Console		44	Satin Ebony	4,690	4,690
Liberty Console		44	Polished Ebony	3,990	3,990
Liberty Console		44	Satin Mahogany	5,490	5,490
Liberty Console		44	Polished Mahogany	4,790	4,790
Studio Upright		50	Satin Ebony	10,690	10,690
Studio Upright		50	Polished Ebony	9,890	9,890
Studio Upright		50	Satin Mahogany	10,990	10,990
Studio Upright		50	Polished Mahogany	10,190	10,190
Grands					
Baby Grand	5		Satin Ebony	15,990	15,990
Baby Grand	5		Polished Ebony	15,190	15,190
Baby Grand	5		Satin Mahogany	16,690	16,690
Baby Grand	5		Polished Mahogany	15,890	15,890
Baby Grand	5		Heritage Victorian Polished Mahogany	26,490	26,490
Studio Grand	5	4	Satin Ebony	17,690	17,690
Studio Grand	5	4	Polished Ebony	16,890	16,890
Studio Grand	5	4	Satin Mahogany	18,390	18,390
Studio Grand	5	4	Polished Mahogany	17,590	17,590
Studio Grand	5	4	Heritage Victorian Polished Mahogany	28,290	28,290

*See pricing explanation on page 201.

Model	Feet	Inches	Description	MSRP*	SMP*
CUNNINGHAM (continued)					
Parlour Grand	5	10	Satin Ebony	20,990	20,990
Parlour Grand	5	10	Polished Ebony	20,190	20,190
Parlour Grand	5	10	Satin Mahogany	21,590	21,590
Parlour Grand	5	10	Polished Mahogany	20,790	20,790
Parlour Grand	5	10	Heritage Victorian Polished Mahogany	30,990	30,990
Chamber Grand	7		Satin Ebony	36,690	36,690
Chamber Grand	7		Polished Ebony	35,790	35,790
Concert Grand	9		Satin Ebony	61,990	61,990
Concert Grand	9		Polished Ebony	60,990	60,990

DISKLAVIER — see Yamaha; see also Bösendorfer

EISENBERG

Verticals

Model	Feet	Inches	Description	MSRP*	SMP*
116		45.5	Polished Ebony	9,043	9,043
121		47.5	Polished Ebony	9,883	9,883
125		49.5	Polished Ebony	10,387	10,387
131		51.5	Polished Ebony	11,227	11,227

Grands

Model	Feet	Inches	Description	MSRP*	SMP*
152	5		Polished Ebony	21,492	21,492
165	5	5	Polished Ebony	23,172	23,172
165	5	5	Phoenix Bass, Polished Ebony	29,900	29,900
178	5	10	Polished Ebony	24,852	24,852

ESSEX

Essex MSRP is the price at the New York retail store.

Verticals

Model	Feet	Inches	Description	MSRP*	SMP*
EUP-108C		42	Continental Polished Ebony	5,490	5,490
EUP-111E		44	Polished Ebony	6,190	6,190
EUP-111E		44	Polished Sapele Mahogany	6,590	6,360
EUP-116E		45	Polished Ebony	6,990	6,580
EUP-116E		45	Polished Walnut	7,990	7,240
EUP-116E		45	Polished Sapele Mahogany	7,290	6,680
EUP-116E		45	Polished White	7,590	6,920
EUP-116FC		45	French Country Satin Lustre Cherry	7,990	7,440
EUP-116CT		45	Contemporary Satin Lustre Sapele Mahogany	7,990	7,400
EUP-116IP		45	Italian Provincial Satin LustreWalnut	7,590	7,400
EUP-116QA		45	Queen Anne Satin Lustre Cherry	7,690	7,540
EUP-116ST		45	Sheraton Traditional Satin Lustre Sapele Mahogany	7,590	7,400
EUP-116EC		45	English Country Satin Lustre Walnut	7,690	7,360
EUP-116ET		45	English Traditional Satin Lustre Sapele Mahogany	7,690	7,340
EUP-116FF		45	Formal French Satin Lustre Brown Cherry	7,990	7,580
EUP-116FF		45	Formal French Satin Lustre Red Cherry	7,990	7,580
EUP-123E		48	Satin Ebony w/Chrome Hardware	8,390	7,760
EUP-123E		48	Polished Ebony	7,490	7,100
EUP-123E		48	Polished Ebony w/Chrome Hardware	7,590	7,200
EUP-123E		48	Satin Sapele Mahogany	8,490	7,780
EUP-123E		48	Polished Sapele Mahogany	8,490	7,600
EUP-123E		48	Satin Walnut	8,490	7,620
EUP-123CL		48	French Satin Sapele Mahogany	8,590	7,860
EUP-123FL		48	Empire Satin Walnut	8,590	7,660
EUP-123FL		48	Empire Satin Sapele Mahogany	8,590	7,860
EUP-123S		48	Institutional Studio Polished Ebony	7,490	7,420

*See pricing explanation on page 201.

Model	Feet	Inches	Description	MSRP*	SMP*

ESSEX *(continued)*

Grands

Model	Feet	Inches	Description	MSRP*	SMP*
EGP-155	5	1	Satin and Polished Ebony	13,500	14,300
EGP-155	5	1	Polished Sapele Mahogany	14,800	15,160
EGP-155	5	1	Satin Lustre Sapele Mahogany	15,100	15,520
EGP-155	5	1	Polished Kewazinga Bubinga	16,900	16,020
EGP-155	5	1	Polished White	18,000	16,020
EGP-155F	5	1	French Provincial Satin Lustre Brown Cherry	17,200	17,120
EGP-173	5	8	Satin Lustre and Polished Ebony	17,100	18,220
EGP-173	5	8	Polished Sapele Mahogany	18,900	19,680
EGP-173F	5	8	French Provincial Satin Lustre Brown Cherry	20,200	20,360

ESTONIA

The Estonia factory can make custom-designed finishes with exotic veneers; prices upon request.
Prices here include Jansen adjustable artist benches.

Grands

Model	Feet	Inches	Description	MSRP*	SMP*
L168	5	6	Satin and Polished Ebony	41,715	39,608
L168	5	6	Satin and Polished Mahogany/Walnut/White	45,125	42,563
L168	5	6	Polished Kewazinga Bubinga	48,948	46,299
L168	5	6	Polished Pyramid Mahogany	54,165	51,299
L168	5	6	Hidden Beauty Polished Ebony w/Bubinga	46,165	43,479
L190	6	3	Satin and Polished Ebony	51,228	48,139
L190	6	3	Satin and Polished Mahogany/Walnut/White	54,569	51,678
L190	6	3	Polished Pyramid Mahogany	65,143	60,350
L190	6	3	Polished Santos Rosewood	65,143	60,187
L190	6	3	Polished Kewazinga Bubinga	58,750	55,530
L190	6	3	Hidden Beauty Polished Ebony w/Bubinga	53,877	50,904
L210	6	10	Satin and Polished Ebony	60,287	57,949
L210	6	10	Satin and Polished Mahogany/Walnut/White	66,315	63,646
L210	6	10	Satin and Polished Pyramid Mahogany	75,358	72,187
L210	6	10	Polished Kewazinga Bubinga	71,140	68,200
L210	6	10	Hidden Beauty Polished Ebony w/Bubinga	64,030	61,279
L225	7	4	Satin and Polished Ebony	75,894	70,807
L225	7	4	Satin and Polished Mahogany/Walnut/White	81,645	76,873
L225	7	4	Satin and Polished Pyramid Mahogany	90,625	86,438
L225	7	4	Polished Kewazinga Bubinga	82,000	79,664
L225	7	4	Hidden Beauty Polished Ebony w/Bubinga	80,605	75,715
L274	9		Satin and Polished Ebony	121,060	107,360
L274	9		Satin and Polished Mahogany/Walnut	132,790	118,595
L274	9		Polished Pyramid Mahogany	137,385	131,013
L274	9		Satin and Polished White	124,930	113,565

EVERETT

Verticals

Model	Feet	Inches	Description	MSRP*	SMP*
EV-112		44	Continental Polished Ebony		4,580
EV-112		44	Continental Polished Mahogany		4,700
EV-113		45	Polished Ebony		4,780
EV-113		45	Polished Mahogany		4,900
EV-115CB		45	Chippendale Polished Mahogany		5,100
EV-121		48	Polished Ebony		5,380
EV-121		48	Polished Mahogany		5,500

Grands

Model	Feet	Inches	Description	MSRP*	SMP*
EV-146	4	9	Polished Ebony		8,980
EV-146	4	9	Polished Mahogany/White		9,480
EV-152	5		Polished Ebony		9,780

*See pricing explanation on page 201.

Model	Feet	Inches	Description	MSRP*	SMP*
EVERETT (continued)					
EV-152	5		Polished Mahogany/Sapele		10,280
EV-165	5	5	Polished Ebony		10,780
EV-165	5	5	Polished Mahogany/Walnut		11,280
EV-185	6	1	Polished Ebony		12,980

FALCONE — see Schumann

FANDRICH & SONS

These are the prices on the Fandrich & Sons website. Other finishes available at additional cost. See website for details.

Verticals

Model	Feet	Inches	Description	MSRP*	SMP*
130-V		51	Polished Ebony	12,850	12,850

Grands

Model	Feet	Inches	Description	MSRP*	SMP*
170-S	5	7	Polished Ebony	19,890	19,890
188-S	6	2	Polished Ebony	23,490	23,490
212-S	7		Polished Ebony	35,990	35,990
212-E	7		Polished Ebony	37,490	37,490

FAZIOLI

Fazioli is willing to make custom-designed cases with exotic veneers, marquetry, and other embellishments. Prices on request to Fazioli.

Grands

Model	Feet	Inches	Description	MSRP*	SMP*
F156	5	2	Satin and Polished Ebony	128,000	128,000
F183	6		Satin and Polished Ebony	128,000	128,000
F212	6	11	Satin and Polished Ebony	143,000	143,000
F228	7	6	Satin and Polished Ebony	160,000	160,000
F278	9	2	Satin and Polished Ebony	214,000	214,000
F308	10	2	Satin and Polished Ebony	234,000	234,000

FEURICH

Verticals

Model	Feet	Inches	Description	MSRP*	SMP*
115		45.5	Polished Ebony	6,200	5,900
122		48	Polished Ebony	7,100	6,800

Grands

Model	Feet	Inches	Description	MSRP*	SMP*
178/179	5	10	Polished Ebony	20,600	19,400
218	7	2	Polished Ebony	34,200	32,600

FÖRSTER, AUGUST

Prices do not include bench. Euro = $1.30

Verticals

Model	Feet	Inches	Description	MSRP*	SMP*
116 C		46	Chippendale Polished Ebony		30,556
116 C		46	Chippendale Satin Mahogany		29,027
116 C		46	Chippendale Polished Mahogany		31,102
116 C		46	Chippendale Satin Walnut		30,392
116 C		46	Chippendale Polished Walnut		32,494
116 D		46	Continental Polished Ebony		22,339
116 D		46	Continental Satin Mahogany/Beech/Alder		22,994
116 D		46	Continental Polished Mahogany		22,994
116 D		46	Continental Satin Walnut/Pear/Oak/Cherry		24,413
116 D		46	Continental Polished Walnut/Pear/Oak/Cherry		24,413
116 D		46	Continental Polished White		24,031
116 E		46	Polished Ebony		25,942
116 E		46	Satin Mahogany/Beech/Alder		26,515

*See pricing explanation on page 201.

Model	Feet	Inches	Description	MSRP*	SMP*

FÖRSTER, AUGUST *(continued)*

Model	Feet	Inches	Description	MSRP*	SMP*
116 E		46	Polished Mahogany/Beech/Alder		26,515
116 E		46	Satin Walnut/Oak/Cherry/Pear		27,880
116 E		46	Polished Walnut/Oak/Cherry/Pear		27,880
116 E		46	Polished White		27,471
125 F		49	Polished Ebony		29,655
125 G		49	Polished Ebony		29,082
125 G		49	Satin Mahogany/Beech/Alder		29,682
125 G		49	Polished Mahogany/Beech/Alder		29,682
125 G		49	Satin Walnut/Oak/Cherry/Pear		31,648
125 G		49	Polished Walnut/Oak/Cherry/Pear		31,648
125 G		49	Polished White		30,610
134 K		53	Polished Ebony		43,005

Grands

Model	Feet	Inches	Description	MSRP*	SMP*
170	5	8	Polished Ebony		60,429
170	5	8	Satin and Polished Walnut		63,814
170	5	8	Satin and Polished Mahogany		61,630
170	5	8	Polished White		63,869
170	5	8	Classik Polished Ebony		68,865
170	5	8	Classik Polished Walnut		78,584
170	5	8	Classik Polished Mahogany		73,260
170	5	8	Classik Polished White		72,741
170	5	8	Chippendale Open-Pore Walnut		97,120
170	5	8	Antik Open-Pore Walnut		116,585
190	6	4	Polished Ebony		67,718
190	6	4	Satin and Polished Walnut		70,940
190	6	4	Satin and Polished Mahogany		68,783
190	6	4	Polished White		70,885
190	6	4	Classik Polished Ebony		75,963
190	6	4	Classik Polished Mahogany		80,413
190	6	4	Classik Polished Walnut		85,709
190	6	4	Classik Polished White		79,894
190	6	4	Chippendale Open-Pore Walnut		104,218
190	6	4	Antik Open-Pore Walnut		130,809
215	7	2	Polished Ebony		77,574
275	9	1	Polished Ebony		142,302

GEYER, A.

Prices do not include bench. Other woods available on request. Euro = $1.50

Verticals

Model	Feet	Inches	Description	MSRP*	SMP*
GU 115		45	Polished Ebony	5,685	4,790
GU 115		45	Polished Mahogany/Walnut	6,135	5,090
GU 115		45	Polished White	5,985	4,990
GU 123		47	Polished Ebony	6,285	5,190
GU 123		47	Polished Mahogany/Walnut	6,735	5,490
GU 123		47	Polished White	6,585	5,390
GU 133		52	Polished Ebony	7,185	5,790
GU 133		52	Polished Mahogany/Walnut	7,785	6,190
GU 133		52	Polished White	7,485	5,990

Grands

Model	Feet	Inches	Description	MSRP*	SMP*
GG 150	4	11	Polished Ebony	12,585	9,390
GG 150	4	11	Polished Mahogany/Walnut	13,185	9,790
GG 150	4	11	Polished White	13,035	9,690
GG 160	5	3	Polished Ebony	14,085	10,390
GG 160	5	3	Polished Mahogany/Walnut	14,685	10,790
GG 160	5	3	Polished White	14,535	10,690
GG 170	5	7	Polished Ebony	15,885	11,590

*See pricing explanation on page 201.

Model	Feet	Inches	Description	MSRP*	SMP*
GEYER, A. *(continued)*					
GG 170	5	7	Polished Mahogany/Walnut	16,485	11,990
GG 170	5	7	Polished White	16,335	11,890
GG 185	6	1	Polished Ebony	17,985	12,990
GG 185	6	1	Polished Mahogany/Walnut	18,885	13,590
GG 185	6	1	Polished White	18,585	13,390
GG 230	7	7	Polished Ebony	28,750	23,990

GROTRIAN

Prices do not include bench. Other woods available on request. Euro = $1.25

Verticals

Model	Feet	Inches	Description	MSRP*	SMP*
Friedrich Grotrian Studio 110		43.5	Satin Ebony		16,170
Friedrich Grotrian Studio 110		43.5	Satin White		16,470
Friedrich Grotrian		43.5	Polished Ebony		18,525
Friedrich Grotrian		43.5	Open-pore Walnut		18,525
Cristal		44	Continental Satin Ebony		21,909
Cristal		44	Continental Polished Ebony		22,932
Cristal		44	Continental Open-pore Walnut		22,932
Cristal		44	Continental Polished Walnut/White		25,059
Contour		45	Polished Ebony		24,804
Contour		45	Open-pore Walnut		24,804
Contour		45	Polished Walnut/White		27,015
Canto		45	Satin Ebony		24,804
Canto		45	Polished Ebony		25,995
Canto		45	Open-pore Walnut		25,995
Carat		45.5	Polished Ebony		28,887
Carat		45.5	Open-pore Walnut		28,887
Carat		45.5	Polished Walnut/White		31,269
College		48	Satin Ebony		31,521
College		48	Polished Ebony		32,880
College		48	Open-pore Walnut		32,880
Classic		49	Polished Ebony		38,838
Classic		49	Open-pore Walnut		38,838
Classic		49	Polished Walnut/White		41,901
Concertino		52	Polished Ebony		48,507
Concertino		52	Open-pore Walnut		48,507
Verticals			Chippendale/Rococo/Empire, add		1,286
Verticals			Sostenuto pedal, add		1,549

Grands

Model	Feet	Inches	Description	MSRP*	SMP*
Chambre	5	5	Satin Ebony		68,462
Chambre	5	5	Polished Ebony		75,638
Chambre	5	5	Open-pore Walnut		75,638
Chambre	5	5	Polished Walnut/White		82,812
Cabinet	6	3	Satin Ebony		80,040
Cabinet	6	3	Polished Ebony		88,682
Cabinet	6	3	Studio Lacquer Ebony		60,079
Cabinet	6	3	Open-pore Walnut		88,682
Cabinet	6	3	Polished Walnut/White		97,164
Charis	6	10	Satin Ebony		93,923
Charis	6	10	Polished Ebony		103,667
Charis	6	10	Studio Lacquer Ebony		74,017
Charis	6	10	Open-pore Walnut		103,667
Concert	7	4	Satin Ebony		111,633
Concert	7	4	Polished Ebony		125,928
Concert	7	4	Open-pore Walnut		125,928

*See pricing explanation on page 201.

PIANOBUYER.COM

Model	Feet	Inches	Description	MSRP*	SMP*
GROTRIAN (continued)					
Concert Royal	9	1	Polished Ebony		168,070
Concert Royal	9	1	Open-pore Walnut		168,070
Grands			Chippendale/Empire, add		4,463
Grands			CS Style, add		4,988
Grands			Rococo, add		14,963

HAESSLER

Prices do not include bench.

Verticals

Model	Feet	Inches	Description	MSRP*	SMP*
H 115		45	Polished Ebony	21,482	20,529
H 115		45	Satin Mahogany/Walnut	21,922	20,929
H 115		45	Polished Cherry	36,911	34,555
H 115		45	Satin Oak/Beech	22,802	21,729
H 115		45	Polished White	22,362	21,329
H 115		45	Polished Mahogany w/Vavona Inlay	36,911	34,555
H 115		45	Polished Cherry and Yew	36,911	34,555
H 118		47	Polished Ebony	23,683	22,530
H 118		47	Satin Mahogany/Walnut	24,783	23,530
H 118		47	Polished Mahogany/Walnut	28,745	27,132
H 118		47	Satin Cherry	25,223	23,930
H 118		47	Polished Cherry	29,185	27,532
H 118		47	Satin Oak/Beech	23,507	22,370
H 118		47	Polished White	25,884	24,531
H 118		47	Polished Bubinga	29,405	27,732
H 118		47	Satin Mahogany w/Vavona Inlay	26,544	25,131
H 118		47	Polished Mahogany w/Vavona Inlay	30,066	28,333
H 118		47	Polished Burl Walnut	29,846	28,133
H 118		47	Satin Burl Walnut w/Walnut Inlay	26,544	25,131
H 118		47	Polished Burl Walnut w/Walnut Inlay	30,066	28,333
H 118		47	Satin Cherry and Yew	26,632	25,211
H 118		47	Polished Cherry and Yew	30,066	28,333
H 124		49	Polished Ebony	25,884	24,531
H 124		49	Satin Mahogany/Walnut	26,852	25,411
H 124		49	Polished Mahogany/Walnut	30,946	29,133
H 124		49	Satin Cherry	26,984	25,531
H 124		49	Polished Cherry	31,386	29,533
H 124		49	Satin Oak/Beech	26,764	25,331
H 124		49	Polished White	28,085	26,532
H 124		49	Polished Bubinga	31,606	29,733
H 124		49	Polished Pyramid Mahogany	34,996	32,815
H 124		49	Satin Mahogany w/Vavona Inlay	28,305	26,732
H 124		49	Polished Mahogany w/Vavona Inlay	33,367	31,334
H 124		49	Polished Burl Walnut	34,556	32,415
H 124		49	Satin Burl Walnut w/Walnut Inlay	28,305	26,732
H 124		49	Polished Burl Walnut w/Walnut Inlay	33,367	31,334
H 124		49	Satin Cherry and Yew	28,305	26,732
H 124		49	Polished Cherry and Yew	34,556	32,415
K 124		49	Polished Ebony	27,997	26,452
K 124		49	Satin Mahogany/Walnut	28,965	27,332
K 124		49	Polished Mahogany/Walnut	33,059	31,054
K 124		49	Satin Cherry	29,097	27,452
K 124		49	Polished Cherry	33,499	31,454
K 124		49	Satin Oak/Beech	28,877	27,252
K 124		49	Polished White	30,198	28,453
K 124		49	Polished Bubinga	33,719	31,654
K 124		49	Polished Pyramid Mahogany	37,109	34,735

*See pricing explanation on page 201.

Model	Feet	Inches	Description	MSRP*	SMP*
HAESSLER (continued)					
K 124		49	Satin Mahogany w/Vavona Inlay	30,418	28,653
K 124		49	Polished Mahogany w/Vavona Inlay	35,480	33,255
K 124		49	Polished Burl Walnut	36,669	34,335
K 124		49	Satin Burl Walnut w/Walnut Inlay	30,418	28,653
K 124		49	Polished Burl Walnut w/Walnut Inlay	35,480	33,255
K 124		49	Satin Cherry and Yew	30,418	28,653
K 124		49	Polished Cherry and Yew	36,669	34,335
H 132		52	Polished Ebony	28,965	27,332
H 132		52	Satin Mahogany/Walnut	29,405	27,732
H 132		52	Polished Mahogany/Walnut	33,807	31,734
H 132		52	Satin Cherry	30,726	28,933
H 132		52	Polished Cherry	34,248	32,135
H 132		52	Polished White	31,166	29,333
H 132		52	Polished Bubinga	34,688	32,535
H 132		52	Palisander Rosewood	36,669	34,335
H 132		52	Polished Pyramid Mahogany	37,549	35,135
H 132		52	Satin Mahogany w/Vavona Inlay	32,267	30,334
H 132		52	Polished Mahogany w/Vavona Inlay	36,669	34,335
H 132		52	Polished Burl Walnut	36,669	34,335
H 132		52	Satin Burl Walnut w/Walnut Inlay	32,267	30,334
H 132		52	Polished Burl Walnut w/Walnut Inlay	36,669	34,335
H 132		52	Satin Cherry and Yew	32,267	30,334
H 132		52	Polished Cherry and Yew	36,669	34,335
K 132		52	Polished Ebony	31,914	30,013
K 132		52	Satin Mahogany/Walnut	32,355	30,414
K 132		52	Polished Mahogany/Walnut	36,757	34,415
K 132		52	Satin Cherry	33,675	31,614
K 132		52	Polished Cherry	37,197	34,815
K 132		52	Polished White	34,115	32,014
K 132		52	Polished Bubinga	37,637	35,215
K 132		52	Palisander Rosewood	39,618	37,016
K 132		52	Polished Pyramid Mahogany	40,498	37,816
K 132		52	Satin Mahogany w/Vavona Inlay	35,216	33,015
K 132		52	Polished Mahogany w/Vavona Inlay	39,618	37,016
K 132		52	Polished Burl Walnut	39,618	37,016
K 132		52	Satin Burl Walnut w/Walnut Inlay	35,216	33,015
K 132		52	Polished Burl Walnut w/Walnut Inlay	39,618	37,016
K 132		52	Satin Cherry and Yew	35,216	33,015
K 132		52	Polished Cherry and Yew	39,618	37,016
Grands					
H 175	5	8	Polished Ebony	74,471	68,701
H 175	5	8	Satin Mahogany/Walnut	80,056	73,778
H 175	5	8	Polished Mahogany/Walnut	87,579	80,617
H 175	5	8	Satin Cherry	79,386	73,169
H 175	5	8	Polished Cherry	89,627	82,479
H 175	5	8	Polished White	79,684	73,440
H 175	5	8	Polished Bubinga	91,266	83,969
H 175	5	8	Palisander Rosewood	95,771	88,065
H 175	5	8	Polished Pyramid Mahogany	100,277	92,161
H 175	5	8	Polished Mahogany w/Vavona Inlay	109,699	100,726
H 175	5	8	Polished Burl Walnut	97,820	89,927
H 175	5	8	Polished Burl Walnut w/Walnut Inlay	109,699	100,726
H 175	5	8	Satin Cherry and Yew	103,964	95,513
H 175	5	8	Polished Cherry and Yew	109,699	100,726
H 175	5	8	Classic Alexandra Polished Ebony	89,217	82,106
H 175	5	8	Classic Alexandra Polished Walnut	102,326	94,024
H 175	5	8	Classic Alexandra Burl Walnut	112,566	103,333

*See pricing explanation on page 201.

Model	Feet	Inches	Description	MSRP*	SMP*
HAESSLER (continued)					
H 175	5	8	Classic Alexandra Palisander	110,518	101,471
H 175	5	8	Louis IV Satin White w/Gold	143,370	131,336
H 175	5	8	Satin and Polished Louis XV Mahogany	109,699	100,726
H 175	5	8	Ambassador Palisander	135,178	123,889
H 175	5	8	Ambassador Walnut	131,082	120,165
H 186	6	1	Polished Ebony	78,977	72,797
H 186	6	1	Satin Mahogany/Walnut	84,900	78,182
H 186	6	1	Polished Mahogany/Walnut	92,085	84,714
H 186	6	1	Satin Cherry	83,892	77,265
H 186	6	1	Polished Cherry	94,133	86,575
H 186	6	1	Polished White	84,505	77,823
H 186	6	1	Polished Bubinga	98,229	90,299
H 186	6	1	Palisander Rosewood	100,277	92,161
H 186	6	1	Polished Pyramid Mahogany	106,422	97,747
H 186	6	1	Polished Mahogany w/Vavona Inlay	114,205	104,823
H 186	6	1	Polished Burl Walnut	102,326	94,024
H 186	6	1	Polished Burl Walnut w/Walnut Inlay	114,205	104,823
H 186	6	1	Satin Cherry and Yew	99,458	91,416
H 186	6	1	Polished Cherry and Yew	114,205	104,823
H 186	6	1	Classic Alexandra Polished Ebony	93,723	86,203
H 186	6	1	Classic Alexandra Polished Walnut	106,831	98,119
H 186	6	1	Classic Alexandra Burl Walnut	117,072	107,429
H 186	6	1	Classic Alexandra Palisander	115,024	105,567
H 186	6	1	Louis IV Satin White w/Gold	147,467	135,061
H 186	6	1	Satin and Polished Louis XV Mahogany	114,205	104,823
H 186	6	1	Ambassador Palisander	147,467	135,061
H 186	6	1	Ambassador Walnut	143,370	131,336
H 210	6	10	Polished Ebony	91,962	84,602
H 210	6	10	Satin Mahogany/Walnut	98,859	90,872
H 210	6	10	Polished Mahogany/Walnut	108,798	99,907
H 210	6	10	Satin Cherry	99,950	91,864
H 210	6	10	Polished Cherry	110,518	101,471
H 210	6	10	Polished White	98,399	90,454
H 210	6	10	Polished Bubinga	112,157	102,961
H 210	6	10	Palisander Rosewood	120,759	110,781
H 210	6	10	Polished Pyramid Mahogany	126,903	116,366
H 210	6	10	Polished Mahogany w/Vavona Inlay	135,096	123,815
H 210	6	10	Polished Burl Walnut	118,711	108,919
H 210	6	10	Polished Burl Walnut w/Walnut Inlay	135,096	123,815
H 210	6	10	Satin Cherry and Yew	118,793	108,994
H 210	6	10	Polished Cherry and Yew	135,096	123,815
H 210	6	10	Classic Alexandra Polished Ebony	106,709	98,008
H 210	6	10	Classic Alexandra Polished Walnut	123,544	113,313
H 210	6	10	Classic Alexandra Burl Walnut	133,457	122,325
H 210	6	10	Classic Alexandra Palisander	135,506	124,187
H 210	6	10	Louis IV Satin White w/Gold	180,237	164,852
H 210	6	10	Satin and Polished Louis XV Mahogany	127,190	116,627
H 210	6	10	Ambassador Palisander	159,756	146,233
H 210	6	10	Ambassador Walnut	155,659	142,508

HAILUN

Verticals

Model	Feet	Inches	Description	MSRP*	SMP*
HU116		45.5	Institutional Polished Ebony	10,782	8,188
HU1-P		48	Polished Ebony	11,502	8,668
HU1-P		48	Polished Mahogany/Walnut	12,366	9,244
HU1-PS		48	Polished Ebony with Nickel Trim	11,970	8,980
HU1-EP		48	Polished Ebony w/mahogany leg, fallboard, cheekblocks	12,402	9,268

*See pricing explanation on page 201.

Model	Feet	Inches	Description	MSRP*	SMP*
HAILUN (continued)					
HU5-P		50	Polished Ebony	12,474	9,316
HU5-P		50	Polished Ebony with Nickel Trim	13,903	10,268
HU5-P		50	Polished Mahogany/Walnut	13,903	10,268
HU7-P		52	Polished Ebony w/Sostenuto	17,982	12,988
Grands					
HG151	4	11.5	Polished Ebony	22,296	15,864
HG151	4	11.5	Polished Mahogany/Walnut	23,955	16,970
HG151C	4	11.5	Chippendale Polished Mahogany/Walnut	24,750	17,500
HG161	5	4	Polished Ebony	24,981	17,656
HG161	5	4	Polished Mahogany/Walnut	26,842	18,548
HG161G	5	4	Georgian Polished Mahogany/Walnut	30,330	19,770
HG178	5	10	Polished Ebony	31,968	22,312
HG178	5	10	Polished Mahogany/Walnut	33,282	23,188
HG178B	5	10	Baroque Polished Ebony w/Birds-Eye Maple Accents	35,064	24,376
HG198	6	5	Emerson Polished Ebony	47,178	32,452
HG198	6	5	Emerson Polished Mahogany/Walnut	49,176	33,784
HG218	7	2	Paulello Polished Ebony	65,257	44,504

HALLET, DAVIS & CO.

Heritage Collection Verticals

Model	Feet	Inches	Description	MSRP*	SMP*
H108		43	Continental Polished Ebony	5,295	4,100
H108		43	Continental Polished Mahogany	5,495	4,190
HC43R		43	Satin Cherry (Roung Leg)	6,280	4,590
HC43F		43	French Provincial Satin Cherry	6,280	4,590
H117H		46	Polished Ebony	5,950	4,300
H117H		46	Polished Mahogany	6,150	4,390
H118F		46	Demi-Chippendale Polished Ebony	5,995	4,500
H118F		46	Demi-Chippendale Polished Mahogany	6,195	4,590

Signature Collection Verticals

Model	Feet	Inches	Description	MSRP*	SMP*
HS114E		45	Classic Studio Polished Mahogany/Walnut	5,995	4,500
HS115M2		45	Classic Studio Polished Ebony	6,995	4,590
HS115M2		45	Classic Studio Polished Mahogany/Walnut	7,195	4,790
HS118M		46.5	Polished Ebony	7,395	4,990
HS118M		46.5	Polished Mahogany/Walnut/White	7,595	5,190
HS121S		48	Polished Ebony	8,795	5,390
HS121S		48	Polished Mahogany/Walnut/White	9,095	5,590
HS131Y		52	Polished Ebony	9,495	6,190
HS132E		52	Polished Mahogany	9,995	6,300

Heritage Collection Grands

Model	Feet	Inches	Description	MSRP*	SMP*
H142C	4	7	Polished Ebony	13,195	8,990
H142C	4	7	Polished Mahogany	13,995	9,390
H142F	4	7	Queen Anne Polished Mahogany	14,995	9,790

Signature Collection Grands

Model	Feet	Inches	Description	MSRP*	SMP*
HS148	4	10	Satin Ebony	14,695	9,790
HS148	4	10	Polished Ebony	13,995	9,390
HS148	4	10	Polished Mahogany/Walnut/White	14,695	9,790
HS160	5	3	Satin Ebony	15,995	10,790
HS160	5	3	Polished Ebony	15,395	10,390
HS160	5	3	Polished Mahogany/Walnut/White	15,995	10,790
HS170	5	7	Satin Ebony	16,995	12,190
HS170	5	7	Polished Ebony	16,495	11,590
HS170	5	7	Polished Mahogany/Walnut/White	16,995	12,190
HS188	6	2	Satin Ebony	20,495	14,590
HS188	6	2	Polished Ebony	19,995	13,990

*See pricing explanation on page 201.

Model	Feet	Inches	Description	MSRP*	SMP*
HALLET, DAVIS & CO. (continued)					
HS188	6	2	Polished Mahogany/Walnut	20,495	14,590
HS212	7		Polished Ebony	29,995	26,990
Imperial Collection Grands					
HD148B	4	10	Polished Ebony	14,995	10,990
HD152B	5		Polished Ebony	17,195	11,790
HD152T	5		Designer Birds-Eye Maple Two Tone	19,195	13,190
HD165B	5	5	Polished Ebony	19,495	12,990
HD165P	5	5	Polished Ebony (fluted leg)	20,995	14,390
HARDMAN, PECK & CO.					
Verticals					
R110S		44	Polished Ebony	5,495	4,090
R110S		44	Polished Mahogany	5,595	4,190
R45F		45	French Provincial Satin Cherry	6,695	4,790
R115LS		45	Polished Ebony	5,995	4,390
R115LS		45	Polished Mahogany	6,195	4,490
R116		46	School Polished Ebony	6,695	4,790
R116		46	School Satin Cherry	6,895	4,890
R117XK		46	Chippendale Polished Mahogany	6,695	4,790
RUE118H		46	Polished Ebony with Silver Hardware	6,695	4,790
R120LS		48	Polished Ebony	6,495	4,690
R120LS		48	Polished Mahogany	6,695	4,790
R132HA		52	Polished Ebony	9,495	6,390
Grands					
R143S	4	8	Polished Ebony	13,695	8,790
R143S	4	8	Polished Mahogany	14,995	9,390
R143F	4	8	French Provincial Polished Mahogany	15,395	9,790
R150S	5		Polished Ebony	15,095	9,590
R150S	5		Polished Mahogany	15,795	9,990
R150SGE	5		Polished Ebony w/Chrome	16,495	10,390
R158S	5	3	Polished Ebony	16,095	10,190
R158S	5	3	Polished Mahogany	16,795	10,590
R158F	5	3	French Provincial Polished Mahogany	17,495	10,990
R168S	5	7	Polished Ebony	17,495	10,990
R168S	5	7	Polished Mahogany	18,195	11,390
R185S	6	1	Polished Ebony	20,295	12,590
R185S	6	1	Polished Mahogany	20,995	12,990
HEINTZMAN & CO.					
Heintzman Verticals					
121DL		48	Satin Mahogany	7,995	7,380
123B		48.5	Polished Mahogany	8,795	7,580
123F		48.5	French Provincial Polished Mahogany	7,995	6,980
126C		50	Polished Ebony	8,795	7,600
126 Royal		50	Polished Ebony	9,795	8,200
132D		52	Polished Mahogany, Decorative Panel	11,795	8,980
132E		52	French Provincial Polished Ebony	11,795	8,780
132E		52	French Provincial Satin and Polished Mahogany	11,795	8,980
132 Royal		52	Satin Mahogany	12,795	9,580
140CK		55	Polished Mahogany	14,995	10,980
Gerhard Heintzman Verticals					
G118		47	Polished Ebony w/Silver Plate and Trim	4,995	4,995
G118		47	Polished Mahogany w/Silver Plate and Trim	5,195	5,195
G120		48	Polished Ebony w/Silver Plate and Trim	5,995	5,700

*See pricing explanation on page 201.

Model	Feet	Inches	Description	MSRP*	SMP*
HEINTZMAN & CO. (continued)					
G120		48	Polished Mahogany w/Silver Plate and Trim	6,195	5,900
G126		50	Polished Ebony w/Silver Plate and Trim	7,995	6,400
G126		50	Polished Mahogany w/Silver Plate and Trim	8,195	6,600
G132		52	Polished Ebony w/Silver Plate and Trim	9,295	7,200
Heintzman Grands					
168	5	6	Polished Ebony	18,995	16,990
168	5	6	Polished Mahogany	19,995	17,390
168 Royal	5	6	Polished Ebony	23,995	17,990
186	6	1	Polished Ebony	21,995	18,980
186	6	1	Polished Mahogany	22,995	20,180
186 Royal	6	1	Polished Ebony	26,995	19,980
203	6	8	Polished Ebony	24,995	20,580
203 Royal	6	8	Polished Ebony	29,995	21,580
277	9		Polished Ebony	89,995	60,995
Gerhard Heintzman Grands					
G152	5		Polished Ebony	9,995	9,995
G152	5		Polished White	11,995	11,995
G152R	5		Empire Polished Mahogany	11,995	11,995
G168	5	6	Polished Ebony	15,995	12,800
G168	5	6	Polished White	19,995	13,800
G168R	5	6	Empire Polished Mahogany	17,995	13,800
HOFFMANN, W.					
Vision Series Verticals					
V112		44	Polished Ebony	12,000	12,000
V112		44	Polished Mahogany/Walnut	13,800	13,800
V112		44	Polished White	13,400	13,400
V120		47	Polished Ebony	13,200	13,200
V120		47	Polished Mahogany/Walnut	15,000	15,000
V120		47	Polished White	14,800	14,800
V126		49.6	Polished Ebony	14,600	14,600
V131		51.5	Polished Ebony	17,000	17,000
Tradition Series Verticals					
T122		48	Polished Ebony	14,800	14,800
T122		48	Satin Mahogany/Walnut	17,000	17,000
T122		48	Polished Mahogany/Walnut/Cherry/White	17,000	17,000
T128		50	Polished Ebony	16,400	16,400
T128		50	Satin Mahogany/Walnut	18,000	18,000
T128		50	Polished Mahogany/Walnut/Cherry/White	18,600	18,600
Vision Series Grands					
V158	5	2	Polished Ebony	37,200	37,200
V158	5	2	Polished Mahogany/Walnut/White	45,000	45,000
V175	5	9	Polished Ebony	41,800	41,800
V175	5	9	Polished Walnut/Mahogany/White	49,800	49,800
V183	6	1	Polished Ebony	47,600	47,600
V183	6	1	Polished Walnut/Mahogany/White	55,600	55,600
Tradition Series Grands					
T161	5	3	Polished Ebony	47,000	47,000
T161	5	3	Polished Mahogany/Walnut	57,400	57,400
T161	5	3	Polished White	54,800	54,800
T177	5	9	Polished Ebony	52,000	52,000
T177	5	9	Polished Mahogany/Walnut	62,800	62,800
T177	5	9	Polished White	60,200	60,200
T186	6	2	Polished Ebony	57,400	57,400

*See pricing explanation on page 201.

Model	Feet	Inches	Description	MSRP*	SMP*
HOFFMANN, W. (continued)					
T186	6	2	Polished Mahogany/Walnut	68,000	68,000
T186	6	2	Polished White	65,400	65,400

IRMLER

Studio Edition Verticals

Model	Feet	Inches	Description	MSRP*	SMP*
P108		42.5	Polished Ebony	6,319	6,319
P108		42.5	Polished White	6,455	6,455
P118		46.5	Polished Ebony	6,575	6,572
P118		46.5	Polished Mahogany/Walnut	6,746	6,717
P118		46.5	Polished White	6,711	6,687

Art Design Verticals

Model	Feet	Inches	Description	MSRP*	SMP*
Mia		47.5	Polished Ebony	8,724	8,393
Gina		48.5	Polished Ebony	9,096	8,708
Monique		49	Polished Ebony	9,096	8,708
Louis		49	Polished Ebony	8,724	8,393
Titus		49	Polished Ebony	9,096	8,708
Alexa		49	Polished Ebony	10,321	9,747
Carlo		49	Polished Ebony	10,321	9,747

Supreme Edition Verticals

Model	Feet	Inches	Description	MSRP*	SMP*
SP118		46.5	Polished Ebony	8,168	7,922
SP121		48	Polished Ebony	8,724	8,393
SP125		49	Polished Ebony	9,578	9,117
SP132		52	Polished Ebony	10,621	10,001

Professional Edition Verticals

Model	Feet	Inches	Description	MSRP*	SMP*
P116E		46	Polished Ebony/White	8,685	8,360
P116E		46	Satin Mahogany/Walnut/Cherry	8,685	8,360
P116E		46	Polished Mahogany/Walnut	8,825	8,479
P116E		46	Polished Cherry	9,127	8,735
P122E		48	Polished Ebony/White	9,242	8,832
P122E		48	Satin Mahogany/Walnut/Cherry	9,242	8,832
P122E		48	Polished Mahogany/Walnut/Cherry	9,381	8,950
P122E		48	Polished Bubinga	10,936	10,268
P132E		52	Polished Ebony/White	10,356	9,776
P132E		52	Satin Mahogany/Walnut/Cherry	10,912	10,247
P132E		52	Polished Mahogany/Walnut/Cherry	11,469	10,719
P132E		52	Polished Bubinga	12,905	11,936

Studio Edition Grands

Model	Feet	Inches	Description	MSRP*	SMP*
F148	4	10	Polished Ebony	17,590	15,907
F148	4	10	Polished Mahogany/Walnut	18,614	16,775
F148	4	10	Polished White	18,273	16,486
F160	5	3	Polished Ebony	20,322	18,222
F160	5	3	Polished Mahogany/Walnut	21,159	18,931
F160	5	3	Polished White	21,005	18,801
F188	6	2	Polished Ebony	29,032	25,603
F188	6	2	Polished Mahogany/Walnut	29,629	26,109
F188	6	2	Polished White	29,715	26,182
F213	7		Polished Ebony	35,521	31,103
F213	7		Polished White	37,229	32,550

Professional Edition Grands

Model	Feet	Inches	Description	MSRP*	SMP*
F160E	5	3	Polished Ebony	32,432	28,485
F160E	5	3	Polished Mahogany/Walnut	33,977	29,794
F160E	5	3	Polished Cherry	34,363	30,121
F160E	5	3	Polished White	32,819	28,813
F160E	5	3	Polished Bubinga	36,680	32,085

*See pricing explanation on page 201.

Model	Feet	Inches	Description	MSRP*	SMP*
IRMLER (continued)					
F175E	5	9	Polished Ebony	34,749	30,448
F175E	5	9	Polished Mahogany/Walnut	36,486	31,920
F175E	5	9	Polished White	35,135	30,775
F175E	5	9	Polished Bubinga	38,417	33,557
F190E	6	3	Polished Ebony	37,066	32,412
F190E	6	3	Polished Mahogany/Walnut	38,803	33,884
F190E	6	3	Polished White	37,452	32,739
F190E	6	3	Polished Bubinga	41,120	35,847
F210E	6	10.5	Polished Ebony	45,560	39,610
F230E	7	6.5	Polished Ebony	54,054	46,808

KAWAI

Verticals

Model	Feet	Inches	Description	MSRP*	SMP*
K-15		44	Continental Polished Ebony	5,245	5,190
K-15		44	Continental Polished Mahogany	5,495	5,390
K-15		44	Continental Polished Snow White	6,995	6,590
506N		44.5	Satin Ebony/Mahogany/Oak	5,245	5,190
508		44.5	Satin Mahogany	5,995	5,790
607		44.5	French Provincial Satin Cherry	6,995	6,590
607		44.5	Queen Anne Satin Mahogany	6,995	6,590
K-200		45	Satin and Polished Ebony	6,995	6,590
K-200		45	Satin and Polished Mahogany	7,745	7,190
K-200NKL		45	Satin and Polished Ebony with Nickel Trim	7,245	6,790
K-200F		45	French Provincial Polished Mahogany	8,745	7,990
UST-9		46	Satin Ebony/Oak/Walnut/Cherry	7,745	7,190
907N		46.5	English Regency Satin Mahogany	9,995	8,990
907N		46.5	French Provincial Satin Cherry	9,995	8,990
K-300		48	Satin and Polished Ebony	10,495	9,390
K-300		48	Satin and Polished Mahogany	11,245	9,990
K-300		48	Polished Snow White	11,495	10,190
K-300NKL		48	Satin and Polished Ebony with Nickel Trim	10,895	9,690
K-400		48	Polished Ebony	11,245	9,990
K-400NKL		48	Polished Ebony with Nickel Trim	11,595	10,290
K-500		51	Satin and Polished Ebony	13,745	11,990
K-500		51	Polished Sapele Mahogany	15,495	13,390
K-800		53	Polished Ebony	21,745	18,390

AnyTime (Silent) Verticals

Model	Feet	Inches	Description	MSRP*	SMP*
K-15 ATX2		44	AnyTime Polished Ebony	8,995	8,190
K-200 ATX2		45	AnyTime Polished Ebony	10,745	9,590
K-300 ATX2		48	AnyTime Polished Ebony	14,995	12,990

Grands

Model	Feet	Inches	Description	MSRP*	SMP*
GM-10K	5		Satin and Polished Ebony	14,995	12,990
GM-10K	5		Polished Mahogany/Snow White	16,495	14,190
GM-10K	5		French Provincial Polished Mahogany	17,995	15,390
GM-11	5		Satin and Polished Ebony	15,495	13,390
GM-11	5		Polished Mahogany/Snow White	16,995	14,590
GM-12	5		Satin and Polished Ebony	19,995	16,990
GM-12	5		Polished Mahogany/Snow White	21,745	18,390
GE-30	5	5	Satin and Polished Ebony	26,495	22,190
GE-30	5	5	Polished Walnut/Sapele Mahogany	29,745	24,790
GE-30	5	5	Satin Walnut	29,245	24,390
GE-30	5	5	Polished Snow White	28,245	23,590
GX-1BLK	5	5	Satin and Polished Ebony	34,995	28,990
GX-1BLK	5	5	Polished Dark Walnut	40,745	33,590
GX-1BLK	5	5	Polished Snow White	39,745	32,790
CR30PL	5	10	Plexiglass	197,500	158,990

*See pricing explanation on page 201.

Model	Feet	Inches	Description	MSRP*	SMP*
KAWAI (continued)					
RX-2C	5	10	Conservatory Polished Ebony	31,495	26,190
GX-2BLK	5	11	Satin and Polished Ebony	40,245	33,190
GX-2BLK	5	11	Satin Walnut/Cherry/Oak	44,745	36,790
GX-2BLK	5	11	Polished Walnut/Sapeli Mahogany	46,495	38,190
GX-2BLK	5	11	Polished Snow White	42,995	35,390
CR40APL	6	1	Plexiglass	209,900	168,990
GX-3BLK	6	2	Satin and Polished Ebony	51,745	42,390
GX-5BLK	6	7	Satin and Polished Ebony	58,745	47,990
GX-6BLK	7		Satin and Polished Ebony	65,745	53,590
GX-7BLK	7	6	Satin and Polished Ebony	76,245	61,990
EX-L	9	1	Polished Ebony	196,795	158,390
KAWAI, SHIGERU					
Grands					
SK-2L	5	11	Polished Ebony	59,800	48,800
SK-2L	5	11	Polished Sapele Mahogany	68,800	56,000
SK-3L	6	2	Polished Ebony	69,500	56,600
SK-3L	6	2	Polished Sapele Mahogany	79,800	64,800
SK-5L	6	7	Polished Ebony	79,900	65,000
SK-6L	7		Polished Ebony	89,900	73,400
SK-7L	7	6	Polished Ebony	99,900	81,000
SK-EXL	9	1	Polished Ebony	223,500	179,800
KAYSERBURG					
Verticals					
KA-121B		48	Polished Ebony	15,995	12,990
KA-121B		48	Polished Dark Walnut	16,995	13,790
KA-126B		50	Polished Ebony	18,495	14,590
KA-126B		50	Polished Cherry	19,995	15,390
KA-132B		52	Polished Ebony	20,995	16,190
KA-132C		52	Polished Ebony w/Sostenuto	21,495	16,990
Grands					
KA-180	5	11	Polished Ebony	59,995	52,990
KIMBALL					
Verticals					
A49		49	Polished Ebony	11,900	10,990
Grands					
K1	5	1	Polished Ebony	14,300	12,990
A2	5	8	Polished Ebony	32,500	30,800
K3	6	2	Polished Ebony	17,300	15,990
KINGSBURG					
Verticals					
LM 116		46	Chippendale Polished Walnut		4,990
KU 120		48	Polished Ebony		5,190
KU 120		48	Satin and Polished Mahogany/Walnut		5,390
KU 123		50	Decorator Satin Walnut		5,990
KU 125		50	Polished Ebony		5,790
KU 125		50	Polished Ebony w/Inlay		6,190
KU 125		50	Satin and Polished Mahogany/Walnut		5,990
KU 133		52	Polished Ebony		6,390
KU 133		52	Polished Mahogany/Walnut		6,590

*See pricing explanation on page 201.

Model	Feet	Inches	Description	MSRP*	SMP*

KINGSBURG (continued)

Grands

Model	Feet	Inches	Description	MSRP*	SMP*
KG 158	5	3	Polished Ebony		11,390
KG 158	5	3	Polished Ebony w/Inlay		11,990
KG 158	5	3	Polished Mahogany/Walnut		11,790
KG 185	6	1	Polished Ebony		12,990
KG 185	6	1	Polished Ebony w/Inlay		13,590
KG 185	6	1	Polished Mahogany/Walnut		13,390

KNABE, WM.

Baltimore Series Verticals

Model	Inches	Description	MSRP*	SMP*
WV 43	43	Continental Polished Ebony	5,376	5,106
WV 43	43	Continental Satin Walnut/Cherry	6,861	6,240
WV 43	43	Continental Polished Mahogany/Walnut	5,926	5,526
WV 43	43	Continental Polished Ivory	6,861	6,240
WV 243F	43	French Provincial Satin Cherry	5,981	5,568
WV 243T	43	Satin Mahogany/Walnut	5,981	5,568
WV 115	45	Polished Ebony	5,981	5,568
WV 115	45	Polished Mahogany/Walnut	6,394	5,882
WV 118H	46.5	Polished Ebony	6,408	5,894
WV 118H	46.5	Polished Mahogany/Walnut	6,820	6,208
WV 118HN	46.5	Satin Ebony	7,150	6,460
WV 118HN	46.5	Polished Ebony	6,875	6,250

Academy Series Verticals

Model	Inches	Description	MSRP*	SMP*
WMV 245	45	Satin Ebony	6,256	5,778
WMV 245	45	Polished Ebony	5,981	5,568
WMV 245	45	Satin Walnut/Cherry	5,981	5,568
WMV 245	45	Polished Mahogany/Walnut/Ivory	6,256	5,778
WMV 245	45	Polished Dark Walnut Lacquer	6,256	5,778
WMV 245	45	Polished White	7,631	6,828
WMV 247	46.5	Satin Ebony	7,411	6,660
WMV 247	46.5	Polished Ebony	7,136	6,450
WMV 247	46.5	Satin and Polished Mahogany	7,411	6,660
WMV 247	46.5	Satin and Polished Walnut	7,411	6,660
WMV 647F	46.5	French Provincial Satin Cherry	7,013	6,356
WMV 647R	46.5	Renaissance Satin Walnut	7,013	6,356
WMV 647T	46.5	Satin Mahogany	7,013	6,356
WMV 121F/M	48	Satin Ebony	7,288	6,566
WMV 121F/M	48	Polished Ebony	7,013	6,356
WMV 121F/M	48	Polished Mahogany	7,288	6,566
WMV 132	52	Polished Ebony	9,611	8,340
WMV 132	52	Polished Mahogany	10,986	9,390

Concert Artist Series Verticals

Model	Inches	Description	MSRP*	SMP*
WKV 118F	46.5	French Provincial Lacquer Semigloss Cherry	11,000	9,800
WKV 118R	46.5	Renaissance Lacquer Satin Ebony	11,000	9,800
WKV 118R	46.5	Renaissance Lacquer Semigloss Walnut	11,000	9,800
WKV 118T	46.5	Lacquer Semigloss Mahogany	11,000	9,800
WKV 121	48	Satin Ebony	11,625	10,300
WKV 121	48	Polished Ebony	10,875	9,700
WKV 121	48	Polished Mahogany	12,625	11,100
WKV 131	52	Satin Ebony	12,625	11,100
WKV 131	52	Polished Ebony	12,125	10,700
WKV 131	52	Polished Mahogany	13,875	12,100
WKV 131	52	Polished Rosewood	16,750	14,400

*See pricing explanation on page 201.

Model	Feet	Inches	Description	MSRP*	SMP*

KNABE, WM. *(continued)*

Baltimore Series Grands

Model	Feet	Inches	Description	MSRP*	SMP*
WG 48	4	9	Satin Ebony	14,011	11,700
WG 48	4	9	Polished Ebony	12,911	10,860
WG 48	4	9	Polished Mahogany/Walnut	14,011	11,700
WG 48	4	9	Polished Dark Walnut Lacquer	15,661	12,960
WG 48	4	9	Polished White	15,661	12,960
WG 50	5		Satin Ebony	14,836	12,330
WG 50	5		Polished Ebony	13,736	11,490
WG 50	5		Polished Mahogany/Walnut	14,836	12,330
WG 50	5		Polished Dark Walnut Lacquer	16,486	13,590
WG 50	5		Polished White	16,486	13,590
WG 54	5	4	Satin Ebony	15,936	13,170
WG 54	5	4	Polished Ebony	14,561	12,120
WG 54	5	4	Polished Mahogany/Walnut	15,936	13,170
WG 54	5	4	Polished Dark Walnut Lacquer	17,311	14,220
WG 54	5	4	Polished Ebony w/Bubinga or Pommele	17,586	14,430
WG 54	5	4	Polished Ferrari Red	19,236	15,690
WSG 54	5	4	175th Anniv. w/Pommele Accents	17,861	14,640
WG 59	5	9	Satin Ebony	19,236	15,690
WG 59	5	9	Polished Ebony	17,861	14,640
WG 59	5	9	Polished Mahogany/Walnut	19,236	15,690
WG 61	6	1	Satin Ebony	20,611	16,740
WG 61	6	1	Polished Ebony	19,236	15,690
WG 61	6	1	Polished Mahogany/Walnut	20,611	16,740

Academy Series Grands

Model	Feet	Inches	Description	MSRP*	SMP*
WMG 600	5	9	Satin Ebony	18,975	15,490
WMG 600	5	9	Polished Ebony	17,600	14,440
WMG 600	5	9	Polished Mahogany/Walnut	18,975	15,490
WMG 610	5	9	Satin Ebony	20,625	16,750
WMG 610	5	9	Polished Ebony	19,250	15,700
WMG 610	5	9	Polished Mahogany/Walnut	20,625	16,750
WMG 650	6	1	Satin Ebony	20,900	16,960
WMG 650	6	1	Polished Ebony	19,663	16,016
WMG 650	6	1	Polished Mahogany/Walnut	20,900	16,960
WMG 660	6	1	Satin Ebony	22,550	18,220
WMG 660	6	1	Polished Ebony	20,900	16,960
WMG 660	6	1	Polished Mahogany/Walnut	22,550	18,220
WFM 700T	6	10	Satin Ebony	27,775	22,210
WFM 700T	6	10	Polished Ebony	26,400	21,160

Concert Artist Series Grands

Model	Feet	Inches	Description	MSRP*	SMP*
WKG 53	5	3	Satin Ebony	26,750	22,400
WKG 53	5	3	Polished Ebony	26,000	21,800
WKG 53	5	3	Polished Mahogany/Walnut/Ivory/White	28,000	23,400
WKG 53	5	3	Lacquer Semigloss Mahogany/Walnut	28,625	23,900
WKG 53	5	3	Polished Bubinga/Pommele	29,125	24,300
WKG 58	5	8	Satin Ebony	31,250	26,000
WKG 58	5	8	Polished Ebony	30,375	25,300
WKG 58	5	8	Polished Mahogany	32,250	26,800
WKG 58	5	8	Lacquer Semigloss Mahogany/Walnut	33,000	27,400
WKG 58	5	8	Polished Bubinga/Pommele	33,750	28,000
WKG 64	6	4	Satin Ebony	38,000	31,400
WKG 64	6	4	Polished Ebony	37,000	30,600
WKG 64	6	4	Polished Mahogany	39,250	32,400
WKG 64	6	4	Lacquer Semigloss Mahogany/Walnut	39,750	32,800
WKG 70	7		Satin Ebony	48,250	39,600
WKG 70	7		Polished Ebony	47,250	38,800
WKG 70	7		Lacquer Semigloss Mahogany/Walnut	54,750	44,800

*See pricing explanation on page 201.

Model	Feet	Inches	Description	MSRP*	SMP*
KNABE, WM. (continued)					
WKG 76	7	6	Satin Ebony	49,750	40,800
WKG 76	7	6	Polished Ebony	48,250	39,600
WKG 90	9		Satin Ebony	120,625	97,500
WKG 90	9		Polished Ebony	118,125	95,500

KOHLER & CAMPBELL

New Yorker Series Verticals

Model	Feet	Inches	Description	MSRP*	SMP*
KC-142		42	Continental Polished Ebony	4,826	4,686
KC-142		42	Continental Satin Cherry/Walnut	4,826	4,686
KC-142		42	Continental Polished Mahogany/Walnut/Ivory	5,101	4,896
KC-243F		43	French Provincial Satin Cherry	5,981	5,568
KC-243M		43	Mediterranean Satin Brown Oak	5,981	5,568
KC-243T		43	Satin Mahogany/Walnut	5,981	5,568
KC-118C		46.5	Polished Ebony	6,408	5,894
KC-118C		46.5	Polished Mahogany/Walnut	6,683	6,104

Millennium Series Verticals

Model	Feet	Inches	Description	MSRP*	SMP*
KM-245		45	Polished Ebony	5,981	5,568
KM-245		45	Satin Cherry/Walnut	5,981	5,568
KM-245		45	Polished Mahogany/Walnut/Ivory	6,256	5,778
KM-247		46.5	Satin Ebony	7,411	6,660
KM-247		46.5	Polished Ebony	7,136	6,450
KM-247		46.5	Satin Mahogany/Walnut	7,411	6,660
KM-247		46.5	Polished Mahogany/Walnut	7,411	6,660
KM-647F		46.5	French Provincial Satin Cherry	7,013	6,356
KM-647R		46.5	Renaissance Satin Walnut	7,013	6,356
KM-647T		46.5	Satin Mahogany	7,013	6,356
KM-121M/F		48	Satin Ebony	7,288	6,566
KM-121M/F		48	Polished Ebony	7,013	6,356
KM-121M/F		48	Polished Mahogany	7,288	6,566
KM-131		52	Polished Ebony	7,838	6,986
KM-131		52	Polished Mahogany	8,113	7,196

New Yorker Series Grands

Model	Feet	Inches	Description	MSRP*	SMP*
KIG-48	4	8	Satin Ebony	14,011	11,700
KIG-48	4	8	Polished Ebony	12,911	10,860
KIG-48	4	8	Polished Mahogany/Walnut/White	14,011	11,700
KIG-50	5		Satin Ebony	14,836	12,330
KIG-50	5		Polished Ebony	13,736	11,490
KIG-50	5		Polished Mahogany/Walnut/White	14,836	12,330
KIG-54	5	4	Satin Ebony	15,936	13,170
KIG-54	5	4	Polished Ebony	14,561	12,120
KIG-54	5	4	Polished Mahogany/Walnut	15,936	13,170
KIG-54	5	4	Polished Bubinga/Pommele	17,586	14,430
KIG-54	5	4	Polished Ferrari Red	17,586	14,430
KIG-59	5	9	Satin Ebony	17,861	14,640
KIG-59	5	9	Polished Ebony	16,486	13,590
KIG-59	5	9	Polished Mahogany/Walnut	19,236	15,690

Millennium Series Grands

Model	Feet	Inches	Description	MSRP*	SMP*
KCM-600	5	9	Satin Ebony	18,975	15,490
KCM-600	5	9	Polished Ebony	17,600	14,440
KCM-600	5	9	Polished Mahogany/Walnut	18,975	15,490
KCM-650	6	1	Satin Ebony	20,900	16,960
KCM-650	6	1	Polished Ebony	19,663	16,016
KCM-650	6	1	Polished Mahogany/Walnut	20,900	16,960
KFM-700	6	10	Satin Ebony	27,775	22,210

*See pricing explanation on page 201.

Model	Feet	Inches	Description	MSRP*	SMP*
KOHLER & CAMPBELL *(continued)*					
KFM-700	6	10	Polished Ebony	26,400	21,160
KFM-850	7	6	Polished Ebony	37,000	32,000

LOMENCE

Verticals

Model	Feet	Inches	Description	MSRP*	SMP*
121		47.5	Polished Black/White/Red	9,450	8,560
121		47.5	Polished Orange/Blue/Lavender	9,490	8,592
123		48.5	Polished Black	9,650	8,720
123		48.5	Polished White	9,785	8,830
123		48.5	Polished Red/Orange	9,740	8,790
123		48.5	Polished Blue	9,970	8,976
123		48.5	Polished Lavender	10,085	9,066
125		50.5	Polished Black	11,063	9,850
125		50.5	Polished White/Red	11,188	9,950
125		50.5	Polished Lavender/Blue	11,375	10,100

Grands

Model	Feet	Inches	Description	MSRP*	SMP*
TRS 186	6		Any Color	44,995	44,995

MASON & HAMLIN

Verticals

Model	Feet	Inches	Description	MSRP*	SMP*
50		50	Satin and Polished Ebony	26,837	26,837

Grands

Model	Feet	Inches	Description	MSRP*	SMP*
B	5	4	Satin and Polished Ebony	59,811	49,065
B	5	4	Satin Mahogany/Walnut	63,923	52,370
B	5	4	Polished Pyramid Mahogany	72,975	59,643
B	5	4	Satin and Polished Rosewood	67,077	54,904
B	5	4	Polished Bubinga	69,557	56,896
B	5	4	Polished Macassar Ebony	72,975	59,643
A	5	8	Satin and Polished Ebony	68,890	56,360
A	5	8	Satin Mahogany/Walnut	73,377	59,966
A	5	8	Polished Pyramid Mahogany	89,194	72,676
A	5	8	Satin and Polished Rosewood	81,443	66,447
A	5	8	Polished Bubinga	84,293	68,739
A	5	8	Polished Macassar Ebony	89,194	72,676
AA	6	4	Satin and Polished Ebony	78,737	64,191
AA	6	4	Satin Mahogany/Walnut	82,881	67,604
AA	6	4	Polished Pyramid Mahogany	95,213	77,514
AA	6	4	Satin and Polished Rosewood	87,462	71,285
AA	6	4	Polished Bubinga	90,308	73,572
AA	6	4	Polished Macassar Ebony	95,213	77,514
BB	7		Satin and Polished Ebony	89,232	72,707
BB	7		Satin Mahogany/Walnut	92,389	75,244
BB	7		Polished Pyramid Mahogany	110,003	89,399
BB	7		Satin and Polished Rosewood	103,425	84,112
BB	7		Polished Bubinga	105,990	86,173
BB	7		Polished Macassar Ebony	110,003	89,399
CC	9	4	Satin and Polished Ebony	132,668	107,613
CC	9	4	Satin Mahogany/Walnut	142,005	115,114
CC	9	4	Polished Pyramid Mahogany	161,670	130,918
CC	9	4	Satin and Polished Rosewood	150,077	121,602
CC	9	4	Polished Bubinga	155,108	125,645
CC	9	4	Polished Macassar Ebony	161,670	130,918
			Monticello Art Case, add	8,000	6,000
			Cambridge Collection (verticals), add	3,091	2,250
			Cambridge Collection (grands), add	8,000	6,000

*See pricing explanation on page 201.

Model	Feet	Inches	Description	MSRP*	SMP*
PALATINO					
Verticals					
PUP-123T		48	Torino Polished Ebony	6,750	5,400
PUP-123T		48	Torino Polished Dark Walnut	7,000	5,600
PUP-123C		48	Carved Contessa French Satin Brown Mahogany	7,000	5,600
PUP-126		50	Capri Polished Ebony	7,500	6,000
PUP-126		50	Capri Polished Dark Walnut	7,750	6,200
Grands					
PGD-50	5		Milano Polished Ebony	16,250	12,200
PGD-50	5		Milano Polished Dark Walnut	17,250	12,800
PGD-59	5	9	Roma Polished Ebony	18,750	14,200
PGD-59R	5	9	Roma Concerto Polished Ebony w/Renner	24,750	18,600
PGD-62	6	2	Firenze Polished Ebony	22,250	16,600
PGD-62R	6	2	Firenze Concerto Polished Ebony w/Renner	28,000	21,000
PEARL RIVER					
Verticals					
UP 108D1		42.5	Continental Polished Ebony	4,495	4,190
UP 110P8		43	French Provincial Satin Cherry	5,595	4,990
UP 110P9		43	Mediterranean Satin Walnut	5,595	4,990
UP 110P10		43	Italian Provincial Satin Mahogany	5,595	4,990
UP 111PA		43	French Provincial Satin Cherry	5,995	5,190
UP 111PB		43	Mediterranean Satin Walnut	5,995	5,190
UP 111PC		43	Italian Provincial Satin Mahogany	5,995	5,190
UP 115E		45	Satin Ebony/Mahogany (School)	5,995	5,190
UP 115M5		45	Polished Ebony	4,995	4,590
UP 115M5		45	Polished Mahogany/Walnut/White	5,395	4,790
UP 118		46.5	Polished Ebony	5,595	4,990
UP 118		46.5	Polished Mahogany/Walnut	5,795	5,190
EU 122		48	Polished Ebony	6,495	5,590
EU 122		48	Polished Mahogany/Walnut/White	6,695	5,790
EU 122		48	Satin Cherry	6,695	5,790
EU 122S		48	Polished Ebony w/Silver Hardware	6,695	5,790
UP 130TS		51.5	Polished Ebony	7,295	6,100
UP 131		52	Polished Ebony	7,395	6,190
Grands					
GP 150	4	11	Hand-rubbed Satin Ebony	11,995	9,590
GP 150	4	11	Polished Ebony	11,495	9,190
GP 150	4	11	Polished Mahogany/Walnut/White	11,995	9,590
GP 160	5	3	Hand-rubbed Satin Ebony	13,395	10,390
GP 160	5	3	Polished Ebony	12,995	9,990
GP 160	5	3	Polished Mahogany/Walnut/White	13,395	10,390
GP 170	5	7	Hand-rubbed Satin Ebony	15,495	11,990
GP 170	5	7	Polished Ebony	14,995	11,590
GP 170	5	7	Polished Mahogany/Walnut	15,495	11,990
GP 188A	6	2	Polished Ebony	18,495	13,990
GP 212	7		Polished Ebony	29,995	22,990
GP 275	9		Polished Ebony	79,995	60,990
PERZINA, GEBR.					
Verticals					
UP-112 Kompact		45	Continental Polished Ebony	8,080	7,260
UP-112 Kompact		45	Continental Polished Walnut/Mahogany	8,590	7,490
UP-112 Kompact		45	Continental Polished White	8,890	7,720
UP-115 Merit		45	Polished Ebony	8,780	7,660

*See pricing explanation on page 201.

PERZINA, GEBR. *(continued)*

Model	Feet	Inches	Description	MSRP*	SMP*
UP-115 Merit		45	Polished Mahogany/Walnut	9,290	7,920
UP-115 Merit		45	Polished White	9,590	8,120
UP-115 Merit		45	Queen Anne Polished Ebony	9,290	7,820
UP-115 Merit		45	Queen Anne Polished Mahogany/Walnut	10,040	8,140
UP-115 Merit		45	Queen Anne Polished White	10,340	8,340
UP-122 Konsumat		48	Polished Ebony	9,990	8,300
UP-122 Konsumat		48	Polished Ebony with Chrome Hardware	10,990	9,180
UP-122 Konsumat		48	Polished Mahogany/Walnut	10,340	8,590
UP-122 Konsumat		48	Polished White	10,530	8,780
UP-122 Konsumat		48	Queen Anne Polished Ebony	10,340	8,580
UP-122 Konsumat		48	Queen Anne Polished Mahogany/Walnut	11,090	8,780
UP-122 Konsumat		48	Queen Anne Polished White	11,360	8,980
DL-122 Balmoral		48	Designer Polished Ebony	11,170	9,380
DL-122 Balmoral		48	Designer Polished Bubinga	12,490	10,380
DL-122 Balmoral		48	Designer Ebony/Bubinga (two-tone)	12,090	9,980
UP-129 Kapitol		51	Polished Ebony	11,130	9,380
UP-129 Kapitol		51	Polished Mahogany/Walnut	11,690	9,580
UP-129 Kapitol		51	Polished White	12,290	9,780
UP-129 Kapitol		51	Queen Anne Polished Ebony	11,430	9,580
UP-129 Kapitol		51	Queen Anne Polished Mahogany/Walnut	12,330	9,780
UP-129 Kapitol		51	Queen Anne Polished White	12,990	9,980
UP-130 Konzert		51	Polished Ebony	13,490	10,580

Grands

Model	Feet	Inches	Description	MSRP*	SMP*
GP-152 Prysm	5	1	Polished Ebony	20,520	14,880
GP-152 Prysm	5	1	Polished Mahogany/Walnut	22,440	15,050
GP-152 Prysm	5	1	Polished White	24,320	16,250
DL-152 Prysm	5	1	Designer Polished Ebony/Bubinga (two-tone)	26,020	16,850
DL-152 Prysm	5	1	Designer Queen Anne or Empire Polished Ebony	20,990	15,190
DL-152 Prysm	5	1	Designer Queen Anne or Empire Polished Mahogany/Walnut	22,878	16,360
DL-152 Prysm	5	1	Designer Queen Anne or Empire Polished White	24,780	16,560
GP-160 Sylvr	5	5	Polished Ebony	26,690	17,050
GP-160 Sylvr	5	5	Polished Mahogany/Walnut	28,600	18,160
GP-160 Sylvr	5	5	Polished White	30,540	18,320
DL-160 Sylvr	5	5	Designer Polished Ebony/Bubinga (two-tone)	34,190	22,050
DL-160 Sylvr	5	5	Designer Queen Anne or Empire Polished Ebony	27,570	17,360
DL-160 Sylvr	5	5	Designer Queen Anne or Empire Polished Mahogany/Walnut	29,550	18,470
DL-160 Sylvr	5	5	Designer Queen Anne or Empire Polished White	31,520	18,620
GP-175 Granit	5	10	Polished Ebony	29,040	17,960
GP-175 Granit	5	10	Polished Mahogany/Walnut	31,560	19,070
GP-175 Granit	5	10	Polished White	33,780	19,250
DL-175 Granit	5	10	Designer Polished Ebony/Bubinga (two-tone)	36,540	22,960
DL-175 Granit	5	10	Designer Queen Anne or Empire Polished Ebony	29,690	18,270
DL-175 Granit	5	10	Designer Queen Anne or Empire Polished Mahogany/Walnut	32,130	19,380
DL-175 Granit	5	10	Designer Queen Anne or Empire Polished White	35,280	19,560
GP-187 Royal	6	2	Polished Ebony	32,520	18,870
GP-187 Royal	6	2	Polished Mahogany/Walnut	33,880	19,990
GP-187 Royal	6	2	Polished White	36,280	20,160
DL-187 Royal	6	2	Designer Polished Ebony/Bubinga (two-tone)	40,020	23,870
DL-187 Royal	6	2	Designer Queen Anne or Empire Polished Ebony	33,380	19,180
DL-187 Royal	6	2	Designer Queen Anne or Empire Polished Mahogany/Walnut	34,490	20,300
DL-187 Royal	6	2	Designer Queen Anne or Empire Polished White	36,680	20,470

*See pricing explanation on page 201.

Model	Feet	Inches	Description	MSRP*	SMP*

PETROF
Most models are also available in finishes other than those shown here.

Verticals

Model	Feet	Inches	Description	MSRP*	SMP*
P 118 C1		46.25	Chippendale Polished Ebony	28,258	28,258
P 118 D1		46.25	Demi-Chippendale Polished Ebony	27,530	27,530
P 118 G2		46.25	Polished Ebony	26,794	26,794
P 118 M1		46.25	Polished Ebony	25,504	25,504
P 118 P1		46.25	Polished Ebony	24,980	24,980
P 118 R1		46.25	Rococo Satin White w/Gold Trim	29,930	29,930
P 118 S1		46.25	Continental Polished Ebony/White	21,968	21,968
P 122 N1		47.75	Polished Ebony	26,100	26,100
P 125 F1		49.25	Polished Ebony	26,990	26,990
P 125 G1		49.25	Polished Ebony	28,490	28,490
P 125 M1		49.25	Polished Ebony	28,090	28,090
P 127 NEXT		49.5	Satin Ebony with Chrome Legs	39,540	39,540
P 127 NEXT		49.5	Satin Wood Tones with Chrome Legs	43,790	43,790
P 131 M1		51	Polished Ebony	38,570	38,570
P 135 K1		53	Polished Ebony	45,980	45,980

Grands

Model	Feet	Inches	Description	MSRP*	SMP*
P 159	5	2	Bora Polished Ebony	75,910	75,910
P 159	5	2	Bora Demi-Chippendale Polished Ebony	81,990	81,990
P 173	5	6	Breeze Polished Ebony	79,990	79,990
P 173	5	6	Breeze Chippendale Polished Ebony	90,958	90,958
P 173	5	6	Breeze Demi-Chippendale Polished Ebony	88,700	88,700
P 173	5	6	Breeze Klasik Polished Ebony	89,240	89,240
P 173	5	6	Breeze Rococo Satin White w/Gold Trim	94,190	94,190
P 194	6	3	Storm Polished Ebony	83,964	83,964
P 194	6	3	Storm Styl Polished Ebony	96,060	96,060
P 210	6	10	Pasat Polished Ebony	119,990	119,990
P 237	7	9	Monsoon Polished Ebony	157,390	157,390
P 284	9	2	Mistral Polished Ebony	217,084	217,084
Grands All Models			Mahogany/Walnut Upcharge	2,400	2,400
Grands All Models			White or Color Upcharge	1,600	1,600

PRAMBERGER

Legacy Series Verticals

Model	Feet	Inches	Description	MSRP*	SMP*
LV-110		43	Continental Polished Ebony	5,376	5,106
LV-110		43	Continental Polished Mahogany	5,926	5,526
LV-43F		43	French Provincial Satin Cherry/Oak	5,981	5,568
LV-43T		43	Satin Mahogany/Walnut	5,981	5,568
LV-115		45	Polished Ebony	5,981	5,568
LV-115		45	Polished Mahogany	6,394	5,882
LV-118		46.5	Satin Ebony	6,820	6,208
LV-118		46.5	Polished Ebony	6,820	5,894
LV-118		46.5	Polished Mahogany	6,820	6,208
LV-118N		46.5	Satin Ebony	7,150	6,460
LV-118N		46.5	Polished Ebony	6,875	6,250

Signature Series Verticals

Model	Feet	Inches	Description	MSRP*	SMP*
PV-118F		46.5	French Provincial Satin Cherry	7,013	6,356
PV-118R		46.5	Renaissance Satin Walnut	7,013	6,356
PV-118T		46.5	Satin Mahogany	7,013	6,356
PV-118S		46.5	Satin Ebony	7,411	6,660
PV-118S		46.5	Polished Ebony	7,136	6,450
PV-118S		46.5	Satin Mahogany/Walnut	7,411	6,660
PV-118S		46.5	Polished Mahogany/Walnut	7,411	6,660
PV-121		48	Satin Ebony	7,838	6,986
PV-121		48	Polished Ebony	7,838	6,986

*See pricing explanation on page 201.

Model	Feet	Inches	Description	MSRP*	SMP*
PRAMBERGER (continued)					
PV-121		48	Polished Mahogany	7,838	6,986
PV-121		48	Lacquer Semigloss Bubinga	8,511	7,500
PV-132		52	Satin Ebony	10,986	9,390
PV-132		52	Polished Ebony	9,611	8,340
PV-132		52	Polished Mahogany	10,986	9,390

J.P. Pramberger Platinum Series Verticals

Model	Feet	Inches	Description	MSRP*	SMP*
JP-132		52	Satin Ebony	15,000	13,000
JP-132		52	Polished Ebony	14,500	12,600
JP-132		52	Polished Mahogany	16,250	14,000
JP-132		52	Lacquer Semigloss Walnut	16,250	14,000
JP-132		52	Satin Bubinga/Rosewood	16,750	14,400

Legacy Series Grands

Model	Feet	Inches	Description	MSRP*	SMP*
LG-145	4	9	Polished Ebony	12,911	10,860
LG-145	4	9	Polished Mahogany/Walnut	14,011	11,700
LG-150	5		Satin Ebony	14,836	12,330
LG-150	5		Polished Ebony	13,736	11,490
LG-150	5		Polished Mahogany	14,836	12,330
LG-157	5	2	Satin Ebony	15,936	13,170
LG-157	5	2	Polished Ebony	14,561	12,120
LG-157	5	2	Polished Mahogany	15,936	13,170
LG-157	5	2	Polished Pommele/Bubinga w/Ebony	16,913	13,916
LG-157	5	2	Polished Ferrari Red	18,563	15,176
LG-175	5	9	Satin Ebony	18,425	15,070
LG-175	5	9	Polished Ebony	16,913	13,916
LG-175	5	9	Polished Mahogany	18,425	15,070

Signature Series Grands

Model	Feet	Inches	Description	MSRP*	SMP*
PS-157	5	2	Satin Ebony	18,686	15,270
PS-157	5	2	Polished Ebony	17,311	14,220
PS-157	5	2	Satin and Polished Mahogany	18,686	15,270
PS-157	5	2	Lacquer Satin and Polished Walnut	18,686	15,270
PS-157	5	2	Polished Pommele/Bubinga w/Ebony	19,236	15,690
PS-158	5	2	Satin Ebony	18,686	15,270
PS-158	5	2	Polished Ebony	17,311	14,220
PS-158	5	2	Polished Mahogany/Walnut	18,686	15,270
PS-175	5	9	Satin Ebony	20,048	16,310
PS-175	5	9	Polished Ebony	18,480	15,112
PS-175	5	9	Satin and Polished Mahogany	20,048	16,310
PS-175	5	9	Lacquer Satin and Polished Walnut	20,048	16,310
PS-185	6	1	Satin Ebony	20,900	16,960
PS-185	6	1	Polished Ebony	19,663	16,016
PS-185	6	1	Satin and Polished Mahogany	20,900	16,960
PS-185	6	1	Lacquer Satin and Polished Walnut	20,900	16,960
PS-186	6	1	Satin Ebony	22,275	18,010
PS-186	6	1	Polished Ebony	20,625	16,750
PS-186	6	1	Polished Mahogany/Walnut	22,275	18,010
PS-208	6	10	Satin Ebony	27,775	22,210
PS-208	6	10	Polished Ebony	26,400	21,160

J.P. Pramberger Platinum Series Grands

Model	Feet	Inches	Description	MSRP*	SMP*
JP-179L	5	10	Satin Ebony	35,250	29,200
JP-179L	5	10	Polished Ebony	34,375	28,500
JP-179L	5	10	Lacquer Semigloss Mahogany/Walnut	37,000	30,600
JP-179L	5	10	Polished Mahogany	37,000	30,600
JP-179L	5	10	Polished Bubinga/Pommele	37,000	30,600
JP-179LF	5	10	French Provincial Satin Ebony	41,500	34,200
JP-179LF	5	10	French Provincial Lacquer Semigloss Cherry	41,500	34,200
JP-208B	6	10	Satin Ebony	44,250	36,400

*See pricing explanation on page 201.

Model	Feet	Inches	Description	MSRP*	SMP*
PRAMBERGER (continued)					
JP-208B	6	10	Polished Ebony	43,250	35,600
JP-208B	6	10	Lacquer Semigloss Mahogany/Walnut	46,000	37,800
JP-228C	7	6	Satin Ebony	49,500	40,600
JP-228C	7	6	Polished Ebony	48,000	39,400
JP-280E	9	2	Polished Ebony	118,125	95,500
RITMÜLLER					
Classic Verticals					
UP 110RB1		43.5	Satin Walnut/Cherry	6,995	5,390
UP 110RB		43.5	French Provincial Satin Walnut/Cherry	6,995	5,390
UP 120RE		47.5	Satin Mahogany	7,995	5,990
UP 121RB		47.5	Polished Ebony	6,995	5,790
UP 121RB		47.5	Polished Mahogany/Walnut/White	7,495	5,990
Performance Verticals					
R1		47	Polished Ebony	8,595	6,790
R2		49	Polished Ebony w/Butterfly Lid	9,595	7,390
RB		49	Polished Ebony	9,595	7,390
Premium Verticals					
UH 118R		46.5	Polished Ebony	8,995	6,700
UH 121R		48	Chippendale Polished Ebony	9,695	7,790
UH 121R		48	Chippendale Polished Mahogany/Sapele	9,995	8,100
UH 132R		52	Polished Ebony	11,995	8,990
Performance Grands					
R8	4	11	Polished Ebony	13,495	9,990
R8	4	11	Polished Mahogany/White	13,995	10,590
R9	5	3	Polished Ebony	15,495	10,790
R9	5	3	Polished Mahogany/White	15,995	11,390
Premium Grands					
GH 148R	4	10	Polished Ebony	15,995	11,590
GH 148R	4	10	Polished Mahogany/Sapele	16,495	12,390
GH 148R2	4	10	Renaissance Polished Ebony	16,495	11,990
GH 148R2	4	10	Renaissance Polished Mahogany/Sapele	16,995	12,790
GH 160R	5	3	Hand-rubbed Satin Ebony	18,995	14,390
GH 160R	5	3	Polished Ebony	18,495	13,590
GH 160R	5	3	Polished Mahogany/Sapele	18,995	14,390
GH 170R	5	7	Polished Ebony	20,995	15,990
GH 188R	6	2	Polished Ebony	25,995	19,590
GH 212R	7		Polished Ebony	31,995	25,990
GH 275R	9		Polished Ebony	84,995	66,990
RÖNISCH					
Verticals					
118 K		46.5	Polished Ebony	20,202	19,182
118 K		46.5	Satin Mahogany	23,054	21,749
118 K		46.5	Polished Mahogany	26,796	25,116
118 K		46.5	Satin Walnut	23,285	21,957
118 K		46.5	Polished Walnut	27,027	25,324
118 K		46.5	Satin European Cherry	23,678	22,310
118 K		46.5	Polished European Cherry	27,420	25,678
118 K		46.5	Satin German Oak	22,823	21,541
118 K		46.5	Polished White	24,324	22,892
118 K		46.5	Waxed Alder	22,014	20,813
118 K		46.5	Satin Heart Beech	20,370	19,333

*See pricing explanation on page 201.

Model	Feet	Inches	Description	MSRP*	SMP*
RÖNISCH (continued)					
118 K		46.5	Satin Ash	22,638	21,374
118 K		46.5	Satin Swiss Pear/Indian Apple	24,324	22,892
118 K		46.5	Polished Indian Apple	28,067	26,260
125 K		49	Polished Ebony	24,324	22,892
125 K		49	Satin Mahogany	24,740	23,266
125 K		49	Polished Mahogany	28,713	26,842
125 K		49	Satin Walnut	24,971	23,474
125 K		49	Polished Walnut	28,944	27,050
125 K		49	Satin European Cherry	25,364	23,828
125 K		49	Polished European Cherry	29,337	27,403
125 K		49	Polished White	26,426	24,783
125 K		49	Satin Bubinga	25,549	23,994
125 K		49	Polished Bubinga	29,522	27,570
125 K		49	Satin Swiss Pear/Indian Apple	25,964	24,368
125 K		49	Polished Indian Apple	29,938	27,944
125 K		49	Carl Ronisch Edition Satin Burl Walnut	28,067	26,260
125 K		49	Carl Ronisch Edition Polished Burl Walnut	32,040	29,836
132 K		52	Polished Ebony	27,235	25,512
132 K		52	Satin Mahogany	27,651	25,886
132 K		52	Polished Mahogany	31,855	29,670
132 K		52	Satin Walnut	27,882	26,094
132 K		52	Polished Walnut	32,086	29,877
132 K		52	Polished White	29,337	27,403
132 K		52	Satin Bubinga	28,505	26,655
132 K		52	Polished Bubinga	32,710	30,439
132 K		52	Carl Ronisch Edition Satin Burl Walnut	31,023	28,921
132 K		52	Carl Ronisch Edition Polished Burl Walnut	35,228	32,705
Grands					
175 K	5	9	Polished Ebony	69,612	63,651
175 K	5	9	Satin Mahogany	71,244	65,120
175 K	5	9	Polished Mahogany	81,232	74,109
175 K	5	9	Satin Pyramid Mahogany	90,427	82,384
175 K	5	9	Polished Pyramid Mahogany	100,416	91,374
175 K	5	9	Satin Walnut	72,412	66,171
175 K	5	9	Polished Walnut	82,401	75,161
175 K	5	9	Satin European Cherry	74,419	67,977
175 K	5	9	Polished European Cherry	84,407	76,966
175 K	5	9	Polished White	73,625	67,263
175 K	5	9	Satin Bubinga	75,632	69,069
175 K	5	9	Polished Bubinga	85,620	78,058
175 K	5	9	Satin Rosewood	82,423	75,181
175 K	5	9	Polished Rosewood	92,412	84,171
175 K	5	9	Carl Ronisch Edition Satin Burl Walnut	90,529	82,476
175 K	5	9	Carl Ronisch Edition Polished Burl Walnut	100,993	91,894
186 K	6	1	Polished Ebony	75,632	69,069
186 K	6	1	Satin Mahogany	77,241	70,517
186 K	6	1	Polished Mahogany	87,230	79,507
186 K	6	1	Satin Pyramid Mahogany	96,425	87,783
186 K	6	1	Polished Pyramid Mahogany	106,413	96,772
186 K	6	1	Satin Walnut	78,410	71,569
186 K	6	1	Polished Walnut	88,398	80,558
186 K	6	1	Satin European Cherry	80,416	73,374
186 K	6	1	Polished European Cherry	90,405	82,365
186 K	6	1	Polished White	79,645	72,681
186 K	6	1	Satin Bubinga	81,629	74,466
186 K	6	1	Polished Bubinga	91,618	83,456
186 K	6	1	Satin Rosewood	88,421	80,579
186 K	6	1	Polished Rosewood	98,409	89,568

*See pricing explanation on page 201.

Model	Feet	Inches	Description	MSRP*	SMP*
RÖNISCH (continued)					
186 K	6	1	Carl Ronisch Edition Satin Burl Walnut	96,812	88,131
186 K	6	1	Carl Ronisch Edition Polished Burl Walnut	107,276	97,548
210 K	6	10.5	Polished Ebony	95,631	87,068
210 K	6	10.5	Polished White	99,622	90,660

SAMICK

Verticals

Model	Feet	Inches	Description	MSRP*	SMP*
JS-042		42	Continental Satin Ebony	5,101	4,896
JS-042		42	Continental Polished Ebony	4,826	4,686
JS-042		42	Continental Polished Mahogany/Walnut/Ivory	5,101	4,896
JS-042		42	Continental Satin and Polished Walnut	5,101	4,896
JS-042		42	Continental Satin Cherry	5,101	4,896
JS-143F		43	French Provincial Satin Cherry	5,981	5,568
JS-143M		43	Mediterranean Satin Brown Oak	5,981	5,568
JS-143T		43	Satin Mahogany	5,981	5,568
JS-115		45	Satin Ebony	6,133	5,684
JS-115		45	Polished Ebony	5,858	5,474
JS-115		45	Satin Walnut/Cherry	6,133	5,684
JS-115		45	Polished Mahogany/Walnut/Ivory	6,133	5,684
JS-118H		46.5	Satin Ebony	6,683	6,104
JS-118H		46.5	Polished Ebony	6,408	5,894
JS-118H		46.5	Polished Mahogany	6,683	6,104
JS-247		46.5	Satin Ebony	7,411	6,660
JS-247		46.5	Polished Ebony	7,136	6,450
JS-247		46.5	Satin Mahogany/Walnut	7,411	6,660
JS-247		46.5	Polished Mahogany/Walnut	7,411	6,660
JS-121F/M		48	Satin Ebony	7,288	6,566
JS-121F/M		48	Polished Ebony	7,013	6,356
JS-121F/M		48	Polished Mahogany	7,288	6,566
JS-131		52	Satin Ebony	8,113	7,196
JS-131		52	Polished Ebony	7,838	6,986
JS-131		52	Polished Mahogany	8,113	7,196

Grands

Model	Feet	Inches	Description	MSRP*	SMP*
SIG-48	4	9	Polished Ebony	12,911	10,860
SIG-48	4	9	Polished Mahogany/Walnut	14,011	11,700
SIG-50	5		Satin Ebony	14,836	12,330
SIG-50	5		Polished Ebony	13,736	11,490
SIG-50	5		Polished Mahogany/Walnut	14,836	12,330
SIG-54	5	4	Satin Ebony	15,936	13,170
SIG-54	5	4	Polished Ebony	14,561	12,120
SIG-54	5	4	Polished Mahogany/Walnut	15,936	13,170
SIG-54	5	4	Polished Bubinga/Pommele w/Ebony	17,586	14,430
SIG-57	5	7	Satin Ebony	17,036	14,010
SIG-57	5	7	Polished Ebony	15,661	12,960
SIG-57	5	7	Polished Mahogany/Walnut	17,036	14,010
SIG-57L	5	7	Empire Satin Ebony	19,250	15,700
SIG-57L	5	7	Empire Polished Ebony	17,875	14,650
SIG-57L	5	7	Empire Polished Mahogany	19,250	15,700
SIG-61	6	1	Satin Ebony	18,563	15,176
SIG-61	6	1	Polished Ebony	17,325	14,230
SIG-61	6	1	Polished Mahogany/Walnut	18,563	15,176
SIG-61L	6	1	Empire Satin Ebony	20,488	16,646
SIG-61L	6	1	Empire Polished Ebony	19,250	15,700
SIG-61L	6	1	Empire Polished Mahogany	20,488	16,646

*See pricing explanation on page 201.

Model	Feet	Inches	Description	MSRP*	SMP*

SAUTER

Standard wood veneers are walnut, mahogany, ash, and alder.

Verticals

Model	Feet	Inches	Description	MSRP*	SMP*
119		46	Peter Maly Concent Satin Ebony	31,654	31,654
119		46	Peter Maly Concent Polished Ebony	33,860	33,860
122		48	Ragazza Polished Ebony	36,680	36,680
122		48	Ragazza Satin Cherry	36,320	36,320
122		48	Ragazza Polished Cherry/Yew	42,870	42,870
122		48	Vista Polished Ebony	40,070	40,070
122		48	Vista Satin Maple	38,250	38,250
122		48	Vista Satin Cherry	39,880	39,880
122		48	Master Class Polished Ebony	46,940	46,940
122		48	Peter Maly Artes Polished Ebony	52,200	52,200
122		48	Peter Maly Artes Polished Palisander/Macassar	53,200	53,200
122		48	Peter Maly Artes Polished White	53,200	53,200
122		48	Peter Maly Pure Noble Polished Ebony/Veneers	48,870	48,870
122		48	Peter Maly Pure Noble Polished White/Red	50,204	50,204
122		48	Peter Maly Pure Basic Satin Ebony/Walnut	39,820	39,820
122		48	Peter Maly Pure Basic Satin White	39,820	39,820
122		48	Peter Maly Pure Basic Satin White/Maple	39,820	39,820
122		48	Peter Maly Rondo Polished Ebony	43,590	43,590
122		48	Peter Maly Rondo Satin Wenge	40,330	40,330
122		48	Peter Maly Vitrea Colored Ebony with Glass	40,860	40,860
122		48	Schulpiano Satin Beech/Black Ash	32,120	32,120
130		51	Master Class Polished Ebony	53,066	53,066
130		51	Competence Polished Ebony	45,350	45,350
130		51	Competence Satin Walnut	43,100	43,100
130		51	Sonder Polished Ebony w/Sostenuto	39,580	39,580
130		51	Sonder Polished Ebony w/o Sostenuto	36,064	36,064

Grands

Model	Feet	Inches	Description	MSRP*	SMP*
160	5	3	Alpha Polished Ebony	95,220	95,220
160	5	3	Alpha Satin Standard Wood Veneers	87,980	87,980
160	5	3	Chippendale Satin Cherry	98,700	98,700
160	5	3	Chippendale Satin Standard Wood Veneers	95,100	95,100
160	5	3	Noblesse Satin Cherry	105,840	105,840
160	5	3	Noblesse Polished Cherry	114,200	114,200
160	5	3	Noblesse Satin Burl Walnut	110,518	110,518
160	5	3	Noblesse Satin Standard Wood Veneers	105,834	105,834
160	5	3	Noblesse Polished Standard Wood Veneers	113,740	113,740
185	6	1	Delta Polished Ebony	105,960	105,960
185	6	1	Delta Polished Ebony w/Burl Walnut	108,600	108,600
185	6	1	Delta Polished Pyramid Mahogany	116,920	116,920
185	6	1	Delta Polished Bubinga	116,040	116,040
185	6	1	Delta Polished Rio Palisander	116,920	116,920
185	6	1	Delta Satin Maple with Silver	99,700	99,700
185	6	1	Delta Polished White	109,240	109,240
185	6	1	Delta Satin Standard Wood Veneers	97,500	97,500
185	6	1	Chippendale Satin Cherry	108,300	108,300
185	6	1	Chippendale Satin Standard Wood Veneers	104,640	104,640
185	6	1	Noblesse Satin Cherry	115,720	115,720
185	6	1	Noblesse Polished Cherry	128,760	128,760
185	6	1	Noblesse Satin Burl Walnut	120,560	120,560
185	6	1	Noblesse Satin Standard Wood Veneers	112,200	112,200
185	6	1	Noblesse Polished Standard Wood Veneers	125,660	125,660
210	6	11	Peter Maly Vivace Polished Ebony	146,920	146,920
210	6	11	Peter Maly Vivace Satin Wood Veneers	137,210	137,210
210	6	11	Peter Maly Vivace Polished White	149,100	149,100
220	7	3	Omega Polished Ebony	133,440	133,440

*See pricing explanation on page 201.

Model	Feet	Inches	Description	MSRP*	SMP*
SAUTER (continued)					
220	7	3	Omega Polished Burl Walnut	148,640	148,640
220	7	3	Omega Polished Pyramid Mahogany	147,300	147,300
220	7	3	Omega Satin Standard Wood Veneers	128,100	128,100
230	7	7	Peter Maly Ambiente Polished Ebony	168,700	168,700
230	7	7	Peter Maly Ambiente Polished Ebony w/Crystals	192,840	192,840
275	9		Concert Polished Ebony	228,320	228,320

SCHIMMEL

Classic Series Verticals

Model	Feet	Inches	Description	MSRP*	SMP*
C 116	46		Tradition Polished Ebony	23,600	19,880
C 116	46		Tradition Polished Mahogany/White	26,600	22,280
C 116	46		Tradition Satin Walnut/Cherry/Beech/Alder	26,600	22,280
C 116	46		Modern Cubus Polished Ebony	27,350	22,880
C 116	46		Modern Cubus Polished White	30,350	25,280
C 120	48		Tradition Polished Ebony	26,100	21,880
C 120	48		Tradition Polished Mahogany/White	29,100	24,280
C 120	48		Tradition Satin Walnut/Cherry/Beech/Alder	29,100	24,280
C 120	48		Tradition Marketerie Polished Mahogany w/Inlay	31,100	25,880
C 120	48		Elegance Manhattan Polished Ebony	24,725	20,780
C 120	48		Elegance Manhattan Polished Mahogany/White	29,100	24,280
C 120	48		Modern Polished Ebony	29,850	24,880
C 120	48		Modern Polished White	32,850	27,280
C 120	48		NWS Edition 80	31,475	26,180
C 120	48		Royal Polished Ebony	28,600	23,880
C 120	48		Royal Polished Mahogany/White	31,600	26,280
C 120	48		Royal Intarsie Flora Polished Mahogany w/Inlays	33,600	27,880
C 126	50		Tradition Polished Ebony	31,100	25,880
C 126	50		Tradition Polished Mahogany/White	34,100	28,280
C 130	51		Tradition Polished Ebony	33,600	27,880
C 130	51		Tradition Polished Mahogany/White	36,600	30,280

Konzert Series Verticals

Model	Feet	Inches	Description	MSRP*	SMP*
K 122	48		Tradition Polished Ebony	34,475	28,580
K 122	48		Tradition Polished Mahogany/White	38,475	31,780
K 122	48		Elegance Polished Ebony	34,475	28,580
K 122	48		Elegance Polished White	38,475	31,780
K 125	49		Tradition Polished Ebony	36,975	30,580
K 125	49		Tradition Polished Mahogany/White	40,975	33,780
K 132	52		Tradition Polished Ebony	42,225	34,780
K 132	52		Tradition Polished Mahogany/White	46,225	37,980

International Series Verticals

Model	Feet	Inches	Description	MSRP*	SMP*
I 115	46		Modern Polished Ebony	19,350	16,480
I 115	46		Modern Polished White	22,350	18,880
I 115	46		Tradition Polished Ebony	19,350	16,480
I 115	46		Tradition Polished Mahogany/White	22,350	18,880
I 119	48		Tradition Polished Ebony	21,850	18,480
I 119	48		Tradition Polished Mahogany/White	24,850	20,880
I 123	50		Tradition Polished Ebony	23,350	19,680
I 123	50		Tradition Polished Mahogany/White	26,350	22,080

Wilhelm Schimmel Verticals

Model	Feet	Inches	Description	MSRP*	SMP*
W 114	46		Modern Swing Polished Ebony	15,225	13,180
W 114	46		Modern Swing Polished White	17,725	15,180
W 114	46		Tradition Polished Ebony	16,225	13,980
W 114	46		Tradition Polished Mahogany/White	18,725	15,980
W 118	48		Tradition Polished Ebony	17,225	15,180
W 118	48		Tradition Polished Mahogany/White	20,225	17,180

*See pricing explanation on page 201.

Model	Feet	Inches	Description	MSRP*	SMP*
SCHIMMEL (continued)					
W 123		50	Tradition Polished Ebony	19,225	16,380
W 123		50	Tradition Polished Mahogany/White	21,725	18,380
Classic Series Grands					
C 169	5	7	Tradition Polished Ebony	64,350	52,480
C 169	5	7	Tradition Polished Mahogany/White	70,600	57,480
C 169	5	7	NWS Edition 80	71,100	57,880
C 189	6	3	Tradition Polished Ebony	68,100	55,480
C 189	6	3	Tradition Polished Mahogany/White	74,350	60,480
C 189	6	3	NWS Edition 80	74,850	60,880
C 213	7		Tradition Polished Ebony	74,350	60,480
C 213	7		Tradition Polished Mahogany/White	80,600	65,480
C 213	7		NWS Edition 80	81,100	65,880
Konzert Series Grands					
K 175	5	9	Tradition Polished Ebony	84,750	68,800
K 175	5	9	Tradition Polished Mahogany/White	92,250	74,800
K 195	6	5	Tradition Polished Ebony	92,250	74,800
K 195	6	5	Tradition Polished Mahogany/White	99,750	80,800
K 213	7		Glas Clear Acrylic and White or Black and Gold	275,000	251,000
K 213	7		Otmar Alt Polished Ebony w/Color Motifs	225,000	181,000
K 219	7	2	Tradition Polished Ebony	99,750	80,800
K 219	7	2	Tradition Polished Mahogany/White	107,250	86,800
K 230	7	7	Tradition Polished Ebony	114,750	92,800
K 256	8	4	Tradition Polished Ebony	129,750	104,800
K 280	9	2	Tradition Polished Ebony	149,750	120,800
International Series Grands					
I 182	6		Tradition Polished Ebony	54,475	44,580
I 182	6		Tradition Polished Mahogany/White	60,725	49,580
I 208	6	10	Tradition Polished Ebony	65,975	53,780
I 208	6	10	Tradition Polished Mahogany/White	72,225	58,780
Wilhelm Schimmel Grands					
W 180	6		Tradition Polished Ebony	39,225	32,380
W 180	6		Tradition Polished Mahogany/White	44,225	36,380
W 206	6	10	Tradition Polished Ebony	47,975	39,380
W 206	6	10	Tradition Polished Mahogany/White	52,975	43,380
SCHULZE POLLMANN					
Studio Series Verticals					
SU115		45	Polished Peacock Ebony	9,595	7,790
SU115		45	Polished Peacock Mahogany	10,495	8,390
SU118A		46	Polished Peacock Ebony	10,995	8,990
SU118A		46	Polished Peacock Mahogany/Walnut	11,995	9,590
SU122A		48	Polished Peacock Ebony	13,995	10,390
SU122A		48	Polished Peacock Mahogany/Walnut	14,995	10,990
SU122A		48	Polished Feather Mahogany	15,895	11,590
Masterpiece Series Grands					
160/GK	5	3	Polished Ebony (spade leg)	55,995	55,995
160/GK	5	3	Polished Briar Mahogany (spade leg)	59,995	59,995
160/GK	5	3	Polished Feather Mahogany (spade leg)	63,995	63,995
197/G5	6	6	Polished Ebony (spade leg)	77,995	76,990
197/G5	6	6	Polished Briar Mahogany (spade leg)	80,995	80,995
197/G5	6	6	Polished Feather Mahogany (spade leg)	84,995	84,995

*See pricing explanation on page 201.

SCHUMANN

Schumann pianos are also distributed under the names Falcone and Hobart M. Cable. Not all styles and finishes are available under all three brands.

Verticals

Model	Feet	Inches	Description	MSRP*	SMP*
U 12TD		44	Polished Ebony	4,800	4,590
U 18TD		46	Polished Ebony	5,000	4,750
C 20FD		47	French Satin Mahogany	5,600	5,170
U 20FD		47	French Polished Ebony	5,100	4,790
U 20ITD		47	Italian Polished Ebony	5,100	4,830
U 22TD		48	Polished Ebony	5,400	5,030
U 22TD		48	Polished Mahogany/Walnut	5,900	5,450
U 22TD		48	Polished White	6,000	5,530
U 25STD		50	Studio Polished Ebony	6,200	5,650
U 25STD		50	Studio Polished White	6,900	6,150
U 32STD		52	Studio Polished Ebony	7,300	6,490

Grands

Model	Feet	Inches	Description	MSRP*	SMP*
G 46TD	4	10	Polished Ebony	12,000	9,990
G 46TD	4	10	Polished Mahogany/Walnut	12,800	10,610
G 46TD	4	10	Polished White	13,100	10,810
G 52TD	5		Polished Ebony	13,300	11,010
G 52TD	5		Polished Mahogany/Walnut	14,200	11,630
G 52TD	5		Polished White	14,400	11,830
G 68TD	5	6	Polished Ebony	16,100	13,070
G 68TD	5	6	Polished Cateye/Ebony	16,900	13,690
G 68TD	5	6	Polished White	17,200	13,910
G 86TD	6	2	Polished Ebony	17,700	14,310
G 86TD	6	2	Polished Mahogany/Walnut	18,600	14,930
G 212TD	7		Polished Ebony	27,600	21,730

SEILER

Seiler Verticals

Model	Feet	Inches	Description	MSRP*	SMP*
SE-116		45	Primus, Polished Ebony	32,813	27,250
SE-116		45	Mondial, Polished Ebony	34,375	28,500
SE-116		45	Mondial, Polished Rosewood	46,875	38,500
SE-126		49	Konzert, Satin Walnut	45,313	37,250
SE-132		52	Konzert, Polished Ebony	45,313	37,250
SE-132		52	Konzert, Polished Ebony w/Rec Panel	46,875	38,500
SE-132		52	Konzert, Polished Mahogany	59,375	48,500

Eduard Seiler ED Series Verticals

Model	Feet	Inches	Description	MSRP*	SMP*
ED-126		49	Primus Satin Ebony	14,250	9,790
ED-126		49	Primus Polished Ebony	13,750	9,306
ED-126		49	Primus Polished Mahogany/Walnut/Ivory	14,250	10,230
ED-132		52	Konzert Satin Ebony	16,750	10,230
ED-132		52	Konzert Polished Ebony	15,000	9,790
ED-132		52	Konzert Polished Mahogany/Walnut/Ivory	16,750	10,670

Eduard Seiler ES Series Verticals

Model	Feet	Inches	Description	MSRP*	SMP*
ES-126		49	Primus Polished Ebony	25,485	19,690
ES-126		49	Primus Polished Mahogany/Walnut	26,985	20,790
ES-126		49	Primus Satin Alder/Beech	26,985	20,790
ES-132		52	Konzert Polished Ebony	28,750	22,110
ES-132		52	Konzert Polished Mahogany/Walnut	30,250	23,210
ES-132		52	Konzert Satin Alder/Beech	30,250	23,210

*See pricing explanation on page 201.

Model	Feet	Inches	Description	MSRP*	SMP*

Johannes Seiler Verticals

Model	Feet	Inches	Description	MSRP*	SMP*
GS-116		45.5	Satin Ebony	7,563	7,050
GS-116		45.5	Polished Ebony	7,013	6,610
GS-116		45.5	Polished Mahogany	7,563	7,050
GS-118		47	Satin Ebony	8,525	7,820
GS-118		47	Polished Ebony	7,975	7,380
GS-118		47	Polished Mahogany/Walnut	8,525	7,820
GS-122		48.5	Satin Ebony	9,061	8,250
GS-122		48.5	Polished Ebony	8,415	7,732
GS-122		48.5	Polished Mahogany	9,061	8,250

Seiler Grands

Model	Feet	Inches	Description	MSRP*	SMP*
SE-168	5	6	Virtuoso, Polished Ebony	101,563	82,250
SE-168	5	6	Virtuoso, Polished Mahogany	114,063	92,250
SE-186	6	2	Maestro, Polished Ebony	109,375	88,500
SE-186	6	2	Maestro, Polished Mahogany	123,438	99,750
SE-186	6	2	Maestro, Polished Rosewood	123,438	99,750
SE-186	6	2	Ziricote, Polished Ebony	139,063	112,250
SE-186	6	2	Louvre, Polished Cherry	173,438	139,750
SE-186	6	2	Florenz, Polished Mahogany	173,438	139,750
SE-208	6	10	Polished Ebony	121,875	98,500
SE-242	8		Polished Ebony	156,250	126,000
SE-278	9	2	Polished Ebony	253,125	203,500

Eduard Seiler ED Series Grands

Model	Feet	Inches	Description	MSRP*	SMP*
ED-168	5	6	Virtuoso Satin Ebony	32,000	24,100
ED-168	5	6	Virtuoso Polished Ebony	31,250	22,780
ED-168	5	6	Virtuoso Polished Mahogany/Walnut	32,000	24,100
ED-186	6	2	Maestro Satin Ebony	41,250	30,690
ED-186	6	2	Maestro Polished Ebony	40,000	29,590
ED-186	6	2	Maestro Polished Mahogany/Walnut	41,250	30,690

Eduard Seiler ES Series Grands

Model	Feet	Inches	Description	MSRP*	SMP*
ES-186	6	2	Maestro Polished Ebony	59,985	44,990
ES-186	6	2	Maestro Polished Mahogany/Walnut	62,985	47,190
ES-186	6	2	Maestro Satin Maple/Cherry	62,985	47,190

Johannes Seiler Grands

Model	Feet	Inches	Description	MSRP*	SMP*
GS-160	5	3	Satin Ebony	19,938	16,950
GS-160	5	3	Polished Ebony	18,975	16,180
GS-160	5	3	Polished Mahogany	19,938	16,950
GS-175	5	9	Satin Ebony	22,688	19,150
GS-175	5	9	Polished Ebony	21,725	18,380
GS-175	5	9	Polished Mahogany	22,963	19,150
GS-186	6	2	Satin Ebony	24,475	20,580
GS-186	6	2	Polished Ebony	23,650	19,920
GS-186	6	2	Polished Mahogany	24,736	20,580

SOHMER

Verticals

Model	Feet	Inches	Description	MSRP*	SMP*
S-126		50	Polished Ebony		10,800
S-126		50	Polished Mahogany		11,200

Grands

Model	Feet	Inches	Description	MSRP*	SMP*
S-160	5	3	Polished Ebony		20,190
S-160	5	3	Polished Mahogany		20,990
S-180	5	10	Polished Ebony		22,190
S-180	5	10	Polished Mahogany		22,990
S-218	7	2	Polished Ebony		31,980

*See pricing explanation on page 201.

Model	Feet	Inches	Description	MSRP*	SMP*

STEINBERG, G.

Verticals

Model	Feet	Inches	Description	MSRP*	SMP*
GS-111 Nicosia		45	Polished Ebony	7,490	6,980
GS-111 Nicosia		45	Polished Mahogany/Walnut	7,690	7,180
GS-111 Nicosia		45	Polished White	7,890	7,380
GS-115 Slate		45	Polished Ebony	7,690	7,180
GS-115 Slate		45	Polished Mahogany/Walnut	7,890	7,300
GS-115 Slate		45	Polished White	8,190	7,520
GS-115 Slate		45	Queen Anne Polished Ebony	7,890	7,300
GS-115 Slate		45	Queen Anne Polished Mahogany/Walnut	8,090	7,400
GS-115 Slate		45	Queen Anne Polished White	8,290	7,620
GS-119 Splendit		47	Polished Ebony	8,090	7,600
GS-119 Splendit		47	Polished Mahogany/Walnut	8,290	7,800
GS-119 Splendit		47	Polished White	8,390	8,000
GS-119 Splendit		47	Queen Anne Polished Ebony	8,290	7,700
GS-119 Splendit		47	Queen Anne Polished Mahogany/Walnut	8,490	7,900
GS-119 Splendit		47	Queen Anne Polished White	8,590	8,100
GS-123 Performance		49	Polished Ebony	8,490	7,800
GS-123 Performance		49	Queen Anne Polished Ebony	8,790	8,000
GS-126 Sienna		50	Polished Ebony	9,490	8,400
GS-126 Sienna		50	Queen Anne Polished Ebony	9,790	8,600

Grands

Model	Feet	Inches	Description	MSRP*	SMP*
GS-152 Sovereign	5	1	Polished Ebony	17,700	14,180
GS-152 Sovereign	5	1	Polished Mahogany/Walnut	19,275	15,250
GS-152 Sovereign	5	1	Polished White	20,875	15,580
GS-152 Sovereign	5	1	Queen Anne or Empire Polished Ebony	18,050	14,580
GS-152 Sovereign	5	1	Queen Anne or Empire Polished Mahogany/Walnut	19,650	15,700
GS-152 Sovereign	5	1	Queen Anne or Empire Polished White	21,350	15,960
GS-160 Stockholm	5	5	Polished Ebony	22,875	16,300
GS-160 Stockholm	5	5	Polished Mahogany/Walnut	24,525	17,300
GS-160 Stockholm	5	5	Polished White	26,175	17,500
GS-160 Stockholm	5	5	Queen Anne or Empire Polished Ebony	23,650	16,580
GS-160 Stockholm	5	5	Queen Anne or Empire Polished Mahogany/Walnut	25,325	17,780
GS-160 Stockholm	5	5	Queen Anne or Empire Polished White	26,975	17,980
GS-175 Schwerin	5	10	Polished Ebony	25,875	16,980
GS-175 Schwerin	5	10	Polished Mahogany/Walnut	27,025	18,380
GS-175 Schwerin	5	10	Polished White	28,975	18,580
GS-175 Schwerin	5	10	Queen Anne or Empire Polished Ebony	25,425	17,500
GS-175 Schwerin	5	10	Queen Anne or Empire Polished Mahogany/Walnut	27,525	18,700
GS-175 Schwerin	5	10	Queen Anne or Empire Polished White	30,175	18,900
GS-187 Amsterdam	6	2	Polished Ebony	27,850	18,100
GS-187 Amsterdam	6	2	Polished Mahogany/Walnut	28,975	19,100
GS-187 Amsterdam	6	2	Polished White	31,050	19,300
GS-187 Amsterdam	6	2	Queen Anne or Empire Polished Ebony	28,575	18,400
GS-187 Amsterdam	6	2	Queen Anne or Empire Polished Mahogany/Walnut	29,525	19,500
GS-187 Amsterdam	6	2	Queen Anne or Empire Polished White	31,375	19,700

STEINBERG, WILH.

Signature Series Verticals

Model	Feet	Inches	Description	MSRP*	SMP*
117		46	Polished Ebony	18,955	18,955
117		46	Satin Alder	21,307	21,307
117		46	Satin Walnut/Mahogany	20,702	20,702
117		46	Polished White	20,702	20,702
124		49	Polished Ebony	20,467	20,467
124		49	Satin Alder	23,138	23,138
124		49	Satin Walnut/Mahogany	22,366	22,366

*See pricing explanation on page 201.

Model	Feet	Inches	Description	MSRP*	SMP*
STEINBERG, WILH. *(continued)*					
124		49	Polished White	22,366	22,366
130		51	Polished Ebony	24,163	24,163
130		51	Satin Alder	27,372	27,372
130		51	Satin Walnut/Mahogany	26,431	26,431
130		51	Polished White	26,431	26,431
Amadeus		51	Polished Ebony	27,523	27,523
Passione		51	Polished Ebony	30,043	30,043
Nomos Series Verticals					
118		46.5	Polished Ebony	16,267	16,267
118		46.5	Polished White	17,746	17,746
123		48.5	Polished Ebony	17,443	17,443
123		48.5	Polished White	19,039	19,039
128		50.5	Polished Ebony	20,803	20,803
128		50.5	Polished White	22,735	22,735
Signature Series Grands					
188	6	2	Polished Ebony	46,692	46,692
212	6	11	Polished Ebony	55,932	55,932
275	9		Polished Ebony	on request	on request

STEINGRAEBER & SÖHNE
Prices include bench. Euro = $1.25

Verticals

Model	Feet	Inches	Description	MSRP*	SMP*
122 T		48	Satin and Polished Ebony	45,994	44,744
122 T		48	Satin and Polished White	46,792	45,542
122 T		48	Polished Ebony w/Twist & Change Panels	50,467	49,217
122 T		48	Satin Ordinary Veneers	45,238	43,988
122 T		48	Polished Ordinary Veneers	52,441	51,191
122 T		48	Satin Special Veneers	47,779	46,529
122 T		48	Polished Special Veneers	55,024	53,774
122 T		48	Satin Extraordinary Veneers	52,336	51,086
122 T		48	Polished Extraordinary Veneers	59,602	58,352
130 T-PS		51	Satin and Polished Ebony	57,145	55,895
130 T-PS		51	Satin and Polished White	57,985	56,735
130 T-PS		51	Polished Ebony w/Twist & Change Panels	61,534	60,284
130 T-PS		51	Satin Ordinary Veneers	55,150	53,900
130 T-PS		51	Polished Ordinary Veneers	62,101	60,851
130 T-PS		51	Satin Special Veneers	57,481	56,231
130 T-PS		51	Polished Special Veneers	64,369	63,119
130 T-PS		51	Satin Extraordinary Veneers	62,101	60,851
130 T-PS		51	Polished Extraordinary Veneers	68,863	67,613
130 T-SFM		51	Satin and Polished Ebony	56,095	54,845
130 T-SFM		51	Satin and Polished White	56,956	55,706
130 T-SFM		51	Polished Ebony w/Twist & Change Panels	60,484	59,234
130 T-SFM		51	Satin Ordinary Veneers	54,121	52,871
130 T-SFM		51	Polished Ordinary Veneers	61,072	59,822
130 T-SFM		51	Satin Special Veneers	56,452	55,202
130 T-SFM		51	Polished Special Veneers	63,340	62,090
130 T-SFM		51	Satin Extraordinary Veneers	61,072	59,822
130 T-SFM		51	Polished Extraordinary Veneers	67,834	66,584
138 K		54	Satin and Polished Ebony	60,631	59,381
138 K		54	Satin and Polished White	61,429	60,179
138 K		54	Polished Ebony w/Twist & Change Panels	64,852	63,602
138 K		54	Satin Ordinary Veneers	58,594	57,344
138 K		54	Polished Ordinary Veneers	65,545	64,295
138 K		54	Satin Special Veneers	60,925	59,675

*See pricing explanation on page 201.

Model	Feet	Inches	Description	MSRP*	SMP*
STEINGRAEBER & SÖHNE (continued)					
138 K		54	Polished Special Veneers	67,876	66,626
138 K		54	Satin Extraordinary Veneers	65,419	64,169
138 K		54	Polished Extraordinary Veneers	72,412	71,162
138 K-SFM		54	Satin and Polished Ebony	62,269	61,019
138 K-SFM		54	Satin and Polished White	63,067	61,817
138 K-SFM		54	Polished Ebony w/Twist & Change Panels	66,532	65,282
138 K-SFM		54	Satin Ordinary Veneers	60,211	58,961
138 K-SFM		54	Polished Ordinary Veneers	67,183	65,933
138 K-SFM		54	Satin Special Veneers	62,584	61,334
138 K-SFM		54	Polished Special Veneers	69,514	68,264
138 K-SFM		54	Satin Extraordinary Veneers	67,078	65,828
138 K-SFM		54	Polished Extraordinary Veneers	74,071	72,821
Grands					
A-170	5	7	Satin and Polished Ebony	103,736	102,486
A-170	5	7	Satin and Polished White	105,689	104,439
A-170	5	7	Satin Ordinary Veneers	117,575	116,325
A-170	5	7	Polished Ordinary Veneers	122,090	120,840
A-170	5	7	Satin Special Veneers	119,297	118,047
A-170	5	7	Polished Special Veneers	123,749	122,499
A-170	5	7	Satin Extraordinary Veneers	123,665	122,415
A-170	5	7	Polished Extraordinary Veneers	128,117	126,867
A-170 S	5	7	Studio Lacquer Anti-Scratch	95,840	94,590
B-192	6	3	Satin and Polished Ebony	120,011	118,761
B-192	6	3	Satin and Polished White	122,300	121,050
B-192	6	3	Satin Ordinary Veneers	133,451	132,201
B-192	6	3	Polished Ordinary Veneers	137,378	136,128
B-192	6	3	Satin Special Veneers	135,110	133,860
B-192	6	3	Polished Special Veneers	139,100	137,850
B-192	6	3	Satin Extraordinary Veneers	139,478	138,228
B-192	6	3	Polished Extraordinary Veneers	143,426	142,176
B-192 S	6	3	Studio Lacquer Anti-Scratch	111,674	110,424
C-212	7		Satin and Polished Ebony	136,664	135,414
C-212	7		Satin and Polished White	139,310	138,060
C-212	7		Satin Ordinary Veneers	152,099	150,849
C-212	7		Polished Ordinary Veneers	156,614	155,364
C-212	7		Satin Special Veneers	154,031	152,781
C-212	7		Polished Special Veneers	158,567	157,317
C-212	7		Satin Extraordinary Veneers	159,008	157,758
C-212	7		Polished Extraordinary Veneers	163,565	162,315
C-212 S	7		Studio Lacquer Anti-Scratch	127,067	125,817
D-232	7	7	Satin and Polished Ebony	166,875	165,625
D-232	7	7	Satin and Polished White	169,248	167,998
D-232	7	7	Satin Ordinary Veneers	184,284	183,034
D-232	7	7	Polished Ordinary Veneers	189,429	188,179
D-232	7	7	Satin Special Veneers	186,426	185,176
D-232	7	7	Polished Special Veneers	191,508	190,258
D-232	7	7	Satin Extraordinary Veneers	191,613	190,363
D-232	7	7	Polished Extraordinary Veneers	196,737	195,487
D-232 S	7	7	Studio Lacquer Anti-Scratch	155,577	154,327
E-272	8	11	Satin and Polished Ebony	249,258	248,008
E-272	8	11	Satin and Polished White	251,673	250,423
E-272	8	11	Satin Ordinary Veneers	268,494	267,244
E-272	8	11	Polished Ordinary Veneers	274,647	273,397
E-272	8	11	Satin Special Veneers	270,972	269,722
E-272	8	11	Polished Special Veneers	277,125	275,875
E-272	8	11	Satin Extraordinary Veneers	276,894	275,644
E-272	8	11	Polished Extraordinary Veneers	283,068	281,818

*See pricing explanation on page 201.

Model	Feet	Inches	Description	MSRP*	SMP*

These are the prices at the Steinway retail store in New York City, often used as a benchmark for Steinway prices throughout the country. Model K-52 in ebony; model 1098 in ebony, mahogany, and walnut; and grand models in ebony, mahogany, and walnut include adjustable artist benches. Other models include regular wood bench. Wood-veneered models are in a semigloss finish called "satin lustre."

Verticals

Model	Feet	Inches	Description	MSRP*	SMP*
4510		45	Sheraton Satin Ebony	32,500	32,500
4510		45	Sheraton Mahogany	36,200	36,200
4510		45	Sheraton Walnut	36,500	36,500
1098		46.5	Satin Ebony	30,800	30,800
1098		46.5	Mahogany	34,200	34,200
1098		46.5	Walnut	34,700	34,700
K-52		52	Satin Ebony	35,800	35,800
K-52		52	Mahogany	40,400	40,400
K-52		52	Walnut	41,800	41,800

Grands

Model	Feet	Inches	Description	MSRP*	SMP*
S	5	1	Satin Ebony	61,300	61,300
S	5	1	Polyester Polished Ebony	63,200	63,200
S	5	1	Polyester Polished Ebony w/Sterling Hardware	65,200	65,200
S	5	1	Polyester Polished White	70,300	70,300
S	5	1	Mahogany	72,900	72,900
S	5	1	Walnut	73,700	73,700
S	5	1	Kewazinga Bubinga	77,900	77,900
S	5	1	East Indian Rosewood	88,100	88,100
S	5	1	Macassar Ebony	95,900	95,900
S	5	1	Figured Sapele	77,300	77,300
S	5	1	Dark Cherry	78,100	78,100
S	5	1	Santos Rosewood	87,500	87,500
S	5	1	African Pommele	90,600	90,600
M	5	7	Satin Ebony	66,300	66,300
M	5	7	Polyester Polished Ebony	68,600	68,600
M	5	7	Polyester Polished Ebony w/Sterling Hardware	70,700	70,700
M	5	7	Polyester Polished White	77,600	77,600
M	5	7	Mahogany	79,100	79,100
M	5	7	Walnut	79,900	79,900
M	5	7	Kewazinga Bubinga	84,400	84,400
M	5	7	East Indian Rosewood	94,700	94,700
M	5	7	Macassar Ebony	103,500	103,500
M	5	7	Figured Sapele	85,100	85,100
M	5	7	Dark Cherry	85,700	85,600
M	5	7	Santos Rosewood	94,600	94,600
M	5	7	African Pommele	98,100	98,100
M 1014A	5	7	Chippendale Mahogany	95,100	94,400
M 1014A	5	7	Chippendale Walnut	97,300	96,600
M 501A	5	7	Louis XV Walnut	122,400	122,400
M 501A	5	7	Louis XV East Indian Rosewood	142,300	142,200
M	5	7	Pops Polished Ebony w/White Accessories	81,700	81,700
M	5	7	Pops Polished Ebony w/Color Accessories	82,500	82,500
M	5	7	John Lennon Imagine Polished White	107,600	107,600
O	5	10.5	Satin Ebony	74,800	74,800
O	5	10.5	Polyester Polished Ebony	77,100	77,100
O	5	10.5	Polyester Polished Ebony w/Sterling Hardware	79,200	79,200
O	5	10.5	Polyester Polished White	85,500	85,500
O	5	10.5	Mahogany	85,800	85,800
O	5	10.5	Walnut	86,700	86,700
O	5	10.5	Kewazinga Bubinga	91,100	91,100
O	5	10.5	East Indian Rosewood	102,900	102,900
O	5	10.5	Macassar Ebony	112,300	112,300
O	5	10.5	Figured Sapele	92,300	92,000

*See pricing explanation on page 201.

Model	Feet	Inches	Description	MSRP*	SMP*
			STEINWAY & SONS (continued)		
O	5	10.5	Dark Cherry	92,700	92,700
O	5	10.5	Santos Rosewood	102,200	102,200
O	5	10.5	African Pommele	106,600	106,600
O	5	10.5	Pops Polished Ebony w/White Accessories	88,700	88,700
O	5	10.5	Pops Polished Ebony w/Color Accessories	89,600	89,600
O	5	10.5	John Lennon Imagine Polished White	115,500	115,500
A	6	2	Satin Ebony	85,300	85,300
A	6	2	Polyester Polished Ebony	88,100	88,100
A	6	2	Polyester Polished Ebony w/Sterling Hardware	90,300	90,300
A	6	2	Polyester Polished White	98,400	98,400
A	6	2	Mahogany	97,100	97,100
A	6	2	Walnut	98,100	97,400
A	6	2	Kewazinga Bubinga	103,500	103,500
A	6	2	East Indian Rosewood	116,900	116,400
A	6	2	Macassar Ebony	127,700	127,600
A	6	2	Figured Sapele	103,900	103,600
A	6	2	Dark Cherry	105,300	105,200
A	6	2	Santos Rosewood	116,500	116,500
A	6	2	African Pommele	121,400	121,400
A	6	2	Pops Polished Ebony w/White Accessories	100,600	100,600
A	6	2	Pops Polished Ebony w/Color Accessories	101,400	101,400
A	6	2	John Lennon Imagine Polished White	129,500	129,500
B	6	10.5	Satin Ebony	96,900	96,900
B	6	10.5	Polyester Polished Ebony	100,400	100,400
B	6	10.5	Polyester Polished Ebony w/Sterling Hardware	104,200	104,200
B	6	10.5	Polyester Polished White	111,800	110,780
B	6	10.5	Mahogany	110,900	110,600
B	6	10.5	Walnut	112,100	110,600
B	6	10.5	Kewazinga Bubinga	118,100	117,800
B	6	10.5	East Indian Rosewood	134,100	132,400
B	6	10.5	Macassar Ebony	145,400	144,000
B	6	10.5	Figured Sapele	117,900	117,200
B	6	10.5	Dark Cherry	118,600	118,400
B	6	10.5	Santos Rosewood	131,200	131,200
B	6	10.5	African Pommele	137,000	137,000
B	6	10.5	Pops Polished Ebony w/White Accessories	114,200	113,100
B	6	10.5	Pops Polished Ebony w/Color Accessories	115,100	113,980
B	6	10.5	John Lennon Imagine Polished White	145,900	144,000
D	8	11.75	Satin Ebony	156,200	148,200
D	8	11.75	Polyester Polished Ebony	157,400	151,400
D	8	11.75	Polyester Polished Ebony w/Sterling Hardware	161,300	155,200
D	8	11.75	Polyester Polished White	173,400	166,440
D	8	11.75	Mahogany	182,700	172,600
D	8	11.75	Walnut	183,900	172,600
D	8	11.75	Kewazinga Bubinga	192,800	183,400
D	8	11.75	East Indian Rosewood	219,400	206,400
D	8	11.75	Macassar Ebony	237,100	226,000
D	8	11.75	Figured Sapele	186,100	177,000
D	8	11.75	Dark Cherry	189,100	178,800
D	8	11.75	Santos Rosewood	206,300	199,000
D	8	11.75	African Pommele	216,800	207,000
D	8	11.75	Pops Polished Ebony w/White Accessories	164,300	164,300
D	8	11.75	Pops Polished Ebony w/Color Accessories	165,300	165,300
D	8	11.75	John Lennon Imagine Polished White	201,600	200,000

*See pricing explanation on page 201.

Model	Feet	Inches	Description	MSRP*	SMP*

Steinway (Hamburg) Grands

I frequently get requests for prices of pianos made in Steinway's branch factory in Hamburg, Germany. Officially, these pianos are not sold in North America, but it is possible to order one through an American Steinway dealer, or to go to Europe and purchase one there. The following list shows approximately how much it would cost to purchase a Hamburg Steinway in Europe and have it shipped to the United States. The list was derived by taking the published retail price in Europe, subtracting the value-added tax not applicable to foreign purchasers, converting to U.S. dollars (the rate used here is 1 Euro = $1.20, but is obviously subject to change), and adding approximate charges for duty, air freight, crating, insurance, brokerage fees, and delivery. Only prices for grands in polished ebony are shown here. Caution: This list is published for general informational purposes only. The price that Steinway would charge for a piano ordered through an American Steinway dealer may be different. (Also, the cost of a trip to Europe to purchase the piano is not included.)

Model	Feet	Inches	Description	MSRP*	SMP*
S-155	5	1	Polished Ebony	77,200	77,200
M-170	5	7	Polished Ebony	79,600	79,600
O-180	5	10.5	Polished Ebony	89,500	89,500
A-188	6	2	Polished Ebony	91,900	91,900
B-211	6	11	Polished Ebony	105,900	105,900
C-227	7	5.5	Polished Ebony	125,400	125,400
D-274	8	11.75	Polished Ebony	159,900	159,900

STORY & CLARK

All Story & Clark pianos include PNOscan, and USB and MIDI connectivity. In addition, all grands now include a QRS PNOmation player-piano system. Prices shown are those for online sales through www.qrsmusic.com.

Heritage Series Verticals

Model	Feet	Inches	Description	MSRP*	SMP*
H7		46	Academy Polished Ebony		5,395

Signature Series Verticals

Model	Feet	Inches	Description	MSRP*	SMP*
S8		48	Cosmopolitan Polished Ebony		5,395

Heritage Series Grands

Model	Feet	Inches	Description	MSRP*	SMP*
H50A	4	11	Prelude Polished Ebony/Mahogany		16,695
H60 QA	5		French Provincial Polished Ebony		17,495
H60 QA	5		French Provincial Satin Lacquer and Polished Mahogany		17,595
H60A	5	3	Academy Satin and Polished Ebony		17,495
H60A	5	3	Academy Polished Mahogany		17,495
H60A	5	3	Academy Polished White		17,995
H70A	5	7	Conservatory Polished Ebony		18,895
H80	6	1	Professional Polished Ebony		21,395
H90	6	10	Semi-Concert Polished Ebony		28,795

Signature Series Grands

Model	Feet	Inches	Description	MSRP*	SMP*
S500	4	11	Manhattan Semigloss Ebony w/Birdseye Maple Accents		25,095
S600	5	4	Cosmopolitan Polished Ebony		24,395
S600	5	4	Melrose Polished Ebony/Mahogany		26,995
S600	5	4	Park West Satin Ebony		24,195
S600	5	4	Park West Polished Ebony		24,495
S700	5	9	Fairfax Polished Ebony w/Bubinga Accents		26,695
S700	5	9	Versailles Satin Lacquer Cherry		26,295
S700	5	9	Park West Polished Ebony		24,695
S800	6	2	Islander British Colonial Satin Walnut		27,895
S800	6	2	Park West Polished Ebony		25,395
S900	7		Park West Satin Ebony		38,495

VOSE & SONS — see Everett

*See pricing explanation on page 201.

Model	Feet	Inches	Description	MSRP*	SMP*

WALTER, CHARLES R.

Verticals

Model	Feet	Inches	Description	MSRP*	SMP*
1520		43	Satin and Polished Walnut		15,264
1520		43	Satin and Polished Cherry		15,226
1520		43	Satin and Polished Oak		14,784
1520		43	Satin and Polished Mahogany		15,504
1520		43	Italian Provincial Satin and Polished Walnut		15,292
1520		43	Italian Provincial Satin and Polished Mahogany		15,532
1520		43	Italian Provincial Satin and Polished Oak		14,798
1520		43	Country Classic Satin and Polished Cherry		15,106
1520		43	Country Classic Satin and Polished Oak		14,870
1520		43	French Provincial Satin and Polished Oak		15,292
1520		43	French Provincial Satin and Polished Cherry/Walnut/Mahogany		15,688
1520		43	Riviera Satin and Polished Oak		14,750
1520		43	Queen Anne Satin and Polished Oak		15,398
1520		43	Queen Anne Satin and Polished Mahogany/Cherry		15,688
1500		45	Satin Ebony		14,338
1500		45	Semi-Gloss Ebony		14,558
1500		45	Polished Ebony (Lacquer)		14,718
1500		45	Polished Ebony (Polyester)		15,216
1500		45	Satin and Polished Oak		13,736
1500		45	Satin and Polished Walnut		14,468
1500		45	Satin and Polished Mahogany		14,658
1500		45	Satin and Polished Gothic Oak		14,482
1500		45	Satin and Polished Cherry		14,620
Verticals			Walter (Chinese) action, subtract		2,000

Grands

Model	Feet	Inches	Description	MSRP*	SMP*
W-175	5	9	Satin Ebony		54,954
W-175	5	9	Semi-Polished and Polished Ebony (Lacquer)		56,356
W-175	5	9	Polished Ebony (Polyester)		57,120
W-175	5	9	Satin Mahogany/Walnut/Cherry		57,400
W-175	5	9	Semi-Polished & Polished Mahogany/Walnut/Cherry		58,856
W-175	5	9	Open-Pore Walnut		56,022
W-175	5	9	Satin Oak		52,834
W-175	5	9	Chippendale Satin Mahogany/Cherry		59,160
W-175	5	9	Chippendale Semi-Polished & Polished Mahogany/Cherry		60,590
W-190	6	4	Satin Ebony		58,432
W-190	6	4	Semi-Polished and Polished Ebony (Lacquer)		59,898
W-190	6	4	Polished Ebony (Polyester)		60,692
W-190	6	4	Satin Mahogany/Walnut/Cherry		60,968
W-190	6	4	Semi-Polished & Polished Mahogany/Walnut/Cherry		62,474
W-190	6	4	Open-Pore Walnut		59,542
W-190	6	4	Satin Oak		56,230
W-190	6	4	Chippendale Satin Mahogany/Cherry		62,830
W-190	6	4	Chippendale Semi-Polished & Polished Mahogany/Cherry		64,278

WEBER

Weber Verticals

Model	Feet	Inches	Description	MSRP*	SMP*
W114		45	Satin Ebony	6,210	5,780
W114		45	Polished Ebony	5,950	5,580
W114		45	Polished Mahogany/Walnut/White	6,210	5,780
W114E		45	Polished Ebony w/Chrome	6,470	5,980
W114F		45	Designer Satin Mahogany/Cherry	6,990	6,380
W121		48	Satin Ebony	7,250	6,580
W121		48	Polished Ebony	6,990	6,380
W121		48	Polished Mahogany/Walnut/White	7,250	6,580
W121E		48	Polished Ebony w/Chrome	8,290	7,380

*See pricing explanation on page 201.

PIANOBUYER.COM

Model	Feet	Inches	Description	MSRP*	SMP*
WEBER (continued)					
W121N		48	Polished Ebony	7,250	6,580
W131		52	Satin Ebony	8,030	7,180
W131		52	Polished Ebony	7,510	6,780
W131		52	Polished Mahogany	8,030	7,180
Albert Weber Verticals					
AW 121		48	Polished Ebony	11,410	9,780
AW 121		48	Satin Mahogany	11,930	10,180
AW 121E		48	Polished Ebony w/Chrome	12,710	10,780
AW 131		52	Satin Ebony	15,050	12,580
AW 131		52	Polished Ebony	14,010	11,780
Weber Grands					
W150	4	11	Satin Ebony	14,270	11,980
W150	4	11	Polished Ebony	13,750	11,580
W150	4	11	Polished Mahogany/Walnut/White	14,270	11,980
W150E	4	11	Polished Ebony w/Chrome	14,530	12,180
W157	5	2	Satin Ebony	15,570	12,980
W157	5	2	Polished Ebony	14,790	12,380
W157	5	2	Polished Mahogany	15,570	12,980
W175	5	9	Satin Ebony	17,910	14,780
W175	5	9	Polished Ebony	16,870	13,980
W185	6	1	Satin Ebony	21,810	17,780
W185	6	1	Polished Ebony	20,770	16,980
Albert Weber Grands					
AW 185	6	1	Satin Ebony	38,970	30,980
AW 185	6	1	Polished Ebony	37,670	29,980
AW 208	6	10	Satin Ebony	47,290	37,380
AW 208	6	10	Polished Ebony	45,990	36,380
AW 228	7	6	Satin Ebony	66,530	52,180
AW 228	7	6	Polished Ebony	65,230	51,180
AW 275	9		Polished Ebony	119,570	92,980
WERTHEIM					
Verticals					
WE123		48.5	Polished Ebony	9,995	7,890
WE123		48.5	Polished Mahogany/Walnut/White	10,295	8,100
WE123 CAB		48.5	French Polished Ebony	10,295	8,100
WE123 CAB		48.5	French Polished White	10,595	8,310
WE133		52.5	Polished Ebony	11,995	9,460
WE133		52.5	Polished Mahogany/Walnut	12,295	9,660
Grands					
WE148	4	10	Polished Ebony	16,695	13,140
WE148	4	10	Polished Mahogany/Walnut/White	18,295	14,400
WE148 CAB	4	10	French Polished White	18,595	15,240
WE170	5	7	Polished Ebony	19,995	15,850
WE170	5	7	Polished Mahogany/Walnut/White	20,995	16,480
WE186	6	1	Polished Ebony	20,995	16,480
WE186	6	1	Polished Mahogany/Walnut/White	21,995	17,340
WYMAN					
Verticals					
WV108		42.5	Continental Polished Ebony	4,500	3,779
WV108		42.5	Continental Polished Mahogany/Cherry	4,575	3,840
WV110		43	Polished Ebony	5,000	4,057
WV110		43	Polished Mahogany/Cherry	5,075	4,118

*See pricing explanation on page 201.

Model	Feet	Inches	Description	MSRP*	SMP*
WYMAN (continued)					
WV115		45	Polished Ebony	5,263	4,225
WV115		45	Polished Mahogany/Cherry	5,325	4,281
WV118DL		46	Polished Ebony w/Chrome Hardware (double leg)	6,190	4,778
WV120		48	Polished Ebony	5,800	4,539
WV120		48	Polished Mahogany	5,875	4,601
WV127		50	Polished Ebony w/Mahogany Trim (straight leg)	8,575	6,585
WV127		50	Polished Ebony w/Mahogany Trim (curved leg)	8,665	6,650
WV132		52	Polished Ebony	7,250	5,713
Grands					
WG145	4	9	Polished Ebony	10,963	8,483
WG145	4	9	Polished Mahogany	11,488	8,903
WG160	5	3	Polished Ebony	13,375	9,973
WG160	5	3	Polished Mahogany	13,875	10,383
WG170	5	7	Polished Ebony	14,950	10,813
WG170	5	7	Polished Mahogany	15,475	11,233
WG185	6	1	Polished Ebony	17,588	12,825
WG185	6	1	Polished Mahogany	18,125	13,250

YAMAHA
Including Disklavier, Silent, and TransAcoustic Pianos

Verticals

Model	Feet	Inches	Description	MSRP*	SMP*
b1		43	Continental Polished Ebony	4,599	4,599
M560		44	Hancock Satin Brown Cherry	6,719	6,719
b2		45	Polished Ebony	6,419	6,358
b2		45	Polished Mahogany/Walnut	6,799	6,668
P22		45	Satin Ebony/Walnut/Oak	7,199	6,998
P660		45	Sheraton Satin Brown Mahogany	8,599	8,599
P660		45	Queen Anne Satin Brown Cherry	8,599	8,599
b3		48	Polished Ebony	7,879	7,298
b3		48	Polished Mahogany/Walnut	8,669	7,928
U1		48	Satin and Polished Ebony	10,699	10,699
U1		48	Satin American Walnut	12,799	12,799
U1		48	Polished Mahogany/White	12,799	12,799
YUS1		48	Satin and Polished Ebony	14,699	14,238
YUS1		48	Satin American Walnut	18,499	17,598
YUS1		48	Polished Mahogany/White	18,499	17,598
U3		52	Polished Ebony	13,699	13,198
U3		52	Satin American Walnut	15,749	15,698
U3		52	Polished Mahogany	15,749	15,698
YUS3		52	Polished Ebony	17,849	16,998
YUS3		52	Polished Mahogany	20,999	20,198
YUS5		52	Polished Ebony	19,949	18,658
SU7		52	Polished Ebony	38,899	36,898

Disklavier Verticals

Model	Feet	Inches	Description	MSRP*	SMP*
DU1E3		48	Polished Ebony	26,999	25,198
DU1E3		48	Polished Mahogany/Walnut/White	28,999	27,198

Silent and TransAcoustic Verticals

Model	Feet	Inches	Description	MSRP*	SMP*
b1SG2		43	Polished Ebony	8,599	8,498
b2SG2		45	Polished Ebony	10,419	9,358
b2SG2		45	Polished Mahogany/Walnut	10,799	9,668
b3SG2		48	Polished Ebony	11,879	10,298
b3SG2		48	Polished Mahogany/Walnut	12,669	10,928
U1SH		48	Satin and Polished Ebony	14,699	14,198
U1SH		48	Polished Mahogany/Walnut/White	16,799	16,398
U1TA		48	Polished Ebony	16,699	16,198

*See pricing explanation on page 201.

Model	Feet	Inches	Description	MSRP*	SMP*
YAMAHA (continued)					
YUS1SH		48	Satin and Polished Ebony	18,699	17,238
YUS1SH		48	Polished Mahogany/Walnut/White	22,499	20,598
U3SH		52	Polished Ebony	17,699	16,198
U3SH		52	Polished Mahogany/Walnut	19,749	18,698
YUS3SH		52	Polished Ebony	21,849	19,998
YUS3SH		52	Polished Mahogany	24,999	23,198
YUS5SH		52	Polished Ebony	23,949	21,658
Grands					
GB1K	5		Polished Ebony	14,199	13,198
GB1K	5		Polished American Walnut/Mahogany	16,799	15,698
GB1K	5		French Provincial Satin Cherry	18,379	17,798
GB1K	5		Georgian Satin Mahogany	17,849	17,398
GC1M	5	3	Satin and Polished Ebony	23,099	22,298
GC1M	5	3	Satin American Walnut	29,399	27,258
GC1M	5	3	Polished Mahogany/White	29,399	27,258
C1X	5	3	Satin and Polished Ebony	35,999	32,198
C1X	5	3	Satin American Walnut	45,449	40,318
C1X	5	3	Polished Mahogany/White	45,449	40,318
GC2	5	8	Satin and Polished Ebony	27,299	25,398
GC2	5	8	Satin American Walnut	32,549	30,398
GC2	5	8	Polished Mahogany/White	32,549	30,398
C2X	5	8	Satin and Polished Ebony	41,599	37,958
C2X	5	8	Polished Ebony w/Chrome Accents	43,899	39,998
C2X	5	8	Satin American Walnut	52,349	46,998
C2X	5	8	Polished Mahogany/White	52,349	46,998
C3X	6	1	Satin and Polished Ebony	57,749	48,998
C3X	6	1	Satin American Walnut	72,749	61,498
C3X	6	1	Polished Mahogany/White	72,749	61,498
S4BB	6	3	Polished Ebony	74,999	69,998
CF4	6	3	Polished Ebony	105,599	105,599
C5X	6	7	Satin and Polished Ebony	60,399	54,398
C5X	6	7	Satin American Walnut	76,199	72,198
C5X	6	7	Polished Mahogany/White	76,199	72,198
C6X	7		Satin and Polished Ebony	67,499	60,658
C6X	7		Satin American Walnut	85,259	76,198
C6X	7		Polished Mahogany/White	85,259	76,198
S6BB	7		Polished Ebony	86,999	80,998
CF6	7		Polished Ebony	119,999	119,598
C7X	7	6	Satin and Polished Ebony	78,499	69,898
C7X	7	6	Satin American Walnut	99,119	87,738
C7X	7	6	Polished Mahogany/White	99,119	87,738
CFX	9		Polished Ebony	179,999	179,999
Disklavier Grands					
DGB1KE3C	5		Classic Polished Ebony	19,999	19,998
DGB1KE3	5		Polished Ebony	24,999	22,598
DGB1KE3	5		Polished Mahogany/American Walnut/White	30,999	28,998
DGC1E3S	5	3	Satin and Polished Ebony	39,999	36,398
DGC1E3S	5	3	Polished Mahogany/Walnut/Whtie	46,999	43,998
DC1XE3S	5	3	Satin and Polished Ebony	50,999	47,798
DC1XE3S	5	3	Polished Mahogany/Walnut/White	57,999	54,998
DGC2E3S	5	8	Satin and Polished Ebony	43,999	40,998
DGC2E3S	5	8	Polished Mahogany/Walnut/White	49,999	46,998
DC2XE3S	5	8	Satin and Polished Ebony	59,999	52,198
DC2XE3S	5	8	Polished Ebony w/Chrome Accents	69,999	60,998
DC2XE3S	5	8	Polished Mahogany/Walnut/White	69,999	60,998
DC3XE3PRO	6	1	Satin and Polished Ebony	73,999	60,998
DC3XE3PRO	6	1	Polished Mahogany/Walnut/White	87,999	72,998

*See pricing explanation on page 201.

Model	Feet	Inches	Description	MSRP*	SMP*
YAMAHA *(continued)*					
DS4E3PRO	6	3	Polished Ebony	119,999	98,998
DC5XE3PRO	6	7	Satin and Polished Ebony	83,999	68,998
DC5XE3PRO	6	7	Polished Mahogany/Walnut/White		
DC6XE3PRO	7		Satin and Polished Ebony	88,999	75,998
DC6XE3PRO	7		Polished Mahogany/Walnut/White	103,999	87,998
DS6E3PRO	7		Polished Ebony	131,999	108,998
DC7XE3PRO	7	6	Satin and Polished Ebony	96,999	81,998
DC7XE3PRO	7	6	Polished Mahogany/Walnut/White	111,999	94,998
DCFXE3PRO	9		Polished Ebony	259,999	232,598
Silent and TransAcoustic Grands					
GB1KSG2	5		Polished Ebony	18,199	16,198
GB1KSG2	5		Polished Mahogany/Walnut/White	20,799	18,698
GC1SH	5	3	Satin and Polished Ebony	27,099	25,298
GC1SH	5	3	Polished Mahogany/Walnut/White	33,399	30,258
GC1TA	5	3	Polished Ebony	31,099	29,298
C1XSH	5	3	Satin and Polished Ebony	39,999	35,198
C1XSH	5	3	Polished Mahogany/Walnut/White	49,449	43,318
GC2SH	5	8	Satin and Polished Ebony	31,299	28,398
GC2SH	5	8	Polished Mahogany/Walnut/White	36,549	33,398
C2XSH	5	8	Satin and Polished Ebony	45,599	40,958
C2XSH	5	8	Polished Ebony w/Chrome Accents	47,899	42,998
C2XSH	5	8	Polished Mahogany/Walnut/White	56,349	49,998
C3XSH	6	1	Satin and Polished Ebony	61,749	51,998
C3XSH	6	1	Polished Mahogany/Walnut/White	76,749	64,498
C5XSH	6	7	Satin and Polished Ebony	64,399	57,398
C5XSH	6	7	Polished Mahogany/Walnut/White	80,199	71,198
C6XSH	7		Satin and Polished Ebony	71,499	63,658
C6XSH	7		Polished Mahogany/Walnut/White	89,259	79,198
C7XSH	7	6	Satin and Polished Ebony	82,499	72,898
C7XSH	7	6	Polished Mahogany/Walnut/White	103,119	90,738
YOUNG CHANG					
Verticals					
Y114		45	Polished Ebony	5,370	5,300
Y114		45	Polished Mahogany/Walnut/White	5,870	5,700
Y114E		45	Polished Ebony w/Chrome	6,120	5,900
Y116		46	Polished Ebony	6,870	6,500
Y116		46	Satin Ebony/Walnut	6,870	6,500
Y118		47	Satin Ebony	6,120	5,900
Y118		47	Polished Ebony	5,870	5,700
Y118		47	Polished Mahogany/Walnut	6,120	5,900
Y118R		47	Designer French Satin Cherry	6,870	6,500
Y118R		47	Designer Satin Mahogany	6,870	6,500
Y121		48	Satin Ebony	6,620	6,300
Y121		48	Polished Ebony	6,370	6,100
Y121		48	Polished Mahogany/Walnut	6,620	6,300
Y131		52	Satin Ebony	7,120	6,700
Y131		52	Polished Ebony	6,870	6,500
Y131		52	Polished Mahogany	7,120	6,700

*See pricing explanation on page 201.

Model	Feet	Inches	Description	MSRP*	SMP*
YOUNG CHANG (continued)					
Grands					
Y150	4	11	Satin Ebony	12,870	11,300
Y150	4	11	Polished Ebony	12,370	10,900
Y150	4	11	Polished Mahogany/Walnut/White	12,870	11,300
Y150E	4	11	Polished Ebony w/Chrome	13,120	11,500
Y157	5	2	Satin Ebony	14,370	12,500
Y157	5	2	Polished Ebony	13,370	11,700
Y157	5	2	Polished Mahogany	14,370	12,500
Y175	5	9	Satin Ebony	16,370	14,100
Y175	5	9	Polished Ebony	15,370	13,300
Y185	6	1	Satin Ebony	20,370	17,300
Y185	6	1	Polished Ebony	19,120	16,300

*See pricing explanation on page 201.

ELECTRONIC PLAYER-PIANO ADD-ON (RETROFIT) SYSTEMS AND PRICES

Prices for electronic player-piano add-on (retrofit) systems vary by installer, and by options and accessories chosen. The following are manufacturers' suggested retail prices for installed systems, options, and accessories. The usual dealer discounts may apply, especially as an incentive to purchase a piano. Prices for player-piano brands that are installed only by the piano manufacturer, such as Yamaha Disklavier and Bösendorfer CEUS, are included in the acoustic piano Models & Prices section of this publication.

Model/Option	MSRP
PIANODISC	
Includes (unless otherwise stated) SilentDrive HD w/1,024 levels of expression, Apple Airport Express (with Air Systems), comp. music where stated. Deduct $108 from iPad systems for iPad Mini.	
iQ Intelligent Player System, factory-installed or retrofitted:	
iQ iPad 128G Air Platinum — iQ Audio Controller module, ProRecord QT, $2,500 preloaded Music & Video package	14,140
iQ iPad 128G Air Premier — iQ Audio Controller module, $2,500 preloaded Music & Video package	11,600
iQ iPad 128G Air — iQ control box, iPad 128G, cables, and comp. music	9,410
iQ iPad 64G Air Platinum — iQ Audio Controller module, ProRecordQT, $2,500 preloaded Music & Video Package	13,910
iQ iPad 64G Air Premier — iQ Audio Controller module; $2,500 preloaded Music & Video package	11,370
iQ iPad64G Air — iQ control box, iPad 64G, cables, comp. music	9,180
iQ iPad 32G Air — iQ control box, iPad 32G, cables, comp. music	8,940
iQ iPad 16G Air — iQ control box, iPad 16G, cables, comp. music	8,730
iQ iPod Touch Air — iQ control box, iPod Touch 32G, cables, comp. music	8,520
iQ Flash — MP3 Player w/remote control, comp. music	7,970
iQ Flex Air — Using customer-provided playback device; includes comp. music	7,990
iQ Flex — Using customer-provided playback device; includes comp. music	7,840
Add for amplified PDS350 speakers (pair)	905

Model/Option	MSRP
PIANODISC (continued)	
QuietTime MagicStar — Control unit w/128 General MIDI (GM) sound module, MuteRail, optical key sensor MIDI Strip, MIDI interface board, cable, power supply, and headphones	3,620
ProScan – Optical Record System – Key strip only	2,430
ProScan QT – ProScan with headphones and MuteRail, cables, etc.	3,189
ProRecord – Optical Record System with Sound Module	2,996
ProRecord QT – Optical Record System, Sound Module, headphones, MuteRail, cables, etc.	3,775
Piano MuteRail only	759
iQ Audio Controller — Dual-balance piano/audio control	198
PIANOFORCE	
Incudes controller and pedal solenoid. Price depends on speaker system and optional components chosen.	6,995 & up
QRS PNOmation	
PNOmation Playback, installation extra	6,195
PNOmation Playback and Record, installation extra	8,195
PNOmation Playback, Record, Perform, and Practice; installation extra	8,595
PNOmation Upgrade Kit, installation extra	2,295
PNOmation MIDI Upgrade Kit, installation extra	2,295
PNOscan II Key Sensor Strip, installation extra	1,995
Qsync	1,995

IF YOU'VE READ any of the "Brand and Company Profiles" on the acoustic side, you'll see that discussions of digital makes and models is of a very different nature. For one thing, although a few manufacturers of digital pianos can trace their roots back over 100 years, such histories, while occasionally fascinating, have little or no relevance to a type of instrument that has existed for only a few dozen years. For another, whereas acoustic piano makers may boast of using slowly grown spruce carefully harvested from trees on north-facing slopes in the Bavarian Alps, there are no stories from digital piano makers of silicon carefully harvested from isolated south-facing beaches during the second low tide of October; no tales of printed circuit boards still crafted by hand as they've been for generations, or descriptions of internal cable harnesses made of only the finest German wire. And while it's interesting to know who was the first to introduce a particular feature, digital pianos, like all modern electronic products, are very much a matter of "What have you done for me *lately*?"

Even more than in the section dedicated to acoustic pianos, the descriptions provided here are only half the story, and must be used in conjunction with the chart of "Digital Piano Specifications and Prices" if you are to have a clear picture of a given brand's offerings. In some cases, little information is available or forthcoming regarding a brand, and much that could have been included would simply be a reiteration of marketing statements. In others, specifications or descriptions available from a manufacturer have been in conflict, as when specifications on their website say one thing and the owner's manual says something else. While every effort has been made to ensure the accuracy of these listings and descriptions, some discrepancies will have undoubtedly slipped through.

Blüthner

Blüthner USA LLC
5660 West Grand River
Lansing, Michigan 48906
517-886-6000
800-954-3200
info@bluthnerpiano.com
www.bluthnerpiano.com

Blüthner, one of the world's preeminent piano makers, has released its first line of digital pianos, called the e-Klavier. (For company background, see the Blüthner listing in the "Brand and Company Profiles" for acoustic pianos.) Engineered and manufactured at the Blüthner factory in Leipzig, Germany, the e-Klavier line comprises five models in three styles: slab, vertical, and a decorator vertical called the Pianette.

Blüthner says it has developed a unique approach to sampling and sound modeling, called Authentic Acoustic Behavior, that allows the e-Klavier to reproduce the effect of the aliquot (fourth) string of Blüthner's acoustic pianos. This system also permits the reproduction of advanced harmonics, such as the coincidental partials produced when two notes are played simultaneously, and the sound the dampers make when lifting off the strings. The e-Klavier actions, sourced from Fatar, feature escapement, and wooden keys with "ivory feel" in some models. In the near future, users will be able to download new sounds to the e-Klaviers via the Internet at no charge, and store the sounds of turn-of-the-century Blüthner pianos and other Blüthner models of interest.

The speaker system and amplifier are unique to the e-Klavier and were designed by Günter Philipp, of PCL

Audio. The e-Klavier 2 and 3 also contain an actual piano soundboard, which enables these instruments to produce certain aspects of acoustic-piano tone that are difficult or impossible to simulate by purely electronic means.

Casio

Casio USA
570 Mount Pleasant Avenue
Dover, New Jersey 07801
973-361-5400
www.casio.com

Kashio Tadao established Casio in 1946. Originally a small subcontractor factory that made parts and gears for microscopes, Casio built Japan's first electric calculator in 1954, which began the company's transformation into the consumer-electronics powerhouse it is today. Perhaps best known for its calculators, digital cameras, and watches, Casio entered the musical instrument business with the launch of the Casiotone in 1980.

Casio's current line of digital pianos consists of six vertical and three slab models. The Privia line's PX-150 slab is the least expensive ensemble model, and all three Privia slabs offer an optional stand-and-pedal module that turns them into three-pedal pianos with support for half-pedaling. At a mere 24 or 25 pounds, they are also the lightest digital pianos. The AP models are marketed under the Celviano label. All Casio digital pianos use the three-sensor, weighted, and scaled (graded) Tri-Sensor hammer action with ebony- and ivory-feel keys. Casio digital pianos are available at music retailers, consumer-electronics and club stores, and online.

Dynatone

Dynatone America Corporation
72 City Stroll
Irvine, California 92620
949-679-5500
www.dynatoneusa.com

Distributed by:
Piano Marketing Group, LLC
752 East 21st Street
Ferdinand, Indiana 47532
812-630-0978
gary.trafton@dynatoneUSA.com

Dynatone, headquartered in Seoul, South Korea, was founded in 1987 as the Electric Instruments Division of the global semiconductor manufacturer Korean Electronics Company (KEC), and was the first maker of electric musical instruments in Korea. It became an independent company in 2000. In addition to digital pianos and MIDI keyboards, Dynatone makes percussion, string, woodwind, and brass instruments, which it exports to more than 30 countries.

Initially, Dynatone is offering in the U.S. market three vertical and three grand models, some as standard digital and some as ensemble models. The cabinets will come in a variety of finishes and distinctive, contemporary designs, including some with smaller, sleeker designs suitable when space is limited. The new ROS V4 sound engine contains the clean, realistic sound of a 12-mega-byte grand piano sound sample. The Advanced Real Hammer Action (ARHA) uses the hammer weight, not springs, to reproduce the touch and feel of an acoustic piano. The flagship model VGP-3000 digital grand also contains a player-piano feature, and its SD memory card can store a library of 1,300 songs. All Dynatone models come with a three-year parts and labor warranty.

Galileo

GW Distribution, LLC
P.O. Box 329
Mahwah, New Jersey 07430
845-429-3712
www.galileopianos.com

Galileo is a division of Viscount International, an Italian company that traces its roots back to accordion builder Antonio Galanti, who built his first instrument in 1890. The Galanti accordion factory was opened in 1898 by Antonio's son Egidio Galanti, and for many years produced some of the finest accordions in the world. In the late 1950s, Egidio's sons, who had joined the business, branched out into making electronic-organ parts for some of that era's best-known brand names. Viscount began manufacturing its own brand of electronic home organs in the 1960s, under the Viscount name. Digital pianos followed in the 1970s, beginning with the Instapiano. Today, Viscount is run by the fourth generation of the Galanti family; distribution in the U.S. is handled by the first of the fifth generation to join the family business.

The Galileo line of digital pianos includes slabs, verticals, grands, and ensemble grands. Some of the grands have a 19-ply wood rim similar to that of an acoustic grand. Galileo offers its Concerto and Aria models in some of the most ornate decorator wood cabinets currently available for a digital piano.

Galileo has taken a step up in both technology and sound with its newly introduced VEGA sound-generation technology, available in its new YP series of digitals.

With this and Galileo's new MAP (mechanical feel) action, the user is brought closer to the experience of playing an actual acoustic grand. The YP series is available in a number of beautiful cabinet finishes.

Kawai

Kawai America Corporation
2055 East University Drive
Rancho Dominguez, California 90220
310-631-1771
800-421-2177
info@kawaius.com
www.kawaius.com

For company background, see the Kawai listing in the "Brand and Company Profiles" for acoustic pianos.

After more than 50 years as a renowned builder of acoustic pianos, in 1985 Kawai entered the market with its first digital piano. Today, Kawai's digital lineup for North America comprises models in four main groups: Concert Performer (CP), Concert Artist (CA), Classic (CS), and CN Series. Other digital models include the CL26, KDP90, KCP90 and CE220. Portable digitals include the ES100 and ES7, and professional models include the MP Series stage pianos and the VPC1 virtual piano controller.

Kawai created the first digital piano to use a transducer-driven soundboard for a more natural piano sound, a feature available in the flagship CA97 and the CS10. Many models offer USB digital audio recording and playback. And if you want a huge library of voices, the models at the upper end of the CP series come with over 1,000 sounds.

Several different types of actions appear in Kawai's digital pianos. Kawai is well-known for its wooden-key digital piano actions, with current versions being the Grand Feel (GF), GFII, RM3II, and AWA PROII. These actions can be found in upper-end models. The Responsive Hammer II (RHII), RHIII, and AHA-IV actions use an industry-standard graded hammer design with plastic keys, and are found in lower-cost and portable models.

Kawai's main lines of digital pianos are sold through a network of authorized local dealers, with certain models also available from Kawai's online store. Professional products and certain other digitals are sold through a combination of authorized online and bricks-and-mortar retailers.

Kohler

See Samick

Korg

Korg USA, Inc.
316 South Service Road
Melville, New York 11747
631-390-6800
www.korg.com

Korg was founded in 1962 to produce its first product, an automatic rhythm machine, and in 1972 entered the electronic-organ market. The LP-10 stage piano appeared in 1980, and its first digitally sampled piano, the SG1, was introduced in 1986. Korg now offers four models of 88-key digital piano, including the entry-level model SP-170 at only $500, plus several models with shorter keyboards. Following Kawai's lead, Korg recently announced plans to sell its home digital pianos online (see Kawai, above).

Kurzweil

Kurzweil Music Systems
6000 Phyllis Drive
Cypress, California 90630
657-200-3470
800-874-2880
www.kurzweilmusicsystems.com

Legendary American inventor Ray Kurzweil, perhaps best known for having developed a reading machine for the blind, and hailed by Forbes magazine as "a modern-day Edison," launched Kurzweil Music Systems in 1983, following conversations with Stevie Wonder about the potential for combining the control and flexibility of the computer with the sounds of acoustic instruments. The result, in 1984, was the Kurzweil K250, recognized as the world's first digital piano. In 1990, Boston-based Kurzweil Music Systems was purchased by Young Chang, which continues to operate the division today. Young Chang is part of Korean-based Hyundai Development Company (HDC), one of the largest companies in the world.

Designed and engineered in Boston, Massachusetts, by a team of American sound architects, all Kurzweil home pianos feature the award-winning PC3X sound engine. Kurzweil piano models also feature USB and audio inputs to allow easy expansion via iPads and other external peripherals. Kurzweil pianos and keyboards are available through a combination of musical instrument dealers, piano-specialty stores, and online sources.

Lowrey

Lowrey
989 AEC Drive
Wood Dale, Illinois 60191
708-352-3388
lowreyinfo@lowrey.com
www.lowrey.com

Lowrey, a division of Kawai, is a developer and distributor of electronic virtual orchestra and digital piano products designed primarily for the home and recreational player. Lowrey currently offers five models of virtual orchestra and two models of digital piano.

Nord

American Music & Sound
22020 Clarendon Street, Suite 305
Woodland Hills, California 91367
800-431-2609
nord@americanmusicandsound.com
www.americamusicandsound.com
www.nordkeyboards.com

The Nord Piano 2 HA88, successor to the Nord Piano 88, is a professional stage piano that comes with a library of more than 1,000 sounds on a DVD, or downloadable from the Nord Piano website to the instrument via USB. Nord Keyboards are made in Sweden by Clavia DMI AB.

Omega

Piano Empire, Inc.
3035 E. La Mesa Street
Anaheim, California 92806
800-576-3463
714-408-4599
info@omegapianos.com
www.omegapianos.com

Omega is the brand name used in the U.S. for Kaino digital pianos. Established in 1986, Kaino, located in Guangzhou, China, began as a manufacturer of portable keyboards. In 1996, the company expanded to manufacture a full line of 88-note digital pianos, quickly becoming a major provider of keyboards throughout China. In 2010, the Omega brand was established for distribution in North America and Europe.

Physis

Physis Piano
P.O. Box 633
Falmouth, Massachusetts 02541
508-457-6771
garyg@physispiano.com
www.physispiano.com

Physis is a division of Viscount International, an Italian company that also makes Galileo digital pianos, among other brands. It has factories and research facilities in San Marino and Italy.

Physis uses physical modeling as the sound source for its instruments. Instead of recorded samples, physical modeling uses advanced mathematical algorithms to reproduce the physical properties of sound, and requires immense computational power that, until recently, was not technologically available. Physis states that it took seven years to develop this technology, and required the assistance of several Italian universities, as well as a team of engineers and musicians. Two international patents have been granted for the Physis technology.

The Physis physical model combines more than 100 elements of the traditional acoustic grand piano sound; e.g., hammer density, string resonance, soundboard size, damper noise, duplex vibration, etc. One of the key advantages of physical modeling is that these elements can be modified by users to create their own unique sounds, and the resulting models can be shared with others, allowing for their continuing evolution. Other advantages include unlimited polyphony, unlimited pedal resolution, and the greater expressiveness that results from the real-time interaction of the physical elements.

Some Physis models have wooden keys with ivory-like keytops and triple sensors, for better expression and a more natural, realistic feel. The H- and V-series pianos have a customizable, multitouch, glass-panel interface that gives the user control of all items on the panel, including display colors. These models also have USB thumb-drive connections for audio and data storage and playback. The Pro and Stage versions are ergonomically designed for portability, and allow maximum flexibility of inputs and outputs.

Physis pianos are sold through a network of professional music retailers.

Roland

Roland Corporation U.S.
5100 South Eastern Avenue
Los Angeles, California 90040
323-890-3700
www.rolandus.com

To simply say that Roland Corporation was established in 1972 is to ignore one of the most compelling stories in the realm of digital pianos. Ikutaro Kakehashi started down the path to Roland Corporation at the age of 16, when he began repairing watches and clocks in postwar Japan. However, his enthusiasm for music meant that his business soon evolved into the repair of radios. At the age of 20, Kakehashi contracted tuberculosis. After three years in the hospital, he was selected for the trial of a new drug, streptomycin, and within a year he was out of the hospital.

In 1954, Kakehashi opened Kakehashi Musen (Kakehashi Radio). Once again, his interest in music intervened, this time leading to his development of a prototype electric organ. In 1960, Kakehashi Radio evolved into Ace Electronic Industries. The FR1 Rhythm Ace became a standard offering of the Hammond Organ Company, and Ace Electronic Industries flourished. Guitar amplifiers, effects units, and more rhythm machines were developed, but as a result of various business-equity involvements, Ace was inadvertently acquired by a company with no interest in musical products, and Kakehashi left in March 1972. One month later, he established Roland Corporation. The first Roland product, not surprisingly, was a rhythm box.

In 1973, Roland introduced its first all-electronic combo piano, the EP-10, followed in 1974 by the EP-30, the world's first electronic piano with a touch-sensitive keyboard. Japan's first genuinely digital pianos for home use were released by Roland in 1975 as part of the early HP series. Next came Roland's portable EP-09 electronic piano in 1980, and the debut of the wood-finish HP-60 and HP-70 compact pianos in 1981. In 1983, Roland released the HP-300 and HP-400, the very first digital pianos with MIDI.

When introduced in 1986, the RD-1000 stage piano was Roland's first entry in what would become the digital piano category. Today, Roland offers more than two dozen models of digital piano covering every facet of the category: slab, vertical, grand, ensemble, and stage instruments, all produced in its factories in Indonesia and Japan.

Of particular interest to those looking for educational features are Roland's HPi models, which include a substantial suite of educational capabilities supported by an LCD screen mounted on a music desk. The new LX models add traditional-looking vertical pianos to the line. Roland can also lay claim to the most extensive collection of model designations in the world of digital pianos. While this is hardly a drawback, it does present a challenge when sorting through the model lineup; the chart of "Digital Piano Specifications and Prices" will help to clarify things.

The Roland V-Piano is the first digital piano to rely entirely on physical modeling as its tonal source. Physical modeling breaks down the sound of a piano note into discrete elements that can be represented by mathematical equations, and creates the tone in real time based on a complex series of calculations. There are no acoustic piano samples. For more information about physical modeling, please see, elsewhere in this issue, "Digital Basics, Part 1: Imitating the Acoustic Piano" and "My Other Piano Is a Computer: An Introduction to Software Pianos."

The HP models are the core of Roland's offerings in home digital pianos; the latest models share the company's new SuperNATURAL® piano sound engine, and differ from each other primarily in the specifications of their audio systems and actions.

Samick

Samick Music Corporation
1329 Gateway Drive
Gallatin, Tennessee 37066
615-206-0077
www.kohlerdigitalpianos.com
www.smcmusic.com

Samick, in the process of expanding its presence in the digital piano market, now makes four grand and nine vertical models. The company's Kohler line of digitals has been discontinued.

Suzuki

Suzuki Corporation
P.O. Box 710459
Santee, California 92072
800-854-1594
www.suzukimusic.com

Suzuki sells its line of digital pianos on its website, through other online outlets, and through Costco. Models change frequently.

Williams

Williams Pianos
P.O. Box 5111
Thousand Oaks, California 91359
www.williamspianos.com

Williams digital pianos, a house brand of Guitar Center, are also available through Guitar Center's Musician's Friend e-commerce website and two other e-commerce sites. There are seven models from Williams, including four verticals, two slabs with optional stand, and one grand.

Yamaha

Yamaha Corporation of America
P.O. Box 6600
Buena Park, California 90622
714-522-9011
800-854-1569
infostation@yamaha.com
usa.yamaha.com

For company background, see the Yamaha listing in the "Brands and Company Profiles" for acoustic pianos.

Yamaha Corporation is the world's largest producer of musical instruments—from the obvious (pianos) to the slightly obscure (bassoon), Yamaha makes it. Yamaha entered the world of electronic instruments in 1959, when it introduced the first all-transistor organ. In 1971, because no manufacturer would develop an integrated circuit (IC) for Yamaha's relatively low-volume demand, the company built its own IC plant. Jumping ahead to 1983, the introduction of the first Yamaha Clavinova, the YP-40, marked the beginning of what we now call the digital piano. Today, Yamaha's three dozen or so models of digital piano (not counting different finishes) constitute the broadest range of any manufacturer. The downside is that deciphering the variety of options—slabs, verticals, grands, stage pianos, ensemble pianos, designer digitals, hybrids—can be a bit daunting. And then there are the sub-brands: Clavinova, Modus, and Arius.

Clavinova digital pianos include the standard CLP line and the ensemble CVP line, and are available only through piano dealers. The Modus models (model numbers beginning with F, H, and R), Yamaha's series of designer digitals, are functionally similar to the CLP line but with modern-looking cabinets. (The Modus H01 and H11 are perhaps the most striking visual designs among digital pianos.) They are now available online through authorized dealers. Arius (model numbers beginning with YDP) represents Yamaha's entry-level line of digital verticals, with the long-popular YDP223 now replaced by the YDP181.

Yamaha has introduced physical modeling technology to its CP line of stage pianos. The CP1 is a physical-modeling instrument featuring Yamaha's new Spectral Component Modeling (SCM) technology. Its less expensive siblings, the CP5 and CP50, feature a combination of SCM and Advanced Wave Memory (AWM) sampling. The CP1 and CP5 also include the new NW-Stage action. The CP and CP stage models are intended for situations that require a portable instrument. Available at several price points, they are suitable for a wide range of applications, from live performance to studio recording.

Yamaha's apps for iPad, iPhone, and iPod Touch are unique in the digital-piano world. The NoteStar app brings sheet music into the 21st century, and puts you in the band with real audio backing tracks that you can slow down or transpose. MusicSoft Manager lets you manage the content of your CVP Clavinova, while Repertoire Finder provides complete keyboard setups for songs you want to play.

Seven different actions are used in Yamaha digitals. In order of increasing quality, they are: Graded Hammer Standard (GHS), Graded Hammer (GH), Graded Hammer 3 (GH3), Natural Wood (NW), Natural Wood Stage (NW-Stage), Natural Wood Linear Graded Hammer (NW-LGH), and the grand piano action used in the AvantGrand models.

A few years ago Yamaha introduced its game-changing AvantGrand hybrid piano. Only time will tell how hybrid pianos will alter the piano landscape, but we predict that the AvantGrand will displace the sales of many similarly priced acoustic models—including Yamaha's own. For more information about the AvantGrand, see the article on "Hybrid Pianos" elsewhere in this issue.

IN THE CHART that follows, we have included those features and specifications about which buyers, in our experience, are most likely to be curious. However, many models have more features than are shown here. Listings are sorted in the following order: first by brand; then, within each brand, by physical form (slab, vertical, or grand); within each form, by type (standard digitals, then ensemble digitals); and finally, by price or model number, whichever seems most appropriate. See the various articles on digital pianos elsewhere in this publication for more information about each of the terms defined below, shown in the order in which they appear in the chart.

Form The physical form of the model: G=Grand, V= Vertical (Console), S=Slab.

Ensemble A digital piano with easy-play accompaniments (not just rhythms).

Finish The wood finishes or colors available for a particular model (not specified for slab models unless multiple finishes are available). Multiple finish options are separated by a slash (/). A manufacturer's own color term is used where a generic term could not be determined. Real-wood veneers are in *italics*. See the shaded box for finish codes.

Estimated Price This is our estimate of the price you will pay for the instrument. For digitals sold online or through chain and warehouse outlets, this price is the Minimum Advertised Price (MAP) and is shown in italics. For digitals sold only through bricks-and-mortar piano dealers, the price shown is based on a profit margin that piano dealers typically aspire to when selling digitals, including an allowance for incoming freight and setup. Discounts from this price, if any, typically are small. For more information on MAP and other pricing issues, please read "Buying a Digital Piano," elsewhere in this issue.

MSRP Manufacturer's Suggested Retail Price, also known as "list" or "sticker" price. Not all manufacturers use them.

Sound Source Indicates whether the sound source is Physical Modeling (M) or Sampling (S).

A	Ash
AG	Amber Glow
Al	Alder
Bl	Blue
Bk	Black
C	Cherry
DB	Deep Brunette
E	Ebony
G	Gold
Iv	Ivory
L	Laquor (used with a wood or color designation)
M	Mahogany
MD	Mahogany Decor
O	Oak
Or	Orange
P	Polished (used with a wood or color designation)
R	Rosewood
Rd	Red
S	Satin (used with a wood or color designation)
Sr	Silver
VR	Velvette Rouge
W	Walnut
WG	Wood Grain (wood type not specified)
Wt	White

Voices The number of different musical voices the instrument can produce.

Key Off Indicates the presence of Key Off samples or simulation.

Sustain Indicates the presence of samples or simulation of the sound with the sustain pedal depressed (allowing the strings to vibrate sympathetically).

String Resonance Indicates the presence of samples or simulation of String Resonance.

Rhythms/Styles The number of rhythm patterns available.

Polyphony The maximum number of sounds the instrument can produce simultaneously. UL=Unlimited

Total Watts Total combined amplifier power.

Speakers The number of individual speakers.

Piano Pedals The number of piano pedals supplied with the model. A number in parentheses indicate the number of optional pedals.

Half Pedal Indicates that the model supports half-pedaling. Many manufacturers do not specify this capability.

Action Indicates the type of action used, if specified.

Triple-Sensor Keys Indicates the presence of three key sensors instead of the usual two.

Escapement Indicates the presence of escapement feel. Models using acoustic-piano actions with actual escapement are indicated by an underlined Y.

Wood Keys Indicates actions with wooden keys.

Ivory Texture Indicates actions with ivory-textured keytops.

Player Moving Keys Indicates that the keys move during playback of recordings.

Vocal Support The model supports some level of vocal performance. This support can vary from the piano simply having a microphone input, to its having the ability to produce the vocalist's voice in multi-part harmony, to pitch-correct the notes sung by the vocalist, or to alter the original voice.

Educational Features The model includes features that specifically support the learning experience. Note that while the ability to record and play back is an important learning tool, it is present on almost all models and so is not included in this definition.

External Storage Indicates the type of external memory accessible.

USB to Computer Indicates the model's ability to interface with a Mac or PC via USB cable.

USB Digital Audio Indicates the ability to record and play back digital audio via a USB flash drive.

Recording Tracks The number of recordable tracks.

Warranty (Parts/Labor) Indicates the manufacturer's warranty coverage period: the first number is the length of the parts coverage; the second number is the length of the labor coverage. Single digits indicate years; double digits indicate days.

Dimensions Width, Depth, and Height are rounded to the nearest inch. If space is particularly tight, refer to the manufacturer's specifications for the model's exact dimensions. Note that grand height measurements sometimes indicate the piano's height with its lid up.

Weight Weight of the model rounded to the nearest pound.

Brand & Model	Form	Ensemble	Finish	Estimated Price	MSRP	Sound Source	Voices	Key Off	Sustain	String Resonance	Rhythms/Styles	Polyphony	Total Watts	Speakers	Piano Pedals	Half Pedal
Blüthner																
e-Klavier PRO-88	S		ESL		3,164	S	25	Y	Y	Y		128	60	2	3	Y
e-Klavier 1	V		ES/WtS		4,924	S	25	Y	Y	Y		128	100	2	3	Y
e-Klavier 1	V		ESL/WtSL		5,276	S	25	Y	Y	Y		128	100	2	3	Y
e-Klavier 2	V		ESL/WtSL		6,684	S	25	Y	Y	Y		128	100	2	3	Y
e-Klavier 2	V		EPL		7,740	S	25	Y	Y	Y		128	100	2	3	Y
e-Klavier 3	V		ESL/WtSL		7,709	S	150	Y	Y	Y		128	150	4	3	Y
e-Klavier 3	V		EPL		8,765	S	150	Y	Y	Y		128	150	4	3	Y
e-Klavier Pianette	V		EPL		19,677	S	25	Y	Y	Y		128	150	4	3	Y
Casio																
PX-5S	S		Wt	999	1,399	S	370	Y		Y		256			1(2)	N
PX-150	S		Bk/Wt	499	899	S	18			Y		128	16	2	1(3)	Y
PX-350	S	E	Bk/Wt	699	1,099	S	250			Y	180	128	16	2	1(3)	Y
PX-760	V		Bk/W/Wt	799	1,099	S	18			Y		128	16	2	3	Y
PX-780	V		Bk	999	1,399	S	250			Y	180	128	40	4	3	Y
PX-860	V		Bk/W/Wt	1,099	1,499	S	18	Y		Y		256	40	4	3	Y
AP-260	V		Bk/W			S	18			Y		128	16	2	3	Y
AP-460	V		Bk/W			S	18	Y		Y		256	40	4	3	Y
AP-650	V		Bk			S	250	Y		Y	180	256	60	4	3	Y

Brand & Model	Action	Triple-Sensor Keys	Escapement	Wood Keys	Ivory Texture	Player Moving Keys	Vocal Support	Educational Features	External Storage	USB to Computer	USB Digital Audio	Recording Tracks	Warranty (Parts/Labor)	Dimensions WxDxH (Inchees)	Weight (Pounds)
Blüthner															
e-Klavier PRO-88	4-zone graded		Y							Y		2	2	55x17x5	40
e-Klavier 1	4-zone graded		Y							Y		1	2	57x22x35	198
e-Klavier 1	4-zone graded		Y							Y		1	2	57x22x35	198
e-Klavier 2	4-zone graded		Y	Y						Y		1	2	55x25x42	220
e-Klavier 2	4-zone graded		Y	Y						Y		1	2	55x25x42	220
e-Klavier 3	4-zone graded		Y	Y	Y				USB	Y		USB	2	55x25x42	230
e-Klavier 3	4-zone graded		Y	Y	Y				USB	Y		USB	2	55x25x42	230
e-Klavier Pianette	4-zone graded		Y	Y	Y					Y		2	2	55x25x42	220
Casio															
PX-5S	Weighted, Scaled, Hammer-Action	Y			Y				USB	Y	Y	8	3/3	52x11x5	24
PX-150	Weighted, Scaled, Hammer-Action	Y			Y			Y		Y		2	3/3	52x11x5	24
PX-350	Weighted, Scaled, Hammer-Action	Y			Y			Y	USB	Y	Y	17	3/3	52x11x5	25
PX-760	Weighted, Scaled, Hammer-Action	Y			Y			Y		Y		2	3/3	53x12x33	71
PX-780	Weighted, Scaled, Hammer-Action	Y			Y			Y	USB	Y	Y	17	3/3	53x12x33	70
PX-860	Weighted, Scaled, Hammer-Action	Y			Y			Y	USB	Y	Y	2	3/3	53x12x33	82
AP-260	Weighted, Scaled, Hammer-Action	Y			Y			Y		Y		2	5/5	54x17x33	87
AP-460	Weighted, Scaled, Hammer-Action	Y			Y			Y	USB	Y	Y	2	5/5	54x17x33	89
AP-650	Weighted, Scaled, Hammer-Action	Y			Y			Y	USB	Y	Y	17	5/5	54x17x36	111

Brand & Model	Form	Ensemble	Finish	Estimated Price	MSRP	Sound Sosurce	Voices	Key Off	Sustain	String Resonance	Rhythms/Styles	Polyphony	Total Watts	Speakers	Piano Pedals	Half Pedal
Dynatone																
SLP-200H	V		RS	1,809	2,495	S	23					64	14	4	3	
SDP-500	V		EP	3,795	5,395	S	23			Y		128	100	4	3	
DPR-2200H	V	E	RS	2,718	3,995	S	128			Y	80	128	100	4	3	
SGP-500	G		EP	5,490	7,195	S	23			Y		128	100	4	3	
GPR-2200	G	E	EP	6,290	8,395	S	128			Y	80	128	100	6	3	
VGP-3000	G	E	EP	9,690	12,995	S	128			Y	80	128	100	6	3	
Galileo																
YP200	V		R	2,495	3,495	S	19		Y	Y		128	80	4	3	
YP300	V		R	2,995	3,995	S	20		Y	Y		128	100	4	3	
YP300	V		EP	3,495	4,495	S	20		Y	Y		128	100	4	3	
Verona II	V		R	2,499	3,499	S	15					64	20	2	3	
Milano II	V	E	R	4,995	5,995	S	138				100	64	40	4	3	
GYP300	G		EP/MP/WtP	6,995	8,995	S	20		Y	Y		128	120	4	3	
Aria	G		EP	8,995	10,495	S	16		Y	Y		64	180	4	3	
Milano 3G	G	E	EP	5,995	7,995	S	138				100	64	120	4	3	
Maestro II	G	E	EP	9,995	11,995	S	128		Y	Y		128	250	5	3	
Maestro II	G	E	WtP	10,495	12,495	S	128		Y	Y		128	250	5	3	
Maestro II	G	E	MP	11,995	13,995	S	128		Y	Y		128	250	5	3	

Brand & Model	Action	Triple-Sensor Keys	Escapement	Wood Keys	Ivory Texture	Player Moving Keys	Vocal Support	Educational Features	External Storage	USB to Computer	USB Digital Audio	Recording Tracks	Warranty (Parts/Labor)	Dimensions WxDxH (Inchees)	Weight (Pounds)
Dynatone															
SLP-200H	AHA											1	3/3	56x16x32	121
SDP-500	ARHA						Y			Y		1	3/3	55x17x39	218
DPR-2200	RHA						Y		SD	Y		2	3/3	56x19x34	165
SGP-500	ARHA						Y			Y		1	3/3	34x55x31	176
GPR-2200	RHA						Y		SD	Y		2	3/3	54x50x34	243
VGP-3000	RHA					Y	Y		SD	Y		2	3/3	56x56x32	440
Galileo															
YP200	Grand Response									Y			4/1	54X17X39	119
YP300	Graded Hammer									Y		3	4/1	54X20x41	137
YP300	Graded Hammer									Y		3	4/1	54X20x41	137
Verona II	Graded Hammer											2	4/1	54X17X40	119
Milano II	Graded Hammer									Y		3	4/1	56x20x34	154
YP300G	Graded Hammer									Y		3	4/1	56x29x35	209
Aria	AGT Pro	Y	Y							Y		2	4/1	54x38x56	315
Milano 3G	Graded Hammer									Y		3	4/1	56x29x35	200
Maestro II	AGT Pro	Y					Y	Y	USB	Y		5	4/1	54x39x35	345
Maestro II	AGT Pro	Y					Y	Y	USB	Y		5	4/1	54x39x35	345
Maestro II	AGT Pro	Y					Y	Y	USB	Y		5	4/1	54x39x35	345

Brand & Model	Form	Ensemble	Finish	Estimated Price	MSRP	Sound Sosurce	Voices	Key Off	Sustain	String Resonance	Rhythms/Styles	Polyphony	Total Watts	Speakers	Piano Pedals	Half Pedal
Kawai																
ES100	S			799	1,099	S	19	y	Y	Y	100	192	26	2	1	Y
MP7	S			1,799	2,199	S	256	Y	Y	Y	100	256	0	0	1	Y
MP11	S			2,799	3,299	S	40	Y	Y	Y	100	256	0	0	3	Y
VPC1	S			1,849	2,149		0						0	0	3	Y
ES7	S	E		1,999	2,399	S	32	Y	Y	Y	100	256	30	2	1 (3)	Y
CL26	V		R	1,099	1,495	S	8		Y			96	30	2	1	Y
CE220	V		ES	1,899	2,199	S	22		Y	Y	100	192	40	2	3	Y
KDP90	V		R	1,149	1,499	S	15	Y		Y		192	26	2	3	Y
CN25	V		R	1,899	2,299	S	19	Y	Y	Y		192	40	2	3	Y
CN35	V		R	2,599	3,199	S	324	Y	Y	Y	100	256	40	4	3	Y
CN35	V		M/ES	2,699	3,299	S	324	Y	Y	Y	100	256	40	4	3	Y
CA67	V		R	3,464	4,199	S	60	Y	Y	Y	100	256	100	4	3	Y
CA67	V		M/ES	3,555	4,299	S	60	Y	Y	Y	100	256	100	4	3	Y
CA97	V		R	4,655	5,899	S	80	Y	Y	Y	100	256	135	6+SB	3	Y
CA97	V		ES	4,755	5,999	S	80	Y	Y	Y	100	256	135	6+SB	3	Y
CS4	V		EP	3,082	3,695	S	15		Y	Y		192	40	4	3	Y
CS7	V		EP	4,536	5,695	S	60	Y	Y	Y	100	256	100	4	3	Y
CS10	V		EP	6,355	8,195	S	80	Y	Y	Y	100	256	135	6+SB	3	Y
KCP90	V	E	R			S	381	Y		Y	100	192	40	2	3	Y
CP3	V	E	R	5,499		S	700+	Y	Y	Y	183	256	100	2	3	Y
CP3	V	E	ES	5,599		S	700+	Y	Y	Y	215	256	100	2	3	Y
CP2	V	E	R	8,399		S	900+	Y	Y	Y	425	256	100	4	3	Y
CP2	V	E	M/ES	8,499		S	900+	Y	Y	Y	425	256	100	4	3	Y
CP1	G	E	EP	19,999		S	1000+	Y	Y	Y	425	256	200	9	3	Y
Korg																
SP170s	S		Wt/Bk/Rd	500	600	S	10					120	18	2	1	Y
SP170DX	S		Bk			S	10					120	18	2	3	Y
SP280	S		Bk/Wt	700	980	S	30					120	22	2	1	Y
SV-1-88	S		Bk	1,700	2,380	S	36					80			1 (3)	Y
LP180	V		Bk/Wt	700	980	S	10					120	22	2	3	Y
LP380	V		Bk/Wt/Rd/R/Bk&Rd	900	1,400	S	30					120	22	2	3	Y

Brand & Model	Action	Triple-Sensor Keys	Escapement	Wood Keys	Ivory Texture	Player Moving Keys	Vocal Support	Educational Features	External Storage	USB to Computer	USB Digital Audio	Recording Tracks	Warranty (Parts/Labor)	Dimensions WxDxH (Inchees)	Weight (Pounds)
Kawai															
ES100	AHA IV-F							Y		Y		1	3/3	52x11x6	33
MP7	RHII	Y	Y		Y				USB	Y	Y	1	3/1	53x13x7	45
MP11	GF	Y	Y	Y	Y				USB	Y	Y	1	3/1	58x18x8	77
VPC1	RM3II	Y	Y	Y	Y				USB	Y			3/1	54x18x8	65
ES7	RHII	Y	Y		Y				USB	Y		2	3/3	54x14.5x6	46
CL26	AHA IV-F												3/3	51x11x31	63
CE220	AWA PROII			Y					USB	Y		2	3/3	54x20x35	137
KDP90	AHA IV-F							Y		Y		1	3/3	56x16x34	84
CN25	RHIII	Y	Y		Y			Y		Y		1	5/5	54x16x34	99
CN35	RHIII	Y	Y		Y			Y	USB	Y	Y	2	5/5	55x19x36	122
CN35	RHIII	Y	Y		Y			Y	USB	Y	Y	2	5/5	55x19x36	122
CA67	GFII	Y	Y	Y	Y			Y	USB	Y	Y	2	5/5	57x19x36	161
CA67	GFII	Y	Y	Y	Y			Y	USB	Y	Y	2	5/5	57x19x36	161
CA97	GFII	Y	Y	Y	Y			Y	USB	Y	Y	2	5/5	58x19x37	192
CA97	GFII	Y	Y	Y	Y			Y	USB	Y	Y	1	5/5	58x19x37	192
CS4	RHII	Y	Y		Y			Y		Y		2	5/5	56x17x36	118
CS7	GF	Y	Y	Y	Y			Y	USB	Y	Y	2	5/5	57x19x37	176
CS10	GF	Y	Y	Y	Y			Y	USB	Y	Y	2	5/5	60x21x41	225
KCP90	AHA IV-F									Y		2	3/3	54x19x34	105
CP3	RHII	Y	Y		Y			Y	USB	Y		16	5/5	56x23x38	224
CP3	RHII	Y	Y		Y			Y	USB	Y		16	5/5	56x23x38	224
CP2	GF	Y	Y	Y	Y		Y	Y	USB	Y	Y	16	5/5	56x23x38	248
CP2	GF	Y	Y	Y	Y		Y	Y	USB	Y	Y	16	5/5	56x23x38	248
CP1	GF	Y	Y	Y	Y		Y	Y	USB	Y	Y	16	5/5	59x63x39	430
Korg															
SP170s	NH												1/1	52x13x6	26
SP170DX	NH												1/1	52x13x31	49
SP280	NH												1/1	54x16x31	42
SV-1-88	RH3									Y			1/1	53x14x6	45
LP180	NH												1/1	54x11x31	51
LP380	RH3												1/1	53x14x30	82

Brand & Model	Form	Ensemble	Finish	Estimated Price	MSRP	Sound Sosurce	Voices	Key Off	Sustain	String Resonance	Rhythms/Styles	Polyphony	Total Watts	Speakers	Piano Pedals	Half Pedal
Kurzweil																
MPS-10	S		Bk	699	995	S	88		Y	Y	78	64	30	2	1	
MPS-10F	S		BK	799	1,295	S	88		Y	Y	78	64	30	2	1	
MPS-20	S		Bk	930	1,495	S	200		Y	Y	100	64	30	4	1	
MPS-20F	S		BK	1,199	1,795	S	200		Y	Y	100	64	30	4	1	
MP-10	V		R	1,299	2,295	S	88		Y	Y	78	64	30	4	3	
MP-10	V		EP	1,439	2,795	S	88		Y	Y	78	64	30	4	3	
MP-10F	V		R	1,449	2,495	S	88		Y	Y	78	64	30	4	3	
MP-10F	V		EP	1,629	2,995	S	88		Y	Y	78	64	30	4	3	
MP-15	V		R	2,499	2,995	S	128		Y	Y	60	64	30	4	3	
MP-20	V		R	1,459	2,795	S	200		Y	Y	100	64	45	4	3	
MP-20	V		EP	1,759	2,995	S	200		Y	Y	100	64	45	4	3	
MP-20F	V		R	2,199	3,495	S	200		Y	Y	100	64	45	4	3	
MP-20F	V		EP	2,499	3,795	S	200		Y	Y	100	64	45	4	3	
CUP-2	V		EP	4,299	5,995	S	88		Y	Y	78	64	130	4	3	
CUP-2	V		Wt	4,495	6,395	S	88		Y	Y	78	64	130	4	3	
CUP2A	V		EP	4,699	5,959	S	88		Y	Y		128	140	4	3	
CUP110	V		R	1,899	2,795	S	88		Y	Y		128	45	4	3	
CUP110	V		EP	2,299	3,395	S	88		Y	Y		128	45	4	3	
CUP120	V		R	2,399	3,595	S	88		Y	Y	78	128	45	4	3	
CUP120	V		EP	2,699	3,995	S	88		Y	Y	78	128	45	4	3	
M3	V		R/Wt	2,399	3,695	S	200		Y	Y	100	64	50	4	3	
MPG-200	G		EP	5,995	6,995	S	200		Y	Y	100	64	200	4	3	
Lowrey																
EZP3	S		Sr	1,518	1,595	S	21					96	32	6	1	
EZP8	V	E	R	2,545	2,795	S	74				24	96	32	2	3	
Nord																
Nord Piano 2 HA88	S		Rd	2,999	3,399	S	1000+			Y		40-60			3	Y
Omega																
CR-202	V	E	M	1,960	2,595	S	96				96	128	40	2	3	
CR-301	V	E	M	2,520	3,360	S	128				100	128	40	2	3	
LX-502	V	E	M	3,240	4,050	S	128				100	128	80	4	3	
LX-505	V	E	M	3,560	4,620	S	128				200	128	80	4	3	

Brand & Model	Action	Triple-Sensor Keys	Escapement	Wood Keys	Ivory Texture	Player Moving Keys	Vocal Support	Educational Features	External Storage	USB to Computer	USB Digital Audio	Recording Tracks	Warranty (Parts/Labor)	Dimensions WxDxH (Inches)	Weight (Pounds)
Kurzweil															
MPS-10	LK									Y		1	2/3	52x14x3.5	39
MPS-10F	Fatar									Y		1	2/3	52x14x3.5	
MPS-20	LK									Y		2	2/3	52x14x3.5	39
MPS-20F	Fatar									Y		2	2/3	52x14x3.5	
MP-10	LK									Y		1	2/3	56x19x35	115
MP-10	LK									Y		1	2/3	56x19x35	115
MP-10F	Fatar									Y		1	2/3	56x19x35	
MP-10F	Fatar									Y		1	2/3	56x19x35	
MP-15	LK									Y		2	2/3	56x19x35	135
MP-20	LK									Y		2	2/3	55x20x34	162
MP-20	LK									Y		2	2/3	56x20x36	162
MP-20F	Fatar									Y		2	2/3	56x20x36	
MP-20F	Fatar									Y		2	2/3	56x20x36	
CUP-2	Fatar		Y	Y						Y		1	2/3	56x17x42	214
CUP-2	Fatar		Y	Y						Y		1	2/3	56x17x42	214
CUP2A	Fatar		Y	Y				Y		Y		1	2/3	56x17x42	224
CUP110	Fatar							Y		Y		1	2/3	56x20x36	132
CUP110	Fatar							Y		Y		1	2/3	56x20x36	132
CUP120	Fatar							Y		Y		1	2/3	56x20x36	162
CUP120	Fatar							Y		Y		1	2/3	56x20x36	162
M3	Fatar			Y						Y		2	2/3	55x35x20	134
MPG-200	Fatar		Y							Y		2	2/3	37x56x36	214
Lowrey															
EZP3										Y		1	2/1	54x14x6	47
EZP8										Y			2/1	53x19x33	112
Nord															
Nord Piano 2 HA88										Y			1/1	51x13x5	40
Omega															
CR-202	Graded Weighted									Y	USB	1	1/90		
CR-301	Fatar Graded									Y	USB	5	1/90		
LX-502	Fatar Graded									Y	USB	Y	7	1/90	
LX-505	Premium Fatar Graded									Y	USB	Y	7	1/90	

Brand & Model	Form	Ensemble	Finish	Estimated Price	MSRP	Sound Source	Voices	Key Off	Sustain	String Resonance	Rhythms/Styles	Polyphony	Total Watts	Speakers	Piano Pedals	Half Pedal
Omega (continued)																
LX-505	V	E	EP	4,388	5,620	S	128				200	128	80	4	3	
LX-802	G	E	EP	6,888	8,610	S	128				200	128	80	4	3	
Physis																
H1	S		Alu	4,390	4,995	M	192+192	Y	Y	Y		UL			3	Y
H2	S		Alu	3,800	4,295	M	192+192	Y	Y	Y		UL			3	Y
K4EX	S		Bl	3,250	3,795	M	192+192	Y	Y	Y		UL			3	Y
V100	V		PE/PRd/PWt/SG/PBl	9,695	9,695	M	192+192	Y	Y	Y		UL	150	6	3	Y
Roland																
RD-64	S		Bk	899	1,165	M/S	12	Y	Y	Y		128			1 (3)	Y
RD-300NX	S		Bk	1,299	2,099	M/S	366	Y	Y	Y	200	128			1 (3)	Y
RD-800	S		Bk	2,499	2,999	M/S	1113	Y	Y	Y	200	128			1 (3)	Y
V-Piano	S		Bk	6,999	7,999	M	24	Y	Y	Y		264			3	Y
F-20	S	E	Bk	899	1,049	M/S	35	Y	Y	Y	32	128	12	2	1	Y
FP-50	S	E	Bk	1,499	1,799	M/S	372	Y	Y	Y	90	128	24	2	1 (3)	Y
FP-50	S	E	Wt	1,499	1,799	M/S	372	Y	Y	Y	90	128	24	2	1 (3)	Y
FP-80	S	E	Bk	1,999	2,399	M/S	372	Y	Y	Y	90	128	26	4	1 (3)	Y
FP-80	S	E	Wt	1,999	2,399	M/S	372	Y	Y	Y	90	128	26	4	1 (3)	Y
DP-90e	V		ES	2,599	2,999	M/S	350	Y	Y	Y		128	24	2	3	Y
DP-90Se	V		EP	3,499	3,999	M/S	350	Y	Y	Y		128	24	2	3	Y
DP-90Se	V		WP	3,599	4,099	M/S	350	Y	Y	Y		128	24	2	3	Y
HP-504	V		R/ES	2,599	2,999	M/S	350	Y	Y	Y		128	24	2	3	Y
HP-506	V		R/ES	2,999	3,499	M/S	350	Y	Y	Y		128	74	4	3	Y
HP-506	V		EP	3,699	4,399	M/S	350	Y	Y	Y		128	74	4	3	Y
HP-508	V		R/ES	4,299	4,999	M/S	350	Y	Y	Y		128	150	6	3	Y
HP-508	V		EP	4,899	5,699	M/S	350	Y	Y	Y		128	150	6	3	Y
LX-15e	V		EP	5,999	7,199	M/S	350	Y	Y	Y		128	160	6	3	Y
LX-15e	V		WP	6,099	7,399	M/S	350	Y	Y	Y		128	160	6	3	Y

Brand & Model	Action	Triple-Sensor Keys	Escapement	Wood Keys	Ivory Texture	Player Moving Keys	Vocal Support	Educational Features	External Storage	USB to Computer	USB Digital Audio	Recording Tracks	Warranty (Parts/Labor)	Dimensions WxDxH (Inchees)	Weight (Pounds)
Omega *(continued)*															
LX-505	Premium Fatar Graded							Y	USB	Y		7	1/90		
LX-802	Premium Fatar Graded							Y	USB	Y		7	1/90		
Physis															
H1	Tri-sensor, Hybrid	Y	Y	Y	Y				USB	Y	Y	16	3/1	54x13x4	58
H2	Lightweight Hammer, 3 sensors	Y	Y						USB	Y	Y	16	3/1	54x13x4	45
K4EX	Tri-sensor, Hybrid	Y	Y						USB	Y	Y	16	3/1	51x14x5	40
V100	Tri-sensor, Hybrid	Y	Y	Y	Y				USB	Y	Y	16	3/1	58x17x46	233
Roland															
RD-64	Ivory Feel-G	Y	Y		Y				USB	Y			3/2	44x11x5	28
RD-300NX	Ivory Feel-G	Y	Y		Y				USB	Y	Y		3/2	57x13x6	39
RD-800	PHA4-Concert	Y	Y		Y				USB	Y	Y		3/2	57x15x6	55
V-Piano	PHA III	Y	Y		Y				USB	Y	Y	1	3/2	56x21x7	84
F-20	Ivory Feel-G	Y	Y		Y				USB	Y	Y	1	5/2	51x12x5	44
FP-50	Ivory Feel-G	Y	Y		Y				USB		Y	2	3/2	53x12x5	37
FP-50	Ivory Feel-G	Y	Y		Y				USB		Y	2	3/2	53x12x5	37
FP-80	Ivory Feel-S	Y	Y		Y		Y		USB	Y	Y	2	3/2	55x15x6	53
FP-80	Ivory Feel-S	Y	Y		Y		Y		USB	Y	Y	2	3/2	55x15x6	53
DP-90e	PHA4-Premium	Y	Y		Y				USB	Y	Y	3	5/2	55x14x31	102
DP-90Se	PHA4-Concert	Y	Y		Y				USB	Y	Y	3	5/2	55x14x31	104
DP-90Se	PHA4-Concert	Y	Y		Y				USB	Y	Y	3	5/2	55x14x31	104
HP-504	PHA4-Premium	Y			Y				USB	Y	Y	3	5/2	55x17x41	114
HP-506	PHA4-Concert	Y			Y				USB	Y	Y	3	5/2	55x17x42	121
HP-506	PHA4-Concert	Y	Y		Y				USB	Y	Y	3	5/2	55x17x42	121
HP-508	PHA4-Concert	Y	Y		Y				USB	Y	Y	3	5/2	55x20x45	177
HP-508	PHA4-Concert	Y	Y		Y				USB	Y	Y	3	5/2	55x20x45	177
LX-15e	PHA4-Concert	Y	Y		Y				USB	Y	Y	3	5/2	55x19x42	201
LX-15e	PHA4-Concert	Y	Y		Y				USB	Y	Y	3	5/2	55x19x42	201

Brand & Model	Form	Ensemble	Finish	Estimated Price	MSRP	Sound Sosurce	Voices	Key Off	Sustain	String Resonance	Rhythms/Styles	Polyphony	Total Watts	Speakers	Piano Pedals	Half Pedal
Roland *(continued)*																
HPi-50e	V	E	R	4,499	4,999	M/S	350	Y	Y	Y	50	128	74	4	3	Y
FP-50BKC	V	E	Bk	1,699	2,099	M/S	372	Y	Y	Y	90	128	24	2	1 (3)	Y
FP-50WHC	V	E	Wt	1,699	2,099	M/S	372	Y	Y	Y	90	128	24	2	1 (3)	Y
FP-80BKC	V	E	Bk	2,199	2,699	M/S	372	Y	Y	Y	90	128	26	4	1 (3)	Y
FP-80WHC	V	E	Wt	2,199	2,699	M/S	372	Y	Y	Y	90	128	26	4	1 (3)	Y
F-130R	V	E	ES/Wt	1,299	1,599	M/S	316	Y	Y	Y	72	128	24	2	3	Y
RP401R	V	E	R/ES	1,599	1,899	M/S	316	Y	Y	Y	72	128	24	2	3	Y
RG-3F	G		EP	10,999	14,999	M/S	337	Y	Y	Y		128	120	4	3	Y
V-Piano Grand	G		EP	19,950	22,999	M	30	Y	Y	Y		264	240	8	3	Y
Samick																
DCP-8	V		R	1,445	1,595	S	8					64		2	3	
DCP-12	V		R	1,627	1,795	S	16					64		2	3	
SSP-10 Stage	V		ES	1,264	1,295	S	16					64	30	2	1 (3)	
SSP-30 Stage Pro	V		ES	1,536	1,595	S	480					64	20	2	1 (3)	
SDP-10	V		R	1,718	1,795	S	9					64	40	2	3	
SDP-31	V		R	1,809	2,095	S	385					64	120	6	3	
SDP-31	V		EP	1,991	2,295	S	385					64	120	6	3	
SSP-12 Stage	V	E	ES	1,627	1,795	S	480					64	10	2	1 (3)	
SSP-20 Stage	V	E	C	1,627	1,795	S	476				260	64	40	2	1 (3)	
SDP-45	V	E	R	1,991	2,295	S	476				260	64	40	2	3	
SDP-45	V	E	EP	2,173	2,495	S	476				260	64	40	2	3	
SG-110	G		EP	3,795	3,795	S	385					64	120	2	3	
SG-210	G		EP	3,890	4,195	S	16					64	120	2	3	
SG-310	G		EP/WtP	4,290	4,595	S	385					64	120	6	3	
SG-450	G	E	EP/WtP	4,890	4,995	S	476				260	64	120	6	3	
Suzuki																
SSP-88	S		Bk&R	699	1,000	S	50					64			3	
CTP-88	V	E	WG	1,200		S	80+ 128GM		Y	Y	100	128	60	4	3	
MDG-200	G	E	EP	1,600	3,000	S	128					100	64	120	4	3	
MDG-300	G	E	EP/MP	1,699	3,390	S	122+ 128GM					100	128	120	6	3	
S-350	G	E	EP	2,000	2,500	S	128					100	64	120	4	3	

Roland (continued)

Brand & Model	Action	Triple-Sensor Keys	Escapement	Wood Keys	Ivory Texture	Player Moving Keys	Vocal Support	Educational Features	External Storage	USB to Computer	USB Digital Audio	Recording Tracks	Warranty (Parts/Labor)	Dimensions WxDxH (Inches)	Weight (Pounds)
HPi-50e	PHA4-Concert	Y	Y		Y			Y	USB	Y	Y	16	5/2	55x17x43	127
FP-50BKC	Ivory Feel-G	Y	Y		Y				USB		Y	2	3/2	53x16x37	64
FP-50WHC	Ivory Feel-G	Y	Y		Y				USB		Y	2	3/2	53x16x37	64
FP-80BKC	Ivory Feel-S	Y	Y		Y		Y		USB	Y	Y	2	3/2	55x15x37	80
FP-80WHC	Ivory Feel-S	Y	Y		Y		Y		USB	Y	Y	2	3/2	55x15x37	80
F-130R	PHA4-Standard	Y	Y		Y				USB	Y	Y	1	5/2	54X12X31	76
RP401R	PHA4-Standard	Y	Y		Y				USB	Y	Y	1	5/2	54X12X31	81
RG-3F	PHA III	Y	Y		Y				USB	Y	Y	1	5/2	58x37x57	242
V-Piano Grand	PHA III	Y	Y		Y				USB	Y	Y	1	5/2	59x59x61	375

Samick

Brand & Model	Action	Triple-Sensor Keys	Escapement	Wood Keys	Ivory Texture	Player Moving Keys	Vocal Support	Educational Features	External Storage	USB to Computer	USB Digital Audio	Recording Tracks	Warranty (Parts/Labor)	Dimensions WxDxH (Inches)	Weight (Pounds)
DCP-8			Y							Y		2	3/1		
DCP-12			Y							Y		2	3/1		
SSP-10 Stage	Graded											2	3/1	54x14x33	64
SSP-30 Stage Pro	Graded								USB	Y		16	3/1	62x13x30	62
SDP-10										Y		2	3/1	54x18x35	148
SDP-31	Graded								USB				3/1	54x20x35	150
SDP-31	Graded								USB				3/1	54x20x35	150
SSP-12 Stage	Graded								USB	Y		16	3/1	52x13x32	57
SSP-20 Stage	Graded								USB	Y		16	3/1	53x13x30	62
SDP-45	Graded								USB	Y		16	3/1	54x20x36	150
SDP-45	Graded								USB	Y		16	3/1	54x20x36	150
SG-110	Graded								USB			16	3/1	57x30x36	170
SG-210	Graded											2	3/1	57x50x36	260
SG-310	Graded								USB			16	3/1	57x50x36	260
SG-450	Graded								USB	Y		16	3/1	57x50x36	260

Suzuki

Brand & Model	Action	Triple-Sensor Keys	Escapement	Wood Keys	Ivory Texture	Player Moving Keys	Vocal Support	Educational Features	External Storage	USB to Computer	USB Digital Audio	Recording Tracks	Warranty (Parts/Labor)	Dimensions WxDxH (Inches)	Weight (Pounds)
SSP-88	Weighted								USB	Y		3	1/1	55x13x5	
CTP-88	Graded						Y	Y	SD	Y		3	1/1	54x20x40	175
MDG-200	Graded						Y		SD	Y		3	1/1	55x29x36	165
MDG-300	Graded						Y		SD	Y		3	1/1	55x30x36	218
S-350	Graded						Y		SD	Y		3	1/1	57x39x36	225

Brand & Model	Form	Ensemble	Finish	Estimated Price	MSRP	Sound Sosurce	Voices	Key Off	Sustain	String Resonance	Rhythms/Styles	Polyphony	Total Watts	Speakers	Piano Pedals	Half Pedal
Williams																
Legato	S		Bk	200	400	S	5					32			(1)	
Allegro	S		Bk	300	500	S	8					64			(1)	
Rhapsody	V		WG	500	800	S	12						20	2	2	
Overture	V		WG	600	1,000	S	15					64			3	
Yamaha																
P45B	S		Bk	450	499	S	10					64	12	2	1	Y
P115	S		Bk/Wt	600	999	S	14				14/10	192	14	4	1(3)	Y
P255	S		Bk&EP/Wt	1,300	1,999	S	24	Y	Y	Y	10	256	30	4	1	Y
CP50	S			1,500	2,199	M/S	322	Y	Y	Y	100	128			1	Y
CP300	S			2,200	2,700	M/S	530	Y	Y	Y		128	60	2	3	Y
CP40 Stage	S			1,699	2,399	M/S	297	Y	Y			128			1(2)	Y
CP4 Stage	S			2,199	2,999	M/S	433	Y	Y			128			1(2)	Y
CP1	S			5,000	5,999	M/S	17	Y	Y	Y		128			3	Y
YDP142	V		W/R	1,100	1,499	S	10					128	12	2	3	Y
YDP162	V		W/R	1,500	1,999	S	10					128	40	4	3	Y
YDP162	V		EP	1,700	2,499	S	10					128	40	4	3	Y
YDPS51	V		Bk/Wt	1,350	2,199	S	10					128	40	4	3	Y
YDPS52	V		Bk/Wt	1,350	2,199	S	10					192	40	2	3	Y
YDP181	V		R	1,700	2,199	S	14					128	40	2	3	Y
CLP525	V		W/E/R	1,700	2,199	S	10		Y			256	40	2	3	Y
CLP525	V		EP	2,000	2,599	S	10		Y			256	40	2	3	Y
CLP535	V		EP	2,600	2,899	S	34	Y	Y	Y		256	60	4	3	Y
CLP535	V		W/R/M	2,200	3,399	S	34	Y	Y	Y		256	60	4	3	Y
CLP545	V		EP	3,400	4,299	S	34	Y	Y	Y	20	256	100	4	3	Y
CLP545	V		W/R/M	2,900	3,699	S	34	Y	Y	Y	20	256	100	4	3	Y
CLP575	V		EP	4,500	5,699	S	34	Y	Y	Y	20	256	160	4	3	Y
CLP575	V		BK/DR	3,900	4,999	S	34	Y	Y	Y	20	256	160	4	3	Y
CLP585	V		EP	5,500	6,999	S	48+480XG	Y	Y	Y	20	256	180	6	3	Y
CLP585	V		BK	4,900	6,299	S	48+480XG	Y	Y	Y	20	256	180	6	3	Y
R01	V		Wt	4,900	7,199	S	1	Y	Y			128	24	2	3	Y
F01	V		EP/BlP/RdP/OrP	5,000	7,699	S	20	Y	Y			128	80	4	3	Y

Brand & Model	Action	Triple-Sensor Keys	Escapement	Wood Keys	Ivory Texture	Player Moving Keys	Vocal Support	Educational Features	External Storage	USB to Computer	USB Digital Audio	Recording Tracks	Warranty (Parts/Labor)	Dimensions WxDxH (Inches)	Weight (Pounds)
Williams															
Legato	Semi-Weighted									Y			1/1	50x11x4	19
Allegro												2	1/1	45x12x20	38
Rhapsody	Weighted									Y		2	1/1	45x12x20	38
Overture										Y		2	1/1	54x20x34	132
Yamaha															
P45B	GHS									Y			3/3	52x12x6	26
P115	GHS									Y		2	3/3	52x12x6	26
P255	GH				Y				USB	Y	Y	2	3/3	53x14x6	38
CP50	GH									Y			3/3	55x13x7	46
CP300	GH									Y		16	3/3	54x18x7	72
CP40 Stage	GH								USB	Y	Y		3/3	52x14x6	36
CP4 Stage	NW-GH	Y		Y	Y				USB	Y	Y		3/3	52x14x6	39
CP1	NW-Stage			Y	Y				USB	Y			3/3	55x17x7	60
YDP142	GHS									Y		2	3/3	54x17x32	84
YDP162	GH				Y					Y		2	3/3	54x17x33	93
YDP162	GH				Y					Y		2	3/3	54x17x33	99
YDPS51	GH									Y		2	3/3	55x12x31	80
YDPS52	GH				Y					Y		2	3/3	55x12x31	80
YDP181	GH								Y	Y		2	3/3	54x34x20	110
CLP525	GH3	Y			Y					Y		2	5/5	53x16x33	94
CLP525	GH3	Y			Y					Y		2	5/5	53x16x33	99
CLP535	GH3X	Y	Y		Y			Y	Y	Y	Y	16	5/5	57x18x36	135
CLP535	GH3X	Y	Y		Y			Y	Y	Y	Y	16	5/5	57x18x36	127
CLP545	NWX	Y	Y	Y	Y			Y	Y	Y	Y	16	5/5	57x18x36	143
CLP545	NWX	Y	Y	Y	Y			Y	Y	Y	Y	16	5/5	57x18x36	135
CLP575	NWX	Y	Y	Y	Y			Y	Y	Y	Y	16	5/5	57x18x36	162
CLP575	NWX	Y	Y	Y	Y			Y	Y	Y	Y	16	5/5	57x18x36	154
CLP585	NWX	Y	Y	Y	Y			Y	Y	Y	Y	16	5/5	57x18x39	199
CLP585	NWX	Y	Y	Y	Y			Y	Y	Y	Y	16	5/5	57x18x39	194
R01	NW			Y	Y									55x15x38	88
F01	NW				Y				USB	Y		1	5/5	56x16x39	168

Brand & Model	Form	Ensemble	Finish	Estimated Price	MSRP	Sound Sosurce	Voices	Key Off	Sustain	String Resonance	Rhythms/Styles	Polyphony	Total Watts	Speakers	Piano Pedals	Half Pedal
Yamaha *(continued)*																
F11	V		EP/BlP/RdP/OrP	7,500	13,999	S	20	Y	Y			128	80	4	3	Y
NU1	V		EP	5,816	6,499	S	5	Y	Y	Y		256	160	4	3	Y
N1	V		EP	8,180	9,999	S	5	Y	Y	Y		256	175	6	3	Y
N2	V		EP	12,362	14,999	S	5	Y	Y	Y		256	500	12	3	Y
DGX650	V	E	Bk&R/Bk&Wt	800	1,299	S	523				165	128	12	4	1(3)	(Y)
YDP-V240	V	E	R	2,000	2,699	S	491				161	64	40	2	3	Y
CVP601	V	E	W	4,127	5,399	S	889	Y	Y	Y	257	128	50	2	3	Y
CVP601	V	E	EP	4,636	6,199	S	889	Y	Y	Y	257	128	50	2	3	Y
CVP605	V	E	W	6,236	8,399	S	1355	Y	Y	Y	420	256	90	4	3	Y
CVP605	V	E	EP	7,018	9,399	S	1355	Y	Y	Y	420	256	90	4	3	Y
CVP609	V	E	W	9,745	13,999	S	1655	Y	Y	Y	566	128+128	200	7	3	Y
CVP609	V	E	EP	10,673	15,399	S	1655	Y	Y	Y	566	128+128	200	7	3	Y
CVP609	V	E	MP	11,145	15,999	S	1655	Y	Y	Y	566	128+128	200	7	3	Y
H01	G		AG/VR/DB	7,500	13,199	S	10	Y	Y			64	80	4	3	Y
H11	G		AG/VR/DB	10,000	20,799	S	10	Y	Y			64	80	4	3	Y
N3	G		EP	18,698	19,999	S	5	Y	Y	Y		256	500	12	3	Y
CVP609GP	G	E	EP	14,500	19,999	S	1655	Y	Y	Y	566	128+128	170	6	3	Y
CLP565GP	G		EP	4,500	5,999	S	34	Y	Y	Y		256	70	4	3	Y

Brand & Model	Action	Triple-Sensor Keys	Escapement	Wood Keys	Ivory Texture	Player Moving Keys	Vocal Support	Educational Features	External Storage	USB to Computer	USB Digital Audio	Recording Tracks	Warranty (Parts/Labor)	Dimensions WxDxH (Inches)	Weight (Pounds)
Yamaha *(continued)*															
F11	NW			Y		Y			USB	Y		1	5/5	56x16x39	198
NU1	Specialized Upright		Y	Y					USB	Y		1	5/5	60x18x40	240
N1	Specialized Grand		Y	Y					USB	Y		1	5/5	58x24x39	266
N2	Specialized Grand		Y	Y	Y				USB	Y		1	5/5	58x21x40	313
DGX650	GHS							Y	USB	Y		6	3/3	55x18x30	61
YDP-V240	GHS							Y	USB	Y		6	3/3	54x20x34	108
CVP601	GH3							Y	USB	Y		16 (MIDI)	5/5	53x24x36	128
CVP601	GH3							Y	USB	Y		16 (MIDI)	5/5	53x24x36	135
CVP605	GH3				Y		Y	Y	USB	Y		16 (MIDI)	5/5	56x24x34	174
CVP605	GH3				Y		Y	Y	USB	Y		16 (MIDI)	5/5	56x24x34	179
CVP609	NW			Y	Y		Y	Y	USB	Y		16 (MIDI)	5/5	56x24x34	179
CVP609	NW			Y	Y		Y	Y	USB	Y		16 (MIDI)	5/5	56x24x34	185
CVP609	NW			Y	Y		Y	Y	USB	Y		16 (MIDI)	5/5	56x24x34	185
H01	NW			Y					USB				5/5	58x30x30	181
H11	NW			Y		Y			USB				5/5	58x30x30	216
N3	Specialized Grand		Y	Y	Y				USB			1	5/5	58x47x40	439
CVP609GP	NW			Y	Y		Y	Y	USB	Y		16 (MIDI)	5/5	57x45x36	240
CLP565GP	GH3X	Y	Y		Y			Y	USB	Y	Y	16 (MIDI)	1	57x45x36	222

ADVERTISER INDEX

PHOTO CREDITS